TO SHAPE OUR WORLD
FOR GOOD

TO SHAPE OUR WORLD FOR GOOD

Master Narratives and Regime Change
in U.S. Foreign Policy, 1900–2011

C. William Walldorf Jr.

CORNELL UNIVERSITY PRESS   ITHACA AND LONDON

Cornell University Press gratefully acknowledges receipt of subventions from the Office of the Provost, the College of Arts and Sciences, and the Jennings Fund, all at Wake Forest University, which aided in the publication of this book.

First published 2019 by Cornell University Press

Library of Congress Cataloging-in-Publication Data

Names: Walldorf, C. William, Jr., 1967 author.
Title: To shape our world for good : master narratives and regime change in U.S. foreign policy, 1900–2011 / C. William Walldorf Jr.
Description: Ithaca : Cornell University Press, 2019. | Includes bibliographical references and index.
Identifiers: LCCN 2018044261 (print) | LCCN 2018045067 (ebook) | ISBN 9781501738289 (pdf) | ISBN 9781501738296 (epub/mobi) | ISBN 9781501738272 | ISBN 9781501738272 (cloth)
Subjects: LCSH: United States—Foreign relations—20th century. | United States—Foreign relations—21st century. | Regime change—History—20th century. | Regime change—History—21st century.
Classification: LCC E744 (ebook) | LCC E744 .W2593 2019 (print) | DDC 327.73009/04—dc23
LC record available at https://lccn.loc.gov/2018044261

To Charlie and Flora

Contents

Acknowledgments

The research and writing of this book has been a narrative of its own, with numerous unexpected hurdles, twists, and turns. Along the way, I have benefited immensely from the support, comments, and encouragement of many people. This book would not exist without them, though all mistakes and oversights are my own.

I am indebted first to my colleagues in the Department of Politics and International Affairs at Wake Forest University. Sara Dahill-Brown and Betina Wilkinson deserve special mention here. Both are co-authors on chapter 2 along with Sandeep Mazumder, my good friend in the Department of Economics at Wake Forest (appendixes for chapter 2 can be found at https://www.willwalldorf.com). Sara and Betina patiently put up with my unending questions about research design and statistical methods. Overall, the skills they and Sandeep brought to the project were most appreciated. I am also deeply indebted to the many individuals who devoted time to reading and commenting on different parts of the manuscript. Two people, John Owen and Mark Haas, deserve special thanks. Both were immensely supportive and helpful as I navigated the waters of their excellent work on elite ideology. Others who deserve mention include Jack Amoureux, Spencer Bakich, Steve Brooks, Jeff Legro, Sarah Lischer, Henry Nau, Dan Philpott, Sue Peterson, James McCallister, Dennis Smith, Hendrik Spruyt, Brock Tessman, Bill Wohlforth, Ben Valentino, Maurits van der Veen, and Andrew Yeo. I also appreciate the provocative and challenging comments from participants in seminars at the Notre Dame International Security Center, University of North Carolina, the Institute for Advanced Studies and Culture at the University of Virginia, the College of William and Mary, and the University of Georgia.

The review process at Cornell University Press made this a far better book than I could have imagined at the start. Roger Haydon's guidance was spectacular as usual. He supported the project from the beginning and offered invaluable constructive criticism to the very end. Two anonymous reviewers offered excellent comments that improved the book immeasurably. Copyediting by Irina Burns helped clarify language and repair numerous mistakes. I appreciate Karen Laun's help in ushering the book through the production process and Ellen Murphy's assistance with the acquisition process. The book also benefitted from the research assistance of many students at Wake Forest, including Payton Barr, Adam Crowley, Sophia Goren, Jacob Hurwitz, Allen Stanton, Brian Hart, Mathew

Layden, Cleo Johnson Miller, Matt Moran, Paige Raudenbush, and Dan Stefany. My son, Will Walldorf, also provided valuable research support while a student at the University of North Carolina. Several of these students stayed on campus during the summer to labor alongside me. Their work was tedious at times, but incredibly valuable to the final product.

On the financial side, I am fortunate to work at an institution with a deep commitment to funding faculty research. Wake Forest provided two semesters of research leave during the writing of this book and was extremely generous in providing additional funds for travel, research assistants, the hiring of coders, and summer salary support. This book would not have been possible without all of that assistance. As to outside funding, New City Commons provided a summer of support. The Earhart Foundation funded a semester leave early on in this project that proved invaluable to the book's framework. It was during that time off from teaching that my knowledge of cultural trauma deepened, which became critical to the book's argument. Finally, I am indebted to the Eudemonia Institute (EI) at Wake Forest University for two summers of salary support that allowed me to undertake major revisions of the book during the Cornell review process. EI is encouraging an important conversation at Wake Forest and beyond about human flourishing in all domains of life. I appreciate the support and space the Institute has granted me to do this kind of work in the domain of international politics.

Many others deserve mention as well for their encouragement and support. My children—Amy, Anson, and Will—grew into adults during the writing of this book. I appreciate their patience with me as research and writing drew me away at times. My wife, Jennifer, is a constant source of loving support. During the writing of this book, she took on the new challenge of becoming an elementary school teacher. Her patience, sacrifice, and care through my professional and personal travails has remained steady, nonetheless. I do not deserve so much. My in-laws, Cartter and Patty Frierson, are always a source of encouragement and came alongside our family in invaluable ways as we dealt with various transitions in life over the past several years. Finally, I thank my parents, Charlie and the late Flora Walldorf. My mom died when I was writing chapter 3. I miss her. She was full of life and a tireless supporter of all my endeavors. My father fits the same description. He sacrificed much for my education, taught me the value of hard work, and gave both space and support as I pursued a career path far removed from the family real estate business. For all the ways that my parents have loved me and my family well, I dedicate this book to them.

TO SHAPE OUR WORLD FOR GOOD

MASTER NARRATIVES AND FORCEFUL REGIME CHANGE

In June 1950, U.S. combat forces entered Korea and eventually crossed the thirty-eighth parallel to unify the peninsula and, in the process, forcibly overturn the regime of Kim Il-sung in the north. At the time, the U.S. president Harry Truman and his advisors admitted they felt deeply constrained against doing otherwise. Truman worried, in particular, that inaction in Korea might hurt his chances at reelection by landing him on the wrong side of a powerful national temperament to stop communism that was part of a popular, almost universally accepted story at the time about world affairs and certain troubling developments abroad.

In 1964 and 1965, President Lyndon Johnson faced a similar set of factors in his decision to send combat troops to Vietnam. Johnson believed that if he did not stop the communist advance into South Vietnam, he too would cross the same narrative and look weak on communism to the U.S. public, which could hurt his political clout in ways that might prevent congressional approval of his prized Great Society reforms. Sending U.S. combat forces to Vietnam was a political necessity, a move he also felt he had to make.

In 2003, similar domestic forces contributed to President George W. Bush's decision to invade Iraq and topple the regime of Saddam Hussein. This time, the big story, or narrative, at work was not anticommunism, but antiterrorism, born out of the trauma of the 9/11 terrorist attacks. As a fairly substantial historical record now indicates, Bush chose a large-scale invasion of Iraq, in part, to bring himself in line with this narrative in order to sustain his politically important image at home of looking tough on terrorism. That image was his political

1

trump card, without which Bush knew he and Republicans might face losses in the 2002 and 2004 elections.

Overall, the three largest and most controversial cases of forceful regime change in United States history—Korea, Vietnam, and Iraq—share something important in common. They all resulted from presidential decisions that were deeply impacted by domestic political pressures associated with broad, public expectations or beliefs that were prominent at the time. Leaders felt pushed to act, in short, by the anticipated political costs at home of appearing out of step with these beliefs, these powerful narratives that emerged around troubling events and carried lasting public expectations for certain kinds of action abroad.

In the study of international relations, the conventional wisdom about forceful regime change grants almost no attention to narratives like these. Instead, most treat broad public dispositions as either irrelevant or epiphenomenal to other factors, like geopolitics or the temperament of powerful elites. In this vein, robust military action for regime change purposes is most likely when a great power, like the United States, has too much power compared with other states in the international system, or is led by ideologically charged policymakers.[1] Conventional arguments blame the wars in Afghanistan and Iraq on the ideological zeal of neoconservatives around President Bush, or the arrogance of power for a United States unbridled by a global challenger in the post–Cold War era. Many talk similarly of the Vietnam War as "Johnson's War," effectively a function of the psychological or ideological makeup of President Lyndon Johnson and his inner circle. Elite dynamics and power are also frequently used to explain why leaders sometimes show restraint in using force to overthrow regimes. The adoption of only limited military means for regime change in Libya in 2011 and general inaction for these ends in Syria are commonly attributed to things like President Barack Obama's (and after him, President Donald Trump's) less ideological, more pragmatic personal sensibilities, or a shift in power to the disadvantage of the United States with the Great Recession and rise of competing powers, like China. In sum, elites and geopolitics dominate our current understanding of forceful regime promotion.

This book shows that this conventional wisdom about forceful regime promotion is, at best, incomplete and in most instances wrong, especially when it comes to wars launched by the United States. Broad story-centric national beliefs—what are called here "master narratives"—are a vital piece to understanding why the United States launches robust, full-scale wars for regime promotion in some cases and not others. When making choices about war, including regime change war, U.S. policymakers indeed look first through the lens of their own ideological and strategic preferences. However, if and to what extent they follow those preferences is often determined by master narrative politics. Sometimes, the master narrative landscape inside the United States around a certain regime crisis abroad allows elites to follow their preferred course of action. In many other important instances, though, the narrative landscape presses presidents and their closest advisors to make choices they would otherwise prefer not to. Truman in Korea and Johnson in Vietnam offer good examples. Prior to invasion, Truman considered Korea strategically irrelevant to the United States and worried about the high costs of a potential war with China. Likewise, Johnson saw Vietnam as an inevitable quagmire with no clear exit strategy and little chance of victory for U.S. forces. Despite their strong preferences for inaction, both presidents approved full combat invasions for regime promotion ends nonetheless due in large measure to narrative pressure centered on anticommunism.

Two factors are especially critical to explain when and what type of narrative-based pressure affects leader choices about forceful regime promotion. The first is the strength of different master narratives at the time of a regime crisis abroad. As discussed more below, two broad master narratives—the liberal narrative (of which anticommunism and antiterrorism are important temporal examples) and the restraint narrative (like the Vietnam or Iraq syndromes)—are especially important in U.S. foreign policy. History demonstrates that both of these master narratives change in strength across time—more robust in some periods, less so in others.

The second factor is the nature of the discourses that certain agents build (if any) around robust narratives at the time of a regime crisis abroad. These discourses are critical to explain the narrative-based pressures that elites feel either for or against robust forceful regime promotion from one case to the next. Sometimes, when a regime crisis occurs abroad and the liberal narrative is strong, certain agents use that narrative to build a broad public discourse for robust military action. In other instances of regime crisis abroad when the restraint narrative is strong, other kinds of agents sometimes draw on the restraint narrative to build discourses for more limited military action or no action at all. This linking of policy arguments for and against action to prevailing strong public narratives raises the profile of specific cases in the policy process. Leaders pay especially close attention to these case-specific narrative discourses. In fact, they tend to choose policies that lineup with these discourses in order to avoid the electoral or political costs of appearing out of step with public expectations (for instance, "be tough on communism" or "stop terrorism") set by prevailing master narratives. In the late 1940s and 1950, Truman faced, for example, intense pressure from a coalition of activists and politicians to use direct force to stop the communist advance in Korea, but not in China. Subsequently, he fashioned policy to match these narrative discourses: a combat invasion in Korea, and only limited action short of direct force in China. Again, sometimes leaders make choices like these willingly, other times they do so against their better strategic or ideological judgement. Overall, the politics of master narratives accounts for the political space in the former and the pressure to act in the latter.

This book does two things primarily. First, it explains the nature, content, and, most important, the strength of the leading master narratives—notably, the liberal and restraint narratives—in U.S. foreign policy from 1900 to the present. Second, the book systematically explores how and when these robust narratives shape patterns of forceful regime promotion through an exploration of the dynamics and impact of different narrative discourses on the policy process.

In tackling these two issues, important contributions follow for the study of international relations and U.S. foreign policy. First, this book offers a more comprehensive explanation of one of the most common types of warfare— forceful regime promotion—in U.S. foreign policy over the past century or more. In this sense, the findings here shed new light not only on when and where the United States launches these wars, but also why it is that forceful regime promotion involves robust combat operations in some cases and more limited military action in others. Second, with its novel explanation of master narratives, this book expands our understanding of long-standing issues at the core of state security: topics like how states see threats, when states use force, and the sources of overexpansion. Narratives and the politics surrounding them often play an important, yet to this point largely underspecified, role here.

Finally, the book offers a cautionary tale about the politics of master narratives. When master narratives (especially the liberal narrative) play a pronounced role in the decision-making process, some positive outcomes result, but for the most part policy under these conditions is not that good by most standards. At the broadest level, discourses centered around a robust liberal narrative often generate collective definitions of both good objectives and good means to achieve those objectives—a sort of passion to "shape our world for good"—that tends to push a country like the United States with a liberal ethos into regime promotion wars that oftentimes do not look that liberal, yield few strategic benefits, and leave behind a trail of postwar violence, as in Libya and Iraq in the 2000s and 2010s.[2] On the other side of the ledger, discourses around a strong restraint narrative often create a healthy degree of national caution and policy forbearance. Yet they can also lead to under-action abroad marked by a reduced national willingness to offer even minimal assistance to alleviate suffering (like Syria) or, more important, inability to counter new strategic challenges in ways that even realists say is necessary (a la the slow response of the United States to match the rise of Nazi Germany).

Beyond broad implications like these, narrative-generated pressure on leaders to either "do something" or "do nothing" also tends to tie the hands of policymakers in ways that leads to myopic and short-sighted decisions marked by motivated biases (especially wishful thinking). Poor strategic decisions generally result. Under narrative pressure, Truman and Johnson both committed to wars that ended in the quagmires they feared most. Facing similar pressure, President John F. Kennedy fell into wishful thinking about the potential success of the poorly planned, and some may say foolhardy, Bay of Pigs invasion, which contributed directly to near nuclear annihilation in the Cuban Missile Crisis. The fulfillment of campaign promises to a restraint-laden U.S. electorate about troop withdrawals from Iraq led the Obama administration to later overestimate the vitality of the Iraqi government and, thus, miss the rise of the Islamic State.

Avoiding a recurrence of these kinds of master narrative-driven policy pitfalls is not easy. Among other things, it requires a degree of responsible political discourse that is especially rare in the highly partisan and divisive U.S. political environment. Yet, without some sort of repair or means to manage the politics of master narratives, the United States will repeat, once again, some of its worst foreign policy mistakes, like Vietnam and Iraq. Managing the politics of master narratives begins with first knowing more about the problem, the sources and essence of master narrative politics. That is the primary task in the pages to follow.

The Origins and Nature of Master Narratives in U.S. Foreign Policy

What are master narratives and where do they come from? At their core, master narratives are collective stories about painful events that include, most important, a moral or lesson. These lessons set expectations on ways for a community or group to be moving forward. In its attention to foreign policy, this book explores master narratives that are national, or public-level in nature, essentially stories that create specific interests for the nation to pursue abroad and sometimes appropriate means by which to pursue those interests.

For the United States, two different types of master narratives are especially important to foreign policy and, more specifically, to explain forceful regime promotion. The first is a story about events that strengthens the collective national will at any given point to advance liberal political order abroad, either by promotion (i.e., expanding democracy and liberal rights) or protection (i.e., preventing the spread of counterideologies to liberalism). This master narrative is called here the "liberal narrative." As a social fact, rather than objective national interest, the liberal narrative with its normative content changes in strength and takes on different temporally specific manifestations over time. Since the late 1930s, a robust liberal narrative has been reflected in deep, national desires to stop the spread of fascism and communism, protect freedom abroad, and combat radical Islam.[3] The second kind of master narrative is a story about events that creates collective national taboos against using military force in certain places, by certain means or for certain kinds of goals abroad. This master narrative is called here the "restraint narrative." Again, the restraint narrative is a social fact that varies in strength and also manifests in temporally specific ways. Among examples from U.S. foreign policy, interwar isolationism, the Vietnam syndrome, and the Iraq syndrome stand out most. Each represented a story-driven set of lessons or norms that centered on national aversion to the use of force abroad, especially for the purpose of nation-building.

The liberal narrative and restraint narrative are distinct social facts (sometimes, varying in strength together, sometimes not) with distinct theoretical foundations. On this score, these kinds of master narratives prove to be especially powerful because of their origins, which has little to do with elites or geopolitics as traditionally conceived.[4] Instead, master narratives emerge from a nation's experience of cultural trauma, the scars of which leave a lasting and powerful mark on collective thinking.[5]

Cultural trauma is the product of two general factors—experienced events (some of which may seem, at first glance, quite mundane) and the arguments of certain kinds of social agents—that together help explain how master narratives strengthen and form. On the liberal narrative side, liberal states naturally care about the plight of liberal political order abroad—it is part of who they are, their identity.[6] For the United States, in particular, this care turns into a collective, national passion to take a more active role in protecting liberal order abroad under conditions of external trauma. More specifically, when ideologically distant, or illiberal, states make geostrategic gains, an opportunity space opens domestically that favors certain kinds of groups who narrate gains like these as traumatic (in essence, a challenge to the national way of life or liberal identity) that requires defense of liberal order abroad. Especially amid ongoing threatening events, these agent stories with their moral to protect/promote liberal order increasingly gain broader salience and become the new collective wisdom—a robust liberal narrative.[7] All major periods of a strong liberal narrative in the twentieth and twenty-first centuries of U.S. foreign policy emerged out of trauma like this. A series of major gains by the Soviet Union in East-Central Europe during the late 1940s coupled with stories told about existential dangers and the need to protect democracy by many prominent figures in the United States at the time sparked, for instance, a near panic inside the United States that created a robust national mentality to defend freedom and stop communism worldwide. This strengthened liberal narrative became a fixture—a *master* narrative—in public thinking about foreign policy that remained strong for most of the next fifty years during the Cold War rivalry between the United States and Soviet Union.[8]

When robust, the restraint narrative takes on a similar kind of status. It emerges and strengthens through an internal trauma process. In the U.S. experience, the nation's liberal creed carries expectations for both liberal outcomes and liberal behavior, especially in times of war. If policy outcomes or behavior (i.e., events in the trauma context) contradict these expectations, other kinds of groups in society, who advocate a less ideological foreign policy, find a favorable opportunity to tell stories about leadership deception and wrongdoing. As widespread collective disillusionment and a sense that national values are under siege sets in, the story-based lessons of restraint that these agents narrate increasingly gain public acceptance. Of special importance for policy, taboos (in essence, the moral of the restraint story) against the kind of behavior that generated the initial trauma gain broad, collective acceptance. These taboos reflect a new robust master narrative—the restraint narrative—for the nation that comes alongside of and sometimes competes with the liberal narrative when the latter is strong.

Each of the major restraint narrative periods of the twentieth and twenty-first centuries in U.S. foreign policy (isolationism in the 1920s–early 1930s; Vietnam syndrome in the 1970s–1980s; Iraq syndrome in the late 2000s to the present) emerged from trauma like this. In the early 2000s, the Iraq War was widely accepted by the U.S. public as necessary in order to stem the tide of terrorism (especially potential attacks with weapons of mass destruction [WMD]) and spread democracy to the Middle East. The postwar political chaos inside Iraq and failure to find WMDs opened space for critics of the war to tell stories about government deception and illiberal policy outcomes, leading to widespread disillusionment and broad acceptance of the moral of the story: no more Iraqs. Marked by a taboo against major combat operations for the sake of nation-building and democracy promotion, the restraint narrative strengthened in the 2000s and remains a mainstay in public discussions in the United States about foreign policy to the current day.

Trauma makes robust master narratives indelible social constructions that, when linked to discourses around specific cases of regime crisis abroad, have a dramatic impact on the policy choices presidents make. As noted already, Korea, Vietnam, and Iraq exemplify this for the liberal narrative. The restraint narrative has similar effects (though in the opposite direction from the liberal narrative) when it comes to using force. In the 1980s, social activists used a robust restraint narrative generated by the trauma of the Vietnam War to build discourses around the possibility of "another Vietnam" in Central America. Worried about the domestic political costs of crossing this narrative discourse, the Reagan administration subsequently chose against direct force for regime promotion in El Salvador and Nicaragua. A similar discourse around the Vietnam syndrome also contributed to President George H.W. Bush's decision against regime change in Iraq in 1991. In the 2010s, antiwar discourse around the Iraq syndrome contributed in important ways to decisions by the Obama administration to use either limited force (Libya) or no force at all (Syria) to topple regimes facing major political crises of late in the Middle East.[9] In each of these instances, restraint narrative discourses elevated costs for action for presidents, who came to fear political losses at home for choosing policies at odds with popular restraint narrative sentiments. Master narratives play far more than a peripheral or epiphenomenal part in the forceful regime change decisions of the United States. They are often the main attraction, in fact the primary force, behind U.S. policy decisions for robust military action in some cases of regime crisis abroad and not others.

The Puzzle, Master Narratives as "Narratives," and Scope Conditions

The purpose of this book is to explain patterns of forceful regime promotion in U.S. foreign policy. Forceful regime promotion is defined here as the use of direct military force (invasions, sieges, military occupations, or aerial bombardments) to either overturn a regime or support a friendly regime in a target state.[10] As to *patterns* of forceful regime promotion, a case is "full scale" or "robust" if when a regime crisis occurs abroad, combat forces are inserted into a country with no major constraints (other than tactical) on efforts to promote a regime. A case falls into the "limited" category if military action is confined to aerial bombardments, special or covert operations.[11] "Non-intervention" cases involve instances of regime crisis where no military action for regime promotion is taken at all.

This book focuses primary attention on the United States for a pair of reasons. First, the United States stands out as the most frequent forceful regime promoting state in international politics since 1900.[12] Added to this, diplomatic history since at least the end of World War II, if not sooner, demonstrates that as the United States goes on using force for regime promotion, so too do other democratic states in the international system. The vital support role of the United States in the 2011 Libyan operation is a case in point, as is Washington's influence over the lack of robust military activity in Syria. Despite talk of U.S. decline, this reality is not one that seems likely to change any time soon. It makes sense, then, to focus primary attention on the United States. All the same, this should not be taken to mean, that some sort of hegemony is required for master narratives to matter. In fact, this book finds strong evidence against that argument. The United States embarked on some of its most robust regime promotion wars (World War II, Korea, and Vietnam) at times and in regions of the world where it did not hold a preponderance of relative power. The impact of master narratives on U.S. foreign policy is not, therefore, a function of the United States possessing overwhelming power.

This book contends that political pressure generated by master narratives is a critical factor in explaining patterns of forceful regime promotion. Some clarifications and qualifications are important here. For starters, the fact that collective beliefs, like the liberal and restraint narratives, are "master" narratives does not mean that they somehow go uncontested in policy debates or society at large. Collective beliefs and stories are often questioned or challenged by some individuals or groups in society. Under certain trauma conditions, this factors into how they change in strength. But contestation does not deny the existence of the narratives in any sense or their ability to shape policy outcomes.

The distinction between collective and individual beliefs helps further clarify this. For some, terms like "narratives" and "beliefs" tend to invoke images related to personal identity or things found inside the heads of individual people. Master narratives are different than these common images, however. Most important, they are "not reducible to individual minds," but instead intersubjective properties of groups, like a nation.[13] Master narratives, like the liberal and restraint narratives, are similar, then, to culture in that they occupy a social space outside of and unique to individual opinion. Sometimes, individual opinion may share, or mirror, the beliefs of extant master narratives. At other points, it may not, as master narratives can be contested at times by individuals who question their efficacy for society. Regardless of this, master narratives still exist as independent and influential social phenomena. A person may have a habit, for instance, that s/he does not like, but that person's individual opinion of his/her habit does not deny the existence of the habit, nor the power of that habit to shape the individual's behavior or thinking. Master narratives, like other collective beliefs, are similar—they are group habits, characteristics, or dispositions that are distinct from and have their existence independent of individual beliefs and opinions. This is what is meant by saying that master narratives, like the liberal and restraint narratives, are *collective*. They are social facts with which individuals grapple.[14]

In this grappling, master narratives often constrain and shape (again, like habits) individual thought, ideas, and actions. This is a widely recognized feature, in fact, of collective beliefs in general. Various scholars demonstrate, for instance, the ways that organizational culture molds the opinions and behavior of individuals in firms and bureaucracies.[15] In a domain important to this study, others find that collective beliefs and ideas shape public opinion. Public opinion is an aggregation or "adding up" of individual opinions, making it a social phenomenon that is distinct from collective beliefs, like master narratives. Yet, through the molding of individual preferences and beliefs, the latter often impacts the direction and content of the former.[16]

Benjamin Page and Robert Shapiro's conception of "collective opinion" captures this best. They note that "values that are relatively enduring" (i.e., collective ideas or beliefs) often determine the contours of individual and, hence, public opinion. "At any given moment," Page and Shapiro contend, "an individual has real policy preferences based on underlying . . . values and beliefs." Collective opinion generates, in short, "*collective* policy preferences," which carry the potential to shape public opinion and voter preferences.[17] It is primarily for this reason, in fact, that policymakers tend to pay such close attention to collective beliefs, like master narratives. The potential that these social phenomena might shape voter opinions, especially in adverse ways for policy elites, helps account for why democratically elected leaders, in particular, worry about policy choices that cross the lessons set by master narratives.[18] The influence of collective beliefs on individual citizens makes elites naturally inclined to care about strong master narratives, especially in instances as this book demonstrates where influential actors raise the profile of certain cases with discourses that draw and center on those master narratives.

When it comes to different categories of collective beliefs, master narratives are defined first and foremost by their narrative component. At first glance, this may seem odd: how can a deep public desire to "stop communism" or avoid "another Vietnam" be considered a story, or narrative? In reality, they can be understood no other way.

Why this is the case requires that we better understand what comprises narratives in general. To this end, there are several interconnected components to a story, including a moral or lesson which is especially important for understanding master narratives. From social scientists to literary theorists, narratives are almost universally understood to start with and center around events. "For there to be a story, something unforeseen must happen," notes Jerome Bruner, "Narrative is a recounting of human plans gone off track, expectations gone awry."[19] Sometimes, these developments can be unexpectedly good things. At many other points, stories stem from troubling developments, such as a car accident or stock market crash. Whatever the case may be, unusual events serve as the foundation, the central point of attention, to narrative.[20] In fact, this is the core feature of narratives that distinguishes them from other collective phenomena like culture (i.e., the most fundamental, "unselfconscious" characteristics of a community at-large) and ideology (i.e., ideas about how state and society should be structured).[21] Unlike both, narratives can only be defined and understood through their origins in events. This is not so for culture or ideology. One does not need to talk about events surrounding the America revolution, for instance, to state the core tenets of a liberal ideology. By contrast, a story, or narrative, cannot exist absent events about which to tell a story. The grounded nature of narratives in the everyday matters of life—in something that happens, essentially— makes them by their very nature unique relative to more detached or abstract ideas and beliefs, such as culture and ideology.

In addressing unexpected events, narratives do far more than simply recount details, however. Instead, they help make sense of those events and set a course going forward for those who know and live the story. Narratives restore meaning and coherence for a group or community amid the confusion and uncertainty that comes with the unexpected.[22] "The sequence of events must form a unified causal chain and lead to closure," notes Marie-Laure Ryan, "The story must communicate something meaningful to an audience."[23] Especially with negative events, people do not live well with uncertainty. They need tools to help make sense of life, for life's developments to be ordered, even if the events remain painful. Narratives bring this order. In doing so, narratives present a simple (often oversimplified) account that downplays the accidental and emphasizes causality instead.[24] To this end, narratives require, according to Burke, an "agent" (who did it), "agency" (how he/she did it), and "purpose" (why he/she did it).[25] Story is defined by someone/something doing something for some specific, identifiable reason. Events do not just happen, they are caused by either a villain or hero— good or bad, there is always someone to blame.

And, if causality is present, lesson or solution is often present as well. Painful stories lead, in particular, to asking "What can be done? What should be done?" according to Maarten Hajer.[26] There is often a moral to the story. This is a final piece to many narratives. Peering through the lens of the past, narratives offer a way forward, often a perceived pathway to repair or reduced pain in the future.[27] As Bruner notes, a major feature of stories is a "coda" which may be "as explicit as an Aesop fable" in helping "to restore or cope with the situation."[28] Scholars find that when it comes to policy narratives like the ones explored in this book, the normative aspect of narratives is especially important. "The final component that must be present for a policy narrative to be a narrative is the moral of the story," observes Michael D. Jones and Mark K. McBeth.[29] A policy narrative cannot be, in effect, a "policy" narrative if it offers no actual direction for policy. The lesson or moral of the story is vital.

These normative components to story can be, in fact, especially critical to narratives over time. Notably, they emerge not just as lessons on how to be but also serve as connection points to—or, a reminder of—the bigger story itself as time passes. By living out or practicing the normative rituals created by the narrative, communities essentially relive or retell the original story. The anthropologist Victor Turner talks of religious rituals this way. As normative practices, these kinds of rituals emerge from a story surrounding certain past events that define a faith. The normative practice of ritual by the faithful over time reinforces a certain way of living explicitly through remembrance of the original faith story. Ritual encompasses objectively or subjectively, then, an intrinsic reliving or retelling of the core, foundational narrative by the faithful.[30] Policy narratives are similar. As Ronald Krebs observes, "National security narratives weave together past, present and future."[31] The practice and verbalization of narrative-centric norms is a link, a marker in the present that conjures up the past, the bigger story of narrative foundations.

All of this (i.e., troubling events, blame, moral, and remembrance) help explain how master narratives are "narratives." The normative essence of master narratives found in collective mantras like "stop communism," "no boots on the ground," and "no more Vietnams" are the end point of a bigger story. Notably, they are the lessons moving forward for the nation. The big story that these morals represent is that of the original trauma, either around external ideological challengers or internal disillusionment. At its core, trauma is story. It reflects all of the above noted characteristics of narratives.[32] As discussed more in the next chapter, trauma centers around unexpected, troubling events; involves narrators, who frame those events as "traumatic"; results in a simple collective tale that identifies a culprit's actions (blame of agent and agency) along with the malicious reasons for those actions (purpose); and sets a new course for behavior moving forward (moral).[33]

Like other policy narratives, this latter piece—the moral of the trauma story—is central to master narratives. Similar to religious rituals, the normative content of master narratives lives on over time and becomes, in fact, a shorthand for the bigger narrative story itself. When uttered in the 1980s, a phrase like "no more Vietnams" did not just dangle, for instance, in the air. Instead, it immediately conjured up or brought to mind a story (and sometimes the emotions that surrounded that story) of government deception, poor decisions, and the violation of certain values in and around a specific event, notably the Vietnam War. A normative phrase like "stop communism" had the same kinds of storied affects during the Cold War, as did "antiterrorism" in the 2000s and 2010s.

This is important for two reasons. First, as a marker or representation of the story that persists over time, the normative content of master narratives often serves as the best way to see and capture the narrative itself in the years after the initial trauma story. The utterance of "no more Vietnams" is essentially a retelling of the story in the present day. It is an indicator of the trauma story's continued strength and presence in the here and now. Second, the normative content of master narratives is also the connection point of the narrative to policy. It is, again, the moral of the story "often portrayed to prompt action and . . . a policy solution."[34] This normative piece of the narrative affects how states behave. Since this book seeks to explain a specific kind of state behavior (i.e., forceful regime promotion), it only makes sense to focus special attention on this part—the lesson or normative content—of master narratives.

Understanding the simple rule-based content of master narratives across time (i.e., "stop communism" or "no more Vietnams") also helps distinguish master narratives from other broad foreign policy concepts, like grand strategies, that international relations scholars often discuss. According to Barry Posen, grand strategies are "a theory states develop about how to cause security for themselves," meaning grand strategies are self-conscious, purposeful, and logical roadmaps for a state and its leaders.[35] The liberal and restraint narratives are far narrower and different than this, however. Regardless of the varied and complex elements of a state's broader grand strategy, a strong liberal narrative is an indication that the public concern about defending liberal political order abroad is especially pronounced at a given point in time. Likewise, a strong restraint narrative is an indication that certain kinds of force for certain kinds of ends are considered collectively taboo. Leaders often build and carry out grand strategies in ways mindful of these master narrative cues, but those cues are not in and of themselves grand strategies.[36]

Finally, master narratives do not explain, of course, all choices for and against forceful regime promotion in U.S. foreign policy. In cases of highest security, for instance, geostrategic considerations generally trump master narrative politics. Toward this end, the United States was not willing to risk a nuclear war with the Soviet Union in order to pursue forceful regime change in Poland, Hungary, or Czechoslovakia when regime crises occurred in each during the Cold War. For policymakers at the time, the extreme strategic costs of action in all of these cases superseded pressure from a robust liberal discourse. Overall, cases like these reflect important boundary conditions for the argument in this book.

Yet, outside of these exceptions, conventional explanations about geopolitics and elites offer insufficient accounts for nearly all of the above-mentioned cases as well as many others like them. President Reagan and his advisors were as ideologically motivated as any foreign policy elites in the twentieth century and fully aware of U.S. geostrategic dominance in Latin America. Yet Reagan chose against full-scale regime promotion in places like El Salvador and Nicaragua due to pressure from the strong restraint narrative discourse around both cases in the 1980s. Likewise, despite knowing that the United States lacked a preponderance of power in Asia, Truman and Johnson both contradicted their more pragmatic personal beliefs and launched wars in the region due to pressure from a robust liberal narrative discourse at the time. Even in instances like those in the early 2000s where we know that ideologically charged advisors and a less threatening strategic environment contributed to Bush administration decisions for regime change, elite disposition and geopolitics only tell part of the story. Policymakers here operated in a political environment marked by a strong liberal narrative discourse that facilitated and encouraged robust military action in important ways.[37] When that master narrative landscape changed later in the decade, so did the robustness of forceful regime promotion.[38] Overall, while it may be especially fashionable in the wake of the U.S. Middle East wars of the early 2000s to blame leaders for poor decisions like Iraq (and before that, Vietnam), choices like these are not usually all about those leaders. Master narrative politics sometimes reinforce and, oftentimes, cause leaders to make ("bad" and "good") policy choices.

Patterns of Forceful Regime Change: Agents, Process, and Discourses

As noted above, to say that master narratives shape policy decisions only gets us so far. Strong master narratives are not monolithic in their impact on policy. In this sense, policymakers are more than mere automatons, who habitually bend policy to match the lessons set by strong master narratives at different points in history. Leaders sometimes make choices, in fact, about forceful regime promotion that seem entirely at odds with the prevailing master narrative orthodoxy of their day. At the height of a robust Vietnam syndrome, Presidents Reagan and George H.W. Bush sent, for example, U.S. combat troops to topple or rescue regimes in Grenada, Panama, and Kuwait. Likewise, when the liberal narrative was especially strong during the 1960s, President John F. Kennedy elected covert military action (rather than a full combat invasion) against the Castro regime in Cuba. As politically salient and powerful as master narratives often are in shaping policy, leaders sometimes find space to defy them. When and how, then, do master narratives shape patterns of forceful regime promotion? This question is important. Without an adequate answer, critics might claim, once again, that master narratives are epiphenomenal to, or little more than a by-product of, other factors, like elite dispositions or geopolitics.

Explaining when and how master narratives matter requires closer attention to process, or the politics that bring the liberal and restraint narratives to the center of policymaking in democratic great powers. On this point, the case-specific discourses that certain kinds of agents, or social carriers, build around robust master narratives at points of regime crisis abroad are, in most instances, of central importance. Two types of agents are especially relevant here: "promoters" who sometimes argue for robust military action and "moderators" who sometimes make the case for military restraint. These different kinds of social carriers gain influence not because of some set of characteristics unique unto themselves. Instead, event-driven robust master narratives empower their arguments. In this sense, when the corresponding master narrative (i.e., the liberal or restraint narrative) is strong, arguments by promoters and moderators work like conveyor belts, essentially thrusting the moral of these collective stories to the center of the decision-making process. They do so by drawing public attention to specific cases of regime crisis and, then, linking those cases to prevailing master narratives in ways that create national movements—strong discourses—for action or inaction.[39] These discourses essentially increase audience costs, or the political price that presidents think they will pay for contradicting voter preferences.[40] As these costs increase, leaders typically respond by bringing forceful-regime change policy in line with the prevailing strong liberal or restraint discourse. When promoters and moderators choose not to build robust discourses like these around a specific case of regime crisis abroad (see chapter 1 for an explanation of choices like these), leaders find more political space to shape policy to their liking. Sometimes, this means they opt for policies—like JFK in Cuba or Reagan in Grenada—that seem out of step with the general master narrative orthodoxy of the day.

As to specific predictions, full-scale military interventions are most likely in cases marked by a *strong-liberal/weak-restraint discourse*. In periods where the liberal narrative is robust, promoters sometimes decide to use that narrative to argue for military action. By playing on elevated national anxiety about protecting liberal order abroad, these arguments generate (or policymakers fear they will generate) powerful national discourses to take a stand in the regime crisis at hand. This kind of pressure looms especially large when parallel syndrome discourses are weak. Overall, in this strong-liberal/weak-restraint context, policymakers face increased political costs at home for inaction, notably potential danger with the voting public, in particular, for doing too little or "for looking weak on the world stage."[41] In this narrative-discourse climate, leaders find a conducive environment to use force, and often get pushed against their will into doing so out of fear of electoral/political losses. This helps explain many cases in U.S. foreign policy, including as mentioned prominent examples in the postwar period, like Korea, Vietnam, and Iraq. In each of these instances, promoters used a strong liberal narrative to build discourses for robust action, which overwhelmed the policy process given weak restraint narratives at the time and pushed leaders to choose large-scale invasions.

Process also matters in explaining how and when master narratives limit military action for regime change purposes in specific cases. Sometimes promoters choose not to use a strong liberal narrative to argue for robust military action, thus creating space for leaders to adopt less forceful policies. As detailed in chapter 4, this was the case with the choice that Kennedy made in Cuba. At other points, strong restraint discourses press leaders to choose more limited forceful regime promotion or no military action at all. When restraint narratives are strong for the nation and moderators choose to argue for military inaction or caution in response to a regime crisis abroad, politically powerful domestic movements that are opposed to using force often emerge. These restraint discourses produce increased costs for action, meaning leaders face the potential of paying a steep political price at home for using force. As a result, this kind of discourse pressure generally causes leaders interested in using force to back down from doing so, or allows leaders with little interest in military action to follow their wishes.[42] Antiwar groups in the United States created a movement around deep national concerns over the possibility of "another Vietnam" when U.S. policymakers were deciding on how to respond to Iraq's invasion of Kuwait in 1991. This restraint discourse made President George H.W. Bush fear that an extended war to topple Iraqi President Saddam Hussein would be politically unpopular and hurt his chances at reelection in 1992. Bush decided consequently against a large ground offensive into Iraq once Kuwait was liberated.

Overall, U.S. forceful regime promotion has varied dramatically over time in what might seem like unpredictable or haphazard ways. In periods of a robust liberal narrative, sometimes democratic great powers pursue full-scale military invasions for regime promotion ends, at other points they do not (Korea versus China in 1950). Amid strong restraint narratives, we see the same kinds of patterns—robust military action in some regime crises abroad, and non-to-limited action in others (Grenada versus El Salvador in 1983). These apparent inconsistencies should not be interpreted as weaknesses or flaws in the power of master narratives to shape policy outcomes, though. Instead, they make sense when one understands the politics of master narratives. Different kinds of traumatic experiences (external or internal) strengthen different master narratives. Different kinds of social agents use those narratives, in turn, to build broad discourses for more or less robust military action abroad, which play a critically important role in shaping the decisions that U.S. presidents make about one of the most controversial forms of warfare—forceful regime promotion—in the history of international politics. The following dives more deeply into this important story.

THE LIBERAL NARRATIVE, RESTRAINT NARRATIVE, AND PATTERNS OF FORCEFUL REGIME CHANGE

Sometimes the United States uses full-scale military interventions to promote or overturn regimes abroad.[1] At other points under similar conditions, the United States does nothing or intentionally chooses more limited military options. How do we explain these patterns in the use of force? This chapter explores potential answers to this question that range from broad public narratives to geopolitics and elite ideology.

Master Narratives and Forceful Regime Promotion

The central argument of this book is that master narratives play a major role in explaining patterns of forceful regime change in U.S. foreign policy. Two interrelated master narratives—the liberal narrative and restraint narrative—are especially important. Discourses that form around these narratives create predictable pressure on policymakers that shape decisions about forceful regime promotion.

Situating the Master Narrative Argument

This is not the first book on either forceful regime promotion or national security narratives. More specifically, John Owen offers the leading work on the former and Ronald Krebs the same for the latter. Owen turns to elite ideology to explain forceful regime promotion. He argues that the normative commitment among elites to spread/protect their political order strengthens (a process that Owen labels "elite polarization") at points of great power war and regime crises abroad. This makes forceful regime promotion more likely. In Owen's framework, polarization involves more than just individual states, however. It is, most important, a structural phenomenon, meaning that when polarization occurs it becomes collective as it reaches across dyads or groups of rival ideological powers. This structural component is the centerpiece of Owen's argument. It helps him explain shortwaves (or focused periods) of especially intense back-and-forth regime promotion invasions by competing ideological rivals. In the end, Owen's structural findings are impressive, expanding our understanding of regime promotion wars across a 500-year period.[2]

The biggest limitation to Owen's argument is that it cannot explain very well the main puzzle at the center of this book—*patterns* of forceful regime change. In this sense, Owen faces a problem common to all structural theories of international relations.[3] Namely, while shedding light on systemic outcomes (i.e., shortwaves), his argument struggles to account for more policy-focused questions of why, when and where great powers pursue forceful regime promotion, and why they use different levels of force when doing so.

A quick glance at history demonstrates the problem most clearly. In periods of high polarization within a state (for example, from the 1930s through most of the Cold War), sometimes a country like the United States pursues robust, full-scale forceful regime promotion in some regime crises (Korea, Vietnam, Lebanon, and Grenada), as Owen might expect. But, at other points marked by near identical conditions, Washington does little to nothing militarily. Just to name a few cases, we can think of U.S. non-to-limited military action at points of regime crises in places like China, Cuba, Guatemala, El Salvador, and Nicaragua during the Cold War. Elite polarization was high in the United States in each of these cases, yet direct U.S. military action remained almost nonexistent. We know, for instance, that President Ronald Reagan and his closest advisors were especially animated (i.e., polarized) about stopping the spread of communism in Central America during the 1980s. So why no military action in places like El Salvador and Nicaragua? Why, furthermore, robust military action in Grenada? What allowed Reagan to follow his ideological preferences and pursue invasion in the latter but not the former? Something important is missing in accounts of forceful regime change that focus exclusively on elite ideology. Again, what explains patterns of forceful regime promotion in U.S. foreign policy?

The argument in this book answers this question by turning attention to a different kind of ideas—public narratives—that exist, most important, at a different level of analysis than elite ideology. In this narrative-based argument, elites are important. But their impact is highly contextualized or conditioned by the political pressure generated around broad narratives in the United States.[4] By restricting his ideational focus to elites alone, Owen misses the impact of these narratives. What the master narrative argument in this book does, then, is build a more integrated, and thus holistic, ideational account of policy by bringing together elite-based and collective or national-based ideas. This approach offers, above all else, a better explanation of case-by-case decisions for and against robust forceful regime promotion in U.S. foreign policy.

This more holistic ideational account makes two specific theoretical moves relative to Owen. First, it starts from Owen's baseline. Notably, leadership elites (i.e., presidents and their top aids in the United States) sometimes prefer forceful regime change due to ideology. Those same elites, as Owen argues, may also sometimes prefer restraint when they reason that the geopolitical costs of pursuing forceful regime promotion are too high.[5] Whether ideological or strategic, the preferences of leadership elites are the starting point for the master narrative argument.

In contrast to Owen, the master narrative argument contends, second, that elite preferences (whether ideological or not) do not automatically, exclusively or, in some cases, even marginally determine forceful-regime-promotion decisions. Here, master narratives enter the picture. The argument centers on the fact that leadership elites in the United States are nested in a wider, national ideational context defined by strong/weak master narratives, and more specifically for policy, the discourses that form around those narratives. Sometimes, narrative discourses create the necessary political space for leaders to follow their preferred course of action (i.e., Reagan in Grenada). At other points, they push leaders to act either for or against forceful regime promotion despite their own preferences to the contrary (i.e., Reagan in El Salvador and Nicaragua).[6] In sum, master narratives are virtually always a necessary condition (working alongside elite ideology) and, in many important instances, more of a necessary and sufficient condition to explain patterns of forceful regime promotion in U.S. foreign policy.

Given the work already done on elite ideology, the primary focus of this book lies with deepening our understanding of master narratives. This leads naturally to Ronald Krebs's work on national security narratives in U.S. foreign policy. Krebs makes two primary arguments. First, he contends that when times are "unsettled" and the president adopts a rhetorical style of storytelling (as opposed to a rhetoric of argument), the president is able to create new narratives that come to dominate policy discourse. For Krebs, the president's role is a key piece, a linchpin of sorts, to his argument. More specifically, executive-branch authority is what elevates presidential stories above the fray, explaining then how a single dominant narrative can triumph amid the cacophony of many competing narratives in unsettled times.[7] Together, unsettled times and presidential storytelling explain, according to Krebs, the emergence of two especially important narratives over the past century in U.S. foreign policy: the global engagement narrative around World War II and the antiterrorism narrative since 2001. Second, Krebs argues that narrative-generated policy success (as opposed to policy failure) is a primary driver of change in the narrative landscape, allowing the president space to reset the nation's dominant story by casting aside old narratives and sometimes adopting new ones in their place. Krebs uses this second argument to explain why the Cold War consensus (formed after the Korean War and defined most centrally by Krebs as a general agreement that the communist bloc was monolithic) lasted only about a decade, declining around 1962, according to Krebs.[8]

Krebs's work is impressive. But it also faces important shortcomings for the task at hand. First, by his own admission, Krebs offers no theoretical explanation for why, when, and how narratives impact policy.[9] His book centers almost exclusively on the narratives alone, not their influence on state behavior. Consequently, Krebs has no way to fully account for policy outcomes, like patterns of forceful regime promotion. Similar to Owen's issues with elite polarization, he cannot explain, most important, variations in policy when the narrative landscape is constant from one regime crisis to the next (i.e., full-scale invasion of Iraq in 2003 versus nonintervention in Syria since 2011). This is not a trivial point. Without a policy-relevant explanation, many will ask whether narratives really matter at all, leading to the bigger question of why bother studying narratives if they do not tell us much about real-world policy events.

Second, structural dynamics and authoritative storytellers are, as Krebs notes, important to any explanation of the formation and change in foreign policy narratives (especially in democratic states like the United States). But these (and other factors) are also either underspecified or too narrowly specified in Krebs's argument to offer an adequate explanation of nearly all of the most powerful and policy-relevant temporal manifestations of the liberal and restraint narrative in U.S. foreign policy since the start of the twentieth century. As discussed more in the chapters to follow, the emergence of a powerful liberal narrative to stem autocracy in Europe around World War I and later anticommunism during the Cold War, were not, for instance, a function primarily of presidential storytelling.[10] Instead, these narratives emerged in response to threatening developments abroad that both presidents Woodrow Wilson and Harry Truman initially tried to downplay, rather than storytell about.[11] Periods of a robust restraint narrative demonstrate the same thing. From interwar isolationism to the Vietnam and Iraq syndromes, presidents Wilson, Lyndon Johnson,

Richard Nixon, and George W. Bush all failed in their attempts to stop robust restraint narratives from setting in across the nation. In short, presidents sometimes do not want, or promote, new collective narratives (they may storytell against those narrative trends, in fact), but the new narratives become the collective wisdom anyway. How does this happen? If not through presidential authority and storytelling, how did these particular narratives at these particular moments gain collective acceptance? In short, what explains master narratives in U.S. foreign policy?

Krebs's other argument about policy success faces problems with master narratives as well. In some situations like the end of the Cold War, dramatic policy success can indeed help generate master narrative change. But, aside from these occasional instances, a collective sense of social pain, not success, has been the main driver—by far—of strengthening and weakening in master narratives over time in U.S. foreign policy. All manifestations of restraint narratives during the twentieth and twenty-first centuries were driven by events seen collectively as wrong or negative. Isolationism emerged from collective disillusionment over the outcomes in World War I, the Vietnam syndrome from the same around the Vietnam War, and the Iraq syndrome from negative developments following the 2003 Iraq War.[12] Painful events like these contributed to weakening of master narratives across this period as well. Disillusionment over World War I and the Vietnam War weakened the liberal narrative substantially, for instance, in the 1920s and 1970s. Negative policy outcomes in the form of Nazi Germany's march across Europe in the 1930s also contributed in unmistakable ways to the decline of interwar isolationism. Overall, a collective sense of policy failure (not success) has been a major engine of change in the master narrative landscape of the United States over the course of the twentieth century or more.

Why is this important? Why in general is a more predictive argument for master narratives important? Above all else, a predictive account of narrative change is critical, again, to explain policy. It is the first step to show how, why, and when narratives matter. Since Krebs focuses so little on policy, we do not know, for instance, how the brief Cold War consensus that he identifies mattered. But, as the chapters that follow show, the liberal and restraint narratives that Krebs cannot explain played a vital role in shaping policies, like patterns of forceful regime promotion. A theory better suited to explain, then, the emergence of these kinds of narratives is essential.

The argument in this book makes two theoretical moves relative to Krebs. First, it develops a clearly specified event-centric, rather than rhetoric-centric, account of narratives. Like others, Krebs rightly criticizes simplistic event-based arguments about ideational change—that is, shock occurs and narratives change or form.[13] But, in countering this weakness in the literature, Krebs overcorrects theoretically. He minimizes the impact of events on narrative formation to the marginal role of simply "shaking things up" (i.e., unsettling times) and elevates, in turn, presidential storytelling as the sole variable that explains the substance, contour and nature that narratives take.[14]

Events do more than this, however. They play a critically important role in not just unsettling the times but also shaping the *substance* and *content* of collectively acceptable narratives. As explored when defining narratives in the prior chapter, events are the critical starting point and ever-present frame of reference for understanding how narratives form and become collectively acceptable.[15] They set the table or direction for how a story can go and develop. In this sense, events bias the space within which storytellers operate, naturally privileging or selecting out some stories as good and deeming others bad or inappropriate. Consider an everyday example. Suppose a person tells a dramatic story about being mugged and ends with the moral that it is best to spend more time walking alone down dark allies at night. Listeners would naturally find the story odd or question the storyteller's sanity. Why? The moral seems inappropriate, it fails to fit or follow naturally from the event—the mugging—around which the story centered. Other alternative morals, like arming oneself, make far more sense by contrast, again because of what happened. In short, event-driven context in this example does more than unsettle things, it shapes narrative content as well, setting the boundaries of good and bad, or collectively acceptable and unacceptable, stories.

National security narratives are similar. More specifically, different kinds of events create varied and predictable political spaces that elevate some agents above others and often shape which stories these agents (many of whom are not the president, by the way) choose to tell. Certain stories resonate, then, in some event-driven contexts and not others. Agents cannot tell just any story in so-called unsettled times and expect it to gain collective resonance. They must tell the *right* kind of story—one that is appropriate for or fits the particulars of the times—in order to matter. Event-driven policy spaces are not a tabula rasa then but biased toward some narratives and not others.[16] Like elite ideology, storytelling is important, but also contextualized, in this case, by events.

A reading of Krebs's own case studies seems to demand more systematic attention to events. By his own admission, Krebs finds that the narrative landscape in the United States around World War II started to shift substantially almost two years *before* President Franklin Roosevelt began to storytell in April 1940, and it took another twenty months after FDR started to storytell for the new antifascism narrative of international engagement (i.e., the liberal narrative in this book) to fully take hold across the public and supplant the previously dominant isolationist narrative.[17] Why was this the case? What else was going on to explain narrative change, because presidential storytelling alone here cannot answer? Although Krebs does not draw this out in any specific or predictable way, the answer one gleans from his case study centers on events, especially threatening events abroad in the form of German aggression in Europe. This raises more questions. Why and how did *these* kinds of events shape narratives the way they did—why privilege a more internationalist (as opposed to isolationist) narrative, how did change begin before presidential storytelling, and what took so long for the new narrative to settle in collectively? Given his theoretically limited conceptualization of events, Krebs cannot answer. But these kinds of questions are important, especially again to policy: the timing of narrative change here played a major part in the timing and nature of U.S. entrance into World War II.[18]

Overall, this book addresses topics like these by developing a well-specified account of event-centric processes around state identity that explains why certain narratives change in strength when they do, why some narratives remain robust for long periods of time, and why narratives that substantially weaken (like the anticommunism narrative in the 1970s) sometimes regain strength and continue on.

The second move that this book makes relative to Krebs centers on how narratives are conceptualized. Krebs treats narratives as atomistic, or historically contingent and disconnected phenomena—each dominant narrative is unique relative to others over time.[19] With its central focus on event rather than rhetoric-driven processes, this book takes a different approach here. Notably, it conceptualizes narratives as broader and cross-temporal in nature. While cognizant of the uniqueness of antifascism, anticommunism, and antiterrorism, it treats narratives like these as being of the same ilk, meaning they share a common essence that involves, at its core, a similar story about protecting and promoting liberal political order abroad. They are considered reflections of a broader narrative phenomenon that shows up in robust form from time to time and for certain long stretches in national discussions about foreign policy. These temporally specific narratives are the historical manifestation, in this sense, of a robust "master" narrative or collective story—the liberal narrative—that is an embedded element in how democratic polities often approach the world.

Temporally specific narratives that restrain action abroad (i.e., isolationism or the post-Vietnam narrative) are also similarly categorized in this book, as reflections of a broader phenomenon. These kinds of narratives are not viewed here as simply different manifestations of anti-interventionist sentiment, unique to certain time periods. They too are of the same ilk, basically similar kinds of stories that show up from time to time. In this sense, each reflects another broad "master" narrative or collective story—the restraint narrative—that also strengthens at points to protect liberal identity in democratic foreign policy. The focus of this book, thus, starts with and centers on these broader, cross-temporal master narrative phenomena—namely, the liberal and restraint narratives.

Overall, this turn is important. By conceptualizing narratives as both phenomenological and temporal, this book explains more about narratives than current accounts allow. It also opens space conceptually to develop more generalizable theories about policy that explain not simply the occasional hit or miss outcome in foreign policy, but instead broad phenomena or regular and repeated events, like patterns of forceful regime change over time. With that, the next section turns to the master narrative argument.

Master Narrative Strength

What explains master narratives in the United States, their emergence and robustness over time? Conventional explanations of ideational change that focus on negative or painful events generally take a more functionalist approach to answer this kind of question. In essence, beliefs change when they do not work or fail to produce outcomes that live up to some sort of preconceived (usually material) expectations.[20] While ideational failure is sometimes relevant, master narratives like the liberal and restraint narratives usually strengthen (and weaken) in ways that are different from this.[21] The reason for this is straightforward: as collective beliefs or stories closely tied to national identity, master narratives tend to change most not when events show the beliefs fail some functional test, but instead when events come to be collectively viewed as either a challenge to or wrong by a society's core (in our case, liberal) values. As alluded to already, identity-based beliefs, like master narratives, generally change by a logic of appropriateness, not functionality.

In order to explain this sort of identity-based change, the more identity-based framework found in sociological work on cultural trauma offers the best approach. Trauma theory offers an explanation of cultural change that explores the processes by which social pain—or identity-challenging events—couple with the stories of important agents to explain how a community comes to accept new ways of getting by in the world. In this trauma framework, events and stories are deeply intertwined. Agents and their storytelling are important. But their impact on the creation of new collective narratives is highly conditioned by specific sorts of events intersecting with identity-based expectations in predictable ways.[22]

Neil Smelser defines cultural trauma as "a memory accepted and given public credence by a relevant membership group and evoking an event(s) or situation(s) which is a) laden with . . . affect, b) represented as indelible, and c) regarded as threatening a society's existence or violating one or more of its fundamental cultural presuppositions."[23] As this definition indicates, trauma is a process that includes several stages. It starts with events, moves to identity, then leaves behind a memory or mark on society. This memory for trauma theorists often turns out to be a new master narrative, or story-based way of being for a community moving forward.

The first stage of trauma occurs when events disrupt identity. Identity sets markers for what a community values, its definition of and expectations for the good life.[24] Trauma is by definition a perceived attack on these most fundamental of values. It centers on developments that become "represented as obliterating, damaging or rendering problematic something sacred," observes Smelser, "usually a value or outlook felt to be essential for the integrity of the affected community."[25] Trauma happens when events are, therefore, more than just vaguely unsettling in some way. For events to be traumatic, they must be existentially challenging as well, going to the core of who the group is in a way that "dislodges patterns of meaning."[26] Since the standard here is the identity-impact of events, one important implication of this is that any event regardless of apparent "size" (i.e., from "big" events like the Great Depression or the Holocaust to "small" events like Nazi Germany's invasion of the Rhineland or the Czech coup of 1948) can collectively traumatize a group or nation in ways that affect master narrative strength, so long as the event is perceived as a challenge to group identity.[27]

These kinds of identity-challenging events create deep emotional reactions (i.e., "laden with affect") for the traumatized group. They tend to throw a community into tumult. Emotions ranging from "disgust, shame, guilt . . . or anxiety" may set in.[28] These emotions lead to the second phase of the trauma process: a collective search for answers. The event-driven "strain" to social expectations "requires fixing," according to Smelser.[29] An emotional and collectively disoriented group will search, then, to find new direction. In this sense, traumatic events set a community on a quest for what Jennifer Mitzen labels "ontological security-seeking." Above all else, a search for new "routines" sets in in order to "pacify the cognitive environment," or to essentially restore a clear, systematic way of being to help actors settle in again to stable, identity routines that help them "get by in the world."[30]

Here, narrative enters the trauma process. The collective, event-driven search for answers opens space for social agents, or carrier groups, to explain what is happening through stories that, under the right conditions, become new master narratives. This is the third phase of the trauma process. "Whether or not the structures of meaning are destabilized and shocked is the result of an exercise of human agency," according to Jeffrey Alexander.[31] Carrier groups do this kind of work. These "cultural specialists" can include any variety of respected individuals in society from priests and politicians to intellectuals, journalists and moral entrepreneurs or activists.[32] In times of identity disruptions, the affected community looks here for guidance and explanation, to the presumed wise figures in society. These actors step in and tell stories that help explain events and set a way going forward.

This raises an important question: which stories become the new collective wisdom? When painful and shocking events happen, multiple carriers often tell, in fact, competing stories about the events, including some who say there is no trauma at all. Some accounts of ideational change claim that a policy context like this with many competing voices is so confusing that the collective tends to retreat to the status quo—too many competing social carriers means less change to master narratives, then.[33] Trauma theory argues something different than this, however. The reason for this lies with the fact that events causing identity pain do far more than simply create space or a tabula rasa for a broader discussion among different groups. They also give specific *content* to the space in which agents operate and build stories. More specifically, events tilt the playing field (or bias the political opportunity structure) to privilege stories from some carrier groups more than others.[34] Thus, even when carriers tell clear and complete stories that match standards set by literary theorists, for instance, they can still be shunned, or fail to set the new master narrative landscape if the story does not fit the prevailing opportunity structure created by traumatic events. Contrary to the standard account, then, not just any well-detailed story will restore ontological security and become a national security narrative.[35] The story must also be right by the times, an appropriate fit given the event-driven experiences of the collective at the moment.

The importance of this "fit" should not surprise us. Event-driven political opportunity structure has been shown to explain strength in identity-based collective ideas in general, especially in U.S. foreign policy. Take the example of human rights norms. In the 1980s, different activist groups battled to determine the strength of human rights values in U.S. foreign policy toward apartheid in South Africa. A series of massacres by the South African government in mid-decade stunned the U.S. public and shattered hopes for liberal change in South Africa, which tilted the debate (i.e., privileging the political opportunity structure) in favor of arguments by human rights advocates. Extant collective beliefs in the form of human rights norms strengthened as a result and two rounds of U.S. government sanctions followed.[36] In this case, certain events (i.e., the repressive acts by the South African government) intersected with the liberal identity of the United States, which in turn, benefited some agents (and their stories) more than others. When it comes to master narratives, different kinds of traumatic events do the same thing. They essentially bend the collective ear of the injured group to listen to some stories more than others, to label some as "good" and others "bad."[37]

So what are "good," or effective, stories that help set the master narrative table? Simply stated, effective stories are those that start with and center around the *affirmation* or *validation* of the disquiet generated by events and which set a course for healing, or repair ("yes, something has changed and we need to do something about it"). This is the fourth, and final, piece of the trauma process. People experiencing identity disruptions want empathy from carrier groups, to hear trusted figures start by saying that the pain is "pain." As Alexander puts it, carriers gain, therefore, a special hearing—or find a space in the political opportunity structure—when they "decide to represent social pain as a fundamental threat to . . . [a group's] sense of who they are, where they came from, and where they want to go."[38] In tandem with the emotions of existential challenge, ongoing or later events that match parts of the story that social carriers tell tend, in turn, to elevate those stories all the more. The pain-validating narratives become indelible, the new collective wisdom. Human rights advocates in the apartheid case did this. Their voices broke through largely because their story matched the identity disquiet (i.e., the collective shock of human rights abuses) created by ongoing events in South Africa.[39] A pain-validating story, then, allowed human rights groups to both set the table for the national conversation and lead the way toward policy change.

The latter—new directions toward repair (or policy)—is almost always a natural part of the pain-validating stories that effective carrier groups tell.[40] In this sense, carriers that matter not only affirm identity pain, they also generally attribute responsibility or name a "perpetrator," then set lessons for how the community should live moving forward.[41] They narrate ways for "defense and coping" or identify "repair work that needs to be done," drawing attention to "mistakes and how they may be avoided in the future" (i.e., blame and moral).[42] Pointing repeatedly to social pain in the past and present, then, effective carrier groups set the community's focus on the future, on new ways of being going forward in light of the pain in the past.[43] These new ways of being and the stories behind them show up as strengthened or new master narratives.[44]

What does this all mean for explaining national security narratives, and more specifically, the vitally important, yet currently underspecified, liberal and restraint narratives in U.S. foreign policy?[45] The answer is straightforward. Notably, we need to understand not just whether groups storytell, or whether shocking events occur. Instead, we need to understand the "fit" between two things: different types of event-driven social pain, and the kinds of carrier group stories that speak effectively into that particular type of pain (or opportunity structure).

Understanding this fit explains liberal and restraint narrative strength over time. For each of these narrative, the fit between events and story type is unique.

TRAUMA AND NARRATIVE STRENGTH

This general framework with its focus on events and carrier group stories offers several pathways to explain change in the strength of the liberal narrative over time and within that the conditions under which restraint narratives emerge in collective thinking.[46]

Pathway 1: Rising Threats, Promoters, and the Strengthening of the Liberal Narrative. Different types of trauma have different effects on collectives. One trauma pathway of particular importance to the liberal narrative involves external events. Trauma theorists find that when a trauma-causing event(s) comes from some force *outside* a community, it can lead to group unity and commitment to a story centered on protecting the ideals of the community as a means of defense, or repair.[47] Event-driven contexts like these often result in a strong collective affirmation of "who we are" as an avenue toward greater future security.[48]

This kind of external trauma explains how the liberal narrative strengthens and one pathway by which it weakens. To understand this, requires starting, of course, with identity. A broad literature in international relations finds that, liberal states (including the public in these states) view other states and developments in the international system through the ideological lens of their own regime type. Along these lines, liberal citizens across borders tend to sympathize with one another or "benefit from a presumption of amity," according to Michael Doyle, while looking with collective suspicion and "enmity" on nonliberals.[49] As one manifestation of this, liberal democratic societies, like the United States, almost instinctually ponder, notice, and worry about the plight of liberal order abroad.[50] They tend, furthermore, to "identify their own interests with the interests of like states."[51] In this sense, liberal societies associate the expansion of the good life with the expansion and thriving of liberalism abroad. They see their security as closely tied to liberal political order beyond their own borders. Liberal polities cannot help but notice, then, when states take positive steps toward democratization, like the changes in East-Central Europe at the end of the Cold War; when governments slaughter their own citizens, as in Rwanda in the 1990s; or when militants like the Islamic State terrorize population groups and behead innocent civilians.

This same identity grid helps explain how the liberal narrative strengthens in the United States. The important identity-centric events here are the geostrategic gains of ideologically different—in this case illiberal—great powers. Geostrategic gains that matter here range on the low end from diplomatic disputes with ideologically distant states to, on the high end, military action against the United States or kindred liberal states. Most important, these kinds of events generate national angst—emotions like fear, panic and worry often emerge, which leads to a collective, national search for explanation and direction (i.e., ontological security-seeking). As this happens, social carriers begin to narrate about the events. For the sake of simplicity, I lump these groups into one of two categories. "Promoters" generally tell stories that center on how geostrategic steps by an ideologically distant state are a challenge to the nation's way of life that demands a robust defense of liberal order. "Moderators," by contrast, tell stories about the importance of not overreacting, downplay ideological differences and offer a less idealistic, more restrained way of approaching foreign policy.[52]

The specific political opportunity space created by external trauma events favors promoters. Geopolitical gains by ideologically distant states raise fears across the public of a challenge to the nation and its core values. Stories from promoters who offer some initial validation of this—saying "yes, something is wrong and we need to defend our way of life"—get a special hearing, as a result.[53] These promoter stories tend to paint a picture of existential danger in the present and future, as well as assign blame (sometimes, to poor government policies for not preventing the challenge) and call for new action to defend liberal order abroad as the moral to the story.

The pace and extent to which the new promoter story becomes the collective wisdom (i.e., strengthens) depends on the nature of events, or the political opportunity structure. If the gains of an ideologically distant state come through direct attack on the United States (i.e., Pearl Harbor or 9/11), the pain of the event is often so intense that promoters carry the day almost immediately. In these circumstances, the liberal narrative strengthens both quickly and substantially, settling in as a new dominant framework for engaging global politics.[54]

A similar but slower process occurs when geostrategic gains are more indirect. If the rival's geopolitical gains come in some other part of the world, the identity challenge may seem ambiguous, especially to the broader public ("it feels painful, but is it really?").[55] Sensing this, promoter storytelling (especially around lessons, or what should be done) are often more modest and national debates more contested. The collective strengthening of the liberal narrative across the public may come with certain fits and starts as a result. In the end, ongoing events become critical. In a path-dependent way, an ideological foe's continued geostrategic gains bring added collective validation to promoter stories.[56] A "see I told you so" response emerges and the liberal narrative strengthens.[57] Most important for policy, this narrative strengthening shows up as an unambiguous national passion to promote liberal political order abroad and/or stop a counter-ideology from spreading.[58] This strengthened liberal narrative will tend to remain strong as long as the rival maintains its great power status and ideological distance from the liberal state (i.e., does not become liberal itself).[59]

The period surrounding World War II offers a good example. Nazi Germany's invasion of the Rhineland in 1936 created a great deal of identity-based angst in the United States, spawning a debate over different stories about these events told by internationalists (promoters) and isolationists (moderators). A subsequent string of additional German gains from the Anschluss to the dismantling of Czechoslovakia and invasions of Poland and France created added space for promoter stories to resonate. National passion to defend democracy in Europe strengthened, paving the way for U.S. entry into World War II.[60]

Pathway 2: Declining Ideological Threats, Moderators, and the Weakening of the Liberal Narrative. The decline of an ideological threat accounts for one way by which the liberal narrative weakens.[61] Sometimes, an extant ideological rival may take conciliatory steps, like initiating negotiations or backing off of prior geopolitical gains, which tends to create a collective response of "What's going on, this seems out of the ordinary." This type of political opportunity tends to favor or give space to moderator stories that the foe may be more normal, or not as ideologically dangerous, as previously thought.[62] As a by-product of moderator storytelling in this event context, the liberal narrative usually weakens, which means, most important, that the collective national passion to protect/promote liberal order wanes. This change may not be dramatic—after all, the rival is still ideologically distant and a great power. But some weakening in the liberal narrative is likely nonetheless.

More dramatic decline in liberal narrative strength can occur when an ideological rival disappears altogether. A rival may change its ideology entirely, or lose its great power status, usually due to a lost war. When either happens, "success anomie"—in essence, a collective sense of lost purpose amid victory—sets in for the nation ("what are we to do now?").[63] With the initial source of external trauma gone altogether, this kind of national uncertainty creates political space for moderators. As moderators narrate the need for pullback and focus on the home front, old stories about the need to defend liberal order seem antiquated or built for a different time. A sharp decline in the strength of the liberal narrative generally follows.

Pathway 3: Disillusionment, Moderators, the Weakening of the Liberal Narrative, and Emergence of Restraint Narratives. A second major form of trauma can come from events *internal* to a community. Sometimes a collective's own behavior traumatizes it by violating "one or more of society's fundamental cultural premises."[64] Under these conditions, sociologists find that collective disillusionment sets in, which is defined by emotions like anger and disappointment around a deep sense of broken trust (especially toward community, business, or political leaders). Social divisions, uncertainty, doubts, and a sense of mistakes sets in. As this happens, space opens for social carriers to tell new stories that cast doubt on conventional ways of doing things as well as propose new lessons on how the group should live. These lessons take hold collectively. "Values become valueless" and "beliefs are refuted," according to trauma theorists.[65] The master narratives behind these kinds of disillusioning events often become labeled wrong-headed and lose collective strength—at least for a time. Perhaps more important, new master narratives can form as a defense mechanism against going down the traumatic road again.

Internal trauma can emerge around the foreign policy of liberal states like the United States, which can, in turn, weaken the liberal narrative and give rise to a strengthened restraint narrative. Identity is again the starting point here. Citizens in liberal states not only view world events through the grid of their own regime type, they also expect policy to generally look good and right by the nation's values. Especially in times of war when the nation is shedding blood and treasure, the public anticipates not simply success against a foe, but that its state's own behavior and policy outcomes match its creed (i.e., broadly liberal, in our case here). Foreign policy elites sometimes encourage this by justifying policy with a robust liberal narrative.[66] This creates collective expectations that the nation is fighting the good fight, for liberal ends by liberal means.

When a series of events demonstrates otherwise, national disillusionment can emerge. Public revelations of illiberal behavior by the United States or its allies in a liberal narrative-justified endeavor (especially war) shakes the nation, creating a sense of broad-based disquiet about current policy. The nation searches for clarity and new direction (i.e., ontological security-seeking). This gives moderators, in particular, an opening. Their stories about immoral leaders and blame of the ideas that caused those policies tend to validate and reinforce the collective sense of national disillusionment. Similar to the process surrounding external trauma, stories like these gain added resonance as further examples of illiberal behavior come to light ("see I told you so").

In the United States experience, the internal trauma that results has distinct short-term and long-term consequences for master narratives. First, in the short-term, internal trauma causes not only doubt about current policy, but discredits the master narrative—that is, the liberal narrative—that justified the policy in the first place. It does so by dampening the effects of threat. In this sense, the stories that moderators tell around the disillusioning events generate so much collective confusion and questioning about liberal order protection/promotion that it distracts publics from—or leads to a downplaying of—challenges posed by ideological rivals. Under these conditions, the liberal narrative often loses collective salience (i.e., weakens) as a guiding story for how the nation should engage world politics. In U.S. foreign policy, Vietnam offers the classic example. Brutal images of U.S. military personnel burning villages in Vietnam, killing innocent civilians, and condoning the human-rights-violating policies of the South Vietnamese regime created anger and disappointment, which kicked off a surge of antiwar protests back home in the United States. From protest leaders to policy pundits and members of Congress, moderators told a story of presidential deception and violation of core U.S. values that gripped the nation. One major byproduct of this was a national retreat from idealistic foreign policy goals (i.e., a weakening liberal narrative) in the late 1960s and 1970s.[67]

These kinds of master narrative effects do not last forever, though—they are generally short-term or temporary. Specifically, the hold of internal trauma on the liberal narrative tends to loosen when the nation extracts itself from the circumstances causing disillusionment. Under these conditions, the emotional fodder for disillusionment fades. Most important, if ideologically distant rivals remain in the system and take steps to achieve new geopolitical gains, promoters will often find a context that increasingly allows them to re-narrate events (something akin to pathway one above). The liberal narrative is likely to strengthen, again, under these circumstances.

Yet, even when this happens, internal trauma is not easily forgotten. It generally has other kinds of long-term narrative consequences too. Disillusionment with its deep self-criticism, internal divisions, and doubts scars a group or a polity in unique ways ("I can't believe we did *that*" or "how did we get into this mess?"). Because of this, moderator stories of events naturally tend to include a moral (i.e., lessons) intended to protect collective identity by preventing a return of the "tear to the social fabric."[68] These lessons settle in as a new collective attitude of "never again." When it comes to foreign policy, this never-again attitude takes the form of restraint narratives that include, most important, normative taboos against certain actions that moderators frame and the nation comes to perceive, therefore, as having generated the initial internal trauma. The Vietnam syndrome, for instance, involved prohibitions against specific kinds of policies that were blamed for dragging the United States into the disillusionment-generating Vietnam War. Hence, while internal trauma may lose its grip on the liberal narrative over time, it generally leaves behind a strengthened restraint narrative which demands that in advancing and protecting liberal order, certain old ways of doing things are off limits. These taboos are powerful, serving as a new master narrative alongside the liberal narrative.[69]

From the above discussion, we can posit the following hypothesis:

> *Geopolitical gains by ideologically distant states combined with promoter stories create external trauma that strengthens the liberal narrative;*

illiberal outcomes in war coupled with moderator stories creates inter-
nal trauma that weakens the liberal narrative; internal trauma generates
restraint narratives.

The Policy Impact of Master Narratives

Explaining the impact of master narratives on policy choices, like patterns of forceful regime change, requires starting with some broad conceptual work. Up to this
point, we have seen the constitutive effects of the liberal and restraint narratives
on the United States, meaning that master narratives shape and determine interests or who the nation sees itself as being abroad. When it comes to actual policy
outcomes, the liberal and restraint narratives can, at times, have these same kinds
of effects.[70] From the beginning of his run for the White House in 2008, Barack
Obama wrapped himself, for instance, in the Iraq syndrome in ways that constituted his presidency by shaping preferences away from the polices of his predecessor. This contributed to Obama's decisions for greater military restraint in regime
crises in Libya and Syria. A second, and what I anticipate to be more common, way
that master narratives effect policy, though, is via a pathway that is less constitutive
and more regulative. To this end, master narratives matter by generally constraining elite decisions rather than determining elite preferences. Sometimes, these narratives create political space for leaders to follow their preferred course of action. In
other instances, they force leaders to choose action they would otherwise prefer not
to take. When and how does this happen? How do we explain the regulative impact
of master narratives on patterns of forceful regime change?

Audience Costs. The answer to these questions is found in the contested nature
of democratic politics, and more specifically, with "audience costs."[71] Audience
costs are the "domestic political price that the leader would pay" for making policy choices that contradict strong public preferences and dispositions.[72] In general, they are costs that leaders face when domestic audiences become "concerned
with whether the leadership is successful or unsuccessful at foreign policy."[73]
Given the nature of their political system, leaders in democratic states are especially sensitive to these kinds of costs. Above all else, leaders fear negative political consequences—such as a loss in future elections or damage to their broader
policy agenda—for being out of step with positions held by domestic audiences,
notably the wider public.

Though not explicitly stated in the current literature, audience costs can take
two different forms, with each having significantly different implications for policy. Sometimes, audience costs consist of *costs for inaction*. These kinds of costs
involve punishment of a leader for doing too little abroad, or "for looking weak
on the world stage" in some way.[74] When a leader faces conditions that generate

these high costs for inaction, it creates incentives for a more robust, active and, if necessary, forceful policy agenda abroad.[75] In other instances, audience costs consist of just the opposite, notably *costs for action*. These kinds of costs tend to press leaders to refrain from aggressive actions abroad, including and especially the use of force.[76] Scholars find that these different kinds of audience costs—costs for action and costs for inaction—have a profound impact on policy, especially when it comes to bargaining in crisis situations. In many instances, audience costs push leaders into taking strong policy positions that they otherwise would prefer not to take.[77]

Audience costs help us better understand patterns of forceful regime change in U.S. foreign policy. More specifically, master narratives shape policy decisions about forceful regime promotion in cases where the liberal and restraint narratives generate audience costs for action and/or inaction. This raises an important question: how and when does this happen?

Standard accounts tell us that audience costs emerge in instances where a president or prime minister makes a public commitment to some kind of action (or inaction) abroad. These public commitments raise, in turn, national expectations that the president will follow through on his/her pledge, thus making it too politically costly (i.e., audience costs) for the president to later back down from the commitment.[78]

Master narrative audience costs form in a different way from this. Notably, they generally emerge not from executive-branch commitments, but instead through a process of social construction.[79] To be more specific, they emerge through public discourses. To this end, the national political discourses that develop around master narratives from one case of regime crisis to the next present presidents and other policy elites with different domestic political cost-benefit scenarios that affect their decisions on whether or not to pursue forceful regime promotion. In some cases, the national discourse generates high audience costs for inaction that encourage or reinforce presidential decisions to utilize more robust force for regime promotion ends. In other cases, the domestic discourse creates high audience costs for action that encourage or reinforce presidential decisions for non-to-limited military intervention for regime promotion goals.[80] These different discourses are shaped in part by the choices that moderators and promoters make about when and how to argue for policy change. Before moving into more specific predictions about forceful regime promotion, we need to briefly discuss what affects these choices given their critical importance to the argument.

The Choices Promoters and Moderators Make. As discussed more below, the case-specific discourses that create audience costs for action and inaction are a function of robust master narratives coupled with arguments by promoters and moderators for and against military action. These agents do not build discourses in every case of regime crisis abroad, however. Instead, they are selective and calculating, choosing to argue or press the case for action in some instances but not others. What explains these choices?

The answer to this question is straightforward and, most important, largely unrelated to any of the alternative explanations below, meaning that an important part of this book's argument is not epiphenomenal to other factors such as geopolitical shifts or the ideological make-up of foreign policy elites. Instead in a nutshell, when regime crises occur abroad, promoters and moderators argue for their preferred option (i.e., robust military action for promoters and no military action for moderators), unless one of the following conditions applies, in which case social groups either create discourses with less stringent demands than they would prefer, or apply no pressure at all on policymakers.[81]

The first potential condition involves the strength of extant master narratives. Notably, when a carrier group's kindred master narrative (such as the liberal narrative for promoters) is weak or the countervailing master narrative for a group (such as the liberal narrative for moderators) is strong, carrier groups tend to show restraint in pressing their agenda(s). The reason for this lies with broader legitimacy or political salience. Groups care about their policy goals, but they are also sensitive not to propose action that will appear extreme to a wider audience, which could cost the group in terms of political capital and effectiveness. In short, promoters and moderators operate like other kinds of social entrepreneurs and activists in that they press their most preferred course of action when they perceive clear windows of opportunity as determined by the master narrative context. When these windows appear to groups as merely cracked (due to strong countervailing narratives) or closed altogether (due to a weak kindred narrative), promoters and moderators pull back entirely or tone down their demands for action.[82] Certain progressives who opposed U.S. entrance into World War I eventually quit advocating for their position altogether, for example, because of the harsh domestic political backlash that they faced amid rising liberal narrative sentiment among the U.S. public to turn back the tide of German autocracy in Europe.[83] This kind of choice happens when kindred/countervailing narrative contexts are not perceived as being to an agent's favor.

Second, similar to other social agents, promoters and moderators often have constituencies or are part of broader coalitions with other groups. Sometimes, interests and philosophical dispositions vary across these broader constituencies/coalitions. Social groups worry, then, that pushing their most preferred course of action could alienate certain constituencies or fracture their coalition in ways that weaken their overall cause. Hence, even if a social group's kindred master narrative is strong, promoters and moderators may choose more restrained discourses when they perceive that acting otherwise could damage broader cohesion.[84] Despite a robust liberal narrative in the late 1940s, cold warriors in the Republican Party chose not to advocate for the deployment of U.S. ground troops to aid Chiang Kai-shek's anticommunist forces in China due, in part, to fears that they might lose the support of the more isolationist, cost-cutting leaders of the party who opposed an expansion of government spending, including for the military.[85]

Third, moderators and promoters are like other social groups in that they have limited time and resources. According to one scholar, groups "worry about costs and benefits" as well as whether they have the "resources to accommodate goals."[86] Groups sometimes build discourses, then, in some cases of regime crisis and not others due to constraints related to available resources. In making these choices, groups again tend to think in terms of perceived windows of opportunity. They want to be heard, so groups usually focus their attention on higher profile cases, meaning regime crises that draw greater media, executive branch, and congressional interest (which again, can be a function of master narratives). Even when a kindred narrative is strong, promoters and moderators might choose not to build a discourse around some cases of regime crisis due to the distraction with other cases.[87]

PREDICTIONS FOR FORCEFUL REGIME PROMOTION

The stage is now set to explore more specific predictions about master narratives and forceful regime promotion. Table 1.1 presents four possible outcomes depending on the strength and weakness of policy discourses centered on the liberal and restraint narratives.

Strong-Liberal, Weak-Restraint Discourse. Full-scale military interventions for forceful regime promotion are most likely when a strong liberal narrative

TABLE 1.1 Predictions for regime change interventions based on strength of liberal and restraint discourses

| | LIBERAL DISCOURSE | |
	STRONG	WEAK
RESTRAINT DISCOURSE STRONG	1 Mixed outcomes more likely	2 Non-to-limited force most likely
WEAK	Full-scale military force most likely 3	Less determinate 4

discourse and weak restraint narrative discourse develops around cases of a regime crisis abroad (cell 3, table 1.1). Two conditions are necessary to produce a strong liberal discourse. First, the liberal narrative itself must be strong, meaning as noted already that the national interest in protecting and/or promoting liberal order abroad is especially elevated. Second, promoters must argue for robust action to deal with the specific regime crisis at hand. Promoters gain a privileged hearing in this master narrative context, not because of qualities unique to themselves (like rhetorical style, government office or ideological passion). Instead, the robust liberal narrative augments their arguments in critical ways. Similar to the external trauma process discussed above, this narrative context grants promoters a special hearing with the public and in policy debates, generally. By tapping into existing national concerns about protecting liberal order abroad (i.e., the strong liberal narrative), these promoter arguments create (or policymakers fear they will create) broad public movements for action in the particular case at hand.

This kind of strong liberal discourse affects, in turn, the decisions that leaders make about forceful regime promotion in one of two ways. Sometimes, presidents with no ideological or strategic interests in taking action come to fear audience *costs for inaction* and, hence, get "pushed to act" into using force. Policymakers worry most that doing nothing could land them on the wrong side of deep public concerns about protecting liberal order, which could in turn threaten future elections or other policy goals.[88] They fear the public will punish them for looking weak on defending liberal order abroad. When the restraint discourse is weak (see discussion below), these kinds of costs for inaction loom especially large for leaders. Under these conditions, leaders choose to use force for regime promotion, even if they think that it makes little sense. President Harry Truman preferred to draw Korea outside of the U.S. defense perimeter but felt compelled to enter the Korean War and cross the 38th parallel in large measure due to fear that inaction might hurt his standing politically at home and with that his chance for reelection in 1952.[89]

At other times, the choice for forceful regime promotion under cell 3 conditions may take more of a "free-hand-to-act" scenario. In these circumstances, the strong liberal discourse plays a more conducive, rather than determinative, role in the decision-making process. Here, a president may already be inclined for ideological reasons to adopt forceful regime promotion. A strong liberal discourse in a weak restraint environment lowers the domestic political costs for the president to follow through on these inclinations. It essentially creates an open political space to take preferred military action.

Regardless of which of these two scenarios plays out, full-scale military invasions are the most likely outcome under cell 3 conditions. A president who opts for more limited methods (like covert operations) does so at great political risk given the especially animated liberal discourse among the public. Leaders would rather be politically safe than sorry, and safety lies with robust military action in this master narrative context.

Weak-Liberal, Strong-Restraint Discourse. This scenario often presents the opposite domestic political incentives for policymakers to those just discussed. Hence, forceful regime change interventions will be least frequent and most limited under these conditions (cell 2, table 1.1). Start with a weak liberal discourse. This might be the result of the broader liberal narrative, itself, being weak at a point when a regime crisis emerges abroad. Under these conditions, moderator arguments about the need for or appropriateness of restraint tend to resonate more with the public, while promoter arguments (if there are any at all) appear odd, or maybe even extreme. Under a different scenario, a weak liberal discourse around a case of regime crisis abroad may be the result of choices made by promoters. For reasons discussed earlier, promoters sometimes opt against arguing for robust military action, even when the liberal narrative is strong. Under either one of these scenarios of weak liberal discourse, costs for inaction are especially low for leaders.

In these cell 2 conditions, a strong restraint discourse amplifies all the more the disincentives to use force for regime promotion. Two factors are necessary to produce a strong restraint discourse around a particular regime crisis. First, restraint narratives must be strong, meaning, as noted already, that story-based taboos resulting from some highly disillusioning prior experience are especially elevated in collective national thinking. Second, moderators must argue for non-to-limited military action to deal with the specific regime crisis at hand. Here again, what gives these agents leverage is the master narrative context. The robust restraint narrative creates a political opportunity space that augments moderator arguments, giving them a special hearing with the public and in policy debates. By tapping into national skepticism around the robust restraint narrative these moderators create (or policymakers fear they will create) broad public movements against military action.

Together, weak liberal and strong restraint discourses make audience *costs for action*, then, exceedingly high for presidents and other policymakers as well. These conditions work to either constrain leadership elites inclined toward force or allow a president with little interest in using force additional domestic political space at home to follow his/her wishes. In general, perceived or real costs for action are so high here that leaders often come to view the use of force as almost prohibited under cell 2 conditions—anything more could potentially hurt their public standing in ways that damage their electoral future or wider policy agenda. Inaction or low-cost and highly conscribed military interventions are most likely. In the 1920s,

President Calvin Coolidge pressed Congress to approve large-scale military operations in Mexico and Nicaragua to prevent the spread of communism. A coalition of progressives and conservative isolationists built national resistance to this plan around restraint-laden and anticrusading public attitudes at the time. Worried about his political future, Coolidge deferred to this pressure and backed down altogether from intervention in Mexico while restricting military action in Nicaragua to nothing more than the protection of U.S. property.[90]

Weak-Liberal, Weak-Restraint Discourse. When discourse around the liberal and restraint narratives are both weak, leaders face a more ambiguous domestic political environment that gives master narratives a less determinate role in decisions about forceful regime promotion (cell 4, table 1.1). The prior section discussed weak liberal discourses. A weak restraint discourse can result from either the broader restraint narrative being weak—that is, there is little taboo-mentality across the nation—or a choice by moderators not to build a restraint discourse around a specific case of regime crisis abroad.

With weak master narrative signals like these, presidents and other policymakers find more space to set policy to their own liking. In fact, this context is one in which elite ideological dispositions tend to matter the most in decisions about forceful regime promotion. This does not mean, of course, that master narratives are altogether irrelevant here. For one, the master narrative context grants elites the domestic political space or freedom to make their own choices. The weak liberal narrative, in particular, may lead presidents to worry about whether the nation will accept costs associated with the use of force. This can incline them toward low-cost military action at most. All the same, these signals are still muddled, making elite dispositions a more prominent factor under these weak narrative conditions.[91]

Strong-Liberal, Strong-Restraint Discourse. Finally, leaders face a deeply conflicted decision- making environment in cases where liberal and restraint discourses are both strong (cell 1, table 1.1). Promoters and moderators find fertile ground nationally to press their arguments in times like these. Audience *costs for action* and *costs for inaction* are high, as a result. All the same, given the close connection between restraint narratives and the use of force, leadership elites are most sensitive to costs for action in this scenario. Augmented by a strong restraint narrative, moderators gain a special hearing with the public and leaders in general. Consequently, mixed policies involving military engagement that leans away from robust military action usually result here.[92] In the early 1980s, for instance, the Reagan administration found enough domestic political space from a strong liberal discourse to defy the prevailing Vietnam-syndrome taboos and provide a limited number of military advisors and sizeable military aid to the noncommunist regime in El Salvador. The desires of

<u>**Stage 1:**</u>
Master narrative strength

<u>**Stage 2:**</u>
Narrative discourses and the use of force

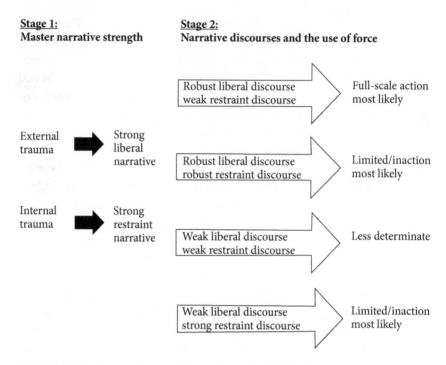

FIGURE 1.1.   The master narrative explanation of forceful regime promotion

some within the administration for even more robust direct military action were stymied, however, by fears of a moderator-fueled backlash across the public that El Salvador might become "Another Vietnam."[93] The policy outcome was a bargain of sorts, then, between the countervailing pressures of two strong master narrative discourses.

Figure 1.1 offers a picture of the entire master narrative argument. The following hypothesis captures the argument as well:

> *In cases of regime crisis abroad where the liberal discourse is strong and restraint discourse weak, robust military action for regime promotion is most likely; In cases of regime crisis abroad where the restraint discourse is strong, limited/nonintervention outcomes are most likely.*

Alternative Explanations

I now turn to explanations for forceful regime change related to factors other than narratives. In discussing each alternative, I develop both a direct explanation of forceful regime promotion and an explanation of change in the strength of the liberal narrative over time.[94] The latter is important, because if the liberal narrative is epiphenomenal to any of these other factors, it means that a direct relationship between the liberal narrative and forceful regime promotion is spurious, a function in essence of some greater cause that deserves more attention than master narratives.

Elite Ideological Polarization

As noted at the outset of this chapter, the master narrative argument is a holistic ideational approach that brings together both elite-based and collective narratives. If that integrated approach fairs no better at explaining outcomes than a stand-alone elite argument, then there is no value to the master narrative argument. Consequently, this book tests a stand-alone elite polarization argument alongside the master narrative argument. As noted earlier, John Owen contends that elite polarization occurs during great power wars and at points of regime crises abroad. When this happens, robust forceful regime promotion becomes most likely. Elite polarization also offers an explanation for liberal narrative strength. While Owen never addresses this directly, he indicates that elites and the broader nation move in lockstep as polarization occurs.[95] By implication, the latter appears to be a product of the former. Simply stated, elites polarize and the nation follows suit, meaning the liberal narrative strengthens when leaders, especially heads of state, press it to do so.

Overall, the elite polarization argument offers the following hypotheses:

> An increase in elite ideological polarization results in the strengthening of the liberal narrative and increases the likelihood of full-scale military interventions for forceful regime promotion.

Geopolitics and Elite Fearmongering

Realists offer a pair of competing arguments about liberal narrative strength as well as an account of the conditions under which forceful regime promotion is most likely. On liberal narrative strength, some realists point to the important manipulative role of elite fearmongering. John Mearsheimer argues, specifically, that when elites perceive threats abroad, they tend to use all available tools, including ideological language, to rally the nation to action.[96] By the logic of this argument, a robust public passion to protect liberal order abroad emerges when elites fearmonger around perceived threats and vice versa.

A second vein of realist thinking that focuses more directly on geopolitics also offers an account of liberal narrative strength and a clear realist explanation for when forceful regime promotion is most likely. According to realists, states care primarily about their security and survival. Consequently, they focus intently on the relative power of other states in the international system. This turns out to be the primary reason that states adjust policy: when geopolitical dynamics shift and threat perceptions subsequently change, policy tends to change as well.[97]

Since states care so much about geopolitics and not the domestic make-up of other states, some realists anticipate that costly endeavors to protect liberal order will be rare and anomalous. These realists view regime change, then, as a topic unworthy of study.[98] Others argue something different, however. While agreeing that forceful regime change is a dangerous waste of resources, some realists note that when a great power like the United States feels secure, the temptation or the space to pursue secondary objectives, like forceful regime promotion, presents itself to that power.[99] This kind of security generally emerges when a powerful state faces a low threat environment, usually resulting from hegemonic or near-hegemonic status in the international system or a particular region of the world. An overwhelming preponderance of power like this creates space for a nation to focus more on its type of political order spreading. Public interest in promoting liberal order (i.e., the liberal narrative) can strengthen under these conditions. This preponderance of power also tempts or creates space for liberal great powers to use force for regime promotion since the threat of great power war or possibility of broader strategic losses appear low. Elites are more likely to think that they will be successful in achieving their aims under these conditions.[100] For realists, this explains policy during the 1990s and 2000s. According to this argument, the hegemonic status of the United States following the collapse of the Soviet Union allowed policymakers to focus on the secondary objectives of regime change in places like Haiti, Afghanistan, and Iraq.[101]

Based on the above, realism offers the following hypotheses:

> A strong liberal narrative is most likely either when policy elites fear-monger, or when national threat perceptions are low; while rare, robust efforts at forceful regime promotion are most likely when threat perceptions are low.[102]

Methods

This book argues that master narratives—the liberal and restraint narrative—play a critical role in explaining levels of force for regime promotion abroad in U.S. foreign policy. It demonstrates this primarily through a set of eight case studies (chapters 3–6). The book also tests major parts of the argument statistically against the alternatives in U.S. foreign policy from 1900 to 2011 (chapter 2). The study begins in 1900 because scholars generally agree that the

United States became a great power around the turn of the twentieth century. The qualitative and quantitative portions of the book assess two things: first, change in master narrative strength over time and, second, the impact of the liberal and restraint narratives on patterns of forceful regime promotion. Here I focus on methods used in the case studies. Statistical methods are discussed in the next chapter.

Case studies allow closer attention to the internal validity of the master narrative argument, especially the role of social carriers and their case-specific discourses that determine patterns of forceful regime promotion. A potential "case" consists of a regime crisis where a foreign government faces, or recently faced, an internal or external resistance movement intent on toppling the regime. Resistance movements can take many forms, from coups to armed domestic insurgents to cross-border invasions by foreign insurgents or another state's military. Chapters 3–6 cover eight cases where the United States adopted different responses (from full-scale military action to nonintervention) between 1900 and 2011 (table 1.2).[103] Each case-study chapter analyzes the state of the liberal and restraint discourses, then weighs the impact of the master narrative argument against the alternatives in explaining cases of forceful regime promotion.

With any ideational argument, tautology is a potential pitfall. In order to avoid this, the case studies use an approach of "symbolic structuring of discourse," that seeks to "understand the patterns and logics" of change in master narratives over time.[104] This approach involves process-tracing prior to and during the period at hand to paint a broad picture of strength in the liberal and restraint narratives. An assortment of sources is used to do this. The secondary literature for each case is substantial. Historians draw from a rich set of primary documents to understand the nature of the times. Patterns in broad statements by members

TABLE 1.2   Cases of forceful regime promotion and date of initial decision

TARGET COUNTRY	TYPE OF ACTION
China (1948–49)	No military action
South Korea (1950)	Full military intervention
Cuba (1961)	Limited military action
Vietnam (1965)	Full military intervention
El Salvador (1981–83)	No military action
Grenada (1983)	Full military intervention
Iraq (2003)	Full military intervention
Libya (2011)	Limited military intervention

of Congress and other political figures about the nation's mood are common and useful as well.[105] At points, these secondary sources are supplemented with commonly used primary sources, like speeches and editorials to capture patterns in collective thinking. Selective polling data is helpful here as well. Polls are especially useful when paired with other more commonly used or well-accepted measures of collective beliefs, like editorials. Polling data is used extensively, then, in this way in the case studies.

If the *liberal narrative* is strong, it will show up in the discussion around major foreign policy events prior to and at the time of decisions about forceful regime promotion. Editorials and congressional debates will talk about the prevailing story, meaning they will highlight major events, assign blame or identify a culprit, and, most important, focus extensively on promoting/protecting liberal order abroad and/or stopping the spread of counter-ideologies. Pundits and commentators at the time will also talk about the same things. Public opinion polls will often show similar trends. Finally, if the liberal narrative is strong, historians will highlight the prevailing story too, notably the national discussion around major events, the assigning of blame, and the nation's interest in protecting liberal order and stopping counter-ideologies. When the liberal narrative is weak, it will show up in the same measures. Above all else, editorials, congressional debate, polls and accounts by historians should talk about or show the public cares less about promoting democracy abroad or stopping counter-ideologies.

Geostrategic changes that spark collective *threat* perceptions and, with that, external trauma are measured in the cases by scanning the historical record for any geopolitical gains of ideologically distant greater powers. These include things like the seizure of new territory, use/demonstration of new weapons, and/or attacks on the United States or ideologically similar allied states. The stories that social carriers tell around these events are also measured using the historical record. Primary and secondary material is used to note the impact of these events and stories on the national disposition. Internal trauma events related to disillusionment are measured by scanning the historical record for publicly known behavior by the United States or its allies that appear to be illiberal, especially when costly to the United States, in essence, where soldiers died or considerable financial resources were involved. Like the above, the stories of social carriers are then detailed along with the impact of all of this on the national disposition.

Restraint narratives are measured using two methods. First, like the above, the case-study chapters use assessments by historians to determine the presence or not of restraint narratives (i.e., collective stories that identify certain painful events, assign blame/responsibility, and set a pathway moving forward) in different periods. Second, these observations are cross-checked by exploring policy debates about the use of force that occur after a period of disillusionment trauma and prior to the main case studies on regime promotion interventions. If restraint taboos exist around some forms of military intervention and not others, one should see contentious debates with references to past trauma across the public, in Congress, and between the executive and legislative branches when policy drifts toward types of force considered taboo. If taboos are real, policymakers and social carriers (especially moderators) will talk about them in applicable situations. Overall, this method allows for the painting of a clear picture of the contours, shape, and boundaries of restraint taboos in certain eras.

Process-tracing through the policy decision in each selected case allows for a close exploration of the impact, if any, of case-specific discourses on policy decisions for or against robust forceful regime promotion. If the master narrative argument is correct, memoirs, private papers, and assessments by historians should demonstrate that in making policy choices master narratives and arguments made by social carriers played a visible and important part in ways predicted above. To this end, leaders should talk about facing fewer domestic constraints to use force and/or the pressure (often reflected in comments about elections or other domestic political fallout) they feel to undertake robust military action when the liberal discourse is strong. When the liberal discourse is weak and/or restraint discourse is strong in turn, decision makers should talk about feeling constrained by public taboos against the use of force. Again reference, perhaps, to future elections or other potential fallout politically should also be common.

The selected case studies (table 1.2) offer extreme values on the dependent variable and are well matched for cross-case comparison which allows for the control of personality (pairing cases under the same presidential administration) and/or context (pairing cases by time period).[106] Sampling on the dependent variable is not a problem with these cases since they include instances of full-scale military force, limited force, and no force in and across different periods. This cross-temporal variation on the dependent variable also allows for the assessment of cross-temporal variation (if any) in the master narrative argument and variables in the competing explanations—all of which helps identify the most prevalent causal factors at work over time.[107] Finally, the selected cases control for issue area by focusing on cases of forceful regime promotion. This also allows for honing in on the causal processes at work without the distraction and complexity of crossing from one issue area to the next. Master narratives may affect other foreign policy decisions and policy tools, like sanctions or foreign aid, neither of which is the focus of this book.

THE BROAD PATTERNS

*(with Sara Dahill-Brown, Betina Wilkinson,
and Sandeep Mazumder)*

Between 1900 and 2011, the United States initiated twenty-seven military regime promotions. This chapter focuses, specifically, on better understanding when the United States pursues these kinds of invasions and how much force it uses in doing so. Table 2.1 notes the target state of each intervention, the year military operations began and ended, and the nature of the intervention (full, limited, or retreating) over time. "Full" interventions were those in which the United States used combat troops for the operation. "Limited" interventions were carried out with light military footprint in the target, most often using air power or naval bombardments. "Retreating" refers to cases where interventions started full-scale and were later pared down significantly, despite ongoing hostilities short of victory or an agreed upon cessation to conflict with a hostile party.[1] On balance, Table 2.1 tells us that when pursuing forceful regime promotion, the United States tends to use full-scale military operations most often (twenty of twenty-seven cases). Furthermore, in the few cases where change of intervention type occurred (Vietnam, Laos, Afghanistan, and Iraq), the dominant pattern was from "full-scale" to "retreating" military operations.

The central argument of this book is that politics around the changing strength of two master narratives—the liberal and the restraint narrative—helps explain forceful regime promotion in democratic foreign policy. This chapter uses statistical methods to test both explanations for change in liberal narrative strength and the impact of master narratives on broad, cross-temporal patterns in the frequency and robustness of forceful regime promotion in U.S. foreign policy from 1900 to 2011.

TABLE 2.1 Cases, dates, and nature of forceful regime promotion,
1900–2011

TARGET COUNTRY	DATES	FULL OR LIMITED
Cuba	1906	Limited
Nicaragua	1912	Limited
Mexico	1914–17	Limited
Haiti	1915	Full
Dominican Republic	1916	Full
Cuba	1917	Full
Soviet Union	1918–20	Limited
Italy	1943–45	Full
France	1944–45	Full
West Germany	1944–45	Full
South Korea	1945	Full
Japan	1944–45	Full
South Korea	1950–53	Full
North Korea	1950–52	Full
Lebanon	1958	Full
Laos	1964–73	Full (1964–68) Retreating (1969–73)
South Vietnam	1963–72	Full (1965–67) Retreating (1968–72)
Dominican Republic	1965	Full
Cambodia	1970–73	Limited
Grenada	1983	Full
Panama	1989–90	Full
Kuwait	1991	Full
Somalia	1993–94	Limited
Haiti	1994	Full
Afghanistan	2001–ongoing	Full Retreating (2009–present)
Iraq	2003–11	Full (2003–8) Retreating (2009–11)
Libya	2011	Limited

These kinds of statistical assessments are hard tests for the argument in this book. Quantitative methods do not allow for the testing of the political process—especially the critical role of social carriers (i.e., promoters and moderators)—that helps account for both change in liberal narrative strength and the case-specific discourses that determine the political pressure faced by policymakers either for or against regime promotion. The central argument of this book is being tested in this chapter, therefore, with one arm tied behind its back. Hence, any findings here to the benefit of trauma theory and the master narrative argument must be considered especially solid evidence—at least, as a starting point—for the claim that broad collective beliefs are an important factor in explaining forceful regime promotion in U.S. foreign policy.

This chapter discusses issues of measurement, then turns to a descriptive overview of master narratives and forceful regime promotion, which is then followed by the statistical analysis.

Measuring Master Narratives and Patterns of Forceful Regime Promotion

As discussed in the introduction, master narratives are distinguished by their *collective* nature, meaning that they are not a sum of individual beliefs but instead intersubjective or a property of groups. Individuals and their interactions affect master narratives, but, at the same time, individuals must also deal with these narratives as "social facts."[2] This determines appropriate methods for measuring narratives. As the sociologist Jeffrey Olick observes, culture (and with that, master narratives) can "be measured only crudely by survey analysis; instead, it must be excavated, observed, and interpreted on its own cultural terms."[3] When it comes to existing public opinion surveys, this assessment turns out to be true for more practical reasons as well. Above all else, survey data faces major limitations that make it less useful for broad statistical analysis when it comes to master narratives. This study of forceful regime change in U.S. foreign policy starts in 1900, yet polling only began in the late 1930s. Furthermore, an extensive search (Gallup, Harris, Chicago Council of Foreign Relations, National Opinion Research Center, and more) finds that survey data is too sporadic for reliable statistical analysis. Questions that ask about threat, disillusionment, and democracy/human rights promotion (or approximate them) come only occasionally, or in compact periods of time that generally range from three to five years.[4] Not enough survey data exists for statistical tests, even if it were the most appropriate or best measure of master narratives and other variables in the master narrative argument.

We need to look in other places, then, to capture master narratives. To this end, master narratives are like other collective beliefs in that they are often embedded in discourse, institutions, and symbols, which offer a useful tool for assessing them.[5] This chapter follows the work of other scholars by using content analysis of State of the Union addresses and newspaper editorials to measure the strength of the liberal narrative across time for the statistical tests. State of the Union addresses are a commonly used tool to assess cross-temporal change in broad narratives. John Markoff comments that they and other similar documents are "sufficiently standardized" to capture public "consensus" or "agreement."[6] Jeffrey Legro contends, likewise, that because they are "highly symbolic," State of the Union addresses "are rightly seen as efforts to capture the character, thought, and direction of the nation."[7] Presidents always discuss foreign policy in these speeches. What varies over time is how presidents frame the policy ideas they discuss. Here, they tend (as the literature on framing expects) to appeal to dispositions and symbols that are especially salient at the time. Again, Legro notes, "Presidents want to present their ideas in ways that sell, and they tend to rally support and legitimacy by reflecting and saluting social traditions and norms."[8] In short, policy ideas will generally be justified using temporally specific phrases/concepts/terms that resonate nationally. If certain concepts are less salient, presidents tend not to use them.[9]

Since policy elites draft State of the Union addresses, some may not be fully satisfied that these speeches capture collective narratives (rather than leader opinions). Hence, this book follows the lead of others and uses editorials as a second measure of master narratives. It analyzes the annual editorial responses to each State of the Union address from 1900 to 2011 in eight newspapers from different regions of the country with different partisan leanings.[10]

Editorialists are quite independent in expressing their opinions on the president's speech, often freely criticizing both domestic and foreign policy. Like others who use this method, focusing on a single point each year around the State of the Union address carries, then, the benefit of offering an annual snapshot of a bipartisan, geographically diverse conversation about the biggest themes and symbols around the nation's thinking and approach to foreign policy. This is an important advantage, in fact, over other alternatives like trying to sample editorials around major annual events. A major-events approach presents more potential for selection bias (i.e., which events are "major" and worth analysis?). Choosing the same point annually around the State of the Union address eliminates this kind of bias and also captures a conversation about the broadest themes driving policy that a major-events approach can miss since the conversation around major events may be focused largely on the event(s) themselves. Overall, editorials collectively approximate the broader discourse and disposition of the nation.[11] They are not a perfect measure since foreign policy discussions in the editorials are limited in some years. All the same, the United States' great power status and the prevalence of values-based language in U.S. foreign policy over the twentieth century especially limits this problem. Themes related to the liberal narrative, especially, and major international trends are common in editorial discussions of foreign policy.

As measured in the State of the Union addresses, the liberal narrative is a continuous variable, ranging from 0 to 170. In symbolic documents like these, the frequency in use of certain kinds of terms or language implies the collective strength or salience of a certain world view or set of concerns in national thinking. The more some language is used, the more it resonates with and reflects audience disposition. For this reason, we used a counting method in the foreign policy section of each State of the Union address to capture the liberal narrative.[12] We counted words, not sentences. Especially in this particular annual speech, presidents and their advisors pour over each word; hence counting words best captures intended meaning and, in keeping with the above discussion, the strength of the liberal narrative. In counting, the obvious words/terms that fit this category include "freedom," "liberty," "democracy," and "human rights" ("human rights" and similar phrases were counted only once, as a single term).[13] As discussed in chapter 1, the liberal narrative is about promoting liberal order *and* protecting it against the spread of counter-ideologies—these are essentially two sides of the same coin. Hence, we also counted words/terms denoting a contrasting identity to that of the United States ("tyranny," "totalitarian," "communist," etc.) and terms referring to specific historical developments/conditions ("elections," "apartheid," "torture").[14] Overall, a higher number of references to these sorts of identity-related terms in the president's discussion of foreign policy approximates greater public interest in the state and protection of liberal order abroad. It reflects a more robust liberal narrative, since as discussed in the introduction, this kind of normative language (i.e., the moral of the story) is a marker of or shorthand for the presence of the broader liberal narrative story both across and at specific moments in time.

We used two methods for counting. First, for all terms that are *not* potential double entendres, we used a computer program, Antconc, to count terms in the foreign policy section(s) of each speech from 1900 to 2011.[15] Second, to count terms with potential dual meanings and those that are more historically contingent, yet still related to liberal identity, coders counted all such terms in each speech.[16] We then added the total computer count and total hand-count of words/terms for each speech, which gave us a raw value score for each year. From there, we controlled for length of the State of the Union addresses, which varies dramatically, to arrive at a final average value score for each year that served as our measure of the liberal narrative in all statistical models and figures below (see Appendix A).

A codebook was used to measure the liberal narrative in the editorials (Appendix A). The reason for this was three-fold. First, it is becoming standard practice to turn to codebooks when measuring narratives and collective beliefs in editorials.[17] Second, while using common identity language, editorials are not written with the same precise concern for audience in mind as the State of the Union addresses. Notably, editors do not parse over individual words, hence a counting method would be less reliable and not capture the same meaning as it does in the State of the Union addresses. Third, with the less extensive conversation in the editorials about foreign policy than the State of the Union addresses, comparability between the two is difficult using a counting method.

For the codebook, we chose keywords and concepts that both match terms counted in the State of the Union addresses and which capture levels of intensity in commitment to liberal values promotion that parallels the theoretical discussion of the liberal narrative in chapter 1. In years with no foreign policy discussion or little to code, a paper was not included in the data. In total, 484 editorials were coded from 1900 to 2011—a figure well above the annual average of a prominent study using this method.[18] The editorial coding from individual papers was averaged for each year in order to create an annual editorial score. We used this score for all editorial figures and models below.

Measuring the restraint narrative is more elusive than the liberal narrative because the restraint narrative does not involve symbols as close to identity and also tends to revolve around past, as opposed to current, events. Consequently, the restraint narrative tends not to show up well in the State of the Union addresses or editorials. This book relies on the large historical literature on U.S. foreign policy from 1900 to 2011 to measure the presence or not of the restraint narrative (for codebook, see Appendix A). In doing so, it follows the lead of William R. Thompson's work, in particular, by using content analysis of diplomatic history sources to capture major trends in foreign policy thinking within states. Thompson adopts this method to measure perceptions of strategic rivals, noting that "we have an extensive foreign policy/diplomatic history literature well-stocked with clues as to which, and when, states are strategic rivals."[19] The same applies to the restraint narrative. Historians of U.S. foreign policy talk about important national/public dispositions. When present, the restraint narrative is commonly mentioned given the constraints it places on decision makers.[20]

The trauma-theory argument contends that event-driven national threat perceptions and disillusionment are central to change in the liberal narrative over time. Both open different kinds of space for narration to begin that affects master narrative strength. Since these broad phenomena—threat and disillusionment— play this vital role and can be quantified, we consider them the best stand-in for, or approximation of, external and internal trauma for statistical analysis (again, the storytelling process involving social carriers around these different event-driven processes is taken up in the case studies). There is no data on collective, national (as opposed to elite) threat perceptions, nor disillusionment, across the same time span as this study in U.S. foreign policy. Consequently, these factors are measured, again, through content analysis of State of the Union addresses and editorials. Paralleling the above discussion, each of these texts offers a picture of threat and disillusionment that reflects the national disposition. Presidents and party leaders discuss, for instance, threats and events in ways the nation relates to and understands. They also talk about national pain (like disillusionment) as a means of connecting with the public. Editorials do the same. Threat and disillusionment are coded on a 0–3 scale. Appendix A discusses the logic and details of codebooks used for this exercise. As with coding for the liberal narrative in the editorials, coding from individual papers was averaged for each year in order to create an annual editorial score for both threat and disillusionment. We used this score for all editorial figures and models below.

Finally, with a total of twenty-seven U.S. interventions (some of which began in the same year) between 1900 and 2011, it is difficult to evaluate in isolation the initiation of new forceful regime change interventions. Hence, we explore the impact of master narratives and the competing explanations on the broad flow in patterns of forceful regime promotion over time. In order to do this, we constructed an index that takes into account the number and type of U.S. interventions (full-scale, limited, or retreating) for each year from 1900 to 2011. Using John Owen's list of cases, we adopted the rules of the Correlates of War dataset to, first, code for start year and end year of all instances of U.S. forceful regime promotion in this time period.[21] From there, we coded each year of these interventions for military robustness (see Appendix B). We, then, added up the coded score for each intervention in each year to produce an annual intervention score. This indexed score—the promotion index—captures both the number and type of interventions in a single variable for each year. Overall, the promotion index offers a more cross-temporal and periodic approach that focuses on patterns and frequency of force from the beginning to end of interventions, which is best for the broad tests that statistical analysis offer and in light of the data. As discussed more at the end of this chapter, questions of case-by-case variation in patterns of forceful regime promotion are best explored through case studies, which come later in the book. We used the promotion index for the statistical models in tables 2.7 and 2.8.

A Descriptive View of the Liberal Narrative

As a starting point, it is important to remember, first, that the liberal narrative is a story that centers on and is reflected across time in (see introduction) the nation's commitment to *promoting* (i.e., expanding democracy and democratic rights) and/or *protecting* (i.e., preventing the spread of counter-ideologies to democracy) liberal order abroad. The collective presence of these normative concerns (i.e., lessons) represent the existence and retelling of the bigger narrative as time progresses. It is also important to remember, second, that the liberal narrative is not stagnant. Instead, it waxes and wanes in strength across time, taking on greater prominence in the public disposition to world affairs at some points compared to others. Figures 2.1 and 2.2 offer a picture of the major periods of strengthening and weakening in the liberal narrative from 1913 to 2011 as measured in the State of the Union addresses and a collection of annual editorial responses to those addresses from eight newspapers nationwide.[22] In both figures, an increase of the black bar on the y-axis reflects a strengthening narrative (the other bars capture threat and disillusionment in these different periods, which are discussed below).

The picture here is one of substantial fluctuation over time in liberal narrative strength. These patterns are interesting for several reasons. The first relates to existing literature on collective ideas, like the liberal narrative. Notably, changes in the narrative from one period to the next do not appear to move on a predictable cycle, like some scholars contend about other broad public dispositions or beliefs, such as internationalism, in U.S. foreign policy.[23] To this end, strengthening periods for the liberal narrative ranged anywhere from two to four to thirteen years. Periods of a weakening narrative followed similarly nonuniform patterns. Furthermore, change in the liberal narrative appears at odds with the other leading study on these kinds of ideas in U.S. foreign policy. Notably, Samuel Huntington contends that aside from one period (1960s/early 1970s) in the twentieth century, the U.S. public tends toward lethargy when it comes to its collective commitment to defending or promoting liberal political order abroad.[24] Figures 2.1 and 2.2 show far more variation than this.

There are two other important things to notice about change in the liberal narrative seen here. The first is the fairly strong correlation (.63) between these two measures (State of the Union addresses and editorials), which suggests that they are tracking the same or very similar phenomena and offers confidence, then, about the validity of these measures. Aside from one period (1952–56), strengthening and weakening in the narrative follows a near identical pattern in both measures. Second, at most points, the degree of change in narrative strength is very similar from one period to the next across both measures.[25] From the 1918–35 period to the 1936–45 period (i.e., around World War II), the liberal narrative strengthened, for instance, by 51 percent in the State of the Union addresses and by 55 percent in the editorials for the same time period. Likewise, it increased by a ratio of 42 percent (State of the Union addresses) to 47 percent (editorials) in 1950–51 (i.e., around start of the Cold War) and declined by a comparison of 36 percent (State of the Union addresses) to 35 percent (editorials) in the 1992–2001 period (i.e., post–Cold War). Together, then, these two

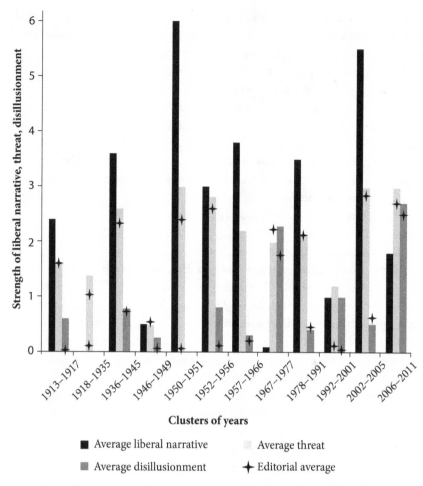

FIGURE 2.1. Liberal narrative, threat, disillusionment by clusters of years in State of the Union addresses

different measures—State of the Union addresses and editorials—are telling a remarkably similar story about changes in the narrative about promoting liberal order abroad over time. This should not surprise us. As discussed earlier, many scholars agree that State of the Union addresses and editorials are especially good at capturing the same kinds of broad public beliefs, like master narratives. The similarities in figures 2.1 and 2.2 reflect this.

A closer look at the editorial data offers another interesting layer to this point. Figure 2.3 depicts the editorial mean for the liberal narrative, plus or minus one

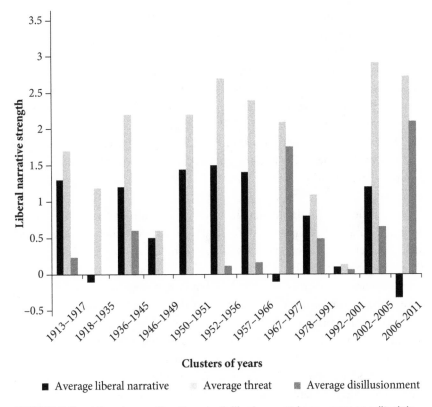

FIGURE 2.2. Liberal narrative, threat, disillusionment in newspaper editorials

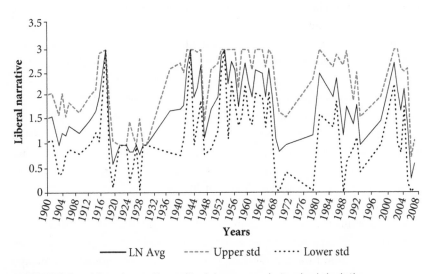

FIGURE 2.3. Liberal narrative editorial mean and standard deviation

standard deviation, in years with data from four or more newspapers from 1900 to 2011 (n = 78). This figure shows two things of special interest. First, the upper and lower standard deviations across the papers tended to rise and fall in sync 76 percent of the time. For instance, the upper standard deviation rose from 2.52 to 3.32 between 1940 and 1942, while the lower standard deviation rose from 1.12 to 1.92 across the same time period. Declines in the liberal narrative showed similar patterns, for example, 3.4 to .79 for the upper standard deviation and 1.92 to .79 for the lower standard deviation from 1944 to 1946. This trend indicates that while values may differ at some points across papers, the papers still reflect a common pattern when it comes to overall strengthening and weakening of the narrative.

Second, figure 2.3 indicates that, in general, the editorials cluster fairly closely around the mean. In 68 percent of the years, the difference between the highest and lowest ends of the standard deviation was minimal, notably one or less on the y-axis scale for the liberal narrative. Again, this clustering points to a robust degree of consensus across the editorials about promoting and protecting liberal order abroad. The years after Vietnam, from 1968 to 1990, indicate the clearest break from this broader pattern. Here, there was only one year with perfect agreement and several where the difference between the lowest and highest observed value was two or more. Many talk of the fracturing of the Cold War consensus in this period, of which collective ideas like the liberal narrative was a critical part.[26] The pattern in table 2.3 seems to bear this out somewhat. Here again, it is worth noting that even with the differences in this post-Vietnam period, upper and lower standard deviation values continued to follow a similar pattern of rise and fall, which still indicates some degree of cohesion and similarity in narrative strength across different newspapers.

Finally, the story being told here of the liberal narrative is not only consistent across the editorials and State of the Union addresses, it is also consistent with how historians talk about the period from 1900 to 2011. Scholars of U.S. foreign policy present a picture of collective national sentiment about promoting democracy abroad and/or protecting it against ideological challenges that is virtually identical to what we see in figures 2.1 and 2.2. The 1913–17 period points, for instance, to a strengthening liberal narrative. Historians confirm this. "The mood of the country demanded a scheme for the future that would curb aggression and perpetuate the victory of liberal-democratic ideals," observed Selig Adler of this period.[27] Senator Henry Cabot Lodge (R-MA) echoed the same in 1917, claiming that Wilson's call to the "great struggle for freedom, democracy and civilization" represented the "sentiments of the American people" and the right lesson to draw from the traumatic story at the time of autocratic Germany's aggression in World War I.[28]

Other periods of strengthening liberal narrative in figures 2.1 and 2.2 are consistent with both historical accounts and, as discussed more in the case study chapters, polling data. Scholars describe a deep public interest in protecting democracy abroad, primarily by stemming the advance of communism in the 1949–66 period. They write at length about "Communism . . . [as] the great 'beast'" for the nation; reference the "rabid anticommunism across the United States"; and note that "vociferous anti-Communism was . . . the lingua franca" of U.S. discourse around foreign policy in this period (all of which reflected a broader existential story as discussed in chapter 3).[29] Scholars also detail how in the late Cold War period (1978–91 in figures 2.1 and 2.2) there was a revival in these collective sentiments to protect freedom. Commentators observed, for instance, that by the early 1980s the public had been "rejuvenated" for "Cold War II," which was reflected in the return of "a degree of idealism" to public discourse.[30] Politicians scrambled to keep in-step with this narrative. Being labelled "soft on communism" or losing any part of the world to communism "was the surest way to lose an election," observes Tony Smith.[31]

Finally, in the 2001–5 period, scholars talk about how "a new narrative literally fell from the sky on September 11" that "became embedded in the popular imagination."[32] It centered on the story of external trauma around 9/11 and, out of that, the lesson to stop radical Islam as a way to protect the national way of life. As part of this, there was an increased sense of the need to advance democracy abroad. In 2002, an opinion poll found that 70 percent of U.S. citizens thought, for instance, that the United States should actively promote democracy worldwide— a steep increase from the forty percent range of the prior decade. Support for these ends remained above 50 percent (and even higher with respect to democracy in Iraq) through 2005.[33] Overall, these periods all reflect the same thing: the national narrative around protecting liberal order was especially strong in the periods where figures 2.1 and 2.2 indicate that the liberal narrative was robust. These figures paint a picture of national beliefs that is true to historical accounts.

Periods of a weak or declining liberal narrative in figures 2.1 and 2.2 also match up well with the historical record (and polling data). For example, when discussing the national climate from 1918 to 1935, historians use phrases like "a rejection of moral leadership" and "slump in idealism" to describe the public's disposition.[34] This remained down to the Second World War.[35] Historical accounts also validate a similarly cynical retreat in liberal narrative strength from the mid-1960s to late 1970s and from 2007 to 2011. The entire Cold War narrative of standing for freedom against democracy came into question during the first of these periods. "Our faith in our values has been shaken," noted the respected historian Arthur Schlesinger in 1970.[36] Others talked similarly about the nation's loss of a "grand narrative" or "vision of the future."[37] From public opinion surveys to the cautious and pragmatic response of the U.S. public to the populist uprisings of the Arab Spring, there has been a sharp decline in public idealism. "The U.S. public has become skeptical about promoting ideals abroad," wrote a pair of scholars in 2009.[38] Overall, figures 2.1 and 2.2 give a historically accurate picture of the liberal narrative from 1913 to 2011.

They do the same for national perceptions of threat and disillusionment. As noted in chapter 1, trauma theory expects that liberal narrative strength starts with and turns, in part, on these two event-driven factors. Figures 2.1 (State of the Union addresses) and 2.2 (editorials) show the state of both in major periods of liberal narrative change between 1913 and 2011. For added comparison, the stars on the threat and disillusionment columns in figure 2.1 indicate the editorial coding for each of these variables as well.[39] There are several things worth noting here. For starters, it is hard to miss the strong correlation between the State of the Union address and editorial results when it comes to threat (correlation of .835) and disillusionment (correlation of .56), which again offers confidence about the validity of these measures. Figures 2.1 and 2.2 show these strong correlations. In the 1936–45 period, for instance, threat in both the State of the Union addresses and editorials measured 2.6 on a three-point scale. Disillusionment in this period measured .78 in the State of the Union addresses and .67 in the editorials on a three-point scale. In the next period, disillusionment in the State of the Union

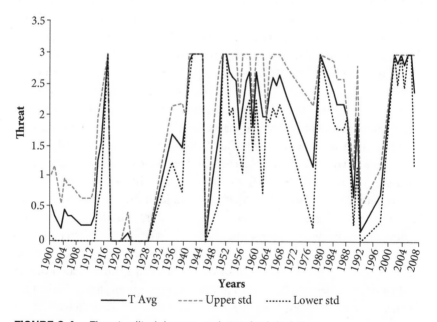

FIGURE 2.4. Threat editorial mean and standard deviation

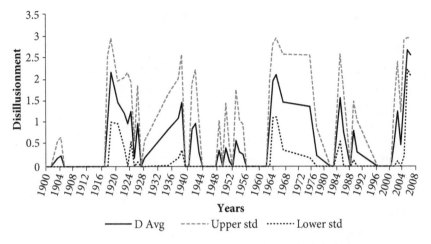

FIGURE 2.5. Disillusionment editorial mean and standard deviation

addresses registered a .25, the editorial figure here was 0, while threat fell similarly to .5 in the State of the Union addresses and .6 in the editorials.

Here again, a closer look at the editorial data provides some interesting additional details. Figures 2.4 and 2.5 depict the editorial mean for threats and disillusionment, plus or minus one standard deviation, in years with data from four or more newspapers from 1900 to 2011 (n = 78). Two things are of special interest. First, the upper and lower standard deviations across the papers tended to rise and fall fairly consistently—85 percent of the time for threat and 72 percent for disillusionment. While values may differ at some points across papers, the papers still reflect a common pattern when it comes to overall strengthening and weakening of threat and disillusionment. Second, figures 2.4 and 2.5 indicate that the editorials generally cluster around the mean. In 85 percent of the years for threat and 82 percent of the years for disillusionment, the difference between the highest and lowest ends of the standard deviation was one or less on the y-axis scale. Again, this clustering points to a robust degree of consensus across the editorials. Like the liberal narrative, the years after Vietnam, from 1968 to 1990, indicate the clearest break from this broader pattern. Even with this, upper and lower standard deviation values still followed a similar pattern of rise and fall, indicating some continued degree of cohesion.

Like the liberal narrative, historians confirm the patterns of change in threat and disillusionment across all the figures. Eminent scholars such as John Lewis Gaddis, Stephen Walt, Paul Kennedy, and William R. Thompson agree that the threats faced by the United States in the twentieth and early twenty-first centuries mirrored what we see in figures 2.1 and 2.2 (as discussed in later chapters, polls show the same). We know three major challengers (all from ideologically distant states) confronted the United States between 1913 and 2011: autocratic and fascist Germany/Japan during the two World Wars (1913–18 and 1933–45); the communist Soviet Union from the late 1940s forward (1948–91); and radical Islamic terrorism after 2001 (2001–11). Threat patterns in figures 2.1 and 2.2 capture all three. Across this time period, there were three major points where ideological threats noticeably declined—1919–33, 1945–47, and 1991–2001. Figures 2.1 and 2.2 capture these patterns as well.[40]

Scholars also widely agree on the three major periods of public disillusionment—the 1920s–1930s, 1967–77, and 2006–11. A large literature discusses the ways that illiberal events/outcomes in World War I, the Vietnam War, and the 2003 Iraq War generated widespread public disenchantment with U.S. policy and engagement abroad. World War I came to be viewed, for instance, by the U.S. public as a senseless loss of life for European imperial repression. Cries went up that the U.S. public had been "lied to, deceived, and misled in the name of democracy and humanity."[41] "'Debunking' set in," claimed one historian, "The ideals of liberalism and democracy were 'unmasked' as hollow pretexts for national egotism."[42] As discussed at greater length in chapter 5, executive branch deception, a repressive ally in the South Vietnamese government, and national impressions of the United States' own immorality during the Vietnam War contributed to widespread public disenchantment in the late 1960s (polls at the time showed the same).[43] "[Vietnam] shattered the veil of government rhetoric and mythology," according to one scholar, "enabling many to see through the veneer of phrases like 'defending freedom' or 'fighting for democracy.'"[44] State of the Union addresses and editorials also accurately capture disillusionment in the wake of the 2003 Iraq War. Polls indicated the public felt deceived on the reasons for entering the war, while sectarian violence in Iraq also fueled public disenchantment with U.S. foreign policy. "Confusion, cynicism and timidity" set in across the nation, noted one observer.[45] Presidents Bush and Obama echoed this when they used terms like "defeatism," "uncertainty in the air," and a "cynical . . . doubtful mood" to describe the late 2000s national discourse around Iraq and the so-called war on terror.[46]

Finally, figures 2.1 and 2.2 hint at a potential relationship between threat, disillusionment and the liberal narrative. Chapter 1 discussed the theoretical expectations here, drawn from trauma theory. Notably, increasing perceptions of ideological threats set the conditions for storytelling that strengthens the liberal narrative, while increasing public disillusionment does the same for storytelling that weakens the liberal narrative.[47] Figures 2.1 and 2.2 give some indication that these expectations may, indeed, be correct. The liberal narrative strengthens most in periods where perceived threats rise and disillusionment is low or declining.

Likewise, the narrative shows its steepest degree of weakening when either ideo-logical threats are declining and/or public disillusionment is strong/rising. More robust statistical tests of these relationships are presented below.

A Descriptive View of Master Narratives and Patterns of Forceful Regime Promotion

Before turning to those tests, it is important to look at a descriptive picture of the relationship between master narratives and forceful regime promotion. Figure 2.6 compares the liberal narrative and the initiation of new forceful promotion change wars (limited or full) between 1900 and 2011. Figure 2.7 compares the restraint narrative and patterns (limited or full) in regime pro-motion interventions. Before discussing these in detail, a few comments on the restraint narrative are necessary. As discussed in the prior chapter, this narrative consists of taboos against using military force in ways, in places, and/or for cer-tain objectives that produced earlier internal trauma for the nation. As with the liberal narrative, these taboos are lessons from and a shorthand for the bigger

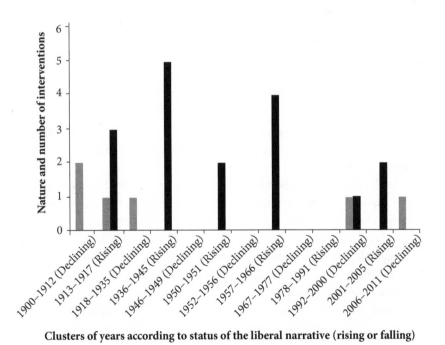

Clusters of years according to status of the liberal narrative (rising or falling)

■ Limited intervention   ■ Full intervention

FIGURE 2.6. Liberal narrative strength and new U.S. military interventions for regime change

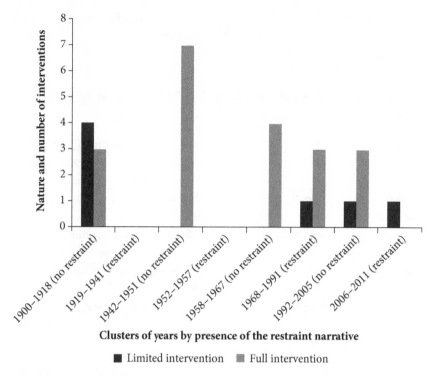

FIGURE 2.7. Restraint narrative strength and new U.S. military interventions for regime change

internal trauma story across time. The x-axis in figure 2.7 points to four major restraint narrative periods in U.S. foreign policy (1919–41, 1952–57, 1968–91, 2006–11) since 1900.

Like the discussion above about the liberal narrative, historians and policy pundits validate that the restraint narrative was especially strong in each of these periods. The collectively accepted story of internal trauma from World War I left behind a strong public restraint narrative, symbolized by Warren Harding's campaign slogan, "back to normalcy" in the 1920 U.S. presidential campaign. The moral of the story here showed up as widespread national aversion to affiliation with Europe and opposition to force for the kinds of regime promotion interventions that President Woodrow Wilson initiated in Latin America.[48] A similar kind of restraint narrative emerged in the wake of the Korean War. President Dwight Eisenhower and other policy elites (including Senator Majority Leader Lyndon Johnson) talked about the public sense of "no more land war's in Asia." Eisenhower's New Look foreign policy was built, in part, around this Korea syndrome.

In the last fifty years, scholars have talked extensively about the two most commonly known periods of a robust restraint narrative—the Vietnam syndrome and, more recently, the Iraq syndrome. Again, both are reflected in figure 2.7. As discussed in more detail in chapter 5, the disillusionment of the Vietnam War scarred the U.S. polity in profound ways. The phrase "No More Vietnams" gained common use. This kind of taboo served as both a lasting reminder of the original trauma story around the war and an imperative against forceful regime promotion in the developing world.[49] Finally, scholars point to similar public restraints in the wake of the wars in Iraq and Afghanistan. John Mueller describes it as the public's "'let's not do that again' attitude."[50] The syndrome has shown-up in common mantras—like "not another Iraq" and "no boots on the ground"—in political commentary, editorials, and public opinion polls in this period. "Iraq . . . was a constant ghost hanging over everything," said a State Department official, in this period—a disillusioning story of the war that haunted the nation then, and continues to do so.[51] Overall, figure 2.7 offers a historically accurate picture of the restraint narrative in U.S. foreign policy from 1900 to 2011.

We can now turn to what figures 2.6 and 2.7 indicate about forceful regime promotion. The argument about master narratives (table 2.2.) anticipates that periods of a strong liberal narrative should witness more frequent and more forceful regime change interventions. When the restraint narrative is strong and/or the liberal narrative weak/declining, forceful regime promotion should be less common and involve more limited forms of military action. Figures 2.6 and 2.7 suggest these expectations may be accurate. Again, this is tested statistically below.

Starting with figure 2.6, twenty of twenty-seven regime promotion interventions came when the liberal narrative was strong. Added to this, all but one of those interventions was full-scale. Likewise of the seven forceful regime promotion interventions when the liberal narrative was weak, only one was full-scale, the others were all limited. We expect this relationship to be lagged, which indeed turns out to be the case (Appendix C). These patterns suggest that a relationship may exist between the liberal narrative and patterns of forceful regime promotion. The length of interventions suggests this too. Interventions begun

TABLE 2.2 Master narratives argument for forceful regime promotion

KEY FACTOR	EXPLANATION
Liberal narrative	Forceful regime promotion becomes more likely and more robust militarily when the liberal narrative strengthens.
Restraint narrative	Forceful regime promotion becomes less likely and less robust militarily as the restraint narrative strengthens.

amid a robust liberal narrative averaged 895 days. By contrast, interventions begun amid a weak/declining liberal narrative were about three times shorter in length, averaging only 345 days. These patterns are not a function of an over-abundance of years where the liberal narrative was robust. The liberal narrative was strong/rising for only forty-six years across this time period as compared to sixty-six years when it was weak/declining. Consistent with the master narrative argument, the United States initiated a forceful regime promotion intervention on average about every two-and-half years when the liberal narrative was strong, and about every seven years when the narrative was weak.

Figure 2.7 shows similarly interesting patterns for the restraint narrative. Out of a total of twenty-seven regime promotion interventions, only five started when the restraint narrative was robust, with the other twenty-two happening in periods of weak restraint narrative. Three of the five interventions (Grenada, Panama, and Kuwait) that started during strong restraint periods were full-scale, with two (Cambodia and Libya) being limited. While this picture about robust-ness of military action is not entirely consistent with expectations from chapter 1, the overall pattern of significantly less-frequent military interventions for regime promotion during periods of a strong restraint narrative is. The length of interventions is interesting too. Interventions begun during nonrestraint periods lasted 845 days on average. Those begun during restraint, were nearly three times shorter in duration, 313 days. Here again, these patterns cannot be attributed to an overabundance of nonrestraint years in the data. The period from 1900 to 2011 is about evenly split in terms of total years between restraint (fifty-nine) and nonrestraint (fifty-three). Hence, a regime promotion intervention occurred about every two-and-a-half years on average when the restraint narrative was weak, and about every twelve years on average when it was strong. Again, this suggests the restraint narrative plays a role in decisions for and against forceful regime promotion.

Testing the Trauma Theory and Master Narrative Arguments

This section turns to more robust statistical tests to assess trauma theory's expec-tations for liberal narrative strength and the relationship between master nar-ratives and forceful regime promotion. It starts with change in liberal narrative strength. As discussed already, trauma theory expects that as national threat perceptions from ideological rivals increase, the liberal narrative strengthens. Likewise, as threats recede or disillusionment strengthens, the liberal narra-tive weakens. This argument is tested against three competing hypotheses dis-cussed in chapter 1 (see table 2.3). Realists focus on threat, though with different

TABLE 2.3 Competing explanations for change in the liberal narrative

SCHOOL OF THOUGHT	EXPLANATION
Geopolitics	The liberal narrative weakens when national threat perceptions rise.
Elite strategic manipulation	The liberal narrative strengthens when elite threat perceptions rise.
Elite (ideological) polarization	The liberal narrative strengthens when elite ideological concerns strengthen.
Economic strength (recession)	The liberal narrative strengthens when the economy strengthens.

expectations than the trauma argument. Notably, when geopolitical changes lead national threat perceptions to increase, realists anticipate the liberal narrative will weaken. Some realists also claim that the more elites perceive threats from abroad, the more the liberal narrative strengthens because elites use ideological language to scare (i.e., strategically manipulate) the public into new policy initiatives abroad to meet the threat. Elite ideology scholars expect that when elites become ideologically polarized (or more fearful of ideological challenges abroad) and share those concerns in public, the nation as a whole follows suit, meaning again the liberal narrative strengthens. Finally, strength of the economy offers another possible argument. Some claim that when the economy is strong, the United States tends to be more internationalist.[52] Since the liberal narrative reflects an amplified interest in activism abroad (at least with respect to liberal order promotion), one can extend this logic with the hypothesis that the liberal narrative strengthens when the economy strengthens.[53]

This book's primary concern is with the effect of national threat perceptions (i.e., an indicator of external trauma) and disillusionment (i.e., an indicator of internal trauma) on the liberal narrative as measured in the State of the Union addresses and editorials.[54] Separate models for these two data sources are created.[55] The coefficients for these models are divided into two broad categories of independent variables: (1) trauma theory and (2) competing explanations.[56]

State of the Union Addresses

We start with tests of the trauma-theory argument using data from State of the Union addresses from 1900 to 2011. Table 2.4 includes two models, where the regression both with and without the interaction between threat level and disillusionment are estimated. This allows for a more accurate testing of trauma-theory hypotheses.

TABLE 2.4 OLS regression results for liberal narrative in State of the Union addresses, 1900–2011

	MODEL 1	MODEL 2
	B (S.E.)	B (S.E.)
Constant	9.339***	5.370
	(5.186)	(5.912)
Lagged liberal narrative (t–1)	0.25***	0.293***
	(0.064)	(0.06)
Trauma theory		
Threat level [+]	21.817***	26.377***
	(2.385)	(2.485)
Disillusionment [–]	–11.922***	0.49
	(1.777)	(3.243)
Threat*disillusionment [–]	—	–6.637***
		(1.619)
Competing explanations		
Elite strategic manipulation [+]	–13.042***	–7.90*
	(3.707)	(3.675)
Elite polarization [+]	1.171	–1.084
	(4.339)	(4.080)
Recession [–]	–3.971	–2.758
	(3.999)	(3.737)
N	111	111
R^2	.72	.76
Adjusted R^2	0.70	0.74

p value: ***0.001 or less; ** 0.01 or less; * 0.05 or less

Note: Directional hypotheses are presented in brackets.

The results in table 2.4 support the trauma argument. Model 1 shows robust support for trauma theory's expectation that national perceptions of threat have a significantly positive effect on the liberal narrative. In sum, collective national passions to advance and protect liberal political order abroad strengthen when the nation sees threats rise. Partially in line with the second hypothesis, the liberal narrative weakens as collective, national disillusionment about foreign policy increases. Furthermore, the coefficients of competing variables to the liberal narrative display that only strategic elite manipulation has significant effects on the liberal narrative over time. But this offers little support for this argument since the coefficient here is negative. This relationship may in the end be spurious, but it could open doors to new research on the relationship between elites and the public. Overall, the results of Model 1 offer strong support for the trauma-theory argument and weak support for the alternatives.

Model 2 in table 2.4 also provides strong validation for the trauma-theory argument.[57] With no disillusionment, a rise in threat perceptions generates a stronger liberal narrative. The results of the interaction variable (Threat* disillusionment) portray the significant moderating effects of disillusionment. An increase in collective disillusionment about foreign policy tends to weaken the effects of high threat perceptions by the nation, causing the narrative to weaken. Similar to the results in Model 1, none of the competing explanations, with the exception of strategic elite manipulation (again, in the wrong direction), explain the dependent variable. It is worth noting here, as well, that endogeneity appears not to be a problem with Models 1 or 2.[58]

What does this mean? Overall, when national perceptions of threat rise, so too does the liberal narrative, or the national sense about the need to protect liberal political order abroad. This stands in direct contrast to realist expectations that perceived geopolitical challenges will cause the nation to focus less on the need to defend or promote liberal political order abroad. Consistent with trauma theory, high levels of collective, national disillusionment about foreign policy moderate this relationship. Disillusionment tends to cloud the effects of threat for the nation, which weakens the liberal narrative over time. Table 2.4 demonstrates that the trauma argument provides a better explanation for the liberal narrative than explanations provided by other schools of thought.

Editorials

Since the liberal narrative is a nationally based story, we should be able to step outside the discourse of policymaking elites and find the narrative in other measures of broad collective ideas as well. Editorials represent one such commonly used measure. The method here of examining editorial responses to the State of the Union addresses allows us to peer into a national discussion annually from 1900 to 2011 about the collective national sense about the desirability of promoting liberal political order abroad.

Table 2.5 details the ordinary least squares (OLS) results, examining the model both with and without the interaction between threat and disillusionment.[59] The results in each model illustrate again solid support for the trauma argument. The findings from Model 1 validate trauma-theory expectations about threat. Notably, collective perceptions of threat generate a strong collective, national desire to protect/promote liberal order abroad. Furthermore, as disillusionment increases, the liberal narrative declines. The results in Model 2 present further support for the trauma argument. When there is no disillusionment

TABLE 2.5 OLS regression results for liberal narrative in editorials, 1900–2011

	MODEL 1	MODEL 2
	B (S.E.)	B (S.E.)
Constant	0.351*	0.009
	(.136)	(0.119)
Lagged liberal narrative (t–1)	–0.088	–0.057
	(0.061)	(0.0494)
Trauma theory		
Threat level [+]	0.423***	0.572***
	(0.046)	(0.042)
Disillusionment [–]	–0.554***	–0.143*
	(0.048)	(0.068)
Threat*disillusionment [–]	—	–0.245***
		(0.033)
Competing explanations		
Elite strategic manipulation [+]	–0.099	0.025
	(0.07)	(0.061)
Elite polarization [+]	0.117	–0.036
	(0.08)	(0.072)
Recession [–]	0.036	.041
	(0.075)	(.061)
N	111	111
R^2	.76	.85
Adjusted R^2	0.75	0.87

p value: ***0.001 or less; ** 0.01 or less; * 0.05 or less

Note: Directional hypotheses are presented in brackets.

(i.e., disillusionment = 0), a rise in national threat perceptions results in strengthening of the liberal narrative. When disillusionment is high, increased perceptions of threat generate less robust strengthening in the liberal narrative. Moreover, including the interaction variable in the model again diminishes the independent impact of disillusionment. As with the findings in table 2.4, endogeneity is not a problem in either of the models in table 2.5. The competing explanations do not seem to play a role in shaping liberal narrative strength.[60]

Overall, the findings indicate that as trauma theory expects an increase in national threat perceptions strengthen the liberal narrative, while an increase in disillusionment tends to weaken the liberal narrative. Furthermore, none of the competing variables explain outcomes as theoretically expected. These findings are important. More than anything else, they suggest the kind of autonomy to collective, norm-centric beliefs that both trauma theory and the master narrative argument expect. Notably, the broad national narrative identified in this book as the liberal narrative is not a function of the strength of the economy, a mere extension of ideologically animated elites or a product of geopolitics and elite fearmongering.[61] Instead, this national belief seems to change in strength independent of these things.

Statistical Tests of Master Narrative Impact on Patterns of Forceful Regime Promotion

We now turn to the effects of master narratives on patterns of forceful regime promotion in U.S. foreign policy from 1900 to 2011. As discussed already, the master narrative argument anticipates for the sake of this chapter that as the liberal narrative strengthens, military interventions for forceful regime promotion will be more common and more militarily robust. As the liberal narrative weakens and/ or the restraint narrative strengthens, military interventions for forceful regime promotion will be less common and, when they occur, more limited militarily.

It is worth remembering that master narratives like the liberal and restraint narratives are rarely the exclusive source of policy outcomes when it comes to the use of force. Master narratives generally work alongside other factors to affect state behavior in this area. To this end, the master narrative explanation is tested against several competing arguments that were discussed at length in chapter 1 (see also table 2.6). The argument about geopolitics anticipates that as elites' perceptions of international threats rise, military interventions for regime promotion become less likely and less robust. Scholars that focus on elite ideology anticipate that as elites polarize ideologically, forceful regime change interventions are likely to increase and be more full-scale. Finally, one can hypothesize here that as the economy strengthens forceful regime promotion becomes common and more robust militarily.[62]

TABLE 2.6 Competing explanations for forceful regime promotion

KEY FACTOR	EXPLANATION
Elite threat perceptions	Forceful regime promotion becomes less likely and less robust militarily when elite threat perceptions rise.
Elite (ideological) polarization	Forceful regime promotion becomes more likely and more robust militarily as elites becomes more ideologically polarized.
Economic strength (recession)	Forceful regime promotion becomes more likely and more robust militarily as the economy strengthens.

TABLE 2.7 Poisson and negative binomial results for military interventions with State of the Union addresses measure of the liberal narrative, 1900–2011

	MILITARY ACTION	PROMOTION ANNUAL (GMM)	PROMOTION INDEX
	IRR (S.E.)	IRR (S.E.)	IRR (S.E.)
Constant	3.051***	0.156***	0.588
	(0.711)	(0.068)	(0.319)
Lagged dependent variable	1.114***	1.59***	0.072**
	(0.032)	(0.15)	(0.02)
Master narratives			
Liberal narrative [+]	1.001	1.006†	1.012**
	(0.002)	(0.003)	(0.004)
Restraint narrative [−]	0.702**	0.493*	0.323***
	(0.556)	(0.144)	(0.109)
Competing explanations			
Elite threat perceptions [−]	0.879	1.71**	1.178
	(0.087)	(0.323)	(0.298)
Elite polarization [+]	1.09	0.74	0.917
	(0.165)	(0.244)	(0.315)
Recession [−]	1.053	0.735	0.763
	(0.124)	(0.182)	(0.230)
N	109	109	109
Pseudo R^2	0.35	0.32	0.14

p value: ***0.001 or less; ** 0.01 or less; * 0.05 or less; † .1 or less

Notes: An IRR score of more than one represents a positive relationship and less than one, a negative relationship. Directional hypotheses are presented in brackets. The conclusions drawn from these models do not change when robust standard errors are applied. Two exogenous events—the Great Depression and 9/11—were significant in the military action model. The September 11 attacks were significant in the promotion annual and promotion index models. We controlled for these significant events in the respective models.

Tables 2.7 and 2.8 assess the relationship between master narratives and force-ful regime promotion. Each table includes three models. The primary interest here is in the results of the third model, promotion index, in each table. This model demonstrates the relationship between master narratives and an indexed variable for military interventions that takes into account both number and type (limited, full, and retreating) of interventions for forceful regime promotion in any given year. Based on the discussion in chapter 1, we anticipate master narratives will have their strongest effects here. The other two models test the liberal and restraint narratives more broadly. The first model, military action, explores the relationship between these two master narratives and all forms of military activity regardless of type (i.e., regime promotion and nonregime promotion) by the United States annually from 1900 to 2011. Finally, the second model, promotion annual, assesses the relationship between master narratives and the number of regime promotion interventions annually, with no distinction made between full-scale or limited interventions for these ends. For the military action and promotion annual models, the expectation is, again, that the liberal and restraint narratives will be less relevant in explaining outcomes.[63]

The models in tables 2.7 and 2.8 include a lag of the dependent variable for the sake of consistency and because the process is autoregressive. Each of these models includes a lag of the liberal narrative variable as well. We do this for theoretical reasons. Military interventions are expensive and unpredictable. In most instances, the initiation of war, then, involves considerable debate, especially in democratic states. Part of this involves, of course, promoters using the liberal narrative to build a robust national discourse for military action in specific cases. In most instances, this work by promoters and the debate for or against war in general takes time. Hence, even when the liberal narrative is strengthening or robust, we generally expect its impact on decisions to intervene to be slow to manifest. Our models therefore include a three-year lag of this variable.[64]

Table 2.7 presents the results for the master narrative argument against the competing explanations, using the State of the Union address as a measure of the liberal narrative.[65] Given that the dependent variable is a count variable, Poisson regression for the military action and promotion annual models is used. Negative binomial is employed for the promotion index model because the distribution of the dependent variable makes negative binomial a better fit than Poisson for the data in this particular model.[66] The results here are interesting and generally in line with the master narrative argument. The Promotion Index model (and to some extent Promotion Annual model) indicates that a strengthening liberal narrative indeed leads to more frequent and robust forms of military action for regime promotion goals—this is in line with expectations for the master narrative argument. In essence, as national concerns grow about the need to protect and promote liberal order abroad, the United States is more likely to use not only force but more robust, full-scale military invasions for regime change or promotion ends. As expected, these effects are lagged. The liberal narrative has its most substantial effects on forceful regime promotion three years out from the point at which the narrative begins to strengthen. This could point to the fact that, as expected, it takes time for promoters to build collectively dense and broadly accepted arguments for forceful regime promotion across the polity.

The findings for the other master narrative—the restraint narrative—in Table 2.7 are equally interesting. Notably, when the restraint narrative increases in strength, the likelihood of using force for regime promotion declines—the promotion annual and promotion index models both point to this conclusion. In fact, the military action model shows the same statistically significant relationship. It appears that the national aversion to using force for regime promotion that comes from a strong restraint narrative makes elites gun-shy about adopting military solutions to any sorts of problems abroad, whether related to regime promotion or not. Finally, it is worth noting that in general there is little evidence to support the competing explanations, especially in the most important promotion index model.[67]

Table 2.8 shows similar findings using the editorial measure of the liberal narrative. Here again, the first two models use Poisson regression, and the third,

TABLE 2.8   Poisson and negative binomial results for military interventions with editorial measure of the liberal narrative, 1900–2011

	MILITARY ACTION	PROMOTION ANNUAL (GMM)	PROMOTION INDEX
	IRR (S.E.)	IRR (S.E.)	IRR (S.E.)
Constant	2.956***	0.141***	0.55
	(0.678)	(0.063)	(0.308)
Lagged dependent variable	1.123***	1.604***	1.191**
	(0.310)	(0.150)	(0.0727)
Master narratives			
Liberal narrative [+]	.936	1.234	1.84*
	(0.08)	(0.213)	(0.456)
Restraint narrative [−]	0.673†	0.564†	0.476*
	(0.89)	(0.175)	(0.16)
Competing explanations			
Elite threat perceptions [−]	0.896	1.78**	1.263
	(0.086)	(0.333)	(0.33)
Elite polarization [+]	1.146	.821	0.806
	(0.180)	(0.254)	(0.301)
Recession [−]	1.077	0.706	0.621
	(0.129)	(0.181)	(0.193)
N	109	109	109
Pseudo R^2	0.35	0.31	0.13

p value: ***0.001 or less; ** 0.01 or less; * 0.05 or less; † .1 or less

Notes: An IRR score of more than one represents a positive relationship and less than one, a negative relationship. Directional hypotheses are presented in brackets. The conclusions drawn from these models do not change when robust standard errors are applied. Two exogenous events—the Great Depression and 9/11—were significant in the military action model. The September 11 attacks were significant in the promotion annual and promotion index models. We controlled for these significant events in the respective models.

negative binomial. A strengthening liberal and restraint narratives offer the best prediction of robust military interventions for forceful regime promotion (promotion index model). Consistent with the findings in the State of the Union address models, the liberal narrative has its most significant effects three years out from points at which the liberal narrative begins to strengthen. The restraint narrative again shows significant effects on the military action and promotion annual models. The competing explanations show no consistently significant impact on decisions for the use of force.

Overall, the results in tables 2.7 and 2.8 add to the credibility of the master narrative argument. A strong national story centered on the need to protect and promote liberal order abroad (i.e., the liberal narrative) appears to open the door to and, perhaps, apply political pressure on, policymakers to pursue full-scale military interventions for regime promotion goals. To this end, the findings in table 2.8 indicate, for instance, that, a one-unit increase in liberal narrative strength may nearly double the incidences of robust forceful regime promotion. It is important to note that this relationship between the liberal narrative and regime promotion does not achieve statistical significance under all specifications of the models in tables 2.7 and 2.8. As is the case at points with time series analysis, there appears to be some feedback between military interventions and the liberal narrative in these models.[68] All the same, if the story told by tables 2.7 and 2.8 is true, these findings add strong support to a key piece of the master narrative argument. The other findings related to the liberal narrative (especially that for general military action) are broadly consistent with the master narrative argument as well. As discussed in chapter 1, the liberal narrative is expected to have its strongest effects on forceful regime promotion, not all forms of military behavior. The findings in tables 2.7 and 2.8 generally support this.

The presence of the restraint narrative appears extremely important as well. As expected, the restraint narrative reduces forceful regime promotion behavior in U.S. foreign policy. When the restraint narrative is especially strong, elites seem to avoid force altogether or choose only limited military action for regime promotion ends. The impact of the restraint narrative, furthermore, is far from marginal. The results in tables 2.7 and 2.8 indicate that the presence of the restraint narrative across the nation reduces the incidences of robust forceful regime promotion by one-half or more. Confidence in these findings is enhanced by the fact that under multiple specifications, we find the same significant results for the restraint narrative time and again. The findings here also indicate that this narrative may have a much more extensive and deeper impact on the use of force than hypothesized in chapter 1. A strong restraint narrative seems to play a constraining role on not just force for regime promotion, but on decisions for any kind of military action abroad. This is an especially interesting finding, pointing to the possibility that scars from highly disillusioning regime promotion wars run very deep for a nation and leave behind particularly powerful taboos that have an extensive impact on policy decisions. Overall, the power of the restraint narrative needs further study.

The strength of these findings for the master narrative argument is bolstered by the weakness of the competing explanations in tables 2.7 and 2.8. Contrary to the leading scholarship on the subject, forceful regime promotion does not appear to become more likely simply because U.S. policymakers become especially polarized about the geopolitical gains of ideological challengers abroad. This does not mean that elites are irrelevant to decisions about forceful regime change. It suggests instead that elite impact here is highly contextualized by master narratives—a point raised in chapter 1 and discussed at length in the chapters to follow. The realist argument about elite threat perceptions seems problematic as well. While this argument shows some significant effects in the promotion annual model of both tables 2.7 and 2.8, the direction of that impact is not what realists expect. Notably, it suggests that forceful regime promotion might become more likely, not less (as realists anticipate), when elites perceive increased threats from abroad. This needs further study. Toward this end, the master narrative argument offers, at least, one possible explanation that brings us back to contextualizing elite impact on policy. Political scientists tend to treat elites and the broader public as separate, autonomous political units. To the extent that one affects the other, most claim the latter drives the former, as discussed already. Maybe, these conceptualizations are wrong. After all, elites hail from the same liberal polity as the public and share the same liberal identity. When threat perceptions rise, it could be that leaders follow (rather than drive) the national disposition and impulse to pursue regime promotion. The collective results from tables 2.4, 2.5, 2.7, and 2.8 indicate that this and not the opposite might be the case more often than not.

This chapter offers sound initial support for the trauma-theory and master narrative arguments. In accord with trauma theory, collective threat perceptions and disillusionment appear to be significant drivers of change in the strength of the liberal narrative from 1900 to 2011 in the United States. Furthermore, the liberal narrative along with a second and related master narrative, the restraint narrative, also appear important to patterns of U.S. forceful regime promotion across this same time period. A strengthening liberal narrative makes this kind of military action more likely and more robust, while a strong restraint narrative has the opposite effect. These findings are validated all the more by the weakness of competing explanations.

Two important conclusions can be drawn at this point. The first deals with the measures of collective beliefs used in this chapter. Many scholars consider texts, like State of the Union addresses, especially good places to capture collective beliefs because those writing these documents are uniquely attuned to the disposition of their audience.[69] They try to connect with and appeal to their listeners in ways that lead them to give voice to popular or mainstream dispositions about things like how the audience views the world.

Overall, the above findings offer at least some confirmation of this. Take the descriptive section at the chapter's outset. The discussion around figure 2.1 indicates that major patterns in liberal narrative strength (along with collective perceptions of threat and disillusionment) matched well with how historians viewed things from 1913 to 2011.[70] The statistical results in table 2.4 show the same thing, though in a different way. Namely, the statistically weak findings for both the elite-polarization and elite-strategic-manipulation arguments are important indicators that the State of the Union address is an especially good measure of collective beliefs. These findings tell us that when elites see threats or become ideologically excited, they are careful about how they communicate that in places like the State of the Union address. In fact, the findings in tables 2.4 indicate that elites may *contradict*, even eschew, their own personal beliefs (sometimes to radical degrees) in what they say in these documents.[71] Talk here is neither cheap, strategic manipulation, or a direct reflection of elite-ideological dispositions. Instead, it is selective and calculating. Why? The explanation that makes the most sense is this: within these particular contexts, elites are sensitive, again, to audience. They want to say what resonates, hence they choose their language carefully to tap symbols and express a view of social reality that captures broad national dispositions in places like the State of the Union address.[72] In sum, the results from this chapter add to the arguments that others make about these measures: they are especially good places to capture powerful collective beliefs and stories, like the liberal narrative.[73]

The second implication relates to the powerful new story this chapter tells. That story defies, most important, a deep and pervasive conventional wisdom. Standard accounts treat regime change wars as a product of either elite dispositions alone or overzealous foreign policies that sometimes come when states have too much power.[74] This chapter indicates that a novel factor—master narratives—may be equally, if not more, important than either of these causes. When strong, the liberal narrative makes robust forceful regime promotion more common. In turn, when the restraint narrative is strong, forceful regime promotion becomes less likely or more limited. These findings stand in sharp contrast to the conventional wisdom. This does not mean that elite views of the world or strategic factors are irrelevant to patterns of forceful regime promotion. Instead, it simply indicates that working alongside these factors is a powerful, under-specified force—master narratives—that deserves more attention.

On this point there is much work to be done. For, even in light of the findings in the above models for the trauma-theory and master narrative arguments, this chapter leaves us with many unanswered questions. For trauma theory, why does a collective like a nation come to see events as threatening and disillusioning when it does? Furthermore, how do these factors affect the liberal and restraint narratives? There are important questions for the master narrative argument too. Chief among them, how do we explain cross-case variation in forceful regime change during periods when a master narrative of one type or another is especially strong, or even more puzzling, when both are strong at the same time? The liberal narrative was robust in 1950, for example, so why did the United States adopt full-scale intervention to address a regime crisis in Korea, but not China? Likewise, the Vietnam syndrome was strong in the 1980s, hence why full-scale military action in Grenada, but not El Salvador?

Questions like these cannot be answered with the statistical models of this chapter. Instead, they require close attention to domestic political process. That means exploring the storytelling around certain events, the moral or lessons those stories generate, and policy discourses constructed by social carriers. For this, we need case study research, which is where this book turns next.

REGIME CHANGE IN KOREA AND CHINA

In the early Cold War period, the United States faced major policy decisions about how to respond to regime crises in two Asian countries: Korea and China. In the former, the United States sent roughly 300,000 military personnel to save the South Korean regime and unify the Korean peninsula under one government. In the latter, Washington gave aid to and eventually moved the 7th Fleet to protect the Nationalist government on Taiwan, but never committed U.S. combat troops to the China area.

This chapter finds the master narrative argument offers a strong explanation for these different outcomes—full-scale forceful regime promotion in Korea, but not China. Starting in 1946, a series of geostrategic initiatives by the ideologically distant Soviet Union created space for promoters to tell a story of existential danger that led to a national crusade-like mentality to protect democracy against the spread of communism.[1] U.S. action in Korea and China were deeply shaped by this strengthened liberal narrative. In the Korea case, promoters built a discourse in 1950 for robust action around the narrative. President Harry Truman subsequently concluded that anything short of full invasion was politically impossible. A similar discourse emerged around China from 1947 forward, but with an important twist. For reasons explored below, promoter appeals to stop communism in Asia never called for the direct use of U.S. military force in China. Hence, while pushing Truman into policies that he preferred to avoid, this weaker liberal discourse dampened audience costs for inaction in ways that gave the president political space to limit engagement in China.

This chapter turns, first, to the strength of master narratives in this period followed by a discussion of the China and Korea cases and the alternative explanations.

The Liberal Narrative Strengthens

The end of World War II generated an "I wanna go home fever" across the U.S. public that carried with it a waning collective interest in pursuing idealistic goals abroad.[2] Fascism was dead. For the public, it was time for a break.

This weakening in liberal narrative strength did not last long, however. By late 1947, a new surge of national passion to protect liberal order abroad emerged in the United States. Rather than fascism, it centered this time on communism. Found in comments by politicians of both parties, newspaper columns, sermons on Sunday mornings, and Hollywood films, "anticommunism took on a momentum of its own," wrote one historian, "It resonated with the fears of many Americans."[3] Across the latter part of the 1940s, the editorial pages across the country were filled with warnings of ideological peril, an existential challenge, and calls for action: "the treacherous tide of Communism is rolling over Europe"; "if freedom dies in Europe and Asia, it will not live in the United States"; "the Communists will not in our time abandon the goal of world revolution."[4]

In sharp contrast to trends in prior years, a 1947 poll found that a plurality (47%) approved of efforts to "suppress Communist-led revolts" that sought control of governments by force.[5] As the New York Times observed in this period, a "pro-Atlantic Charter policy" to prevent efforts to "Bolshevize small countries ... has the full support of the leaders of both political parties in the United States and of the overwhelming majority of the American people."[6] The focus was not only abroad. Targeting communists at home became a passionate issue as well. One 1946 poll found strong support for government action to "kill or imprison" communists in the United States.[7] Newspapers reflected this too, with many calling for loyalty probes and curbs on communist party activity.[8] Overall, anticommunism became "totally centrist and politically safe," notes David Halberstam, "Anything else was politically dangerous."[9] It all reflected a clear trend: the liberal narrative soared in strength across the late 1940s.

This strengthened liberal narrative grew out of external trauma. Two things contributed to this: the perceived geopolitical gains by an ideologically distant state (in this case, the Soviet Union) and a common story told by promoters. This trauma process began in February and March 1946, with new public revelations about Soviet behavior. On February 3, a nationally syndicated radio show exposed a Soviet atomic espionage operation run out of Canada. Six days later on February 9, Soviet Premier Joseph Stalin gave his famous Bolshoi Theatre speech, in which he called on his people to prepare for war between capitalist and communist states. The speech made headlines across the United States. A few weeks later in early March, the U.S. public became aware, for the first time, of the fact that the Soviet Union was looting industrial resources from Manchuria and stonewalling on its prior commitment to withdraw troops from Iran.[10]

These steps by the Soviet Union eclipsed all other media stories of the time and left U.S. citizens "stunned" and in "near hysteria," according to historians.[11] Editorials carried headlines like: "What's Russia's Goal?"; "The Red Riddle: What to Do about Russia"; and "Where Is Russia Going?"[12] A number of papers talked about "these baffling times" and "a time of fear and foreboding."[13] Others commented on how the spy case and Manchuria were "most disquieting," "disturbing," and "arousing the fears of Americans."[14] Fears of a new existential challenge to democracy took hold, with the Soviet Union suddenly looking like an ideological menace. "Is Russia pursuing a policy of pushing out, mile by mile, country by country—a sort of Communist imperialism—or does she truly wish only security?" asked the *Milwaukee Journal*.[15]

The national panic created a political opportunity space for promoters, who stepped in and told a story about the February events that validated the nation's concerns. Many commentators (least of which was President Truman) contributed to the story's development, especially in this early period. Promoters in Congress stood out most. For starters, they narrated the events in existential terms as a real danger for Western liberalism. In a February 26 speech, Congressman Paul Shafer (R-MI) laid out the details of the spying revelations, Soviet subjugation of Eastern Europe, and communist infiltration of the State Department before asking rhetorically: "Do we want to continue the American system of free enterprise, or do we want to abandon it?"[16] It was a typical statement for promoters. "Democracy is under challenge as it has not been at any other time during the last century and a half," said one congressman in February, as he discussed current events. Another castigated Stalin's speech, saying "there is no more freedom in a Communist country today than there is in the penitentiary of Michigan, Mississippi, Ohio or Texas."[17] Others told the story of existential danger in historical terms. Congressman Wiley Mayne (R-IA) contextualized Stalin's speech and Soviet spying with President George Washington's Farewell Address, which he quoted at length. "Never was this truer than today," he said, of Washington's comments, "when all the tricks and subterfuges of foreign-inspired propaganda are being used to beguile us from the American way to the alien way, the collectivist way."[18]

Blame was a big part of the promoter story as well. Soviets drew their fair share of criticism, of course. But so too did the Truman administration. For Truman, cooperation with the Soviet Union remained a chief policy objective.[19] With the February 1946 events, promoters went after Truman for being too conciliatory and not tough enough with the Soviets. The highly respected senator Arthur Vandenberg (R-OH) led the charge with an especially important late February speech. "What is Russia up to? It is of course the supreme conundrum of our time," Vandenburg said, echoing the national dialogue around the February events before criticizing the administration. Dealing with communist states "calls for patience and goodwill, but not for vacillation," Vandenberg claimed, "There is a line beyond which compromise cannot go."[20] The speech made national headlines. Similar statements of blame did too. Many charged that the administration's tolerance for communists in government led to "weak" policies toward the Soviets. "Has this administration finally become interested in saving America from communism?" one member of Congress said, reflecting a typical statement here, "If this administration is disturbed by Russian expansion, why do they go on supplying the Russian Bear?"[21] Some challenged the president to be more loyal to the United States, rather than cater to Soviet wishes.[22] Others went after Secretary of State James Byrnes for being too compliant toward the Soviets on Europe. Senator Harlan Bushfield (R-SD) accused Byrnes, in fact, of complicity in the fall of democracy here. "In Eastern Europe it appears that we are encouraging the Communists," he charged on February 13, "Russia goes right ahead lapping up new territories and proclaiming what amounts to a modern version of the Monroe Doctrine for Europe and Asia."[23] Bushfield blamed Byrnes and the Truman administration more widely for these events.

Finally, every good story has a moral. That was true with promoter narrating around the 1946 events as well. From Capitol Hill to media pundits and policy experts, a resounding call went up for United States policy to get tougher with the Russians in order to defend freedom and democracy. "This is our Nation—not the Kremlins," said one member of Congress in mid-February, after discussing Stalin's speech, "We will protect our country against all comers from without."[24] Similar statements from promoters saturated the public discourse. Many referenced the recent past against Nazism ("The greatest nations of the world cried to America to save them when their freedom was at the point of destruction") and put out a clarion call for the same against communism in the present.[25] Others called for a tighter alliance with Great Britain as the only hope for "the protection of human liberty and man's gradual progress toward a better world."[26] Together, one statement after another reflected the critical final piece to the promoter story: a call to defend liberal political order abroad.

All of this was impossible for the Truman administration to ignore. The president and his closest advisors had no interest in creating a crusade-like mentality across the nation (strategic manipulation and the stand-alone polarization argument offer, then, little help in explaining the strengthening liberal narrative in this period). But they also knew that political necessity required they not appear out of step with the nation. In classic trauma-theory terms, they had to keep pace with the story that gripped the times. In a late February meeting amid the national panic, Secretary of State Byrnes told the cabinet that he "was being accused by his colleagues at home of having turned an appeaser."[27] This worried Truman as well. He admitted privately that these charges of blame could have devastating effects for the 1946 midterm elections.[28] Truman had to tact to the political winds of the budding liberal narrative. Consequently, the president told Byrnes to "stiffen up and try for the next three months not to make any compromises" with the Soviets. He also instructed Byrnes to take a firmer position with the Soviets in an upcoming speech.[29] On February 28, Byrnes did just that. Adding his voice to that of the promoters, Byrnes offered a near mirror-image of Vandenburg's speech, so similar, in fact, it was dubbed the "Second Vandenberg Concerto" by the press.[30] Byrnes talked of the uncertainty of the times and claimed in references to Iran and Manchuria, that no nation has the right to station troops in another country without that country's consent.[31] The speech sounded all the prevailing themes of the promoter story, notably existential challenge and the need to be more forceful with the Soviets.

The tough talk continued when Winston Churchill visited Fulton, Missouri and delivered the Iron Curtain speech, in which the British prime minister warned about the growing power of Soviet totalitarianism in Europe.[32] The speech was a watershed. Covered extensively in the media, Churchill told the entire liberal narrative story with dramatic effect. "From Stettin in the Baltic to Trieste in the Adriatic, an iron curtain has descended across the continent," Churchill said. He talked of the existential danger with "Communist fifth columns" across Europe, then cited the peril of indifference in the West (i.e., blame)—"Our difficulties and dangers will not be removed by closing our eyes to them." The prime minister closed with a robust call for repair—the moral of the story. "The Western democracies must stand together" he said, before warning of doing otherwise, "If they become divided or falter in their duty . . . then indeed catastrophe may overwhelm us all."[33]

The speeches by Vandenberg, Byrnes, and Churchill are part of Cold War history lore. For our purposes here, they played the critical role of legitimating the growing public unease in the United States over the ideological challenge abroad and, in turn, galvanizing the liberal narrative around anticommunism. "Byrnes and Vandenburg were moving with their times," observed Westerfield, "not far ahead, not far behind."[34] Various commentators said the same at the time of the speeches. "Secretary Byrnes was undoubtedly responding to a rising popular demand when he broadcast from the Overseas Press Club," said commentator Anne McCormick, "Mr. Byrnes has committed himself to a policy which the country must desire and therefore that the government will carry out."[35] The influential columnist, James Reston, agreed: "The country is now prepared to support a more courageous foreign policy in general and a sterner policy toward the Soviet Union in particular."[36] Churchill's speech was cast in a similar light. The *San Francisco Chronicle* called it a "service for the world" and noted that "Churchill pointed quite rightly to Russia's present pattern of projecting communism throughout Western Europe, and many other parts of the world, as a threat to the Western world."[37] Similar comments about Churchill's speech in newspapers across the country reflected the emerging unity among citizens around the need to challenge communism abroad as a means to defend liberal order.[38] This proved, furthermore, to be more than a fleeting or momentary phenomenon. The liberal narrative settled in as "a rigid political absolute," observed Frederik Logevall, becoming a standard fixture in the national discourse from 1946 forward.[39]

Politicians who tried to tell an alternative story learned this the hard way. In late 1946, for instance, Secretary of Commerce Henry Wallace sharply criticized Byrnes's "get tough" policy in a speech, claiming among other things that the Soviets had every right to "socialize their sphere."[40] The speech created "a mighty uproar," all of which centered on the strengthened liberal narrative.[41] Above all else, commentators across the country (and the political spectrum) attacked Wallace for being out of step with the national mood to defend democracy against communism's encroachment. "Byrnes is trying to maintain the principles for which American boys fought," wrote the *Milwaukee Sentinel*, "Mr. Wallace wants to nail up the iron curtain for good. Which is more democratic?"[42] Polls showed the same trends. Gallup found that 76 percent supported Byrnes's approach of being "firm with Russia" as opposed to Wallace's policy of being "easy with Russia; appeasing her."[43] This kind of national reaction makes sense. As trauma theory expects, external trauma like that of the late 1940s privileged promoters and ostracized moderators (like Wallace) with their alternative stories centered on restraint. The historian Melvin Small observes, for instance, that Wallace and others like him were considered "unpatriotic or dupes of the communists."[44] President Truman again scrambled to respond, eventually firing Wallace in order to calm public anger.[45] Overall, the Wallace incident demonstrated that by late 1946 a strengthening liberal narrative meant safety in U.S. politics was coming to lie with taking a stand against communism, both at home and abroad.

Liberal Narrative Strengthening, 1947–1949

Trauma theory anticipates that when threats are distant and less direct to a collective, the strengthening of the liberal narrative (especially its normative content) often occurs in fits and starts. One way that this evidenced itself in this period was the lack of clarity over *what* the U.S. public seemed willing to do in order to combat communism in 1946 and 1947. Specifically, it was right, as we have seen, to "get tough" in negotiations with the Soviets—this moral took hold collectively. Beyond that there was little action that seemed collectively acceptable to the nation—nothing forward-leaning or proactive. Things like shoring up democratic or anticommunist states, forming new alliances and, especially, rebuilding defenses were not on the nation's agenda. As one indication of this, cost-cutting on foreign policy remained a major theme through 1946. Congress showed no inclination to end the rapid demobilization begun in the prior year. "When asked 'Get tough' with what to back it up?" notes Larson, "Congressmen merely shrugged." The public lay behind this. The American people showed no interest in "increased arms expenditures and 'saber rattling.'"[46]

The Truman Doctrine speech in March was instrumental in helping to change this. Here, Truman arguably played his most important role as a promoter in the postwar period. The main purpose of the speech was rather mundane: namely, to generate public support to take on what had been to that point British responsibility for economic assistance to Greece and Turkey. The way he framed that request—that is, with the now standard Cold War story—to Congress had far-reaching implications, however, for the liberal narrative (and, as we see below, China and Korea). The following part of Truman's speech was especially important, reflecting the promoter story of the time and adding to that a call to greater action:

> The peoples of a number of the countries of the world have recently had totalitarianism forced upon them against their will [i.e., events and blame] . . . At the present moment in world history nearly every nation must choose between alternative ways of life. The choice is often not a free one [i.e., existential challenge] . . . It must be the policy of the United States to support free peoples who are resisting attempted subjugation by armed minorities or by outside pressures . . . Our help should be primarily through economic and financial aid which is essential to economic stability and orderly political processes [i.e., moral/repair].[47]

Truman's appeal linked the defense of liberal order abroad with a new active element—namely, foreign aid. The president charged that defending freedom demanded more than protests in direct negotiations with the Soviet Union. The bolstering of friendly, noncommunist nations abroad was now required as well. The survival of democracy in Europe and the United States demanded nothing less.

The U.S. public received Truman's call to action with enthusiasm. An April 4 Gallup poll found that 56 percent of the U.S. public approved of the speech.[48] As the broad narrative around the speech demonstrated, this support went hand-in-hand with and reflected a strengthening liberal narrative. "Whatever complacency that existed here up to that moment dissolved," said the *San Francisco Chronicle*. "It was something like the feeling on the day of Munich . . . The frontier of freedom in the world is our frontier, and if freedom dies in Europe and in Asia, it will not live in the United States."[49] The *Washington Post* commented that the danger of communism was "sensed in the public mind," and Truman "pitched the exact note from the people's point of view."[50] Other commentaries at the time said much the same: "we must check the spread of communism and totalitarian government"; "insure the survival of our freedom without waiting for an Armageddon"; and fight for "our way of life" and "protect our political system."[51] Some like the *Chicago Tribune* opposed the speech for fear that it could lead to war. But even here the editors admitted the surge of interest in actively curbing Soviet expansion: "Almost everybody in this country would like to see Russia checked."[52]

The Division of Press Intelligence (DPI) inside the White House concluded much the same. A DPI survey of 225 newspaper editorials between March 13 and 16 found a top theme in the response to Truman's speech was that "the outcome of the situation may decide our destiny as a free people."[53] Historians attest to the extensive impact of the speech as well, noting that it resonated with existing public concerns and deepened national sentiments to protect democracy against communism.[54] "Victory over the Soviet anti-Christ" settled in as the new national mood, observed one scholar, due "in great part. . . . to the rhetoric of the Truman administration."[55] Overall, the Truman Doctrine speech pressed the liberal narrative toward greater robustness in 1947, as the collective acceptance of greater activism to stop communism deepened.[56]

This raises an important question, though. Was the strengthening of the liberal narrative here simply a function of elite polarization or strategic manipulation? The answer, in short, is no, pointing us back again to trauma theory's attention to the mutually constitutive effects of master narratives and promoter arguments. As Truman's private comments reveal, the president worried about Soviet-inspired communism. But this was not the primary reason for the March speech. He still had little interest in—in fact, was quite leery about—rallying the nation to action around a crusade for democracy in 1947. Cooperation with the

Soviets remained a top priority for the president.[57] So why did he become such an ardent promoter in March 1947? The answer is straightforward. Like 1946 with the Byrnes speech, the strengthening liberal narrative pushed Truman into the promoter role, largely against his will. This evidenced itself most clearly at two points in the months leading up to the speech.

The first came in response to the 1946 midterm elections. The issue of anti-communism and defense of freedom played a major part in these elections.[58] As one writer observed, "The word 'Communism' was whooped about like an Indian war cry."[59] Truman was the main target in this conversation. A number of first-time-winning candidates for national office (from Richard Nixon (R-CA) to Joseph McCarthy (R-WI)) focused their campaigns, for instance, on Truman's failure to combat "Red Fascism" at home and abroad.[60] The GOP took control of both the House and Senate for the first time since 1932 on the back on this kind of anticommunist message.[61] As had been the case with the February events, the administration recognized that it again needed to tack to the prevailing liberal narrative winds. Consequently, Truman moved to beef up his anticommunist credentials the day after the election by, among other things, approving an executive loyalty program intended to investigate and root out federal workers suspected of affiliation with communist groups.[62] Truman's advisors defended the move as a necessary evil. "Truman was going to run in '48, and that was it . . . The President didn't attach fundamental importance to the so-called Communist scare," said Clark Clifford, White House Counsel and close confidant to the president, "He thought it was a lot of baloney. But, political pressures were such that he had to recognize it."[63] Truman advisors saw anti-communism as a way of "attracting votes and building a political reputation" by avoiding "being denounced as a fellow traveler," according to Logevall.[64] Again, Truman was not the driver of the liberal narrative here. Instead, he was pushed along by it.

The same was the case to a large extent with the Truman Doctrine speech in March. A meeting with congressional leaders prior to the speech on February 27 demonstrates this most clearly. The purpose of the meeting was to secure initial congressional support for Greek and Turkish aid. The new secretary of state George Marshall opened the meeting with the administration's main justification for aid. He made no mention of communism or totalitarianism. Instead, Marshall tried to sell the program exclusively on realpolitik and humanitarian grounds, noting the geostrategic importance of the eastern Mediterranean to the British. The appeal fell flat. As Truman advisor George Elsey described it, "The reaction of the Congressional leaders [to Marshall] was rather trivial."[65] Congress had no interest in propping-up British imperial interests.[66] Sensing a disaster, Undersecretary of State Dean Acheson, jumped in. To counter "the audience's indifference" to Marshall's appeal, Acheson offered a long, ideologically charged justification for aid, pointing to the inevitable collapse of one regime after another to communist totalitarianism if Greece and Turkey fell. Acheson's argument struck a chord. This was the kind of talk that constituents understood, said the members of Congress. Vandenberg told Truman, "If you will say that to the Congress and the country, I will support you and I believe that most of its members will do the same." He then told the president to "Scare the Hell out of the American people."[67]

Truman agreed to do so.[68] In the days that followed the meeting, mundane geopolitical language in the speech was replaced with justifications for aid—focused on the need to protect freedom—that resonated with the liberal narrative.[69] Those raising realpolitik complaints were rebuffed. Marshall told Truman, for instance, that he was "somewhat startled to see the extent to which the anticommunist element of the speech was stressed" and wondered if the speech was "overstating the case a bit." Truman brushed him aside, saying that "from all contacts with the Senate, it is clear that this was the only way in which the measure would pass."[70]

The main point is this: the president adopted a more ideological line in the Truman Doctrine speech not primarily because of his own polarization. Instead, he did so out of necessity, under pressure (via the peoples' representatives in Congress) from the broad liberal narrative disposition of the U.S. public. As trauma theory anticipates, promoters, like the president of the United States, are at times *both* product and driver of change in liberal narrative strength.[71] That was all too evident with Truman in the mid-1940s.

So, if not ideological polarization, what about the other elite-based account—strategic elite manipulation or fearmongering? At first glance, there appears good evidence for this argument: as indicated by accounts of the February 27 meeting, Truman clearly adopted ideological language for instrumental reasons, notably to create national support for what he viewed as the strategically important goal of aiding Greece and Turkey.

The problem with this argument is that it places too much weight on elites, and, like the stand-alone polarization argument, misses how the liberal narrative conditions, circumscribes, and sometimes trumps elite influence. In addition to the fact as already noted that Truman was pushed into the ideological language of the speech by an already strengthening liberal narrative, Truman's ideological language in the speech would have fallen flat in its own right had it not been for that narrative. This is what Melvin Small means when he says that in 1947 Truman did not create the national, anticommunist mood "whole cloth"—he helped consolidate that national mood on a preexisting collective narrative that emerged the year prior.[72] Added to this and in sharp contrast to the elite-manipulation argument, Truman helped create something in a strong liberal narrative that became much more powerful and independent of elite control than anything he intended. "Vigilance against Communism . . . [became] a national priority," observed Stephen Whitfield, of the political environment from 1947 forward, "[as] politicians vied with one another to demonstrate their devotion to the cause of the 'Free World.'"[73] The liberal narrative took on a life of its own, independent of elite control. As this happened, the politics surrounding the liberal narrative not only pressed the Truman administration to *say*, but also *do* (as Marshall feared), things it otherwise might have chosen to avoid.[74] All Truman wanted in March 1947 was aid for Greece and Turkey. The liberal narrative he helped consolidate in order to get that aid pushed him, however, into far more than that. China and Korea demonstrate this all too well.

China, 1947–1949

Following retired-general George Marshall's failed 1946 attempt to negotiate an end to the Chinese civil war, the Truman administration sought to avoid forceful regime promotion on behalf of Chiang Kai-shek's anticommunist Nationalist regime. In fact, the administration's preferred course of action was full disengagement from Chiang. From mid-1947, Truman tried to take several steps toward this end: continuation of a 1946 arms embargo against the Nationalists, termination of direct aid to Chiang, and normalization of relations with Mao Zedong's communist insurgency in hopes of encouraging independence from the Soviet Union.[75] In the end, the administration got part of what it wanted: it avoided robust forceful regime change in China. Yet it also never fully disengaged from Chiang, providing him instead with large amounts of aid and eventually moving the 7th Fleet to protect Taiwan.[76] Normalization with Mao never came either. The liberal discourse that developed around China in this period helps explain these various outcomes.

The story starts with promoters. The "China bloc" in the United States included a loose coalition of influential private citizens (like publisher Henry Luce), lobbying organizations, popular mainstream publications (such as Luce's *Time* and *Life* magazines), religious groups, and a small cadre of vocal members of the U.S. Congress, like Representative Walter Judd (R-MN) as well as Senators Owen Brewster (R-ME) and Styles Bridges (R-NH)).[77] The bloc's cause was support for Chiang's anticommunist Nationalists. It began activities in 1947, following the collapse of the Marshall mission, with charges that communists were running U.S. Asia policy. The lobby drew heavily on liberal narrative themes. China bloc magazines/publications talked of the "Red Propaganda" that filtered into the Roosevelt Administration leading to the "Sins of Yalta," such as giving away Manchuria to Mao's communists.[78] The bloc charged the same of the 1946 Marshall mission. From the negotiated truces to arms embargo, the China bloc claimed that communists at the State Department duped Marshall into a pro-Mao policy.[79]

Above all else, the lobby demanded direct U.S. aid to the Nationalists, especially as Chiang's forces lost ground in 1947 and 1948.[80] William Bullitt, a Democrat and first U.S. ambassador to the Soviet Union, played a big role here. He published a mid-October 1947 report that appealed for approximately $600 million in U.S. military and economic aid to the Nationalists. Given his expertise, Bullitt's report created an immediate sensation.[81] On Capitol Hill, promoters used it and the robust liberal narrative in appeals to aid Chiang. In hearings on Greece and Turkey, bloc members hounded State Department witnesses about China. Some pointed to the inconsistency of aiding Europe but not China: "define the subtle differences between Chinese communists and Greek communists," charged Senator Brewster to Marshall, at one point.[82] Others claimed the loss of Asia would hurt freedom in Europe.[83]

Bullitt's report also moved aiding China into the political mainstream. Non-China bloc Republicans like Vandenberg, John Foster Dulles, Speaker of the House Joseph Martin, and eventual GOP nominee for president, Thomas Dewey, all began to voice support for aiding China in order to stop communist expansion.[84] Others did too. *Newsweek* and the *Atlantic* endorsed, for instance, the idea of more aid to combat Chinese communists. So did the *New York Times* and many other newspapers.[85] Public opinion changed as well. Support for economic aid to the Nationalists rose from 43 percent in the spring of 1947 to 53 percent in December. By mid-1948, polls showed that 55 percent of the public supported military aid for the Nationalists as well.[86] "A general orthodoxy of opinion was clearly emerging," Lewis Purifoy notes, of this period, "As there was one 'world Communist conspiracy,' so there was one 'containment,' and in Asia Chiang Kai-shek was its prophet."[87] The China bloc helped generate this broad discourse, tying China to the now increasingly robust liberal narrative.

This impacted policy. Notably, the promoter surge raised audience costs for inaction in ways that the administration could not ignore. "House committee took me down a lot of side streets with reference to China, Communism, etc.," Marshall reported, in a memo to Truman on the November 1947 European aid hearings, "Opposition does not take a stand on what we are trying to do but how we are trying to do it [i.e., aid for European anticommunism only]."[88] Privately, Marshall said he wanted to challenge the China bloc.[89] But fearful of the political fallout from crossing the liberal discourse, the administration did just the opposite instead. "The government did not have the choice of 'abandoning' Chiang's government; the option was foreclosed by the clamor of the Asialationists [i.e., China bloc]," observed Purifoy, "The president could not very well rebut the arguments of men who employed his own logic and mouthed his very clichés," all of which were about communism and democracy.[90] Citing the bitter domestic political climate, a China specialist at State observed simply, "We couldn't appear to push ... [Chiang] out."[91]

Consequently and in an effort to "appease pro-China groups in Congress and the public," Marshall lifted the arms embargo on the Nationalists in May.[92] He also removed John Carter Vincent (a frequent target of promoter attacks) as director of the Department of State Far Eastern Affairs.[93] Aid flowed to the Nationalists as well. In late October 1947, Truman agreed to attach $30 million in assistance for the Nationalists to the Greek-Turkish aid bill. In early 1948, Marshall proposed a $570 million aid program to China over fifteen months, which nearly matched Bullitt's number. Congress approved both measures. For Marshall, none of it made any sense. "I wash my hands of the problem which has passed altogether beyond my power to make judgments," he wrote privately, after passage of the China bill. Truman called it "pouring money down a rat hole."[94]

Two questions are important here. First, why did the administration capitulate to promoters on China? Some argue it was about votes for European aid.[95] While this holds some truth, the vote-swapping explanation misses the important impact of the liberal discourse. First, it understates the *indirect* influence of the liberal narrative. It took the robust narrative of defending democracy against communism to make China bloc threats of opposition to European aid salient. As Richard Freeland observes, Republicans in Congress used the national "sentiment" of a "growing, wide-ranging, anti-communist emotionalism" to "force the Executive into unwanted commitments to Nationalist China."[96] The liberal narrative called for *universal*, or global, defense against communism, giving political life to China bloc arguments. Aid to Europe was impossible without aid to China. The liberal narrative trapped the administration into aid for *both* regions.[97]

The vote-swapping argument also misses the liberal narrative's *direct* impact on policy too. The administration feared public backlash on China. "The United States should extend the minimum aid necessary to satisfy *American public opinion*, and if possible, to prevent any sudden and total collapse of the Chinese Government," argued the State Department Policy Planning Staff in late 1947.[98] An especially poignant example of direct capitulation to liberal narrative pressure came in early 1949. By this point, Congress had approved European aid (vote-swapping was not an issue) and in 1948 Democrats regained control of Congress. Given both of these realities, the new secretary of state Dean Acheson proposed ending China aid. That idea was quickly shelved under direct pressure from the liberal discourse, though. In a meeting with members of Congress, Vandenberg (a Republican) stiffly opposed the move:

> If we take this step at this fatefully inept moment, we shall never be able to shake the charge that we are the ones who gave poor China the final push into disaster. Millions of our people will be shocked . . . I make it plain that I have little or no hope for stopping the immediate conquest [of communist forces in China]. That is beside the point. I decline to be responsible for the last push which makes it possible.[99]

His appeal worked. Truman sided with Vandenberg, who also did not want public responsibility for abandoning the noncommunist forces in China (i.e., audience costs for inaction). Military aid continued and even increased later that year. In the end, the need to convey to the public an image of standing for democracy against communism was simply too strong for the administration to resist, especially when the China bloc raised the issue repeatedly.[100]

A second important question relates to the use of force. If the discourse around China was so strong and policymakers (like Marshall and Vandenberg) knew Chiang had no chance of military victory, why not direct force to save the Nationalist regime in this period? The answer lies, at least in part, with this: the liberal discourse never demanded a robust application of force in China. "Even the most outspoken critics of the Marshall-Truman policy never proposed publicly the use of American ground forces in China for combat duties," observes Tang Tsou.[101] On Capitol Hill, Chiang's supporters went out of their way, in fact, to say that U.S. support of Chiang did not and never would imply a commitment to use force. In testimony before Congress in 1947, Bullitt stated plainly, "I do not propose that American troops be sent to China."[102] Representative Judd said, at one point, "Not for one moment has anyone contemplated sending a single combat soldier in."[103] In a 1949 congressional debate, Brewster stated emphatically, "I never proposed to send an army to China."[104]

Why so much promoter restraint? The answer centers again on master narratives. "American public opinion and demobilization . . . rendered such a policy [i.e., military force] unthinkable," Freeland argues.[105] Protecting democracy abroad was important for the nation, but not with force, at least not yet. Until mid-1950, communist gains that animated the liberal narrative were still geographically distant from the U.S. polity and, furthermore, a product of internal subversion, not overt, cross-border invasions by military forces from communist states. As discussed above, the national discourse focused on military or economic aid—and, explicitly not military force—to defend liberal order abroad. Editors at the *Los Angeles Times* noted that the Truman Doctrine's "defense . . . against Communists" involved a policy of "economic intervention," and not military action, to stop "Russian expansion."[106] Likewise, the *Atlanta Constitu-tion*'s ringing endorsement of the Truman Doctrine came with this caveat: "We will, if Congress approves, send money, equipment, technicians and advisers to Greece and to Turkey—but not troops."[107]

Comments like these reflected broader thinking. Polls in early 1950 showed public reticence about using force to combat communism abroad as well.[108] Coupled with pressure from cost-cutters in the China bloc, this shaped promoter arguments. Promoters knew that to remain politically salient they had to limit their appeals on China to aid only, and no troops.[109] The China bloc was "careful not to advocate American military intervention in China," observed Donovan, "They expounded proposals far more acceptable to voters than that."[110] In the end, then, promoters used, but were also constrained by the state of the liberal narrative in this period. Consequently, a liberal discourse for robust military action never materialized around China—audience costs for inaction did not reach the point, then, of expecting a direct U.S. role.

The Truman administration responded accordingly. It structured China policy between 1947 and 1950 to match the liberal discourse built by promoters. That discourse focused on aid, not force. This helps explain why the U.S.-supported Chiang up to but not to the point of forceful regime promotion prior to 1950.

The "Loss" and "Soft" Discourse, 1949–1950

In 1949 and 1950, the promoter discourse and national disposition around U.S.-Asia policy became noticeably more strident. The change revolved around events that created new fears about liberal order abroad. Developments here included China's fall (December 1949) and alliance with the Soviets (February 1950); the first Soviet nuclear bomb test (August 29, 1949); and new espionage cases (i.e., January 1950 conviction of Alger Hiss and arrest of Klaus Fuchs) that accentuated national panic around the Soviet nuclear test.[111] Collectively, these events "slashed the American psyche like the repeated thrust of a dagger."[112] The collapse of China, in particular, "shocked the American public" causing "hysteria," according to historians.[113] Some claimed China's fall shook the public like the Great Depression. Overall, there was a deep national sense that "something was amiss."[114]

Building on this, promoters went after Truman directly. The bloc attacked the administration for a weak, "do-nothing" policy against communism following the Soviet nuclear test and formation of the People Republic of China (PRC) in the latter part of 1949.[115] Other charges included appeasement, being "soft" on communism, and "losing" China.[116] Due to pressure from the liberal discourse, all of these assaults on administration policy went virtually unopposed. "Only a few Senators or Representatives dared voice a contrary view," observes Nancy Tucker, "Worried about the attitude of the voting public, they feared the action of the China bloc."[117]

The power of the China bloc's liberal discourse (and with it, political pressure on the administration) expanded all the more with the emergence of Republican Senator Joseph McCarthy as a promoter in early 1950. McCarthy came onto the scene at an opportune time, just as news of the espionage cases broke and the Sino-Soviet alliance formed. Armed with information from Luce, Kohlberg, and others in the China lobby, McCarthy launched the torrid anticommunist campaign that is well documented by many scholars.

The early phases of that campaign focused almost exclusively on foreign policy, especially in Asia. His attacks included a new wrinkle: disloyalty, not just of a few advisors, but Truman and Acheson themselves. Administration softness on communism resulted from more than miscalculation, claimed McCarthy. Instead, it was intentional, a product of communist traitors in government, whom FDR, Truman, and Acheson supported and defended.[118] Into the summer of 1950, McCarthy went after "card-carrying" communists, name-by-name at the State Department—all of whom were aided by Acheson, he charged.[119] The State Department is "loyal to the ideals of Communism rather than those of the free, God-fearing half of the world," McCarthy charged.[120]

Although McCarthy was, as many note, a "creature, not the creator" of the times in which he operated, he and other promoters impacted the national discourse in important ways.[121] By the spring of 1950, accusations of traitors in government and Truman administration "softness" became standard themes in the wider national discussion about Asia policy. The *Washington Post* commented on how the "attacks from fanatics and commiphobics" over China had "whipped up a fury" that fueled national "anxiety about communism."[122] The *Los Angeles Times* derided Acheson as a "late joiner to the 'get tough with Russia policy'" and called for a "fumigation of the State Department."[123] The *San Francisco Chronicle* talked at length in the spring of 1950 about national anxiety over Asia and blamed the administration as well. "Russia is away and running while we stand, tethered by indecision, at the starting line," the editors claimed. Comments like these were abundant across 1950.[124]

Other indicators showed similar trends. By late 1949, the most frequent poll responses on China were that the "U.S. blundered" and that the Truman administration's performance was "very poor" in Asia.[125] Another poll showed that 68 percent thought the administration was "too soft" on communism.[126] By May 1950, a plurality considered McCarthy's efforts good for U.S. national security.[127] Historians shed light on these trends too, claiming McCarthy and others "scarred the political landscape" and "certified the authenticity of anticommunism" for the U.S. public in ways that contributed to a "hardening attitude over the fight against communism."[128] The environment was treacherous for moderators. "Less and less do people dare raise their voices lest they be called Communist or pro-Communist," a new deal Democrat wrote, in April 1950, "It is a poisonous sort of atmosphere."[129]

The Truman administration scrambled again to accommodate this surge of liberal narrative pressure. Steps here were many: State abandoned efforts to normalize relations with Mao; new aid flowed to noncommunist regimes in Southeast Asia; and government officials made more stridently anticommu-nist statements in public.[130] Added to this, the State Department saw wholesale changes in personnel. In an effort to appease McCarthy, old China experts were moved out and new advisors supported by promoters brought on board.[131] The two most prominent were Dean Rusk to head the Department of State Far East-ern Affairs and the Republican, John Foster Dulles, as special advisor.[132] Both appointments were, according to one scholar, "a reflection of changing domestic politics . . . bringing that pressure right into the room."[133]

None of these steps seemed to ward off promoter demands or calm national anxiety, however. Pressure built for something more, notably an *active* policy in Asia. "We have got to start doing," said the *San Francisco Chronicle* in mid-June 1950.[134] A "positive program" is needed in Asia, noted the *New York Times*.[135] "Russian force is a fact, American force must become a fact," the *Milwaukee Jour-nal* commented in March, "The main issue is the need for democracy to win the cold war or be swept under the advancing tide of totalitarianism."[136] In June 1950, the strengthening liberal-discourse demands for action came home to roost in U.S. policy toward Korea and China.

China and Korea, 1950

On June 25, North Korean forces invaded South Korea in order to unify the pen-insula under a single, communist government led by North Korean Premier Kim Il-Sung. Korea's attack "heightened, not diminished, the anti-Communist hys-teria in America," notes Kaufman.[137] It created, above all else, an instantaneous surge of liberal narrative pressure for robust action. "In the face of an aggres-sor, the United States must take the risks to preserve freedom here and for the non-Communist world," argued the *Milwaukee Journal*, two days after the inva-sion.[138] Stopping communism demands the nation "meet strength with strength," claimed the *Atlanta Journal Constitution*.[139] The *San Francisco Chronicle* said that North Korean action could not be met with a "hands-off policy" since "what's at stake out there . . . [is] the freedom of every one of us, and we can't dodge that and have our freedoms too."[140] Of the forty statements made by members of the

House and Senate in the first two days after North Korea's invasion, only one opposed defending South Korea.[141]

Support for robust force was also strong. Telegrams to the White House ran ten-to-one in favor of military action in Korea.[142] Papers across the country called for a policy to "meet strength with strength" and claimed it "would be folly" to stop short of ground troops.[143] Before Truman even announced his first steps, Congress demanded force. During the first two days of congressional discussion on Korea, nearly half of the House and Senate members who spoke called for a ground invasion. Comments here were unambiguous: "I . . . hope that he [Truman] will not shrink from using the army"; "let us now send jet planes, fighter planes, bombs, munitions, and men to protect Korea"; and "I am dedicated to the proposition of defending our far eastern line . . . to the last man, if necessary, in order to offset the Communist movement of Moscow."[144] As one demonstration of the strong national impulse to stop communism, cost-cutters in the GOP jumped on board too. With extensive reference to protecting freedom, they dropped, without reservation, all former opposition to aid for Korea and a larger military in general. Moderators were almost impossible to find—even Henry Wallace supported force to save South Korea.[145]

Korea, June 1950

The Truman administration saw little strategic value in Korea. In January 1950, Acheson drew Korea outside the U.S. defense perimeter in Asia—U.S. military personnel were withdrawn soon after. Like China, geopolitics and not ideology was the main driver here—the administration saw danger in unnecessary competition with the Soviets and, thus, sought limits to U.S. activity in Asia. North Korea's June invasion reversed this policy entirely. On June 26, the administration ushered through a U.N resolution to defend South Korea. Four days later, two divisions of U.S. ground troops left for the Korean peninsula.[146]

Historians widely agree that the liberal narrative discourse had an unmistakable impact on these decisions in June. Observers differ here only on how it mattered. Some claim the liberal discourse raised audience costs for inaction for the Truman administration in ways that pushed the president to act in Korea. "Eager to score political points at home by demonstrating his anti-communist credentials," Craig and Logevall argue, "[Truman] almost immediately decided on a military response."[147] Zelizer indicates similarly that a "passive response" would have aided conservatives, making it "hard for . . . [Truman] to refrain from a military response," especially in the wake of the administration's choice against military action in China the year before.[148]

There is good evidence to support the pushed-to-act argument. Secretary of Defense Louis Johnson said that avoiding the "soft-on-communism" label contributed to Truman's decision to enter the war.[149] Likewise, a Democratic senator close to both Truman and Acheson claimed at the time that "if the Republicans hadn't been hammering on Harry Truman, he'd never have gone into Korea."[150] On this score, Truman knew he had to protect Democrats on Capitol Hill from liberal narrative charges of being soft on communism.[151] On June 27, for instance, Senator Joseph O'Mahony (D-WY), an influential member of the Senate Appropriations Committee, told Truman that testimony that day in the committee about South Korea's under-preparedness for the attack "will undoubtedly be used to support the charge that our policy was soft toward the Communists." After committing air and naval forces on June 28, Truman responded to O'Mahony that by his assessment Democrats were now off the hook. "I think," He said, "We have now covered the situation to a point where we will either get results or we will have to go all-out to maintain our position."[152]

Internal discussions also support the pushed-to-act argument. Rusk and Acheson both pressed Truman in the hours after the attack, for example, to go to the United Nations quickly so that the U.S. resolution would appear in the morning papers alongside the announcement of the North Korean attack. Why the haste? Historians agree that quick action at the United Nations signaled to the U.S. public toughness against communism just as news broke publicly about North Korean troops crossing the 38th parallel. It was a move, then, to head-off charges of administration softness. Commentators agree the same drove Truman's decision to send ground troops. "In the atmosphere in Washington vicious domestic political repercussions damaging to the president would have been inevitable if the 'loss' of China were to be followed by the 'loss' of Korea," observes Truman's official biographer, Robert Donovan.[153] Acheson told Truman something to the same effect on June 29, the day before the president decided to commit ground troops. It would be a domestic political disaster, Acheson said, if North Korea won the war after the United States had committed military aid and air power to the South. In light of the robust liberal narrative around Asia policy generally, the administration had little choice but to use robust force for regime promotion in South Korea.[154]

Other historians argue that instead of pushing the administration to act in Korea, the liberal discourse played a more conducive, free-hand-to-act role in June 1950. Most here contend that Truman chose to enter the Korean War primarily for reasons of international credibility and prestige, in essence to communicate resolve as a means to prevent the Soviets from trying to use force in other places later on down the line.[155] The robust liberal discourse helped most by facilitating this action. "Had it been radically different from what it was, the domestic political climate might have prevented large-scale American involvement," observes Stueck, "As it was, it merely reinforced Truman's and Acheson's strong inclination to commit American troops."[156]

Again, internal deliberations offer good evidence that the liberal narrative played this free-hand-to-act role. For starters, top policy elites saw the public disposition as something that was not holding them back from action, but instead had the potential for the opposite, to push them farther than they wanted to go in Korea and beyond.[157] Prior to North Korea's invasion, Truman and Acheson were aware of rising public expectations of a coming war with the Soviet Union.[158] When the Korean War came, then, the State Department advised caution. "We must exercise a high degree of self-discipline under the present situation and should carefully consider any measure likely to cause hysteria," a State Department advisor said in late June.[159]

Truman followed this line. He told his National Security Council on June 28, for instance, that a State Department report on the possibility of direct Soviet involvement in the war needed to be kept secret, so as to avoid alarming the public.[160] During the early days of the conflict, the administration also tried to temper the liberal-discourse fervor at home, rather than fan it, by using less ideological language in public statements. The White House warned reporters, for instance, not to be too alarmist.[161] Likewise, Truman intentionally waited four days after North Korea's invasion to make a much-anticipated public statement on Korea. When he finally spoke, the president took a subdued approach, offering a bland detailing of events and making only a single passing reference to "communist forces" in order to avoid exciting public opinion too much.[162] In sum, Truman not only felt little constrained by the public's disposition, he knew the burgeoning liberal discourse to stop communism in Asia granted him a wide-open field of play to use all necessary means, including robust force.

Deliberations about a war declaration from Congress offer a good example of this kind of thinking inside the administration as well. When Secretary of the Army Frank Pace suggested to Truman on June 27 that he ask Congress for a declaration of war, the president responded, "Frank, it's not necessary. They're all with me."[163] Pace brought the matter up because members of Congress had raised the subject for the first time that morning in a meeting with the president. This caught Truman by surprise. Neither he nor his advisors had even considered asking congressional permission to use force in two solid days to that point of internal discussions on Korea.[164] The deep anticommunist fervor across the nation gave Truman the impression that he faced no constraints at home on the use of force. The president simply took national support for granted. Overall, the liberal discourse-charged political climate gave Truman a free-hand to use robust force to save South Korea in June 1950.

China, June 1950

The Chinese Nationalists fled to Taiwan in December 1949. The Truman administration anticipated Mao would take the island by mid-1950, an eventuality that Washington had no plans to prevent. Here again, elite preferences centered on geopolitics (and, hence, restraint) not ideology when it came to China. Like Korea, Truman was unable to stick to this policy entirely, however. Two days after North Korea's invasion, the president sent the 7th Fleet into the Taiwan Straits to neutralize Formosa. With that move, the United States assumed a permanent role in the Chinese civil war with commitments to Taiwan that lasted throughout the Cold War.

The decision to protect Taiwan (as well as the reasons why that protection did not include full-scale forceful regime promotion) is best explained, again, by the liberal discourse around China in June 1950. In the weeks prior to North Korea's invasion, promoters inside the administration pressed Truman to protect Taiwan. Rusk and Dulles (again, the newcomers close to promoters outside of the administration) both argued internally that Taiwan offered a place to win political points at home. To this effect, Rusk said in a May 30 meeting that "world and U.S. opinion" was disappointed with Truman's approach to Taiwan—policy change would be "politically useful." A few days later, Dulles claimed a strong stand on Taiwan could "establish our policies toward the Far East on a broad bipartisan basis."[165]

North Korea's invasion of South Korea both amplified arguments like these and significantly raised political costs for not complying with them. On June 25, Truman called his advisors to Blair House for meetings on Korea. He faced immediate pressure from promoters to protect Taiwan. Secretary of Defense Louis Johnson led the charge. He had the chairman of the Joint Chiefs of Staff Omar Bradley read a letter from General Douglas MacArthur on the need to deny Formosa to the communists.[166] The highly popular MacArthur warned Bradley that if Truman did not move to defend Formosa, he would return home from the Pacific and tell the U.S. public the facts.[167] Whether the latter was conveyed by Bradley at the Blair House meeting, we do not know. But given the fact that the media at the time knew about MacArthur's letter, one finds it hard to believe that the president was not also aware of the "threat of political attacks by MacArthur and the China lobby."[168]

These promoter arguments mattered in critical ways. "The political costs of appearing soft on communism compelled the President and his Secretary of State to shield the Kuomingtang for the duration of the Korean conflict," observes Nancy Tucker.[169] More specifically, long-standing promoter carping about saving Taiwan from communism made it politically impossible for the administration to pursue a strong anticommunist policy in Korea, but not Taiwan. Truman knew that aiding only the former would leave him out of step with the liberal narrative and open to fresh "weak-on-communism" charges. "Truman had little practical choice but to abandon neutralization on Formosa . . . [due to] the need for home front unity," argues David Halberstam.[170] The forceful and immediate push by promoters prior to the war and at Blair House along with MacArthur's threat made this all too clear. "Defending Formosa would help win support for the Korean policy in Congress," according to Donovan.[171]

This reasoning eventually won over Truman and Acheson during the Blair House meetings. Reflecting their preferences for a more pragmatic approach to China, neither went down that road willingly, though. Truman was slow to approve, for instance, the request from Johnson and Bradley to shield Taiwan, delaying a decision for twenty-four hours. When he finally capitulated, Truman claimed with frustration that it was his last step to aid the Nationalists. The United States would not give "a nickel" more to Chiang, he said. Acheson agreed, warning against getting "mixed up" in the Chinese civil war.[172] Acheson then went one step further, in fact, and encouraged Truman to have the 7th Fleet stop outside of the straits rather than enter them immediately in hopes that a firm commitment to defend the Nationalists might still be avoided. Overall, Truman and Acheson had no change of heart about Chiang, nor a sudden awakening to the strategic importance of Taiwan. The Nationalists looked much as they had since 1946 for the president: not worth defending.[173]

So why move the 7th Fleet in their defense? The pressure of the liberal narrative offers the strongest explanation. According to several scholarly accounts, Acheson dropped his resistance because he realized that a PRC attack on Taiwan *now*, amid communist gains in Korea, would be devastating at home. In light of the pressure from McArthur/Johnson/Bradley, inaction could become a domestic political disaster for an administration already under attack for being weak on communism.[174] Richard Freeland captures this well, "In the Formosa intervention, it is difficult to avoid the conclusion that the Administration felt the need, at the inception of a potentially difficult and divisive war in Korea and four months before a national election, to establish clearly for a skeptical public and critical Congress its determination to do everything possible to oppose communism in Asia."[175] In sum, "the unbridled hysteria of the times" that came with a robust liberal discourse drove policy toward Taiwan.[176]

This all raises an important question. If costs for inaction were prevalent, why did the administration not do more, like send ground troops to Formosa or invade the mainland? Strategic calculation mattered some here—the United States was preparing to launch a major war in Korea, meaning the reality of a two-front war discouraged action in China (see discussion below). An equally (if not more) important factor, though, was the political space created by the types of arguments promoters were making about China in 1950.

Well before the Korean War, promoter discourse around China had narrowed in two critical ways. First, the China bloc abandoned the goal of saving the mainland, focusing instead solely on Taiwan. This turn came in early 1950, showing-up in debates over the administration's January decision to exclude Taiwan and Korea from the U.S. defense perimeter in Asia. Senator Smith led the way. "I cannot express how shocked I was when I read [about] . . . the President's 'hands off policy' on Taiwan" said Smith, "The most urgent question facing us today . . . [is] the action which should be taken with respect to the remaining core of Nationalist resistance . . . whose vital center is Formosa."[177] China bloc members followed Smith, one statement after another took a scripted line: criticize the administration for the loss of China and argue for more action—not for mainland China, but Taiwan. "Assistance should be given to the legal Government of China to defend . . . Formosa," said Senator William Knowland (R-CA).[178] "We should prevent Communist occupation of Formosa," argued Senator Robert Taft (R-OH).[179] "We must save Formosa from the Communists," said Senator Stiles Bridges.[180] Again, no one in the January debates (or later) advocated regime promotion on the mainland.[181] Promoter discourse around anticommunism in China narrowed to Taiwan alone.

Second, in their attention to Taiwan, promoters were careful. They intentionally advocated only limited military action. The China bloc endorsed sending the navy—and no other troops—to prevent a PRC attack from the mainland.[182] "We would not be putting any military force there [Taiwan], or any military mission," argued Senator Smith in January.[183] Other "save-Taiwan" members of Congress echoed this. "I will say that I am not advocating the sending of armed forces to Formosa," said Senator Bourke Hickenlooper (R-IA).[184] On January 11, Taft clarified earlier comments about protecting Formosa: "I did not suggest the occupation of Formosa, nor the sending of any army."[185] Promoters (including Dulles and Rusk) wanted a strong stand for Formosa, with limited means alone—a position that remained down to the Korean War.[186]

This mattered to Truman in June 1950. The promoter discourse gave the president the political space *not* to act on the Chinese mainland and *not* to use robust regime promotion force in Taiwan (i.e., a weaker liberal discourse that limited costs for inaction). "As with the pattern over the preceding three years, it seems that the administration intervened in the Chinese Civil War only to the minimum degree necessary to guarantee consensus on other policies," observes Christiansen.[187] And that consensus required only limited military action. To this end, a State Department official at the Blair House meeting wrote that moving the fleet should be enough to "get popular approval."[188] This assessment turned out to be accurate. The public announcement of the 7th fleet move won high praise at home. "It was all a wonderful answer to prayer," wrote Senator Smith, in his diary on June 27, "The saving of Formosa was clearly God guided."[189] The editorial pages, *Congressional Record*, and opinion polls showed similar enthusiasm for the move.[190] Of special note, no member of the China bloc responded with calls for more action. Instead, promoters were satisfied. At the Blair House meetings, Johnson and Bradley did not demand additional military action on China.[191] Again, this is how many historians explain the policy outcome here. "The very nature of the President's decision disarmed critics of the Truman-Acheson foreign policy," observes Goldman, "They had demanded American arms to protect Formosa from the Chinese Reds; the Seventh Fleet shielded the island."[192] In sum, Truman fit, or matched, policy with the unique liberal discourse around the regime crisis in China. The result was limited regime promotion activity for the Nationalists on Taiwan in 1950.

Korea, September 1950

General MacArthur's famous mid-September attack at Inchon turned the tide of the Korean War. By the end of the month, United Nations forces retook South Korea.[193]

MacArthur's success also created a groundswell of national enthusiasm to unify the Korean peninsula under a single democratic regime.[194] A week after MacArthur's invasion, a poll found that 64 percent of Americans supported crossing the 38th parallel to "keep fighting."[195] The national discussion here was fixated on liberal narrative themes. "The crusade for freedom is underway," proclaimed the *Milwaukee Journal*.[196] Choosing not to cross the 38th parallel would be a "blow to the hopes of the free world," said another paper.[197] Others echoed these themes, talking of "upholding freedoms" and "a free, democratic, and united Korea."[198] Many commentators saw the danger of war with the Soviets or Chinese, but advocated going ahead anyway. "It is unthinkable that we should not finish what we so boldly started," noted the *Los Angeles Times*, "because some timid souls in the State Department fear the Russians, or the Chinese Communists, or both, will jump into the fray the moment we cross the 38th parallel."[199]

Truman also faced a wave of domestic, liberal narrative-based attacks across the summer. New charges of being "soft on communism" rose to a fever pitch. The subdued tone that Truman took in the first week of the war (as seen above, to avoid overheating public opinion) coupled with a string of U.S. defeats early in the war set the stage for the attacks.[200] Charges surfaced in the media that the president was complacent, pressure built for full mobilization.[201] Republicans harped on the complacency theme as well. In a July statement, fifteen House GOP members criticized Truman's lack of leadership.[202] Soon after, Republicans released a white paper as part of the run-up to the November midterm elections. Garnering front-page headlines in papers across the country, the white paper centered on liberal narrative themes, citing administration "blunders" in combatting communism. "World domination by communism is still the goal of the Kremlin," the report said.[203] Pressure also increased around domestic communism. The Korean War gave renewed energy to charges of communists in government. In August, the Democratically controlled Congress folded to the powerful liberal discourse when it abandoned the White House and passed the McCarran Internal Security Act, which included severe restrictions on civil liberties meant to root out communists across the country.[204] As one Democrat observed, the "fever of fear was on my colleagues."[205]

Officials inside government responded to this rising liberal narrative discourse as well. The publicity around the white paper alarmed Paul Nitze, director of Policy Planning. He encouraged the administration to take steps to ensure national solidarity, which he said was vital to successfully implementing foreign policy.[206] The administration did so by bending policy on Korea to accommodate the liberal discourse. On July 10, for instance, the Indian government proposed a peace agreement to U.S. officials. George Kennan, a counselor at the State Department, supported it and was immediately "shouted down" by Dulles. It would "look to our public as if we had been tricked into giving up something for nothing," Dulles argued, drawing attention to the political disaster (i.e., costs for inaction) that the administration would face for crossing the liberal narrative.[207] Later in the year, Truman and Acheson took a similar line toward a British peace plan. "Americans would not accept surrender in the Far East," said Acheson in response to the plan, "Americans demand that we must be vigorous everywhere."[208] Both peace offers were summarily rejected. For Kennan, these outcomes were all about the liberal discourse. Given the "McCarthyist hysteria" and "China Lobby," he noted that negotiations were impossible "without blowing the domestic situation sky-high."[209]

The September decision by the administration to send U.S. forces across the 38th parallel in order to overturn the Kim regime followed the same script.

Scholars are virtually unanimous in concluding that the robust liberal discourse of the summer and fall of 1950 pushed the Truman administration into this move, largely against the administration's better judgment. It would have been a "political catastrophe" not to cross the 38th parallel, notes one scholar.[210] Especially with the November elections on the horizon, "the prudent but not anti-communist enough decision" was to halt at the 38th parallel, said Small.[211] "Given the storm of protest" at home, observes Caridi, "it would have been exceedingly difficult to ignore the calls for movement north of the line."[212] Costs for inaction were simply too high not to take decisive action.

Internal deliberations support this assessment. Even before Inchon, State Department officials talked, for instance, about the public pressure to go north. In July, promoters like Rusk and Dulles hammered the theme of crossing the 38th parallel in hopes of trumping doves, like the Policy Planning Staff at the State Department. With public sentiment on their side, the pressure worked. Despite objections again from Kennan, a series of memos shows a progressive turn by the Policy Planning Staff on the need to go north due to liberal-discourse pressure.[213] "Present public and Congressional opinion in the United States would be dissatisfied with any conclusion falling short of what it would consider a 'final' settlement," noted a Policy Planning memo on August 1, "A sentiment favoring a continuation of military action north of the 38th parallel already is rising."[214]

This swelling liberal discourse also drove policy in late September and early October. Fearful of war with China or the Soviet Union, Truman, Acheson and the JCS initially had no interest in regime promotion in North Korea. Truman talked about this from the very start of the war. In July, he gave explicit orders to the military not to send ground forces across the 38th parallel. "I wanted it clearly understood that our operations in Korea were designed to restore peace there and to restore the border [i.e., the 38th parallel]," Truman later noted.[215] In early September, the administration line remained unchanged. Acheson warned about the dangers of how "fooling around in North Korea" might incite a Soviet/Chinese military response.[216] The preferences of top policy elites still centered on geopolitics, not ideology.

But, following Inchon, the administration cast all such caution to the wind and sent troops across the 38th parallel. Louis Halle, a member of the Policy Planning Staff, explained that the liberal discourse lay behind this decision. "This was a time when the American people were becoming convinced that the foreign policy of the United States had fallen into the hands of communist conspirators," observed Halle, "For the government now to order MacArthur to desist from giving the beaten Communists the coup de grace would have appeared to conform to this view."[217]

Several examples from internal policy discussions support Halle's assessment. First, officials found it impossible to again cross MacArthur. To the wider public, the already popular leader was viewed almost like a superstar in the wake of Inchon.[218] "There is no stopping MacArthur now," Acheson said, upon receiving the news of Inchon. When one of Acheson's aids complained to him that MacArthur's orders to cross the 38th parallel were too vague, Acheson snapped back at him in frustration, "Are you willing to take on the entire Joint Chiefs of Staff?" The aid interpreted Acheson's anger as a reflection of just how much the Secretary of State was a prisoner of events.[219] One of Truman's closest advisors, Averill Harriman, said in this vein, "It would have taken a superhuman effort to say no" since a "political tempest" at home would have followed any attempt to deny MacArthur.[220]

Another example of narrative-driven costs for inaction at work on decision makers came in late August, when Kennan sent Acheson a memo arguing against going north. Among other points, Kennan claimed that it was neither strategically necessary nor feasible given existing resources to establish an anticommunist regime in North Korea. Acheson read the memo, then brushed it aside. He called Kennan's analysis a view of "national interest in the abstract," devoid of any appreciation of domestic context. Bowing to the discourse of the day, Acheson then conceded, "In view of public opinion and political pressures [i.e., the liberal discourse] in the concrete, ideas such as these could only be kept in mind as warnings not to be drawn into quicksand."[221] Acheson, of course, knew the narrative-driven domestic context here all too well. He told the British prime minister Clement Atlee that he had "probably been more bloodied than anyone else" by Asian policy.[222] It is little wonder, then, that costs for inaction factored into the Truman-Acheson decisions on Korea. "A greater political risk would be incurred by showing hesitation and timidity," Acheson said privately on October 4, "The only proper course to take was a firm and courageous one."[223] Especially with elections approaching, those political risks for Truman lay in being out of step with the nation's elevated concern about following the moral of the liberal narrative to stand firm against communism. "In the midst of a heated congressional election campaign," writes Stueck, "the momentum for sending American troops across the thirty-eighth parallel was nearly irresistible."[224] Truman "had little choice," according to Treasury Secretary, John Snyder. In the end, it seems no coincidence, then, that the president informed advisors of his final decision to cross the 38th parallel at a cabinet meeting devoted almost exclusively to the upcoming elections.[225]

Overall, the costs of inaction were too high for the administration to do nothing in North Korea. They were also too high for the administration to do too little. In order to avoid, a return of the politically damaging "soft-on-communism" debate, robust action had to be taken. On this score, the administration never considered anything other than a full-scale combat invasion of North Korea.[226] This is expected when the liberal narrative and promoter appeals are strong. The nation wanted MacArthur's army to take the fight against communism across the 38th parallel. Truman reluctantly complied.

Alternative Explanations

This section explores the strengths and weaknesses of several other alternative explanations of U.S. forceful regime promotion in China and Korea. Generally, each fails to offer as comprehensive an account as the master narrative argument.

Geopolitics

Realists anticipate robust forceful regime promotion when a great power possesses large differentials of power either globally or in a certain region of concern. In the absence of these power differentials, states refrain from or use limited force.

There is some good evidence for this argument, especially in the China case. The United States did not hold a preponderance of power either globally or in Asia in 1950. In light of the potential for a two-front war once the Korean War started, limited intervention in China matches realist expectations to some degree. So too does a decision by Truman not to expand the Korean War to China after the PRC came into the conflict on the side of North Korea in late 1950. Truman feared this would lead to war, perhaps even nuclear war, with the Soviet Union. He turned down the request.[227] At one level, this decision clearly supports the realist argument.

The problem for realism comes with explaining why the United States acted *at all* in China and, especially, Korea. For one, decision makers repeatedly claimed China carried no strategic value to the United States, even after the start of the Korean War.[228] Added to this, Marshall and other advisors feared in 1947 and 1948 that aid to Chiang would lead to wider military commitments. Acheson and the JCS said the same when drawing Taiwan outside the U.S. defense perimeter. As seen above, when deciding to send the 7th Fleet, both Truman and Acheson expressed concern about getting involved directly in the Chinese civil war.[229] Knowing the strategic dangers of escalation, inaction on China seems to make the most sense from a realist perspective. Adding to the puzzle for realism, the United States took its boldest steps to insert itself into the Chinese civil war— sending the 7th Fleet—*after* the Soviets both tested their first nuclear weapon (September 1949) and established a formal alliance with the PRC (February

1950). The limited military action of sending the 7th Fleet would have made far more sense from a realist perspective prior to these major geostrategic shifts, not after them when the Soviets were even stronger. Overall, U.S. policy toward China presents some problems for realism in this period.[230]

Korea is even more problematic. First, U.S. officials saw no strategic value in Korea, which like Taiwan was drawn outside the U.S. defense perimeter in Asia in January 1950. Those strategic assessments did not change by June when the North Korean invasion began.[231] Differentials of power is also problematic here. Truman and Acheson worried about Soviet/Chinese entrance into the war.[232] In fact, the United States saw many indicators that China would enter the war if U.S. forces crossed the 38th parallel. In September alone, these included a direct warning from Chinese Premier Zhou Enlai, a second warning from China via the Indian government, reports of Chinese forces being captured by South Korean troops in August, and intelligence showing that Chinese citizens along the border with North Korea were preparing for war.[233] Some note how these warnings were downplayed in the policy process.[234] To focus too much on this, though, misses the bigger point: the credibility of Chinese warnings aside, the very hint of possible Chinese retaliation should have forestalled U.S. action of any type in North Korea, according to realist logic. U.S. action to the contrary forces us to look beyond geopolitics to explain robust forceful regime promotion in Korea.

Elite Polarization

A stand-alone elite polarization argument expects robust forceful regime promotion when leadership elites are polarized. Since most policy elites were polarized in the late 1940s and 1950s, the fact that the United States adopted at least some degree of regime promotion in China and Korea appears, at first glance, to be good evidence for this argument.[235]

A closer look, though, demonstrates weaknesses along the lines of those discussed in chapter 1. Above all else, cross-case variation in the use of force is puzzling here. With elites polarized in 1950, one wonders specifically why there was no full-scale intervention in *both* China and Korea (and, furthermore, why robust action in Korea, but not China). An elite-based argument is not without an answer here, of course. As John Owen and others argue, strategic pragmatism sometimes trumps elite polarization, leading to restraint even when polarization is high.[236] This helps the argument some, since leaders like Truman and Acheson were thinking this way about China and, in the end, used no direct force there. The problem with this explanation is, however, the same as that noted above for realists. Truman and Acheson preferred no military action for strategic reasons not just in China but Korea as well. They got what they wanted (in part) in only one case.[237] Why? In short, we are left with the original question: what allowed leaders to follow at least some of their strategic preferences in one instance but not the other?

A stand-alone elite-based account cannot answer this question. The more holistic master narrative argument can, however. The Truman administration did not want (again, for strategic reasons) to create a crusade-like public mentality to defend liberal order abroad. It helped do so, regardless, because of budding liberal narrative pressures. Likewise, the administration wanted no action in China or Korea. Yet it acted anyway (and to varying degrees) because of different pressures, again, from promoter discourse built around the robust liberal narrative. Those narrative-based discourses created political space for Truman to follow more of his preferences in China, while largely precluding the same in Korea. In this sense, leadership dispositions mattered—a two-front war might have materialized if Truman had been more ideological in his thinking. But the impact of that disposition on policy was also highly conditioned by master narratives. Stated simply, elites mattered in ways and at moments determined by the politics of master narratives.

Prestige

Finally, prestige offers an important counterargument. Perhaps leaders wanted to protect the nation's reputation for resolve. This argument explains some things but faces important shortcomings as well.

The late 1940s was a period of rising anticolonialism in Asia. U.S. leaders knew that interfering in the Chinese civil war, in particular, would be interpreted as great power imperialism and have a negative impact on the U.S. reputation in the region. In fact, avoiding this image stood behind much of the Truman administration's efforts, as discussed above, to distance the United States from the Nationalist Chinese. European allies also saw little value to U.S. action in China—they feared it would draw resources away from the Cold War in Europe.[238] U.S. support for Chiang and eventual bolstering of his regime with the 7th Fleet makes little sense then. U.S. officials knew that both of these moves would fuel anti-Americanism in Asia to the benefit of communists. Yet it acted anyway and, as expected, faced harsh criticism abroad for doing so.[239]

As to Korea, prestige undoubtedly motivated U.S. action in June 1950. U.S. leaders believed that inaction would hurt the nation's reputation with allies in Asia and Europe. At the Blair House meetings, policymakers frequently referenced the Munich analogy, arguing that a stand in Korea would prevent further

Soviet aggression elsewhere in Asia and, even more important, reassure European and Asian allies of U.S. resolve.[240] Prestige, thus, helps explain the June decision. The argument falters, though, when it comes to the September decision to cross the 38th parallel. Policy elites barely mentioned prestige here, largely because they knew that crossing the 38th parallel could hurt the image of the United States in both Asia and Europe. Toward this end, European allies saw no value in an invasion of North Korea, with many telling Truman it was an "unwise move."[241] Since going north would also mean killing more Asians, it is hard to see how taking down the North Korean regime could aid U.S. regional prestige. Overall, the Truman Administration's *domestic*, not international, credibility, appears more important to the 38th parallel decision. "The war was a symbol for the American people and for no one else," observes Purifoy, "After all, it was only in America . . . that the administration's anti-communist faith was in doubt."[242] Explanations like this lead us back, of course, to master narratives, the liberal narrative in particular.

The United States faced the challenge of dealing with regime crises in Korea and China during the early Cold War. It responded to both very differently—full-scale military action for regime promotion in Korea and non-to-limited military action in China. The master narrative argument offers an especially strong explanation of these different outcomes. The trauma of Soviet geostrategic gains just after World War II galvanized a robust national interest in protecting liberal order abroad. Promoters used this robust liberal narrative to build case-specific arguments for regime promotion in China and Korea. Largely against its will, the Truman administration folded to this pressure. The varying levels of force used in Korea relative to China are explained by the nature of the liberal discourse around each case. For various reasons related to domestic coalitions and the contours of the broader liberal narrative, promoters constructed a weaker liberal discourse that urged only limited action in China. In Korea, promoters constructed a strong liberal discourse that demanded full-scale military action. Worried about the power of public sentiment, the administration complied with the discourses on both counts.

As detailed in chapter 1, the liberal narrative is not the only master narrative that affects patterns of forceful regime change. The restraint narrative does as well. The above discussion of China and Korea said nothing about this narrative, though. This is for good reason: the restraint narrative was weak in this period. U.S. citizens emerged from World War II wanting, as noted earlier, to bring troops home from Europe and the Pacific. But this general mood was not one of retreat into the restraint-driven isolationism of the interwar years. As many historians note, collective taboos about becoming enmeshed in European affairs, in particular, died with World War II and were replaced by a broadly accepted internationalist posture that reflected a dearth of restraint narrative thinking among the U.S. public in the late 1940s.[243]

With the exception of a few years in the wake of the Korean War (see chapter 2), this weak restraint narrative remained the norm until the late 1960s. Coupled with a robust liberal narrative across this period, it is little surprise that the United States pursued a flurry of forceful regime promotions in this period. None was more robust and controversial than the Vietnam War, to which we turn next.

REGIME CHANGE IN CUBA AND VIETNAM

In the 1960s, two prominent U.S. attempts at regime promotion occurred in Cuba and Vietnam. In Cuba, President John F. Kennedy approved invasion by U.S.-trained Cuban exiles in an attempt to overthrow the regime of Fidel Castro. This operation failed, its fate sealed with Kennedy's decision not to send in the U.S. military to support the exiles or overthrow Castro directly. In Vietnam, President Lyndon B. Johnson committed to maintain a decade-old U.S. policy to preserve an independent regime in South Vietnam. He escalated U.S. military action with the 1965 deployment of U.S. combat forces, which eventually grew to nearly 550,000 U.S. soldiers.[1]

Master narratives played a critical role in explaining limited action in Cuba versus a full-scale invasion in Vietnam. In both cases, Kennedy and Johnson preferred no military action. Promoter arguments, though, pushed them to act against their wishes. In the case of Cuba, promoters built a weaker liberal discourse that called only for limited military action (similar to China in chapter 3). Kennedy complied, and went no farther. On Vietnam, promoters used the liberal narrative to argue for progressively greater military action. As they did, Johnson also reluctantly complied. This chapter tells these stories, while also considering the strengths and weaknesses of competing arguments.

The Master Narrative Landscape

The liberal narrative was strong and restraint narrative weak in the United States during the first half of the 1960s. On the restraint side, the residue of the Korean War dissipated by 1960. Though not the internal trauma that the Vietnam War would eventually turn out to be (see chapter 5), the 1951 military stalemate in Korea created enough disillusionment and, with that, space for moderator storytelling to generate some aversion across the U.S. public to the use of conventional warfare to combat communism. The lesson of this moderator story—"No more Koreas"—was a common mantra in the early 1950s. A 1954 survey found, for example, that 72 percent opposed stationing U.S. ground troops in Asia.[2] President Dwight Eisenhower built his foreign policy around this restraint narrative. Ike's New Look de-emphasized conventional force and focused instead on nuclear weapons to deter communist geopolitical gains abroad.[3] "The president's goal was to win victories in Asia without getting bogged down in 'another Korea,'" observe Campbell Craig and Frederik Logevall, "to prevent left-wing and communist expansion in that part of the world, but to do so on the cheap."[4]

This Korea syndrome did not last long, however. This was due in large measure to major new events, especially *Sputnik*, which became traumatic in ways that, among other things, made the restraint narrative appear anachronistic.[5] Referred to as a "disaster comparable to Pearl Harbor" by one observer, the 1957 Soviet orbiting of the *Sputnik* satellite caused "ripples of panic" across the United States, "a wave of near-hysteria," according to President Eisenhower.[6] A deep existential fear of falling behind the Soviets set-in across the country. "The great question," commented *Time* of the post-Sputnik atmosphere, "is whether the U.S. has the plan and purpose to hold its lead against the threats of the Soviet Union."[7] The entire New Look and restraint mindset behind it came into question. A November 1957 poll found only 26 percent satisfaction with current U.S. defense policies.[8] Newspapers charged the administration with being "indecisive, uncertain, and hesitant."[9] Many in Congress agreed. Senator Henry "Scoop" Jackson (D-WA) called for a "national week of shame and danger."[10]

This panicked context gave promoters a favorable space to narrate. Using *Sputnik* to tell a story of lost ground to the Soviets, promoters attacked the New Look policy and directly challenged the Korea syndrome. They claimed Ike's policies granted too little attention to the conventional forces necessary to combat communism in the Third World.[11] In classic trauma-theory form, existential danger, blame and repair stood, therefore, at the center of how promoters narrated about *Sputnik*. Their story gained added validation with a wave of late 1950s decolonization wars. U.S. newspapers wrote daily, for instance, about countries (mostly Cuba and Congo, but also Algeria, Kenya, Uganda, North/South Rhodesia, and Sierra Leon) where communists were making new inroads with Soviet and Chinese help.[12] In this anxious, "get-going" environment of post-Sputnik America, this promoter story of falling behind settled in collectively. In sharp contrast to earlier polls, 68 percent agreed in 1960 with the statement that "the United States should keep soldiers overseas where they can help countries that are against Communism."[13] Overall, polls like this and the public discussion at the time signaled an important turn: the Korea syndrome looked antiquated and ill-suited for the "new" Cold War. The restraint narrative waned, then, in this period.

The liberal narrative took a different turn. The events that weakened the Korea syndrome coupled with other developments abroad to create external trauma for the U.S. public, which reinforced an already strong liberal narrative to fight communism. By far, the two most important additional events here were the May 1960 Soviet downing of a U.S. U-2 spy plane and the growing alliance between Castro's Cuba and the Soviet Union. The U-2 incident led to the cancellation of a May summit in Paris between Eisenhower and Soviet premier Nikita Khrushchev.[14] That same month, Castro's leftist regime in Cuba established diplomatic ties with the Soviet Union, followed a few weeks later with a visit by Khrushchev to Cuba. Soon after, Castro nationalized U.S. oil refineries with no compensation to U.S. companies, leading to a flurry of Cold War jabs that included Ike's termination of the Cuban sugar quota and threats from Khrushchev to use Soviet rockets to protect Cuba.[15]

Similar to the late 1940s, this series of quick-hitting events shook the U.S. public, creating a high degree of ontological insecurity. Editorials and commentators from across the country described both events in strident terms: "alarming"; an "intolerable danger"; and a "shock to . . . pride and confidence." Others commented that the dramatic events and harsh words in Paris "have aroused understandable tension and anxiety among the people" and "confronted the world with a dark night of crisis."[16] Congress responded similarly, members spoke daily about these events into the summer and fall. Many used terms like "shocked," "heavy clouds," and "a tragic development" to describe the U-2 incident and cancellation of the summit.[17] Cuba generated similar responses. "Castro's repeated irrational rantings against the United States and his tolerance of Communists makes me shudder," said Congressman Charles Porter (D-OR), in mid-June.[18] The geographic proximity of Cuba accentuated the trauma of Castro's rise. As one historian observes, Castro's leftist drift made it "downright existential" for U.S. citizens to know where Castro was headed.[19] Between the U-2 incident and Cuba, the U.S. public worried about danger ahead. "Americans began to feel that the Russians had thrown them on the defensive around the globe," observes the historian Robert Divine, "Everywhere they looked, the Soviets were pushing ahead to turn unstable situations to their advantage."[20]

These events created a political opportunity for promoters, who began to immediately tell the familiar Cold War story. The main actors here came not from the White House. For his part, Eisenhower took a subdued tone, trying to calm the public. The promoter charge came, instead, from Capitol Hill and opinion leaders outside of government.

The story with its focus on the existential danger posed by Soviet actions, blame, and lesson/moral was both identical from one speaker to the next and showed up everywhere, saturating foreign policy debates in late 1960. First, there was a narrating of specific events as both linked together and posing an existential challenge to the United States. "The deliberate scuttling of the recent summit conference by the Soviet Premier clearly demonstrated that the Sino-Soviet bloc is not ready to abandon its conquest of the free world," said Senator Jackson, "This threat to our security is made clearer with . . . Cuba, where the Communists are taking advantage of the troubled situation to make inroads into the Western Hemisphere."[21] This kind of existential interpretation of events came repeatedly, like a beating drum, from promoters in Congress: "the present Cuban Government is being used to further the international communistic conspiracy"; "world communism has launched a massive offensive to . . . weaken the United States"; and "here again, the . . . very future of mankind is at the mercy of a psychopathic dictator."[22]

Second, this kind of interpretation of events led naturally to blame by promoters. Khrushchev and communism in general were, of course, one source of blame. So, too, was the Eisenhower Administration. Members of Congress (especially Democrats) again went after the President repeatedly for an overly reserved foreign policy, even calling Ike soft on communism. "Our Government has suffered a serious setback at a critical moment," charged Congressman Chester Bowles (D-CT), who then went on to claim Eisenhower "embarrassed" the United States.[23] Critics like this went after Eisenhower for all sorts of things. Many criticized him for not taking a tougher stand with Khrushchev and that his Third World policy lacked creativity. Others claimed he was too budget conscious and spent too much time on the golf course. Some called for congressional investigations.[24] For example, Senator Ernest Gruening (D-OR) charged in June 1960 that Eisenhower's foreign policy is "leading us downhill." Drawing direct parallels to the China debate a decade earlier (see chapter 3), he further stated: "I should like to ask Republicans, Who has lost Cuba, right at our very door?"[25]

And, of course, like any good story, there was a moral. Almost without fail, each promoter ended his/her existential narration with a call for renewed vigor in defending freedom abroad. "The United States must be ever vigilant," said Congressman Albert Bosch, "This is indeed a dangerous period in the history of our country and the world . . . No appeasement."[26] Senate majority leader and presidential candidate, Lyndon Johnson (D-TX), said much the same. In a speech on June 17, he told the familiar story of the ideological challenges from Paris to Havana ("The massive Communist attack against our way of life is being felt on many fronts"), then ended with a call to action: "Without strength we cannot survive, because the Communists will always resort to brute force."[27] Others drew near identical lessons, calling for things like "imagination and foresight" and a "renewed effort to integrate the free world."[28]

The promoter story resonated with and took root across the nation. The liberal narrative strengthened, then, in this period. "The cold air mass from the Soviets created an entirely new atmosphere in U.S. political life," observed *Time*.[29] One survey found that 50 percent of the U.S. public expected war with the Soviets "sooner or later." Poll numbers like these remained steady through the mid-1960s.[30] Above all else, the public adopted the moral at the center of the promoter story. "The American people are in a 'get tough' mood," observed one commentator.[31] Nearly all major newspapers reflected this mood. Typical comments sounded like this: "The United States will not permit Cuba or any other country in the Western Hemisphere to be made a cat's paw of international communism"; "we can deny to the Communists any hope of world conquest by military force"; and "we cannot let Cuba become an American funnel for Communist infiltration, propaganda, and sabotage."[32] For the U.S. polity, "the Cold War had never been colder."[33]

One especially prominent way that the robust liberal narrative showed itself was in the rhetoric of the 1960 presidential campaign. "The public is going to expect a hard, tough line," predicted Senator Jackson of the fall campaign.[34] And, that is what the public got. Vice President Richard Nixon and Senator John Kennedy punched and counterpunched repeatedly in hopes of carrying the public mantle of freedom and democracy's protector against communism. To combat the post-McCarthy-era image of Democrats as "soft on communism," Kennedy hit liberal narrative themes early in the campaign.[35] He published, *Strategy for Peace*, a collection of his Senate speeches laced with anticommunist rhetoric.[36] "Mr. Nixon is experienced, experienced in the politics of retreat, defeat and weakness," Kennedy asserted in a late August speech, "The real issue is who can stand up and summon all the resource of this land to the defense of freedom."[37]

Nixon counterpunched. After Kennedy refused in an October 7 debate to commit to defend the islands of Quemoy and Matsu against communist China, Nixon pounced. "These two islands are in the area of freedom," Nixon snapped. He accused Kennedy, like Truman, of "surrendering the islands to Communist China," then committed to protect Quemoy and Matsu if elected president.[38] It turned into a "serious setback" for Kennedy.[39] Many charged him weak on communism.[40]

Kennedy scrambled to recover lost liberal narrative ground. Cuba came to the fore.[41] On October 19, Eisenhower embargoed all goods from Cuba. Despite seeing no better alternative, JFK bowed to "political necessity."[42] "What the hell, they [Republicans] never told us how they would have saved China," Kennedy said privately in reference to the McCarthy era.[43] On October 20, Kennedy publicly labeled the embargo "too little too late," then pledged support to Cuban rebels in their fight to unseat Castro, adding "these fighters for freedom have had virtually no support from our government."[44] Kennedy aids admitted the term "fighters for freedom" was one they thought "Americans would like to hear."[45]

This liberal narrative counterpunch proved fatal for Nixon. He could not publicly reveal that Eisenhower was planning a covert operation to unseat Castro. The vice president criticized, then, JFK's remarks as "reckless"—a move that "was wrong politically," landing Nixon out of step with the robust liberal narrative. Consequently, Kennedy won the mantle of more vigorous defender of liberal order abroad, which helped propel him, commentators note, to victory in the November election.[46]

Overall, the national discussion here points to a clear bottom line. The liberal narrative was robust in the early 1960s, "virtually the third rail of American politics," according to one scholar.[47] Politicians scrambled to keep up with this almost universally accepted story centered around the defense of freedom and stopping communism abroad. Forceful regime promotion in Cuba and Vietnam demonstrate this all too well.

The Bay of Pigs Invasion, 1961

Ten days after being elected president, John Kennedy received his first briefing on a covert operation to topple the Castro regime. The effort began with Eisenhower, who approved a November 1960 Central Intelligence Agency (CIA) request to plan Castro's ouster.[48] The plan involved landing U.S.-trained Cuban exile soldiers to spark a general rebellion leading to Castro's removal.[49]

In sharp contrast to his campaign statements, Kennedy showed no enthusiasm for the operation. Never a "knee-jerk anti-communist," JFK wanted a new direction in U.S.-Latin American relations and toppling Castro would not help that.[50] In fact, two days before the CIA briefing, the president-elect asked advisors for estimates of the U.S. embargo's effectiveness and prospects for normalization of relations with Cuba as first steps toward improved Latin America relations.[51] "Immediately after the election, his concern was with an affirmative program for Latin America rather than with Cuba," observed Arthur Schlesinger, a close advisor to Kennedy.[52] The center-piece was the Alliance for Progress—a large-scale development program to improve the U.S. image and help dampen communism's appeal in the region. Kennedy campaigned on the Alliance for Progress and presented the program to Congress in March 1960.[53] He knew that a U.S.-backed Cuba invasion would undermine the program's effectiveness— a point his advisors brought up repeatedly in the following months. Kennedy thought the same. When Schlesinger once asked him what he thought of the CIA plan, Kennedy responded, "I think of it as little as possible."[54] As Schlesinger later observed, "It is inconceivable to me that Kennedy would have initiated such a project" on his own accord.[55]

Why, then, did he go forward with the invasion? Furthermore, why was the operation limited to covert methods? The liberal discourse that developed around Cuba helps answer both questions. Promoters built pressure, on the one hand, around the robust liberal narrative that undoubtedly pushed JFK to act against Castro (i.e., audience costs for inaction). But, in doing so, these promoters only argued for the use of limited military means, which gave the president space, in the end, to hold action in Cuba to covert operations alone and avoid a full-scale combat invasion (i.e., a weakened liberal discourse).

Start with how the liberal discourse pushed Kennedy to act in Cuba. By the time Kennedy took office, the Cuban amphibious/airborne force of approximately 750 men had been training at a CIA-constructed base in Guatemala for more than two months.[56] Leading up to the invasion, promoters inside the administration, like the CIA director Allen Dulles and the CIA deputy director for plans Richard Bissell, drew Kennedy's attention to liberal narrative political costs by focusing on the "dispersal" or "disposal" problem. Notably, if Kennedy chose to cancel the operation, Dulles and Bissell warned, 750 rabidly anticommunist Cuban soldiers would be freed up to return to (or "disperse" across) the United States and tell the story about how Kennedy failed to help bring freedom back to Cuba. At a time of heightened public concerns about communism (i.e., the moral of the liberal narrative), the political fallout for Kennedy would be devastating. As the historian Jim Rasenberger observes, this problem was "one that no U.S. politician could ignore, certainly not one who had gained a narrow victory over his opponent by trumpeting a hardline policy against Castro."[57]

Promoters raised the dispersal argument repeatedly in memos and at nearly every meeting on Cuba down to the invasion on April 17. Dulles hit on it, for instance, at the first post-inauguration meeting on Cuba (January 22). "[Dulles] then went on to mention the difficult problem of keeping them [the Cuban exile army] in Guatemala," records a memo of the meeting, "At best, we had six weeks to two months before something had to be done about them."[58] Six days later Dulles raised dispersal again with Kennedy, Secretary of State Dean Rusk and Secretary of Defense Robert McNamara. After detailing the current plan, Dulles pressed for a quick decision, citing the dispersal problem.

"A particularly urgent question is the use to be made of a group of such Cubans now in training in Guatemala, who cannot remain indefinitely where they are," Dulles argued.[59] Dispersal was at the center of a February 8 meeting too. When Bissell again called for prompt action, Rusk interjected. He raised concerns about the "grave effects" on the U.S. image in Latin America.[60] In doing so, he took on the dispersal problem directly, which was now settling in as a leading argument for taking action. "U.S. policy should not be driven to drastic and irrevocable choice by the urgencies, however real, of a single battalion of men" in Guatemala, Rusk argued.[61]

Opposition from Rusk and other moderators did not deter the CIA, however. In fact, it only made Dulles and Bissell more forceful in pressing the argument. A week after Rusk's criticism, Bissell gave the president an extensive memo. He again raised the dispersal problem. The operation needed to happen soon, Bissell argued, otherwise the exile army would need to be let go. "The resettlement of the military force will unavoidably cause practical problems," Bissell continued, "Its members will be angry, disillusioned and aggressive with the inevitable result that they will provide honey for the press bees and the U.S. will have to face the resulting indignities and embarrassments."[62] At two other critical meetings in March, Dulles and Bissell hammered this same line. The administration could not stand the political embarrassment of cancelling the operation, they claimed.[63] It is "well understood," said a CIA memo in March, that "demobilization of the paramilitary force and return of its members to the United States . . . involves certain risks."[64] In a memo trying to persuade the president against the operation, Schlesinger admitted the weight of the dispersal problem as well. "Abandonment would conceivably suggest a failure of U.S. nerve," he wrote to Kennedy on April 5, "It would confront us with the problem of demobilizing and resettling these men [and] the fact that the expedition was conceived, prepared and then called off at the last moment would increase Castro's prestige and power. These are powerful points."[65]

The ongoing 1961 public conversation around the liberal narrative augmented the CIA's argument and raised audience costs for inaction for Kennedy. JFK faced "unrelenting and pervasive pressure to act against Castro," in early 1961, observes one historian. Hardly a press conference passed without Kennedy facing a question about Cuba. He heard it from promoters on Capitol Hill too. "Republicans and Democrats alike peppered the White House with demands for action against Castroism," notes the historian Thomas Paterson.[66] On February 24, Senator Kenneth Keating (R-NY) presented a plan, for instance, to unite the anti-Castro forces in the hemisphere, form a Cuban government-in-exile, and rally support in the Organization of American States (OAS) to help bring the exile government to power in Cuba. Keating justified action on the robust liberal narrative. "We see a nation . . . turned into a Communist base," he argued, "How long must the free world tolerate this menace?"[67] Ideas like these found wide, bipartisan support because they tapped into deep sympathy for the Cuban exiles in their bid to end communism in Cuba. "All of us are concerned, and properly so, about the presence of a Communist-dominated government in Cuba," said Senator Styles Bridges (R-NH), in endorsing Keating's plan.[68] We need to "get rid of" the government in Cuba, said Senator George Smathers (D-FL), "It is a matter our survival."[69] "We must fight," argued Congressman Daniel Flood (D-PA), in a statement endorsing U.S. aid to Cuban rebels.[70]

National sympathy along these same lines grew stronger after leaked plans of the invasion showed up (much to the chagrin of Kennedy) in the *New York Times* on April 7.[71] "Americans whose credo is liberty have nothing to be ashamed of . . . in their support for Cubans who are seeking to liberate their country from tyranny," observed the *Washington Post* in April.[72] Many other leading papers said much the same: "American public sympathy for the anti-Batista, anti-Castro forces is clear"; "Secretary Rusk undoubtedly spoke the national mind when he expressed official sympathy for the anti-Castro forces . . . as an army of liberation"; "Castro has invited . . . revolt by opening the doors wide to communism."[73] In late 1960, 81 percent rated Castro "unfavorable" and 50 percent expected his ouster within the year.[74] Overall, promoters both inside and outside the Kennedy administration built a clear liberal discourse for action in Cuba.

Facing audience costs for inaction, Kennedy had little choice but to approve the Bay of Pigs operation. "He [Kennedy] . . . decided that the political costs of not acting would be higher and that the potential gains of success would be substantial," observes Lawrence Freedman.[75] Fear of domestic backlash around the dispersal problem fueled these calculations. When Kennedy told Schlesinger on April 8 about his final decision to go forward, JFK justified it this way: "If we have to get rid of those 800 men, it is much better to dump them in Cuba than in the United States, especially if that is where they want to go."[76] Kennedy said much the same in mid-May to General Maxwell Taylor. "It is much better . . . to put the guerrillas on the beach in Cuba than bring them back to the United States and have them state that the United States would not support their activities," Kennedy told Taylor, "The end result might have been much worse had we done this than it actually was."[77] This led Taylor to conclude that the disposal problem "forced his [Kennedy's] hand."[78] For Kennedy, the domestic political costs of appearing soft on communism were just too great to ignore.

Kennedy's closest advisors confirmed this to be the case. "If we didn't do it, the Republicans would have said: 'We were all set to beat Castro, and this chicken, this antsy-pantsy bunch of liberals,'" said the national security advisor

McGeorge "Mac" Bundy, "There would have been a political risk in not going through with the operation."[79] Kennedy's political rhetoric was compounded by his own campaign rhetoric and the fact that Eisenhower, a war hero whom Kennedy charged with being weak on communism, hatched the plan. The president would have looked like "an appeaser of Castro, Eisenhower made a decision to overthrow Castro and you dropped it," observed Kennedy's chief political advisor Kenny O'Donnell.[80] Schlesinger noted much the same. "The fear of sounding soft on communism was a very strong one," he said, about Kennedy's decision, "A liberal Democrat like Kennedy had to be constantly concerned with this issue."[81]

Out of sensitivity to the invasion's regional impact, JFK toned down the operation to conceal the U.S. hand. The result was a nighttime (rather than the previously planned daytime) landing at the Bay of Pigs, a more remote part of the island than originally planned by the CIA.[82] Beyond that, Kennedy could do no more.[83] Cancelling was not an option because the president, as Howard Jones concludes, was overwhelmed by "the felt need to do something" in order prevent "embittered Cubans" from "publicly accusing the administration of betraying their trust and cowing before communism."[84] Pressed forward, then, by the "momentum of Cold War politics" and, with that, the powerful liberal narrative, the Kennedy administration launched the hapless Bay of Pigs invasion to overthrow Cuba's Fidel Castro on April 17, 1961.

This raises a question, though. If Kennedy felt so much pressure from the liberal narrative, why not use the full weight of the U.S. military to topple Castro? Part of the answer lies with Kennedy. Namely, he did not want a full invasion, for reasons related again to the U.S. image in Latin America. "I'm not going to risk an American Hungary," he told aides, referring to the international backlash that the Soviet Union faced after the 1956 invasion of its wayward satellite in Eastern Europe.[85] But understanding Kennedy's personal preferences only get us so far here. After all, Kennedy did not want to use force of *any kind* in Cuba due to these same concerns, yet he ended up approving the Bay of Pigs invasion anyway. Something else, then, must have allowed, or opened space for, Kennedy to limit military action on Cuba.

On this point, master narratives (especially the nature of the liberal discourse around Cuba) reenter the picture.[86] Above all else, none of the most strident promoters argued for a full-scale invasion of Cuba. Despite constant public rants about Cuba, Senator Keating never demanded, for instance, direct U.S. military action. In detailing his plan to unseat Castro, he said, explicitly, "I am not proposing unilateral U.S. action . . . [and] I am not proposing that the OAS send a military force into Cuba."[87] Others took the same position. On March 2, Senator Dodd discussed the "rapid Communization of Castro's Cuba" and railed against Kennedy's "timorous policy," but then proceeded to propose not direct use of force against Cuba, but a full trade embargo and naval blockade instead.[88] Five days later, Congressman Seymour Halperin (R-NY) warned, likewise, of the "deadly peril to the free world" of a communist Cuba, then proceeded to call only for a ban on Cuban imports with no mention of force.[89] On April 14, another strong opponent of Castro, Senator Smathers, followed suit. After citing at length the existential danger of a communist Cuba, he backed away from direct force and advocated a multilateral solution. "I can think of no better time for all free peoples of this hemisphere to begin to organize their efforts to get rid of communism," he said. Senators Keating and Hubert Humphrey both spoke in support of Smathers's comments.[90]

This kind of restraint on force dominated behind the scenes too. None of Kennedy's hardline advisors advocated sending Marines to Cuba and none suggested a follow-on U.S. invasion if the initial operation failed.[91] Overall, then, while the liberal narrative, itself, was robust in this period, the promoter-generated discourse around that narrative was weaker when it came to Cuba. This made, in turn, audience costs for inaction lower than they otherwise could have been.

Why was this the case? The answer lies with political salience. Despite its fear of communism, the U.S. public remained hesitant about direct force in Latin America in the wake of the 1958 attack on Vice President Nixon's entourage in Venezuela during a goodwill tour. The event sensitized U.S. citizens to the Latin American impression of U.S. regional policy as overly militarized, even imperious. This sensitivity showed up, for instance, in the 1960 presidential campaign when Kennedy was forced, amid skeptical media attention, to clarify that his attack on Eisenhower's Cuba policy did not mean he supported force in violation of hemispheric treaty obligations.[92]

The same national hesitancy about direct force showed up in other places as well. In response to an open-ended Gallup question on the best policy for Cuba, only 3 percent of the public answered "the U.S. should send troops to Cuba."[93] Every major newspaper in the United States spoke out against an overt U.S. invasion as well.[94] "We do not want to accept a blanket responsibility for expeditions bent on overthrowing [Castro]," said the hawkish *New York Herald Tribune*, "If there is to be a new revolution in Cuba, it will have to be a genuinely Cuban revolution."[95] The same showed up in editorial comments after the *New York Times* article broke the story of the invasion. One editorial after another pushed the no-force line: "American moves must be quiet, discreet, and guarded"; "fortunately, nobody wants to land the marines"; "our government has wisely announced that U.S. armed forces will not intervene on their [the Cuban exiles] behalf"; and "the approach taken by the new Cuban rebels is clearly preferable to any course which smacks of direct United States intervention."[96] Overall, the public shared JFK's sensitivity about Latin American opinion and with that support for the OAS system. "We do not want a 'Hungary' of our own in Cuba," said one paper in April.[97]

Promoters, like Smathers and Keating, were keen to these concerns. They wanted action against Castro, but worried about political relevance as well. The result was a restrained promoter discourse, focused on limited methods, to stop communism in Cuba.

This mattered to U.S. policy. It gave Kennedy political space not to pursue full-scale forceful regime change in Cuba. This was evident in several ways. For starters, unlike the dispersal problem, there was never any pre-invasion conversation among Kennedy and his advisors about pressure from the national discourse to send Marines into Cuba.[98] In fact, the opposite was the case. Some advisors argued a lack of public support for a U.S. invasion meant a delay was possible.[99] Since "public opinion is not ready for an invasion," one advisor argued, action could be put off "for a number of months."[100] Schlesinger made a similar comment. "A great many people," he said, do not see Cuba as justifying direct force, pointing out that only two Democratic senators openly supported the exile invasion, much less direct U.S. action.[101] With the administration viewing the domestic climate this way, it is little surprise that plans included no contingency for a direct U.S. intervention if the exile invasion failed.[102] In sum, the liberal discourse pushed Kennedy to do something short of a U.S. invasion of Cuba—the administration developed a plan to match that discourse, nothing less and nothing more.

That same discourse also helps explain why the administration did not change course and send the Marines once the covert invasion failed. Most important, when news of failure broke, there was no surge of promoter or public demands for a full-scale invasion by the U.S. military.[103] The Kennedy administration probably bears some responsibility for keeping the liberal discourse in check here. A week before the invasion, Schlesinger saw potential trouble brewing at home. "A great danger is that the U.S. prestige will become committed to the success of the rebellion: that if the rebellion appears to be failing, the rebels will call for U.S. armed help; that members of Congress will take up the cry; and that pressures will build up which will make it politically hard to resist the demand to send in the Marines," he detailed, in an April 10 memo to Kennedy.[104] In short, given the elevated national concerns about anticommunism, Schlesinger knew a failed invasion offered a golden opportunity for promoters to build support for a direct U.S. invasion. Kennedy agreed to Schlesinger's suggestion of two steps to help prevent this. First, he recommended pre-invasion public statements by government officials pledging not to use force in Cuba in order to harden the already prevalent sentiments in the national discourse against force. "When senatorial voices are raised demanding overt U.S. intervention," Schlesinger argued, "our people must be primed to oppose this demand."[105] Kennedy followed this advice. He stated emphatically in a speech on April 12 that the United States would not use force in Cuba—Rusk followed this up two days later with a similar statement.[106] The plan seemed to work. Both statements were widely praised in the media, especially.

Second, Schlesinger suggested the need for a frank conversation with Miró Cardona, president of the Cuban Revolutionary Council. The Council was a coalition of Cuban political leaders who would land in Cuba to create a new government once the exile army established a beachhead on the island.[107] Schlesinger worried that Cardona might call for quick U.S. recognition and trigger, as a result, a promoter surge in the U.S. demanding intervention on Cardona's behalf.[108] He told Kennedy it was critical to prevent this, by controlling Cardona. Cuban leaders must hear "clearly and emphatically," Schlesinger argued, that there will be no U.S. recognition of the provisional government postlanding until the Cuban exiles achieve "better than a 50–50 chance of winning under their own steam."[109] Kennedy again complied with Schlesinger's suggestion. He dispatched Schlesinger to New York City prior to the invasion to inform Cardona that no formal U.S. recognition would come until the Revolutionary Council was in full control of the Cuban government.[110]

How much these two moves affected the liberal discourse on Cuba is hard to tell (if nothing else, it points again to the importance of that discourse to JFK's policy decisions).[111] In the end, what is clear is that the postinvasion discourse worked to Kennedy's advantage, at least when it came to the issue of using direct force in Cuba. News of the invasion's failure on April 20 brought a variety of responses from the media and members of Congress. Some expressed dismay, many called for renewed vigor against communism, and others criticized the planning of the Bay of Pigs invasion.[112] In all of this, one thing was noticeably absent, though: calls for a U.S. military invasion. Most important, promoters took a soft line. "The trouble was that our intervention was deficient in planning and determination and scope," said Senator Dodd, "I do not suggest that we should have sent in the Marines to put down the Castro dictatorship."[113] Likewise, conservative GOP Senator Barry Goldwater (AZ) called for a region-wide blockade of Cuba, while praising Kennedy's policy. "This is not Jack Kennedy's fault," said Goldwater, "When he's right, I'm with him. I think he's right."[114] Senator Styles Bridges (R-NH) stated simply, "I approve of the position our government has taken on Cuba."[115] This was a common theme. Of all the statements made on the floor of the House and Senate from April 20 until the end of the first week of May, only one (Congressman Abraham Multer [D-NY]) openly called for U.S.

military action in Cuba.[116] Editors from across the country were equally tame as no major newspaper from New York to Los Angeles, San Francisco, or Chicago advocated a full-scale U.S. invasion of Cuba in late April 1961. Instead, most spoke against using force.[117] Public opinion surveys showed this disposition was widespread. A Gallup poll taken two weeks after the Bay of Pigs debacle indicated that 61 percent of the public approved of "the way President Kennedy is handling the situation in Cuba."[118]

Why so much unity behind Kennedy and why were promoters so tame? Part of it was continued support for hemispheric treaty obligations and avoiding the Hungary stigma.[119] Another reason had to do with partisanship. It was difficult for Republicans, in particular, to attack Kennedy since Eisenhower, a Republican, hatched the idea for and planned most of the exile invasion. "The Republicans, of course, were a little inhibited by their own role in conceiving the operation," observed Schlesinger.[120]

Kennedy took steps to reinforce those Republican inhibitions by arranging highly publicized meetings with GOP heavyweights (Nixon, Eisenhower, Goldwater, and New York governor Nelson Rockefeller) starting April 20, the day the operation's failure became public. Kennedy got just what he needed out of these meetings, namely photo-ops shaking hands with the GOP leaders and a ringing endorsement from Eisenhower.[121] Nixon and Republican leaders in Congress privately agreed to "hold their fire" against Kennedy until after the crisis passed.[122] Overall, this bipartisan response closed the political space for promoters, especially in the Republican Party, to charge the administration with being soft on communism. "No president ever got himself into a more embarrassing jam in faster time than John F. Kennedy in Cuba," observed the *Chicago Daily Tribune*, at the time, "And few presidents have shown more adroit footwork at disarming the opposition."[123]

This was a welcome outcome for Kennedy. The failed invasion was "an incident, not a disaster," he told a reporter, in reference to the mild response at home.[124] In the end, JFK granted a Joint Chiefs of Staff (JCS) request to allow air cover for a few hours on April 19 in order to help the Cuban landing force evacuate, but that was it in terms of direct U.S. military action. Due to the weakened liberal discourse around Cuba, Kennedy felt no domestic political pressure to do anything more.[125] As a result, U.S. forceful regime change in Cuba remained a militarily limited affair in April 1961.

Vietnam

When Lyndon Johnson assumed the presidency after the November 1963 assassination of John Kennedy, he faced an immediate decision on Vietnam. Earlier in the month, a coup removed the heavy-handed president of South Vietnam Ngo Dinh Diem from office. At the time, the United States had approximately 16,000 advisors in noncombat roles in Vietnam and was providing South Vietnam with military assistance.[126] Johnson faced the decision to continue the U.S. commitment or leave Vietnam altogether.

Prior to Johnson, the liberal narrative played a major role in U.S. policy here. In 1961, Kennedy created a taskforce to stop communism in South Vietnam.[127] In a joint memo, McNamara and Rusk endorsed the move because South Vietnam's fall "would stimulate bitter domestic controversies in the United States and would be seized upon by extreme elements to divide the country and harass the administration."[128] This rationale drove Kennedy to progressively triple the number of U.S. advisors in Vietnam. "If I tried to pull out completely now from Vietnam we would have a Joe McCarthy red scare on our hands," he said in March 1963.[129] At another point, JFK said that he would be "charged with being soft" if South Vietnam fell.[130] In short, the liberal narrative pushed Kennedy toward deeper involvement in Vietnam.

It did the same to Johnson. When LBJ became president, liberal-discourse pressure on Vietnam remained intense. Seventy-two percent of the public favored helping "the non-communist government there [South Vietnam] resist a communist take-over."[131] Editorial and congressional commentary after the Diem coup echoed the same.[132] Editorials were full of resolve for the sake of freedom: "America's reason for being in South Viet Nam is to help to save that nation from communism"; "we can press forward with the sticky, unpleasant job of stopping and rolling back the spread of communism"; and "the anti-Communist war can be won and South Vietnam saved as a bulwark against a Communist conquest of all of Southeast Asia."[133]

On Capitol Hill, Senate Majority Leader Mike Mansfield faced a torrent of liberal narrative-laced criticism when he supported a plan in February 1964 to neutralize Vietnam.[134] "The people of the United States want Communist aggression defeated in Vietnam," said Congressmen Clement Zablocki (D-WI), in response to Mansfield, "We cannot give way . . . before the expansionist policies of Communist China." Jacob Javits, a moderate New York Republican senator and future opponent of the Vietnam War echoed Zablocki. "[The American people] will accept the risks," he said, "if they believe there is the remotest chance to keep the Communist grip from encompassing Vietnam."[135] At the time, other Democrats, like Senators Eugene McCarthy (MN), Frank Lausche (OH), Paul Douglas (IL), Russell Long (LA), Thomas Dodd (CT), and Gale McGhee (WY) sounded the same themes.[136] Overall, agreement to stop communism in Vietnam was everywhere in the mid-1960s. It was like a pillar—a "dominant consensus"—in the national discourse, from Congress and the press to the man on the street. "There was no need to doubt the importance to the United States of preventing the forced Communist domination of Vietnam," observe Leslie Gelb and Richard Betts, "It was self-evident . . . a nondebate."[137] In short, audience costs for inaction in Vietnam were strengthening around the liberal narrative in 1963 and early 1964.

Johnson was deeply influenced by this. Within days of Kennedy's assassination, LBJ held two meetings with advisors on Vietnam. From the start, Johnson was hesitant. He confessed to "serious misgivings" about Vietnam—"I didn't like the smell of it," he said.[138] But fear of the crossing the liberal narrative outweighed this for LBJ. "I am not going to lose Vietnam," he said to his advisors right off the bat. He worried, in particular, about suffering Truman's fate. "I am not going to be the President who saw Southeast Asia go the way China went," said Johnson, "I don't think Congress wants us to let the Communists take over South Vietnam."[139] The president pressed his advisors to approach Vietnam with greater vigor, telling them not to go to sleep at night until they were certain they had done everything they could to assist South Vietnam.[140]

This toughness generated by the liberal narrative pressure shaped the administration's posture toward neutralization. In a December 1963 memo to Johnson, Mansfield argued for neutralization, warning of Vietnam becoming unpopular like Korea.[141] On January 9, Rusk, McNamara, and Bundy argued emphatically against this, saying that neutralization would lead to communist control of South Vietnam and, thus, "the same sort of political fallout we had over China."[142] McNamara wrote that this was politically unacceptable. "The stakes in preserving an anti-Communist South Vietnam are so high that in our judgment, we must go on bending every effort to win," he said.[143] Bundy claimed Mansfield had the Korean analogy all wrong. "The political damage to Truman and Acheson from the fall of China arose because most Americans came to believe that we could and should have done more than we did to prevent it," he argued, "This is exactly what would happen now if we should seem to be the first to quit on Saigon."[144] Bundy posited that neutralization should follow a more determined effort to save South Vietnam. Anything else would land Johnson on the wrong side of the liberal narrative and threaten his administration. Neutralization "would be regarded as betrayal by the new regime in Saigon and by all anti-Communist Vietnamese," Bundy concluded, "*There are enough of them to lose us an election.*"[145]

These arguments swayed Johnson. In mid-January, the president rejected neutralization. "We do not want another China in Viet-Nam," he said to Mansfield.[146] Johnson also approved increased military aid and new covert operations to assist with South Vietnamese military strikes along the North Vietnamese coast.[147] The political danger of crossing the liberal narrative stood at the center of these decisions. "Johnson would have been the subject of attacks for turning his back on Kennedy's policies and giving something to the communists," said the under-secretary of state George Ball at the time.[148] Many historians agree. "Given the existing assumptions about . . . a long term struggle between democracy and totalitarianism," Robert Dallek observes, "no President, especially an unproven, unelected one, could simply have withdrawn."[149]

Escalation to Air Power, 1964

1964 brought more liberal narrative pressure to save Vietnam. As this hap-pened, U.S. military engagement deepened. The situation inside South Vietnam started this process of change. Amid mounting protests, General Nguyen Khanh unseated General Duong Van Minh, Diem's successor, in a January 1964 coup. The military situation deteriorated substantially as well in early 1964 with the VC making gains in the countryside. A CIA report in early February warned, "the tide is against us."[150]

Promoters ramped up the liberal-discourse pressure. Internally, the JCS were the most hawkish. General Maxwell Taylor, chair of the JCS, pressed Johnson in early March for air and naval strikes against North Vietnam.[151] Pressure from outside the administration grew as well. Looking to gain ground ahead of the November elections, Republicans grew increasingly vocal. Wrapped in the liberal narrative, these arguments dominated the political discourse in 1964. "The for-eign policy of this administration has been vacillating and contradictory" in the face of "Communist exploited" crises around the world, charged New York gov-ernor John Rockefeller in March.[152] In "the death struggle with Communists . . . we have been playing blindfolded against a team that sees clearly," said Senator Keating.[153] Some Democrats echoed these themes as well.[154] Media commentary pointed to growing public impressions of "confusion," "mistakes," "faint-hearted apprehensions," and "weakness" in U.S. policy toward Vietnam.[155]

By summer, these criticisms and questions about U.S. policy developed into two distinct streams of promoter arguments for more action in Vietnam. The first came from the "win the war" camp. Consisting mostly of Republicans, this group of promoters called for (at this point, limited) force to defeat the Vietcong. A group of thirteen House Republicans released a much-publicized "Report on American Strategy and Strength" in late June that attacked the administration for a "no win" strategy of "indecision in the prosecution of the war against the sources of Communist strength" in Vietnam. The report advocated a policy that would bring "a victory for freedom in Vietnam," rather than simply a "compla-cent commitment" to deterring communist gains. This became a prominent GOP theme in the presidential campaign of 1964. "Yesterday it was Korea, tonight it is

Vietnam," claimed the Republican presidential nominee, Barry Goldwater, at the Republican National Convention in July, "[The president] refuses to say whether the objective there is victory."[156]

The second vein of promoters were the "don't lose Vietnam" camp. While skeptical about achieving military victory, these promoters did not want to give up Vietnam either. They argued for U.S. resolve as a means to negotiations that ensured an independent, noncommunist regime in South Vietnam. "Any nation is likely to get, at the bargaining table, what that nation can hold in the field," said Senator Frank Church (D-ID) in June 1964, "It is certainly to be hoped that the military situation in South Vietnam may improve to the point, where the prospects brighten for a peaceful settlement."[157] In his advocacy for neutralization, Mansfield sounded the "no lose" theme at points as well. "Indeed there can be no peace in Indochina, except a Communist dictated peace, unless an improvement is brought about in the situation in South Vietnam such as the President is trying to achieve," said Mansfield in May.[158] While many like Mansfield, Church, and the Senate Foreign Relations Committee chair William Fulbright, did not publicly advocate military force to bring this kind of peace settlement, there arguments left that door open.[159] "They either will go down the drain or we must step in," said Fulbright in a June statement.[160] Others were forthright about what "stepping in" might look like. To ensure that "we are . . . not going to lose," argued the *New York Times*, "an increase instead of a diminution of American military participation" may be required.[161] Overall, "don't lose" promoters often stood—at least tacitly—with "win the war" promoters on a critical point: the United States needed a more robust military effort to save South Vietnam. From mid-May to mid-July, sixty of the ninety-three floor statements by members of Congress on Vietnam fell into one of these two camps.[162]

Johnson remained conflicted, though. On the one hand, he saw danger at home and abroad in escalating the war. "It looks to me like we're getting into another Korea," he told Mac Bundy in March, "I don't think it's worth fighting for and I don't think we can get out."[163] He also worried about the Great Society. In 1964, the first key pieces of Great Society legislation were before Congress. LBJ saw danger here. "Once the war began, then all those conservatives in Congress would use it as a weapon against the Great Society," he later said. The war would essentially eclipse everything—"all my hopes . . . and dreams," LBJ argued.[164] But, politically, Johnson also knew that he could not allow Vietnam to fall—audience costs for inaction weighed on the president. "I knew that if we let Communist aggression succeed, . . . there would follow in this country an endless national debate—a mean and destructive debate—that would shatter my Presidency, kill my administration, and damage our democracy," Johnson said, in a 1969 interview.[165] He said the same thing in 1964. When Senator Smathers encouraged LBJ in June to abandon Vietnam altogether, Johnson mimicked back the likely Republican charge if he did so: "We can't retreat, because . . . it'll be very disastrous to the United States to give up all of our interests in Southeast Asia."[166] Overall, the political danger of crossing the liberal narrative bore down on LBJ in 1964.

Torn between these competing pressures, LBJ initially tried to find a middle way. In the spring of 1964, he approved the planning (but not execution) of a sustained air and naval campaign along with several steps "designed to demonstrate U.S. determination to key constituencies at home," including the deployment of 5,000 additional U.S. troops to Thailand and appointment of a high-level diplomatic team to Saigon headed by Maxwell Taylor as the new U.S. ambassador.[167] Taylor saw domestic politics behind it all: "It is quite apparent that he [Johnson] does not want to lose South Vietnam before next November [i.e. the election] nor does he want to get the country into a war."[168]

None of these steps helped Johnson's domestic standing, though. Advisors warned Johnson in early summer that he looked "wishy-washy" to the public— tough one week and soft the next.[169] Even more politically dangerous, Goldwater was gaining ground on Johnson with Vietnam. A mid-summer survey found that 58 percent viewed Johnson's Vietnam policy negatively. The survey also found that Johnson's sizeable lead over Goldwater dropped when questions about who would best handle Vietnam were folded into the mix. Vietnam is "clearly an issue working for Goldwater," warned LBJ's pollsters.[170] This worried the administration. Bill Moyers suggested a speech by Johnson on Vietnam to "defuse a Goldwater bomb before he got a chance to throw it."[171] Likewise, foreign policy advisor William Bundy recommended a congressional resolution before the GOP convention to steal Goldwater's thunder.[172]

Johnson turned these ideas down, but the promoter discourse still worried the president. In the spring for instance, Johnson asked a close friend, Senator Richard Russell (D-GA), to make a speech advocating U.S. withdrawal from Vietnam. LBJ told Russell, "It could protect me against Goldwater throughout the South." Though opposed to escalation, Russell also worried about political costs with crossing the liberal narrative—he refused LBJ's request.[173] Overall, the historian Stanley Karnow describes how the administration saw things. "If a Communist victory in Vietnam knocked over the dominoes, Johnson would be the biggest domino to topple," observed Karnow, "This real or imaginary prospect haunted him during the summer of 1964, as he campaigned for election against Barry Goldwater."[174]

This political context, driven by the robust liberal narrative, helps explain the Gulf of Tonkin incident in August. In short, the liberal discourse around Vietnam pushed Johnson to use military force here, which in the end also shored him up politically against Goldwater by removing Vietnam as an issue from the fall campaign. Despite his own preferences and concerns, audience costs for inaction came, again, to shape LBJ's policy decision.

On August 2, North Vietnamese warships attacked a U.S. destroyer, the USS *Maddox*, in the Gulf of Tonkin. Johnson assumed the strike accidental and took no additional steps. On August 4 reports came in of a second attack on another destroyer, the *Turner Joy*.[175] For Johnson and his advisors, the two incidents together looked intentional. The domestic political climate required a decisive response. "The attack was going to come from the right and the hawks," political advisor Kenny O'Donnell told Johnson on the morning of the *Turner Joy* attack, you "must not allow them to accuse" you of "vacillating or being an indecisive leader."[176] McNamara and Mac Bundy took a similar line later that morning, fearing that "an orgasm of outrage" could lead to all-out war. "Some of the right-wing hawk Republicans might take such action that would be in effect a declaration of war or would put the administration in a position where we had to do things which we thought would be unwise, that might involve bringing the Chinese in or offending someone else," Bundy and McNamara argued.[177] Johnson got the same advice from Democrats on Capitol Hill. On August 4, Democratic leaders told Johnson he must take a firm stand, which included going to Congress for a resolution on Vietnam.[178] Given the liberal discourse of the time, the president could not afford to look weak on communism.

Johnson moved quickly. "You know that resolution your brother's been talking about for a few months?" He said to Mac Bundy, after meeting with O'Donnell, "Well, now's the time to get it through Congress."[179] Later that day, he met with a bipartisan group of congressional leaders who all (except Mansfield) gave their support to military reprisals and a congressional resolution for a firmer policy in Southeast Asia. Senator George Aiken (R-VT), who shared Mansfield's doubts, admitted that the groundswell of national support for a tough position would make passage easy. "By the time you send [the resolution] up here there won't be anything for us to [do] but support you," he said.[180] That evening, Johnson told the nation about the retaliatory airstrikes against Hanoi. This was the first application of overt military force by the United States in Vietnam.[181]

The Tonkin Gulf Resolution went to Congress the next day. It was broad, authorizing the president "to take all necessary steps, including the use of force, to assist any member or protocol state of the Southeast Asia Collective Defense Treaty that requests assistance in defense of its freedom."[182] As Aiken predicted, the liberal narrative groundswell around the resolution was intense. In Senate debate on the measure, approximately thirty-three senators spoke on the resolution—twenty-four expressed support by referencing themes at the heart of the liberal narrative, such as "Communist provocations"; "foremost defender of freedom"; and "protection of the idea of freedom and independence."[183] Fearful of crossing the liberal discourse, doubters of the resolution came onboard as well. Fulbright, for instance, worked tirelessly to usher the resolution through the Senate. While he later confessed this was a mistake, Fulbright admitted that looking tough on communism at home was his chief concern in 1964. "At the time, I was not in a suspicious frame of mind," he said, "I was afraid of Goldwater."[184]

In fact, Fulbright used this line to squash dissent. When Senator Gaylord Nelson (D-WI) told Fulbright he wanted military limits in the Tonkin Resolution, Fulbright told him that this move would frustrate Johnson's effort to "pull the rug out from under Goldwater." Nelson backed off. Pat Holt, a staff member on Fulbright's Senate Foreign Relations Committee, explained the liberal-discourse pressure that all Democrats felt. "Goldwater was taking a very hardline about Vietnam," Holt said, "The politics of it were such that Democrats almost had to support this thing . . . because if they didn't, they would be in the position of opening themselves to the charges of knuckling under to this little two-bit communist power in Southeast Asia."[185] Costs for inaction from the liberal discourse around Vietnam were simply too great to ignore—the administration and other Democrats had to act in order to look right by the moral of the day's main story to stop communism. The resolution passed unanimously in the House and with only two dissenting votes in the Senate.[186]

Johnson reaped the political benefits. According to historians, the entire incident "effectively neutralized Goldwater on Vietnam" as Johnson proved his mettle against the liberal narrative.[187] Polls in the fall showed that 61 percent disagreed that Johnson was "soft on Communism."[188] LBJ's choice of limited means—air power—also fit neatly with the national discourse. Promoter calls in the spring and summer for "more action" to combat communism in Vietnam were often vague on substance, with little definition of what kind of "action" actually needed to be taken. Above all else, almost no major voice here, including that of the hawkish Goldwater, proposed combat troops in South Vietnam.[189] In general, the liberal discourse in 1964 called for limited action to stop communism in South Vietnam, and that is what Johnson gave the nation.

Full-Scale Regime Promotion in Vietnam, 1965

In November 1964, Lyndon Johnson won the U.S. presidential election over Barry Goldwater by the widest popular-vote margin since President James Monroe's reelection in 1820. Likewise, Democratic congressional majorities increased to their largest since 1938. Many of those Democrats were leery of or opposed to escalation in Vietnam.[190] This all mattered little to Johnson, though.

Despite large majorities, the newly elected president worried most about the danger of crossing the robust liberal narrative to defend freedom in Asia. In 1965, this discourse coalesced around robust military action. Johnson complied with a full invasion in July.

Across late 1964, VC gains in the countryside brought more political turmoil to South Vietnam. "The situation in Vietnam is now likely to come apart more rapidly than we had anticipated," William Bundy told the president, just after the election.[191] This brought promoter demands for U.S. military escalation. Internally, the president's closest advisors were at the forefront of this emerging discourse. On November 19, Johnson received policy options from a National Security Council sub-committee on Vietnam. McNamara, Rusk, Taylor, and Mac Bundy recommended the president give closest consideration to one of two proposals: a rapid and massive full-scale military escalation (Option B); or gradual escalation from airpower against VC supply lines in Laos to bombing in North Vietnam, followed by ground operations (Option C). Johnson's advisors favored Option C, noting it would boost morale in South Vietnam and bring gradual pressure on Hanoi to enter negotiations. LBJ's advisors said continuing existing policy (Option A) looked "too soft." Immediate withdrawal was not an option.[192]

Johnson hesitated—his desires to stay out resurfaced. He gave no answer at the November 19 meeting. In a follow-up meeting on December 1 when his advisors expected a decision, Johnson instead poked holes in the assumptions behind Option C and talked about potential casualties. He also ranted about South Vietnam's political chaos and complained about the escalation's impact on the Great Society. The president agreed only to reconnaissance flights along the Vietnamese-Laotion border. He refused to approve any other parts of Option C without a stable government in Saigon.[193]

The president's reluctance did not sit well with promoters. After hearing about Johnson's position, the influential syndicated columnist Joseph Alsop wrote a series of scathing pieces that historians point to as having a big impact on the policy discourse at home.[194] Alsop charged that inaction would produce a "chain reaction" of losses for the United States in Southeast Asia, resulting in the "greatest defeat in American history." He challenged Johnson to adopt a tough line like Kennedy during the Cuban missile crisis, then issued a warning. "As the losses mount and are registered at home, the bitterness will mount proportionally," wrote Alsop, "Since the President has the means to avert defeat, he cannot disclaim responsibility."[195] Other commentators and important voices picked up on these same themes.[196]

These appeals resonated with and paralleled public sentiment as well. Above all else, the moral of the liberal narrative—to stop communism—remained widely accepted when it came to policy toward Vietnam. A late December poll (that deeply troubled Johnson) showed 50 percent thought LBJ was "handling affairs [in Vietnam] badly."[197] Other polls showed support for a tough stand in Vietnam. A February survey registered 57 percent support for holding the line in Vietnam or carrying the fight to the North.[198] Amid these trends, moderators with deep reservations about the war took political cover in "don't lose" arguments. In January, Senator Church made the case for neutralization with the important caveat that negotiations should not, however, "camouflage for a Communist takeover." Future antiwar presidential nominee, Senator George McGovern, took an even stiffer line. "We cannot simply walk out and permit the Vietcong to march into Saigon," he said, "We [are] prepared to wage a [prolonged] conflict rather than surrender the area to communism."[199]

Johnson caved again to the costs for inaction generated by this liberal discourse. In late January 1965, another coup led to speculation of South Vietnam's imminent collapse. Frustrated by Johnson's hesitation, Mac Bundy and McNamara wrote a joint memo to the president on January 27. "Bob and I believe that the worst course of action is to continue in this essentially passive role which can lead only to eventual defeat, . . . it is time for harder choices," read the memo.[200] They ended with a veiled threat to resign if policy did not change: "McNamara and I have reached the point where our obligations to you simply do not permit us to administer our present directives in silence and let you think we see real hope in them."[201] Lloyd Gardner claims the message of the memo was simple (coming back to an argument Bundy made in 1963 and would make later in 1965): "If we lose the war because we withheld military power, you will be blamed and it will be the end of your administration."[202] As Kennedy men, the president must have also worried that McNamara and Bundy would be right out front talking about how weak Johnson was on communism, relative to his predecessor. When Johnson finished reading the memo, he looked at Bundy and McNamara and said, throwing all reservations aside, "Stable government or no stable government, we'll do what we have to do—we will move strongly."[203] LBJ confessed to friends at the time that the Great Society played in here too. "If I don't go now and they show later that I should have, then they'll be all over me in Congress," he said, "They won't be talking about my civil rights bill . . . No sir, they'll push Vietnam up my ass every time. Vietnam. Vietnam. Vietnam."[204]

The door was now open to escalation. Much like the Tonkin Gulf incident, the February 7 Vietcong bombing of the U.S. airbase at Pleiku generated a surge of domestic pressure for more action. Bundy again reminded Johnson of this. Action now will blunt "the charge that we did not do all that we could have done, and this charge will be important in many countries, including our own."[205] Johnson confessed that the costs for inaction were high. "Suddenly I realized that doing nothing was more dangerous than doing something," LBJ said of the national reaction to Pleiku.[206] McNamara and Ball suggested only retaliatory strikes. Johnson wanted more, though. "We have kept our gunpowder dry for a long time," LBJ said in a meeting at the time, "We can't ask our boys to fight with one hand tied behind their backs."[207] Following an attack on a second U.S. base a few days later, Johnson ordered the start of a sustained bombing campaign against North Vietnam—Rolling Thunder—on February 13. Audience costs for inaction were front and center here. "Losing the Great Society was a terrible thought, but not so terrible as the thought of being responsible for America's losing a war to the Communists," Johnson later said of the decision, "Nothing possible could be worse than that."[208] Two weeks after the start of Rolling Thunder, Johnson approved a request from General William Westmoreland for the dispatch of two battalions of Marines to protect the airbase at Danang.[209]

Within days of approving sustained air power, pressure mounted to take the next step: U.S. ground troops. On March 6, Rusk, Bundy, and McNamara said that while the air war had raised morale in Saigon, communists were still gaining ground in the countryside. Bombing alone would not work, they argued.[210] Johnson felt stuck between the domestic pressure to avoid a loss to communism and his own reservations about escalating the war. "I can't get out and I can't finish it with what I've got in," he said, at the time, "So what the hell can I do?"[211] Two weeks later, Johnson was stunned by an assessment of the military needs in Vietnam. The Army chief of staff told LBJ that it would take 500,000 combat troops and five years to defeat the Vietcong. "The alternative was that Vietnam fell to North Vietnam," said General Johnson.[212] Bundy took this as an opportunity to remind LBJ of familiar themes about measuring up to the liberal narrative. In a March 21 memo he told Johnson to avoid the impression at home of being a "paper tiger." "In terms of domestic U.S. politics, which is better: to 'lose' now or to 'lose' after committing 100,000 men?" Bundy argued, "The latter, for if we visibly do enough in the South, any failure will be, in that moment, beyond our control."[213]

Bundy's warnings made sense given the emerging national discussion around Vietnam. Resolve was stiffening around the liberal narrative moral to stop communism in Asia. A host of polls in February and March pointed to this: 78 percent agreed that "Communists would take over Southeast Asia if we withdrew now"; 79 percent said it was "very important" that "communist control over Southeast Asia be prevented"; 64 percent agreed "the United States should continue its present efforts in South Vietnam" rather than "pull our forces out." In late April, another survey found 63 percent agreed that the United States should "hold the line" or "go North" in Vietnam.[214]

Promoters contributed to and took advantage of this powerful liberal narrative context to go after the administration. "It is apparent we have no clear policy but an aimless patchwork . . . that becomes more confused every day," said a conservative in Congress.[215] Nixon called for an end to the "evasions" in U.S. policy so as to meet "communist resolution to take the world, segment by segment."[216] "Tit-for-tattery," wrote Alsop, "can never add up to a policy for waging the Vietnamese war."[217] Even moderate voices, like that of the columnist James Reston, concluded in late April that the United States was not "free to submit to the triumph of Communist guerrilla techniques without making them pay dearly in the process."[218] In this context, equivocation would set off, as one commentator noted at the time, politically devastating charges of "Johnson's appeasement."[219]

LBJ knew this, which helps explain his response to JCS requests for combat troops. In April, the president agreed to deploy two additional Marine battalions to Vietnam and a change in the mission of the Marines at Danang from base security to active combat. The big request from the JCS came on May 8. Amid another wave of intense political chaos in Saigon, the commander of U.S. military operations in Vietnam, General William Westmoreland, asked to increase U.S. combat troops to 125,000. He also requested permission for troops to fully join the war by taking on active search and destroy missions.[220]

As Johnson considered Westermoreland's request, the liberal narrative's high costs for inaction bore down upon him. His advisors talked about it repeatedly. "Academics [opposing the war] . . . are currently out of step with the mainline American conviction and purpose," Bundy said, in an early June reference to protests on college campuses, "Any President who was asked to choose between the understanding and support of the American people, and the understanding and support of the intellectuals, would choose the people."[221] Likewise, McNamara told the columnist Arthur Krock in late April that "if Asia goes Red" due to the loss of Vietnam, "a disastrous political fight that could . . . freeze American political debate and even affect political freedoms" would break out. Johnson felt the weight of the liberal narrative too. He feared a quagmire, but saw no way out of it given the domestic discourse. "When I land troops they call me an interventionist and if I do nothing, I'll be impeached," he told a reporter at the time.[222]

On July 26, Johnson agreed to increase combat troops by 100,000 and approved Westmoreland's request for full combat operations. "We intend to convince the Communists that we cannot be defeated by force of arms or superior power," LBJ said, in a public statement announcing the move.[223] The decision was widely praised. Polls showed 65 percent supported the administration's Vietnam policy with a plurality favoring "more ground troops."[224] Editorial commentary from across the country was equally supportive. "If the Communists continue to reject all courses except war, then they will have war," the *Atlanta Constitution* stated, "The President's position is sound, it is right, and it deserves the solid backing of the American people."[225] The *Sun* [Baltimore] commented that getting the North Vietnamese to the negotiating table begins with "proving a military solution is impossible."[226] "It is better than the alternative of pulling out," claimed the *Des Moines Register.*[227]

Lyndon Johnson had once again brought foreign policy in line with the robust liberal discourse in the United States.[228] The end result was a full-scale regime change war in Vietnam.

Alternative Explanations

Geopolitics, elite polarization, and prestige offer alternative explanations. This section explores each in turn.

Geopolitics

For realists, robust forceful regime change becomes most likely when a state possesses a preponderance of global or regional power. This argument struggles to offer an adequate explanation of the Cuba and Vietnam cases. To realism's credit, there are indications that the United States considered wider geopolitical dynamics in its choices about how to move forward in both cases. In Vietnam, for instance, Johnson chose not to pursue Option B in 1965 (an immediate, full-scale attack on North Vietnam) out of fear that it might bring Chinese and/or Soviet retaliation. For this reason, the gradual escalation of Option C was better. "If China reacted to our slow escalation by threatening to retaliate, we'd have plenty of time to ease off the bombing," Johnson said.[229] This statement also suggests the central problem for a realist account in this case. The very fact that Johnson worried about China attests to a reality—namely, small differentials of power in Asia—that according to realists should have discouraged any use of U.S. force in Vietnam. As seen above, Johnson feared the United States would get bogged down like Korea. Moreover, he worried constantly that even the gradual application of force might bring China into the war. "I never knew as I sat there in the afternoon, approving targets one, two, and three, whether one of those three might just be the one that sets off the provisions of those secret treaties," said Johnson, "What if one of those targets you picked today triggers Russia or China?"[230] This was an ongoing concern for Johnson through 1965.[231] For realists, the potential of a great power war should have deterred or limited U.S. military action. Something other than differentials in power accounts for robust U.S. forceful regime promotion in Vietnam.

On one level, Cuba appears a stronger case for realists. During and after the invasion, Kennedy worried that U.S. escalation might result in a Soviet strike against Berlin and in turn lead to a nuclear war.[232] Given these considerations, limited U.S. action in Cuba matches realist expectations.

By the same token, questions arise as to *how much* these geopolitical factors mattered in Kennedy's estimation. Moderators like Rusk, Fulbright, and Schlesinger never mentioned Berlin or the possibility of nuclear war with the Soviets in their appeals to cancel the mission or warnings about the implications of an overt invasion (they focused instead almost exclusively on regional prestige and another Hungary).[233] Kennedy's own decision making raises questions here too. At 1 AM on April 19, for instance, as the invasion was failing, Kennedy initially resisted JCS pressure for U.S. air support to help evacuate the exile army due to concerns, as he said, about "a general war with the Soviets." Five hours later, he changed course despite Rusk's reminder of JFK's earlier position. This marks a "deeper commitment," Rusk warned the president. Kennedy held his hand up to his nose and responded, "We're already in it up to here."[234] In general, a wider great power war mattered little to JFK's decision making.

Finally, cross-case comparisons raise problems for the realist argument. The United States held far greater differentials of power in Latin America during the 1960s than it did in Asia. Even with the global reach of the Cold War, Latin America was a sphere of U.S. influence in ways that Asia was not. From the realist perspective, full-scale military action made far greater sense, then, in Cuba than Vietnam. Overall, geopolitics has less leverage than the master narrative argument when it comes to explaining patterns of forceful regime change.

Elite Polarization

A stand-alone elite polarization argument contends robust forceful regime promotion is most likely when elites become polarized. Kennedy and Johnson, as well as their advisors, were clearly polarized in the 1960s.[235] Like the cases in chapter 3, the problem here is that the constant of elite polarization is not sufficient enough to explain the levels of force—limited action in Cuba and full-scale in Vietnam—adopted by the United States for regime change. If elites were so polarized, why was there no full-scale invasion of Cuba? Two additional points compound this puzzle. First, given its proximity to the United States, policymakers arguably sensed greater ideological danger (i.e., more elite polarization) over potential communist gains in Cuba than in Vietnam. Second, unlike the China case in chapter 3, there were fewer pragmatic considerations (such as fighting a two-front war in both China and Korea in 1950) to constrain elite decisions in Cuba. The United States also had a long history of using force in Latin America. Arguably, then, from a polarization stand point, full-scale regime promotion seems at least as likely in Cuba as Vietnam.

A second strain of the elite polarization argument faces explanatory problems as well. According to John Owen, policy elites sometimes show restraint in pursuing forceful regime change when geostrategic factors become especially pronounced for leaders. Concerns like these can trump ideological preferences. This variant of the argument helps explain some aspects of the Cuba case, especially. JFK's more pragmatic sensibilities undoubtedly helped keep the intervention against Castro limited. The problem here comes, again, with cross-case variation. LBJ held similarly powerful misgivings against war in Vietnam, but went ahead with robust action anyway. Why did elite preferences against military action not shape policy here in ways they did on Cuba? The answer turns, again, on master narratives. Notably, elite dispositions mattered to varying degrees because of the master narrative context. In the Cuba case, a more restrained-liberal narrative discourse allowed space for elite preferences to shape policy, while in the Vietnam case a more robust liberal narrative discourse overwhelmed elite preferences and pushed LBJ to act in a way he would have preferred to avoid.[236] Overall, elite ideology and strategic dispositions mattered in the sort of contextualized way that is expected with the more holistic ideational approach of the master narrative argument.

Prestige and Length of Commitments

Prestige and the importance of prior commitments are two counterarguments that deserve attention. On the former, concerns about the U.S. image abroad—either for resolve or restraint—undoubtedly impacted U.S. decision making in both cases. Kennedy felt constrained by regional opinion on Cuba.[237] On Vietnam, Kennedy/Johnson officials talked often in private about protecting the U.S. image of resolve to deter Soviet/Chinese aggression. In 1964, Rusk argued, for instance, that if the United States abandoned Vietnam, "our guarantees with regard to Berlin would lose their credibility."[238] Demonstrating resolve, then, was an important part of decision making on Vietnam.

While these factors related to image played a part in the Cuba and Vietnam decisions, they cannot explain the patterns of forceful regime change in each case. Take Cuba for instance. With the details of the Bay of Pigs invasion (including the U.S. role) exposed in the *New York Times* on April 5, it was obvious to everyone that the United States had a hand in the invasion before it ever launched. "We will be blamed," Kennedy said, in reference to regional opinion, when the news broke.[239] Rusk and Schlesinger agreed. They predicted widespread regional protests (which indeed happened) and damage to U.S. prestige if the U.S. went ahead with the operation, even in its limited form.[240] Overall, if protecting an image of restraint was that central to JFK's decision on Cuba, he never should have approved any invasion, regardless of size.

On Vietnam, the resolve argument faces similar problems. First, Johnson and his advisors questioned whether the U.S. reputation for resolve was at stake here. In March 1965, Mac Bundy claimed Vietnam mattered little to U.S. credibility. "Win or lose," he said, "The result elsewhere would not be earthshattering."[241] This uncertainty about whether or not prestige was on the line stands in sharp contrast to how Johnson and his advisors talked about the liberal narrative. Here, they never questioned the negative domestic political implications of losing Vietnam. This tells us that fear of audience costs from a liberal narrative backlash were an accepted fact, a staple in the decision-making process, in ways that prestige was not. Second, if U.S. credibility was so important in Vietnam, why did Johnson not commit to a full invasion as soon as he came into office? Nothing would have demonstrated U.S. resolve more profoundly than this. Likewise, one can also ask why the United States chose only limited military action with the Gulf of Tonkin incident or attack on the airbase at Pleiku? Again, if demonstrating international resolve was so vital, a full-scale military response to these earlier incidents makes the most sense.

Finally, perhaps the greater length of time behind the U.S. commitment to regime promotion in Vietnam (starting with the 1954 Geneva accords, ten years prior to direct U.S. military action) as opposed to Cuba (starting with the embargo, one year prior to U.S. intervention) somehow explains why the United States pursued combat operations in one but not the other. The historical record does not support this argument very well. If anything, the opposite appears to be the case. As the appeals for neutralization show, the United States' long relationship with the highly unstable, illiberal South Vietnamese government produced a degree of deep hesitation and skepticism among many U.S. policy elites (including LBJ) about the potential for success in sustaining a free, independent South Vietnam. The familiarity of time brought caution, therefore, not resolve to use force. With Cuba, by contrast, there was no questioning the U.S. ability to bring off successful regime promotion by toppling Castro. Given the United States' long history of successful regime change interventions in Latin America, the short time horizon of this case (especially with an ongoing rebellion against Castro in 1961) seemed to favor robust military action, not the limited approach that transpired.

Overall, it appears that something other than prestige or length of commitments best explains patterns of forceful regime promotion in Cuba and Vietnam. As this chapter demonstrates, the politics of master narratives fill this gap.

In the 1960s, the United States faced two major regime crises in Cuba and Vietnam. In the former, it applied limited, covert force to try to topple the Castro regime. In the latter, a series of escalatory steps ended with full invasion in 1965.

The discourse around master narratives offers a strong account of these outcomes. The restraint narrative was weak and the liberal narrative robust in this period. Promoters used that liberal narrative to press Kennedy and Johnson to reluctantly take military action in both cases. One fascinating point to consider here is the fact that the most vocal promoter voices came from Republicans, who were the minority party during this period. These particular voices carried so much policy weight not because of their numbers, oratorical skill, or some other factors unique to Republicans at the time. Instead, the discourses they built mattered because of master narratives. As the discussion in chapter 1 anticipates, the robust liberal narrative essentially augmented or leveraged promoter appeals in ways that gave these agents an oversized role in the policy process. Aware of the power of the liberal narrative, Kennedy and Johnson could not risk being "soft on communism" in an age when being labeled as such was nothing short of political suicide. Promoter arguments mattered because they brought political costs like these home to roost for both JFK and LBJ in this period.

The different levels of force applied in Cuba and Vietnam is also best explained by the liberal discourse. For various reasons, promoters helped build a progressively stronger discourse in favor of full-scale military operations in Vietnam, but not Cuba. The policy choices made by Kennedy and Johnson fell in line with these discourses. Neither president could risk the political danger of being out of step with the national discourse around the liberal narrative. Yet both also went only as far as the discourse demanded in terms of military action in Cuba and Vietnam.

REGIME CHANGE IN EL SALVADOR AND GRENADA

This chapter turns to U.S. regime promotion in the late Cold War. In a few instances such as Grenada, Panama and Kuwait, the United Stated took on full-scale military invasions. In many others like El Salvador, Nicaragua, and Iraq (1991), Washington took no military action for regime promotion. The master narrative argument best explains these patterns. Both the liberal and restraint narratives were especially strong in the 1980s. Internal trauma from the Vietnam War left behind a robust restraint narrative, reflected in a common mantra—"no more Vietnams." Sparked by new communist bloc geopolitical gains, the liberal narrative also strengthened into the 1980s. Discourses around these two narratives affected patterns of forceful regime promotion down to the end of the Cold War.

This chapter looks closely at a pair of cases—El Salvador (nonintervention) and Grenada (full-scale intervention)—during the 1980s. With El Salvador, a robust liberal narrative contributed to the most extensive U.S. involvement in a regime crisis since the Vietnam War. But a strong restraint-based discourse limited U.S. involvement to security assistance alone—direct force was never adopted. With Grenada, certain idiosyncrasies of the decision-making process prevented a restraint discourse from emerging in this case. This lowered audience costs for inaction opening the door for the Reagan administration to pursue a full-scale invasion in October 1983. As noted in the conclusion, master narratives help account for decisions in numerous other cases during this period as well.

The Master Narrative Landscape

Understanding the strength of master narratives in the late Cold War begins with the internal trauma created by the Vietnam War. As the prior chapter detailed, U.S. military engagement in Vietnam was fully wrapped up in the liberal narrative.[1] Policymakers commonly mentioned Vietnam in the same breath with terms like "free nations," "the free world," and "defense of democracy."[2] As one scholar noted, "At stake in Vietnam was each American's place in the divine drama of democracy and freedom."[3]

By the late 1960s, a national groundswell emerged against the war and this entire liberal narrative justifying it. Social activists, student groups, writers, clergy, and political figures led the charge here.[4] The movement sprang from a series of inhumane actions by the United States and its South Vietnamese ally. These events combined with moderator stories to make the war look anything but liberal, leading to widespread disillusionment and a strengthened restraint narrative.

The first major event was the August 1965 torching of Cam Ne. In a television report that carried on-site footage, CBS reporter Morley Safer told the story of U.S. troops burning 150 houses, wounding three women and killing one baby in a cluster of villages, known as Cam Ne. To that point, no reporter had strayed from the U.S. government's official line on the war. "People saw American troops acting in a way they had never seen American troops acting before," Safer later said.[5]

Cam Ne turned out to be far more than an isolated incident. In October 1966, media reports surfaced that U.S. aircraft and artillery leveled a series of villages in Ngai Province and, in 1967, razed the village of Ben Suc.[6] In 1968, disturbing events also occurred during and around the first Tet offensive. A stunning series of candid photographs showed Saigon's police chief carrying out a summary-execution of a Vietcong captive. The photos appeared in media outlets across the United States. Another widely reported incident was an off-handed remark by a U.S. army officer about the burning of yet another village, Ben Tre. "We had to destroy the village to save it," the soldier said. The soldier's comment stood in stark contrast to not only the pro-democracy reasons for the war, but also the official government report that lauded the successful "liberation" of Ben Tre.[7] A third major incident from Tet—the massacre at My Lai—came to light in December 1969. A task force from the 23rd Infantry Division led a slaughter in the village of My Lai on March 16, 1968. Five hundred and two unarmed civilians, including 170 children, were killed and 300 homes destroyed. *Life* magazine published a spread of photos in November 1969 that captured the entire incident.[8]

These events shocked the U.S. public. Pictures of women and children flee-ing burning houses in places like Cam Ne turned all noble justifications for war on their head.[9] "Both Safer and the American public were stunned to see U.S. soldiers casually setting fire to huts in the village while Vietnamese cowered in fear," observed historian Charles Neu, of the Cam Ne incident, "Americans were accustomed to viewing their soldiers as liberators, not avengers."[10] Safer's report caused an uproar at home. As one indication of this, CBS was barraged by phone calls. Coming early in the war and indicative of public dismay, most callers crit-icized the network, labelling the report antiwar propaganda.[11] A similar thing happened with My Lai. Photos of the My Lai incident were first unveiled to a civic group in Cleveland, Ohio. The response was "disbelief and denial," according to one scholar. Historians offered similar descriptions. "It caused a sort of national shockwave," notes Tom Engelhardt, "My Lai had taken Americans to the edge of what they could bear to see. Where the enemy had once been were now innocent victims."[12] Overall, the events of Tet, in particular, were "titanic" in shaking the confidence of the U.S. public in the war.[13]

These developments created a political opportunity space for moderators. Historians such as George Herring claim that all of these events in Vietnam "starkly symbolized the way in which violence had triumphed over moral-ity and law."[14] And, this was, the story that the antiwar movement told about Vietnam—notably, that these war-time events were not just one-off aberrations but, instead an existential challenge to who the nation was at its core, its liberal values. "Immoral and illegal," a United Church of Christ minister called the war following the 1968 Tet offensive. "The United States . . . [has] lost its leadership of the free world," said Dr. Benjamin Spock, a leading antiwar activist, in January 1968.[15] Blame was a big part of the protest movement story too. Soldiers were repeatedly portrayed by the antiwar movement as "hired killers in an 'immoral war.'" Political figures in Washington, DC, were the main target though, charged with perpetrating "American imperialism" and "genocide."[16] By mid-1968, pro-testers regularly blamed President Johnson for the war and worked to debunk the standard Cold War narrative of falling dominoes in Southeast Asia. In re-narrating these events, they charged that the problem was not communism but instead the United States. "To these protestors the United States is the aggres-sor in Vietnam, the war is immoral . . . inhumane," observed one reporter of the protest movement's story.[17]

The inhumanity of the South Vietnamese government, the U.S. ally in the war, added fuel to the immorality story in ways that validated both the public sense that something was wrong and the stories that moderators told. By 1968, reports were streaming out of Saigon about government torture, summary executions, repression of the political opposition, and fraudulent elections.[18]

This fueled moderators all the more. One commentator summed up the existential core (centering on blame and repair) of the protest movement story this way: the antiwar movement wants "a cessation of the American adventure in Vietnam because they cannot live comfortably with selective morality—with a government that proclaims democracy at home and supports puppet dictators abroad . . . [and] winks at torture on the Mekong Delta."[19] The purpose of demonstrations, sit-ins, and the like was to produce, as one observer noted at the time, "moral shock" in order to wake a "dormant, insensitive society into recognizing its moral failures."[20] For moderators, Vietnam was a national tragedy that reflected the nation's violation of its deepest values. "We're not on the wrong side," said Daniel Ellsberg, who leaked the Pentagon Papers on the war, at a rally in 1972, "We are the wrong side."[21]

This kind of existential narration of events showed up in moderator claims that the war was unconstitutional as well. "This war is illegal," charged Representative Ron Dellums, at an antiwar protest. Dellums blamed his colleagues for being "caught up in their own aggrandizement and expediency" at the expense of defending the U.S. Constitution.[22] Moderators hammered this theme, in fact, about the lack of democratic accountability and runaway executive power. Charges of cover-up and deception (again, blame) were common and, often, justified. Take Cam Ne, for instance. In sharp contrast to Safer's story, the official military report on Cam Ne claimed that only one building burned and 1,287 enemy combatants were killed in an "impressive military victory."[23] In a way that helped increase the salience of moderator stories, television footage from the war and photographs like those of My Lai showed the U.S. public a different picture from official government accounts like these.[24]

Military developments on the ground did the same thing. The 1968 Tet offensive is illustrative. In sharp contrast to government reports that victory was "just over the horizon," the powerful and well-coordinated North Vietnamese attack told a different story to the public. The result was traumatic, sending "shockwaves" through the country, according to one scholar.[25] At the center of this shock was a deep sense of deceit. "Tet exposed a lie," according to one historian, as it "shattered the veil of government rhetoric and mythology."[26] Moderator charges of presidential abuse of power gained added public resonance with events like these. Again, blame was everywhere in the moderator story. "Freaks are running this communistic country," a protester leader charged at one rally.[27] "Cease fire— Nixon is a Liar," others chanted after President Richard Nixon resumed bombing of North Vietnam in 1972.[28] "Nixon . . . has badly misled and deceived" the nation in what one newspaper called a "new reign of terror."[29] Events like the "secret" bombing of Cambodia, horror of the protesters shot at Kent State University, and Watergate further deepened a "see, I told you so" reaction across the nation.

The moderator narrative about the immoral, unconstitutional behavior of an "imperial presidency" outside the bounds of accountability took hold.[30] "The contention that the war is immoral is widely accepted as fact and anyone who says otherwise these days can expect to be laughed down as a relic of another age," wrote one commentator in late 1971. In this vein, My Lai with all of its brutality came to be viewed cynically, he said, by the U.S. public as a typical combat operation in Vietnam.[31] Opinion surveys told the same story. By 1968, 68 percent of the public felt that Vietnam was a mistake—that number had been well below 50 percent until 1967. By 1971, 58 percent said the war was immoral—a complete reversal from a 1966 survey where 59 percent regarded the war in Vietnam as "morally justified."[32] Sentiments like these only hardened as time passed. A 1977 survey found that 70 percent believed that Vietnam was "more than a mistake, fundamentally wrong and immoral."[33]

The war created widespread disillusionment, which is common with internal trauma. "The United States is a country torn by self-doubt," said Representative Richard Ottinger (D-NY), in a 1969 congressional debate on Vietnam, "This is surely the most devastating war for our national spirit in our whole history." Another member of Congress commented that national unity had collapsed in "an acid sea of hate, self-doubt, and self-recrimination." Assessments like these were held by both Democrats and Republicans.[34] In his 1969 State of the Union address, President Nixon referred, for instance, to the Vietnam experience in existential terms, calling the war years the "long dark night of the American spirit."[35] He later complained that the "guilt-ridden carping" of the antiwar movement proved "traumatizing" for the United States.[36] Historians described disillusionment similarly, commenting on it as a "lack of confidence"; "wave of disengagement sentiment"; "loss of nerve"; and noting that "guilt has . . . paralyzed us."[37] In sum, disillusionment flourished in the late Vietnam War years. For our purposes, this opened space for a restraint narrative to take hold across the nation—a tale that centered on events in a distant land, villainous government policies, and, most important, lessons for the nation moving forward. That narrative became a fixture in U.S. foreign policy to the end of the Cold War.

The Vietnam Syndrome

Over the final two decades of the Cold War, "the lens of Vietnam" dominated national foreign policy discussions.[38] More specifically, "no more Vietnams" became a new collective mantra for the nation. Historians and commentators describe this Vietnam syndrome as a deep national aversion to the direct use of military force for regime promotion, especially in the developing world.[39] This restraint narrative was, in essence, the moral of the internal trauma story of the 1970s. It showed up repeatedly in moderator storytelling about the war. "Now I feel that although we can't end this war," one protest leader said, in 1968, "We will prevent the country from getting into the next one."[40] That moral—to prevent "the next one"—indeed settled in with the nation and eventually showed up everywhere across the political landscape. A 1975 Gallup survey that asked, for instance, how the United States should respond to "an attack by communist-backed forces" on specific U.S. allies found that support for sending U.S. troops was well below 50 percent in each case, except Canada (Germany 27%, Japan 16%, Brazil 15%, and Turkey 9%). The most common response was "do nothing."[41] As trauma theory anticipates, the lessons of the restraint narrative lasted well beyond the events of the 1970s too. A 1985 survey found that less than 50 percent supported using force to stop communism from spreading, with 83 percent agreeing that the United States should "remember the lesson of Vietnam—that there are limits to American power."[42] As Stanley Karnow observed, in a 1980 column, "The legacy of Vietnam has been to instill in Americans a sense of caution."[43]

The syndrome was evident in and became further entrenched across the public with major policy debates in the 1970s. Congress adopted legislation to ensure "No More Vietnams" as a means to repair the existential damage from the war. Above all else, it curbed the kinds of commitment-making authority that led to Vietnam. The war started small, for instance, with a commitment of military aid and advisors to South Vietnam and progressively dragged the United States into all-out combat operations from there. In order to prevent these "escalating entanglements" and "creeping commitments" in the future, Congress cut military training programs and aid as well as reduced arms sales to allied states.[44] The moves were widely praised. The *Washington Post* commented, for instance, that the new restrictions "belong right up there with the War Powers Act as one of the most valuable pieces of foreign policy legislation in the post-Vietnam era."[45]

Congress also barred aid to governments that violated human rights. Here again, the move was a repair, or an "emotional reaction to Vietnam."[46] It reflected the moral of the Vietnam story. Stephen Rosenfeld observed, in 1975, for instance, "The Vietnam experience gave a powerful stimulus to the feeling in the country that we ought to stop supporting the 'wrong side' or the 'bad guys' around the world and, instead, get with the democrats, the liberals, and the partisans of political liberty."[47] Congressional human rights conditions on military aid satisfied this inclination. They were also meant to, again, prevent creeping commitments. In the 1970s, a prevailing lesson from Vietnam—again, part of the restraint narrative that moderators constructed at the time—was that inhumane, nondemocratic client regimes (like the one in South Vietnam) were more likely to need direct U.S. military intervention to avoid being toppled.[48] Weapons to "notoriously unstable [countries] . . . could trap us as we were trapped in Vietnam," noted the editors of the *Boston Globe*, in defense of the new restrictions on military aid.[49] Intended to repair the causes of the Vietnam trauma, aid conditioned on human rights was part and parcel of the "usurpation of policymaking that . . . marked the post-Vietnam era."[50]

These same themes drove the 1973 War Powers Resolution, the marquee piece of commitment-curbing legislation. The measure centered on the lesson of preventing "another Vietnam."[51] Of the twenty-eight senators who spoke in the final Senate debate on this legislation, twenty-three talked about the need to prevent a repeat of the Vietnam War. The "tragic experience" of Vietnam produced commitments that "have come to haunt us," said one supporter of the legislation.[52] "The Vietnam war divided our country," said Senator Pete Dominici (R-NM), "This was not an 'American war' because in a real way Congress had not declared it as such."[53] This theme of constitutionality, which of course reflected the broader existential story that moderators told about the war, ran through many statements. "We have reaped, in the Vietnam conflict, the whirlwind of our failure to abide by our constitutional principles," said Senator Edward Brooke (R-MA). He went on, then, to emphasize repair: "however, if out of this tragedy comes the impetus to correct our mistakes, we may avoid a repeat of past follies."[54] Other members of Congress told the prevailing restraint story too, linking the events in Vietnam to the solutions (i.e., repair) found in the legislation with trauma-related terms like "tribulation," "wounds," "tragic experience," and "enormous injury."[55] These same elements of the restraint narrative—existential danger, blame, and repair—pulsed through the broader national discussion at the time as well. "The mood to curb presidential war-making power [i.e., moral] . . . followed the long tribulation in Indochina [i.e., events and trauma]," wrote the *Los Angeles Times*, "The unchecked authority of a President to commit this nation to war is more power than a President should have [i.e., blame]." Papers ranging from the *Des Moines Register* and *Denver Post* to *Atlanta Constitution* and *Chicago Tribune* echoed similar themes, all of which centered on the conventional restraint story.[56]

Finally, the restraint narrative shaped policy outcomes in the 1970s, particularly in situations that resembled Vietnam. The debate over aid to Angolan rebels offers a poignant example. In September 1975, news broke of a covert aid program to anticommunist rebels in Angola. U.S. engagement in a chaotic, tropical Third World country looked too familiar for most. It conjured up, again, the story and lessons at the heart of the restraint narrative. Fears of another Vietnam created, above all else, a political firestorm.[57] "With the bitter experience of intervention in a complicated civil war in Asia, the United States should take great care to avoid involvement in [Angola]," noted the *New York Times.*[58] "The situation is enough like that which prevailed in Viet Nam a decade and a half ago to be chilling," the conservative *Chicago Tribune* warned.[59] The *Washington Post* claimed that "Angola already is another Vietnam."[60]

Members of Congress attacked the aid request along the same lines. "In poll after poll in recent years, the American people have made it clear—no more Vietnams," said Senator John Tunney (D-CA).[61] "We ought not to get in on the ground floor of a budding Vietnam," said Senator Dominici.[62] Themes of trauma and blame from the Vietnam story surfaced. We need to avoid "growing and undesired commitments" and becoming entangled with a faction that has "no popular support to establish a legitimate government," said a pair of senators.[63] Supporters of aid, like Senator Jake Garn, admitted that "Vietnam . . . [is contributing] to our paralysis in Angola."[64] Garn's appeal to combat communism fell on deaf ears (an expected outcome in this narrative context). Congress passed the Clark Amendment (named after its main sponsor, Senator Richard Clark [D-IA]), which prohibited further covert operations in Angola.[65] The Vietnam syndrome helped generate this limited policy outcome as it did in other cases like the Carter administration's effort to counter Soviet/Cuban activity in Ethiopia later in the decade.[66]

It is important to note that the Vietnam syndrome did not necessarily make every foreign policy initiative—including some that required force—taboo. President Ford's 1975 decision to rescue by force captive U.S. sailors aboard the *Mayaguez* was overwhelmingly popular in the United States, for instance. The same goes for the 1975 decision to send U.S. troops back into South Vietnam to evacuate U.S. personnel prior to the fall of Saigon.[67] What made these situations different? Unlike Angola or Ethiopia, they showed little resemblance to Vietnam, since force in neither case was intended for regime promotion. This helped mitigate fears of a drawn-out military engagement for ends that looked messy, and maybe illiberal. As seen below, similar dynamics also mattered in explaining differences in forceful regime promotion in El Salvador and Grenada.

The Liberal Narrative

The 1970s were a tumultuous time for the liberal narrative. Trauma theory anticipates that during periods of disillusionment, the liberal narrative often weakens. This happened in the United States in the late 1960s and early 1970s. According to many scholars, one disillusioning revelation after another created uncertainty and deep confusion across the U.S. polity about the country's role abroad. "A lack of confidence in the innate superiority of the American way of life" emerged along with the loss of a "grand narrative" or "vision of the future."[68]

Many across the political spectrum shared these assessments. Neoconservatives, like Ben Wattenburg, talked in 1973, for example, about "a lack of passion, of conviction in the essential idea of freedom and human liberty" that seemed to grip the United States at the time. Secretary of State Henry Kissinger talked of a pervasive national "self-hatred," centering on the "myth that the enemy is us."[69] Indicative of the weakened liberal narrative, a 1972 poll found Americans cared little if a noncommunist government took power in Vietnam. A 1974 survey demonstrated, likewise, that Americans ranked "containing communism" as only the fourth most important foreign policy goal behind things like securing jobs for American citizens and arms control.[70] Overall, the nation's sense of purpose around the Cold War objectives of protecting and promoting liberal order abroad flagged in the early 1970s.

As anticipated by trauma theory, this weakening in the liberal narrative did not last long, though. A series of geostrategic gains by the Soviet bloc coupled with a new wave of promoter storytelling strengthened the liberal narrative into the early 1980s and through the remainder of the Cold War. This new wave of storytelling started with Angola and Ethiopia. While the policy discussion around both of these cases reflected the strong restraint narrative of the times, Soviet bloc intrusion into both countries also sparked something else in the United States: a growing chorus of promoter tales sounding the alarm of the communist challenge and calling for a more robust defense of liberal order abroad. A 1975 editorial by James Kilpatrick is illustrative. Kilpatrick told a detailed story of a country becoming "a virtual satellite of the Soviet Union"; elaborated on the dangers this presented (i.e., "consider the worst prospect") to other noncommunist states in southern Africa and to U.S. security; blamed Kissinger's détente ("indifferent" and "flabby" policies) for the outcomes; and called for repair ("decisive action") on the part of the United States.[71] Stories like this—ones that centered on telling/retelling of threatening events, blaming weak U.S. policies, and calling for greater defense of liberal order—proliferated across the late 1970s and into the 1980s.

At the center of this promoter surge stood a group of Democrats who disagreed with the prevailing trend in the Democratic Party (which President Jimmy Carter reflected) to downplay the ideological challenge from the Soviet Union to the United States. In 1976, these neoconservatives formed the Committee on Present Danger and began to attack Carter's foreign policy.[72] The standard promoter story showed up repeatedly. "Can Freedom and traditional American values survive once the lights go out in the rest of the world?" Walter Lacquer asked, rhetorically about existential danger in a column that told stories about communist advances in Africa and blamed the Carter administration for its weak response.[73] Wattenburg argued similarly in 1979: "There *are* Communists and their footprints are still menacing."[74] Some hawkish Democrats in Congress echoed the same themes. Our policy in Africa has "the mark of appeasement," said Senator Henry Jackson (D-WA) in 1978.[75]

As the Soviet bloc made further gains, these promoter stories found broader traction. By late 1978, liberal narrative themes of existential danger abroad and blame surfaced more in mainstream political discourse. Comments to this effect centered on things like Soviet "world domination," the expanding list of "Marxist-Leninist client states," and the "indecisiveness" of Carter's foreign policy.[76] The 1979 Soviet invasion of Afghanistan amped up and validated this story all the more, generating a renewed sense of national mission to stand for freedom against communism. Reminiscent of the late 1940s, editorials used terms like "disturbing," "Satan Russia," and "rape of Afghanistan" to describe the invasion and the sense of existential danger across the nation.[77] Super-charged by debates in the 1980 presidential campaign, promoters repeatedly told the story of Afghanistan's collapse, warned of grave danger ahead for other noncommunist states, and demanded policy change. Carter became a symbol of U.S. paralysis (i.e., blame) as calls went up for a more active defense of liberal order (i.e., lesson and moral).[78] "Adversaries large and small test our will and seek to confound our resolve but the Carter administration gives us weakness when we need strength, vacillation when the times demand firmness," said Republican presidential nominee Ronald Reagan.[79] Many others, including Democratic contenders for the presidency, made similar charges.[80]

These tales about the international scene resonated with the nation. By 1980, a national panic to combat communism became mainstream once again. Commentators talked about how the fear of a Soviet "plan for global domination" "rejuvenated" the nation for "Cold War II."[81] The *Dallas Morning News* noted that Carter's talk in 1977 about the "inordinate fear of communism . . . was not so 'inordinate' after all."[82] Stanley Karnow observed of the national conversation that "a degree of idealism has been revived and some of the old jingoism has come back" in what he now called "the post-post-Vietnam period."[83] A headline in a major newspaper read, in February 1980, "Crises Stir Militant Mood."[84] Others echoed the same: "America Aroused" and "Caging the Bear."[85] Historians also talked of the "major shift in public attitudes" and "altered ideological environment" that came with the 1980 events.[86] For the first time in twenty years, a majority (60%) of the American public supported an increase in military spending.[87] Furthermore, 67 percent agreed in January 1980 that the United States needs to "get tougher in its dealings with the Russians"—up from 35 percent in June 1978.[88] A poll later in the decade found that 57 percent of U.S. citizens believed that "in thinking about all the different kinds of government in the world today (communism) is the worst kind," while 73 percent agreed that "more than ever . . . it is the duty of the United States to prevent the communists from taking over the world."[89] Statements and poll numbers like these reflected a return of liberal narrative strength—the moral of the promoter story to stop communism settled in again as a conventional approach to world affairs.

This narrative shift helped propel the conservative Republican, Ronald Reagan, to victory in the November 1980 presidential election. He soon learned the challenges of making regime promotion policy in an age of two strong and competing master narratives.

El Salvador

When Ronald Reagan took office, the anticommunist military junta in El Salvador faced a powerful leftist resistance movement, the Frente Farabundo Martí de Liberación Nacional (FMLN). Before leaving the White House, President Carter loosened congressionally imposed, human rights sanctions with the provision of $5.7 million in military aid to the junta.[90] Promoters inside the new Reagan administration (led by Secretary of State Alexander Haig) wanted far more than this. With the robust liberal narrative, they saw an opportunity—a free hand of sorts—to press a bold anticommunist initiative, or "take a stand" as Haig would say, in El Salvador. These promoters got Reagan's attention early in his administration. The president agreed to a counterinsurgency plan—the first of its kind since Vietnam—to bolster the Salvadoran junta. This led to the dispatch of four teams of U.S. military advisors to El Salvador, reprogramming of $25 million for military assistance, and a request to Congress in late 1981 for an additional $70 million in military aid.[91]

Promoters used the liberal narrative to build a discourse to generate support for the new policy. The State Department released, for instance, a February white paper to paint a picture of increased Soviet/Cuban interference in El Salvador. Following the white paper's release, promoters claimed that U.S. military force might be next. Along these lines, Deputy Assistant Secretary of State William Clark said publicly that the administration was prepared to use "whatever means" necessary to save El Salvador. Haig called publicly, as well, for a "full range of economic, political, and security measures" to curb Cuban/Soviet influence in Central America.[92]

The white paper resonated and sparked a wider liberal discourse. "Of course, a communist takeover in El Salvador would not be in the American interests, nor the interests of the average Salvadoran," wrote the editors of the *Raleigh News and Observer*.[93] The new chairman of the Senate Foreign Relation Committee, Senator Charles Percy (R-IL), charged that the United States needed to take all steps necessary to "prevent a Communist takeover in El Salvador." House Major- ity Leader Jim Wright (D-TX) commented on the vital importance of Central America and Senator Robert Byrd (D-WV) called Soviet/Cuban interference in El Salvador "totally unacceptable." The nation needed, Byrd said, to get past the paralysis of Vietnam and actively combat communism.[94] Overall, political pres- sure linking the liberal narrative to El Salvador became especially pronounced in 1981.

By late March, a powerful restraint discourse emerged to challenge this liberal discourse, however. A wide-coalition of moderators that included antiwar activ- ists, human rights groups, the Catholic Church and former government officials like Robert White (President Carter's ambassador to El Salvador) led the charge here.[95] Many challenged the white paper, claiming that conflict was fueled not by the Soviet Union but the inhumanity of the Salvadoran regime instead. The argu- ments of Maryknoll priests in El Salvador were especially important, providing direct evidence of human rights abuses. Critics drew parallels to Vietnam, with aid to the Salvadoran junta and U.S. advisors cast as first steps down a slippery slope to full-scale intervention for a weak, unpopular ally.[96]

These arguments by moderators touched a nerve for the nation, sparking a broad restraint discourse around El Salvador. Parallels to Vietnam were every- where. "The 'next' Vietnam?" asked the *Des Moines Register*, in response to the vague statements by Haig about the use of force.[97] "Currently the government says there are 54 military advisors in El Salvador . . . Does that sound familiar?" said the *Atlanta Constitution*, in drawing parallels to Vietnam, "Advisors. More advisors. A few troops. More troops."[98] Commentators talked extensively of how arms, advisors, and support for a brutal regime in El Salvador all pointed to another dangerous "slide into Vietnam."[99] A popular bumper sticker at the time read, "El Salvador is Spanish for Vietnam."[100] Supporters of Reagan's policy, like the *Wall Street Journal*, conceded that Vietnam was "cropping up in the news- paper cartoons and columns."[101] This broad discourse was reflected in opinion polls too. A 1982 survey found that two out of three U.S. citizens believed that it was "very likely" or "fairly likely" that "U.S. [engagement] in El Salvador could turn into a situation like Vietnam."[102] Another found 89 percent of the public opposed sending U.S. troops to El Salvador. White House mail ran 10-1 against Reagan's policy.[103] "Vietnam provides the emotional kindling, the passion, as well as frame of reference for the national debate," observed Don Oberdorfer, of the discourse around El Salvador.[104]

The same restraint narrative discourse showed up on Capitol Hill too. Rep- resentative Clarence Long (D-MD) was especially vocal. He worried most that casualties among U.S. advisors would become an excuse for escalation—"a kind of Gulf of Tonkin resolution," he said.[105] Long was not alone. Many feared the loss of El Salvador, but were even more frightened by the prospects of another Vietnam. This was reflected in a running dialogue in the spring among members of Congress from both parties about the dangers of advisors, military aid and human rights conditions in El Salvador.[106]

Overall, by mid-1981, the master narrative landscape generated high audience costs for both action and inaction. Congress took steps to reconcile these competing pressures. It approved military aid to El Salvador, but at a much lower level ($25 million) than the $70 million Reagan requested. Congress also conditioned military aid on a report from the administration every six months certifying progress on human rights by the Salvadoran government.[107] This outcome was essentially a bargain between the two robust master narrative discourses of the day. On the one hand, continued aid (rather than full termination) and approval of some military advisors showed resolve in preventing the spread of communism. Congress appeared, therefore, in-step with the liberal narrative. For Democrats, this was especially important to their public image. It meant that they avoided "the chilling . . . examples," according to one Democratic staffer on Capitol Hill, "of Senators [Dick] Clark and [Frank] Church," who led the charge to curb anticommunist legislation in the 1970s, but then lost their Senate seats in subsequent elections, in part, for being perceived as "weak on communism."[108] Allowing some aid to El Salvador reflected, then, the power of costs for inaction associated with the liberal discourse in this period.

On the other hand, the reduced aid levels and certification matched the restraint narrative moral for a not-too-militarized solution to problems like El Salvador. By pressuring the Salvadoran regime to improve human rights and hence become more legitimate at home, the United States could avoid being dragged into the conflict. This found wide appeal on Capitol Hill, including with moderate Republicans, like Senator Percy.[109] "I don't want another Vietnam," Percy said, during the foreign aid debate, "The nation doesn't want another Vietnam . . . We must have a government down there that we can support."[110]

This syndrome-based pushback also constrained Reagan's policy decisions at two points in 1981. First, the restraint discourse (or better yet, the prospect of it) limited policy from the very start of the administration. In a January meeting at Blair House prior to Reagan's inauguration, Haig pressed the president to take robust military action in El Salvador and the Caribbean. In addition to a major increase in aid and advisors (far more, in fact, than what the administration eventually proposed), Haig wanted an "augmented U.S. military presence in the region."[111] A chief component of this was an invasion of Cuba. By making Cuba "a parking lot," Haig argued, the United States would end, once and for all, the flow of arms to the Salvadoran rebels (and the Sandinista regime in Nicaragua).[112] Like neoconservatives, he believed that incrementalism was the chief reason for defeat in Vietnam. Haig advocated, then, quick, robust action in El Salvador. "Mr. President, this is one you can win," he said at one of the first National Security Council (NSC) meetings.[113]

Haig's proposals faced major resistance—all of which centered on the restraint narrative—from moderators inside the administration. This group included Secretary of Defense Caspar Weinberger, Chief of Staff James Baker, Deputy Chief of Staff Michael Deaver and Counselor to the President Edwin Meese.[114] All shared one thing in common: a sensitivity to public worries about "another Vietnam." Weinberger's concerns reflected those of the military establishment more widely. Appalled by the public's post-Vietnam backlash against the U.S. military, he felt that force should only be used at points when military action had strong public support. "You can't fight Congress and public opinion and an enemy at the same time," said Weinberger, "That's why Vietnam was the crime of the century."[115] For the others, the issue was about domestic priorities. These more pragmatic advisors were leery of initiatives that drew valuable political capital away from the administration's chief goal of moving beyond the economic stagnation of the late 1970s. From the start, Haig's Central America policies sparked these kinds of concerns. "It scared the shit out of me," said Deaver of Haig's plan.[116] Given the political costs of crossing the powerful Vietnam syndrome, Deaver and his cohorts saw "Central America as a political loser," likely to distract from plans to improve the economy.[117] Overall, administration moderators worried extensively about the costs for action from a robust restraint discourse.

Weinberger set the tone for this group at the January Blair House meetings, openly opposing Haig's ideas for military action in Central America and the Caribbean. "I told the President," Weinberger later recounted, "One of the principal lessons I had learned from the Vietnam experience was that we could not suddenly explode upon the American people a full-fledged war and expect their support."[118] Syndrome pushback like this grew more intense in a series of NSC meetings on El Salvador beginning January 23. All agreed on more economic aid, combatting the communists and a new ambassador to El Salvador. Dissension arose, though, over two syndrome-related issues: military advisors and security assistance.[119] Moderators in the late January meetings hammered the domestic costs of these actions, drawing attention, according to Haig, to the "background noise in the press and Congress" that might come with "another tropical war into which American troops and money would be poured with no result different than Vietnam."[120] Indicative of apprehension over a syndrome-driven backlash, large amounts of time were spent during the January meetings on how to limit the role of the advisors, both in number and scope of mission. At one meeting, an entire hour was devoted, for instance, to whether or not advisors should carry rifles and appear in civilian clothes or uniforms. Topics like procedures on consulting Congress and how to handle the press also led to long, drawn-out discussions. Overall, each of these internal debates shared one thing in common: a deep concern about avoiding syndrome-generated political fallout and the costs for action that would come as a result. Haig described the incessant deliberations as "anguishing."[121]

In the end, the power of the restraint narrative augmented moderator arguments in the January meetings. Reagan eventually came to share moderator concerns about costs for action posed by policy options at odds with the moral of the prevailing restraint narrative.[122] Hence, the president turned aside Haig's more bellicose policy suggestions on Cuba in early 1981. He agreed with the moderators that U.S. advisors in El Salvador be increased by only twenty-six and prohibited from entering combat zones. On military aid, the president also decided to ask Congress for far less in security assistance than what the pentagon (and Haig) felt was necessary for the Salvadoran government to win the war. According to historians and administration officials, each of these steps was intended to avoid inciting syndrome concerns. Moderators also succeeded in delaying the release of the State Department's white paper until after Reagan announced his plan for economic recovery.[123]

The second major point in 1981 where the restraint discourse constrained the Reagan administration came with the public and congressional outburst following release of the white paper. "The White House did not appreciate how rapidly El Salvador would take off in the minds of the press as another Vietnam," said one White House aide.[124] Another aid agreed, "Al Haig opened the jar and he didn't, perhaps, realize how many genies were in it."[125] Throughout March, Haig and El Salvador dominated the headlines in ways that, most important for the moderators inside the administration, eclipsed Reagan initiatives to revive the economy. "Important as Central America was, it diverted attention from our top priority [i.e., the economy], which we wanted to be the only priority," said Reagan political advisor David Gergen, "We decided we had to cut off his [Haig's] story."[126] Baker did just that. He commissioned the White House pollster Richard Wirthlin to conduct a survey on El Salvador. Wirthlin's poll (conducted March 6–8) found deep public suspicion of Haig's discussion of Central America and Cuba. Baker went to Reagan, who, upon review of the poll numbers, agreed that the audience costs around the administration's El Salvador policy were daunting. He instructed Baker to kill Haig's message.[127]

Baker used the president's backing in March to get Haig to, as Baker noted, "knock it off" about El Salvador.[128] As the secretary of state became less bellicose and El Salvador faded from the headlines, Haig's imprint on policy further diminished.[129] Of greatest importance, the administration altered policy to accommodate the restraint discourse and with it, congressional concerns about policy toward El Salvador. In mid-April, Reagan said for the first time that violence *"by all sides,"* including the government, must end. In July, the administration went one step further. Assistant Secretary of State for Latin American Affairs Thomas Enders delivered a speech that laid out a new approach to El Salvador. Enders downplayed the Cold War nature of the Salvadoran conflict and, most important, adopted the congressional two-track policy—military aid for counterinsurgency *in tandem* with democratic reform in El Salvador. Enders criticized the violence of the far right and spent nearly half of the speech discussing upcoming elections in El Salvador.[130]

State Department memos show that the Enders speech was all about bringing policy in line with the lessons of the Vietnam syndrome. As one document noted, the central objectives of the speech was to "accommodate fears of Vietnam-escalation among the public and Congress" and demonstrate that "human rights is the core of our policy."[131] Neoconservatives referred to the new approach as "badly muddied."[132] While meant derisively, descriptions like these were accurate. In accommodating congressional/public concerns, the Reagan administration indeed retreated to a mixed policy toward El Salvador in late 1981 that, at its core, reflected a bargain between the audience costs associated with two powerful narratives—the liberal narrative around anticommunism and restraint narrative of the Vietnam syndrome. The latter ensured, in particular, that direct force would not be (at least for the time being) a part of Washington's regime promotion strategy in El Salvador.

El Salvador, 1983

Promoters were not done in 1981. Sudden bursts of FMLN military gains over the next two years again brought out hardliner arguments for a more robust military approach in El Salvador. By drawing on liberal narrative concerns, these appeals yielded some increases in military aid. Yet, like 1981, the more promoters pushed, the more they fueled national concerns around the restraint narrative moral—"no more Vietnams." This augmented moderators, who successfully helped steer policy away from force in El Salvador. In the end, then, promoters only helped deepen the constrained, "muddled" policy that they so disdained.

Developments in 1983 demonstrate this. In January, an unexpected series of FMLN military gains in El Salvador caused panic inside the White House. Led by National Security Advisor William Clark and CIA Director Bill Casey (Haig resigned in July 1982), a group of promoters attacked Enders' policy toward El Salvador, marginalized the State Department, and took control of Central

America policy.[133] The intent was the "wholesale Americanization" of the war in El Salvador.[134] Promoters pushed for an additional 160 military advisors for El Salvador and convinced the president to request $110 million in emergency military aid—more than a four-fold increase from the prior year.[135]

The administration also launched a broad public relations campaign that, again, cast the civil war in Cold War terms. The intent was to elevate costs for inaction in such a way as to bludgeon Congress into supporting more aid. "I'm in favor of doing what we can and not being afraid of Congress," said Casey, in a January NSC meeting.[136] By tapping into the robust liberal narrative, Casey reasoned that members of Congress would go along with the administration request in order to avoid being blamed for having "lost all of Central America."[137] Reagan became an especially powerful voice here. On April 27, he gave a nationally televised speech before Congress that focused exclusively on the new aid request. After laying out the Cold War implications, he ended the speech with this: "Who among us would wish to bear the responsibility for failure to meet our shared objectives?"[138]

The administration's anticommunist campaign had the effect of again sparking wide discourse around both the restraint and liberal narratives. The nation was deeply conflicted. On the one hand, the pressure of the liberal narrative was palpable. A 1983 NBC News poll found that 68 percent of Americans believed that "communist activities in Central America are a threat to our national security."[139] It is little wonder, then, that Reagan's final comment in his April speech hung over legislators and the conversation around aid to El Salvador. "Everyone agrees with the objectives of the President," said Senator Wyche Fowler (D-GA), "We all don't like communism."[140] Liberals, like Christopher Dodd (D-CT) commented similarly, "We will oppose the establishment of Marxist states in Central America. . . . All patriotic Americans share this goal."[141] From Capitol Hill to newspaper editorials, comments like these were common in early 1983.[142] Casey's assessment, then, turned out to be right. Legislators recognized public hesitation about using direct force in El Salvador, but also feared possible electoral implications if communism spread in Central America.[143] "No one wants to be blamed for 'losing El Salvador,'" observed the liberal *New York Times*.[144] The liberal discourse around El Salvador was strong in the United States, creating powerful audience costs for inaction for legislators, especially in 1983.

The restraint discourse was robust as well, however. The Reagan administration's ideological campaign once again drew out fears of "another Vietnam." The same NBC poll mentioned above found, for instance, that 50 percent disagreed (and only 30% agreed) that "in some cases U.S. troops should be used to overthrow communist-controlled governments in Central America and the Caribbean."[145] Likewise, 60 percent in 1983 felt that U.S. military aid to El Salvador "will inevitably lead to another Vietnam for the United States."[146] Similar to 1981, the syndrome concerns reflected in these poll numbers were everywhere in the political discourse. "Vietnam is in the air"; "the Vietnam analogy"; and the "lessons of the Vietnam War" were the kind of phrases that repeatedly showed up in media and congressional circles.[147] To most members of Congress, the regime in El Salvador looked as "fatally flawed" as the one in Saigon—fear abounded of a slippery slope to war.[148] Audience costs for action were high.

Overall, the nation was torn again between competing narrative pressures in 1983. The *New York Times* summed it up this way: "What is it . . . [that] politics demands? Don't 'lose' El Salvador and don't get involved in another Vietnam. No lose, no win."[149]

Like 1981, policy came to reflect a bargain between the competing master narratives, which resulted again in no forceful regime promotion by the United States. Pressure from the liberal narrative led Congress to approve a major increase in military aid. Reflecting the Vietnam syndrome, the approved aid was, however, at a level ($64 million) far below the nearly $140 million requested by the administration. Furthermore, Congress conditioned 30 percent of the new military assistance on Salvadoran progress in solving certain cases of human rights abuses involving U.S. citizens. Leery of Vietnam-style creeping commitments, Congress also capped the number of U.S. advisors allowed in El Salvador at fifty-five and limited those advisors to noncombat support roles.[150]

As with 1981, the powerful restraint discourse augmented Reagan's more pragmatic advisors. In a March 4 meeting, Secretary of State George Shultz told the president that hardliners, like Clark, were creating a "self-inflicted wound" for the administration by playing "straight into the argument that El Salvador was the next Vietnam."[151] Others sounded the same theme. "The crazies want to get us into war," warned Baker in April, "We cannot get this economic recovery program going if we get involved in a land war in Central America."[152] Audience costs for inaction bore down, in short, on Reagan's advisors. Eventually, they bore down on the president too. As the restraint discourse brewed outside of government, pragmatists slowly won the president over. In watching the 1983 congressional aid debate as well as the political uproar created by a series of promoter-conceived U.S. military exercises (Big Pine I and II) meant to mimic a regime change invasion in Central America, Reagan recognized that his policies made him look "too pugnacious [and] . . . like a warmonger," according to Shultz.[153] The president later conceded, "The post-Vietnam syndrome . . . [generated] a depth of isolationism in the country that I hadn't seen since the Great Depression."[154]

With hardliners taking the administration into a political black hole, Reagan concluded that the audience costs of a more aggressive, militarized approach in

El Salvador were too high. This helped temper U.S. policy. In March, Shultz convinced Reagan not to increase the number of U.S. advisors and to publicly commit not to use force in El Salvador. To ease syndrome concerns and bring policy in line with the restraint narrative, Reagan hit on the latter issue directly, in a March 10 speech: "Are we going to send American soldiers into combat? The answer to that is a flat no."[155] He repeated the pledge several times across the rest of the year.

The intensification of the restraint discourse in the summer led to even more policy adjustments. By August, the president turned his back entirely on promoters inside the administration.[156] Shultz now regained full control over Central America policy. Admitting that policy on El Salvador was "like walking through a swamp," Shultz moved expeditiously to accommodate moderator demands by matching policy to the lessons of the restraint narrative.[157] Starting in the fall of 1983, the State Department initiated an unprecedented, high-profile campaign for human rights improvements and democratization in El Salvador that eventually led to free and fair presidential elections in 1984. In response to this, Congress approved large increases in military and economic aid to El Salvador. But, most important for our purposes, the use of direct force never again entered U.S. policy discussions on El Salvador. The powerful restraint discourse around the Vietnam syndrome made certain of that.[158]

Grenada

Grenada in 1983 resembled El Salvador in many ways. Located in the same general region of the world as El Salvador, a leftist regime took control of the island nation in 1979. Like El Salvador, a communist bloc presence emerged in Grenada as Cuban military aid and advisors arrived to support the new leftist government. Like El Salvador, President Reagan publicly highlighted the dangers of the communist drift in Grenada at several points in 1982 and 1983.[159]

The parallels between U.S. policy toward Grenada and El Salvador end there, however. For unlike El Salvador, the United States opted for a full-scale forceful regime change invasion of Grenada on October 25, 1983. How do we explain this? The answer is two-fold. First, the possibility of American hostages in Grenada brought additional costs for inaction (beside those related to communism's spread) that pressed the Reagan administration toward regime change. Second and just as important, the Grenada case was marked by a weak restraint discourse. More specifically, certain idiosyncrasies of the decision-making process—namely the distraction of other issues for moderators, the secrecy around the policy debate on Grenada, and, again, the hostages—helped prevent (or led Reagan officials to believe they would prevent) the emergence of a strong restraint discourse here. This opened political space in the restraint narrative landscape, lowering the administration's costs for action in ways that encouraged the gamble on full-scale regime change in Grenada.

The story begins with a regime crisis. On October 13, 1983, a radical communist faction inside Grenada's government placed the leftist prime minister, Maurice Bishop, under house arrest and took over the regime. This led to widespread protests. The new government responded with violence. On October 19, it executed Bishop, imposed a strict curfew and initiated a repressive campaign to maintain order.[160]

These events alarmed the U.S. government. While some hardliners worried about communism, the overwhelming concern for nearly all administration officials was the plight of close to 1,000 U.S. citizens on the island, especially 600 students at St. George's Medical School.[161] This issue dominated policy debates.[162] The new government's brutality raised fears of a repeat of the Iran-hostage crisis, a politically loaded scenario given the political damage the crisis inflicted on Jimmy Carter's presidency. "Once the announcement of the twenty-four-hour curfew, with its open license to kill, was made," noted Secretary of Defense Weinberger, "We naturally had to think about how we could . . . prevent [U.S. citizens] being seized as hostages in a reprise of the Iranian seizure of our citizens and capture of our Embassy in Tehran."[163] In a meeting on October 19, Deputy Secretary of State Kenneth Dam said that without action soon, the administration "might have some dead students on its hands."[164] With no assurances that the Grenadian government would protect foreign nationals, parallels to Iran drove policymakers toward taking robust action.[165] "We . . . had the searing memory of Tehran," Shultz said, after a meeting with Assistant Secretary of State Tony Motley on the 19th, "We had to avoid such a situation."[166]

The first cabinet-level meetings on Grenada came on October 20. In an afternoon session, Under Secretary of State Lawrence Eagleburger raised the specter of Iran. Chairman of the Joint Chiefs John Vessey, said that medical students were scattered across the country, making it necessary to secure the entire island and remove the regime in the process. This meant a full-scale invasion.[167] "There were six hundred U.S. citizens in four different locations," said Motley, "That gave cause for alarm . . . It was a situation ripe for hostages."[168] Reagan felt the same pressure. A few days later, he commented, to close advisors, "I am no better off than Jimmy Carter."[169] The October 20 meeting ended with a lengthy discussion about the added benefits of stopping communism and restoring democracy to Grenada. The JCS was given authority to plan an invasion.[170] In short, hostages coupled somewhat with worries about further communist gains (i.e., Cuban troops/bases on the island) raised the perceived costs of inaction for the

Reagan administration exponentially.[171] These costs laid the foundation for an invasion of Grenada.

They were, however, not the only factors that mattered in the administration's policy calculations. The restraint discourse—or better yet, lack thereof—did so as well. In sharp contrast to El Salvador, there was virtually no domestic conversation in the United States around Grenada during the days of the October crisis. Between Bishop's arrest on October 14 and the day of the U.S. invasion (October 25), the *Washington Post* and *New York Times* published a combined total of one article and one editorial on Grenada.[172] The tone of both was generally neutral, with neither critical of administration policy. This was, in fact, common for media coverage of Grenada even before the October crisis. In a February 1983 speech, Reagan talked, for instance, at length about Soviet-Cuban activity in Grenada. But no media outlets granted attention to this portion of the speech. Bridgette Nacos sums up the national discourse around Grenada in 1983: "The reaction of American politicians and of the American media seemed to indicate a 'so what?' attitude."[173]

Here, the first decision-making idiosyncrasy—the distraction of other policy issues—played a key part in creating the weak restraint discourse around Grenada. As Nacos argues, moderator groups outside the administration were focused on Central America in 1983. Grenada was not on their radar. Compounding this inattention, information was limited, especially in October 1983. Following Bishop's arrest, all foreign press were kicked off the island. This stifled media attention to Grenada all the more during the crucial days of the October crisis—moderators outside of government knew little about what was happening.[174] As a result (and in sharp contrast to El Salvador), no restraint discourse formed around Grenada in October 1983.

This mattered to policy. Notably, it was the first major factor that reduced perceived costs for action in ways that helped moderators inside the administration (who blocked the use of direct force in Central America) come on-board with the Grenada invasion.[175] Most important, moderators became optimistic that the administration could manage the domestic conversation, and thus avoid a Vietnam-syndrome backlash. This was the conclusion that White House advisors (especially, Baker, Deaver, and Richard Darmon) came to by October 20.[176] "We knew that no one [outside of the administration] knew much about the situation in Grenada and that this was not a place television could get easily," Deaver said later, in explaining his willingness to gamble on an invasion of Grenada.[177]

The terrorist bombing of the U.S. Marine Corps barracks in Beirut, Lebanon on October 23 factored in here as well. The bombing did not create new reasons to act for Reagan's more pragmatic advisors—as seen above, planning for the Grenada invasion was underway prior to Lebanon. Instead, Beirut created further political distraction, enhancing moderator confidence of a weak restraint discourse around Grenada going forward. The historian Gary Williams observes that "what [Beirut] did that Sunday was to provide cover as the press overlooked the presence of the Grenada group at the White House."[178] Beirut made Grenada "a kind of sideshow," noted Secretary of Defense Weinberger.[179] This again helped clear the way for administration moderators to support military action in Grenada. Williams observes that Shultz and the White House advisors pursued intervention "with more fervor post-Beirut."[180] Beirut further dumbed down an already mute restraint discourse (with all of its potential political costs) around Grenada.

One other factor—hostages—helped moderators come to support using force as well. This represented, in fact, the second idiosyncrasy of the Grenada case. In essence, moderators concluded that restraint narrative fallout could be kept at bay if rescuing Americans took center-stage in the operation. From the very beginning of the Grenada crisis, Reagan's more pragmatic advisors firmly opposed (like El Salvador) hardline proposals in Grenada based exclusively on the need to stop communism. National Security Advisor Bud McFarlane shot down, for instance, an anticommunist-based plan for regime change put forward by hardline NSC staffer, Constantine Menges, at an October 18 meeting. McFarlane did not want a repeat of El Salvador, which forced his predecessor, William Clark, to resign. He considered Menges, like Clark, too much of a cold warrior and, after October 18, pushed Menges to the periphery of policymaking through the remainder of the crisis.[181]

The hostage-based justification for military action that surfaced a few days into the crisis changed political calculations for the pragmatists altogether, though. Above all else, rescuing hostages offered moderators, like McFarlane, political cover from the costs of crossing the Vietnam syndrome.

An NSC meeting late in the day on October 23 was especially significant here. The discussion centered on a memo drafted by Menges suggesting that the operation's public justification focus exclusively on rescuing Americans. Menges learned from his experience the week before—he knew a Cold War justification would raise moderator fears about a restraint narrative backlash.[182] According to scholars, this October 23 meeting was the final straw that brought the White House moderators to fully support the operation.[183] Deaver explained why: the "deliberate effort" to focus on hostages "would be a much more easily accepted decision if it didn't look like it had cold war overtones. This was something that could be justified and easily explained to the American people."[184] Pragmatists saw the opportunity for the public to see Grenada as more like Mayaguez, rather than "another Vietnam." By casting Grenada as an exception to the syndrome rule, Reagan officials saw another way to mute the restraint discourse and, perhaps, even gain a political victory at home by rescuing U.S. citizens. This possibility further reduced perceived costs of action for moderators, allowing them to support military action. Unlike El Salvador then, a faction of presidential advisors (augmented by a publicly robust restraint discourse) never coalesced to stop robust forceful regime change in Grenada.

One final idiosyncratic feature of the Grenada case—the secrecy of the decision-making process—also muted the restraint discourse and affected policy, especially for the president. Reagan was fully aware that regime promotion "flew in the teeth of fashionable opinion . . . given the mood of retreat" in the country.[185] Secretary of Defense Weinberger warned the president, for instance, on October 22 that there "would be a lot of harsh political reaction" at home to intervention. "I know that, I accept that," Reagan responded.[186] As Reagan later described it, secrecy tamped down the restraint narrative around Grenada in a way that helped him accept this risk:

> Frankly, there was another reason I wanted secrecy. It was what I call the "post-Vietnam syndrome" . . . We were already running into this phenomenon in our efforts to halt the spread of Communism in Central America . . . I knew that if word of the rescue mission leaked out in advance, we'd hear this from some in Congress. "Sure, it's starting small, but once you make that first commitment, Grenada's going to become another Vietnam." Well, that wasn't true. And that's one reason why the rescue operation on Grenada was conducted in total secrecy. We didn't ask anybody, we just did it.[187]

One can hear echoes of thinking by the president's more pragmatic advisors here. The lack of a restraint discourse (which secrecy helped ensure) gave Reagan more of a free hand to launch the Grenada operation by offering a political space that he did not have, by his own admission, with El Salvador.

Shultz, who was one of those pragmatists, shared Reagan's assessment about secrecy and how the space created by the limited restraint discourse affected the choice for action. "Delay [of military action] would undoubtedly have meant leaks and much more opposition," the secretary of state, later noted, "Quite possibly, time and leaks could have meant the U.S. hostages would have been taken."[188] Together with the distraction of other issues and the hostage justification, secrecy helped keep the restraint discourse at bay, essentially preventing or reducing the potential for the political "swamp" that Shultz said engulfed policymaking on El Salvador.[189] In the end, this opening in the master narrative landscape lowered perceived costs for action for administration officials. In short, the administration felt a Grenada operation did not and would not look to the nation like it violated the moral of the Vietnam-syndrome story, thus allowing political space for military action to go forward.

On October 25, the invasion began.[190] As planned, it was publicly justified (much to the frustration of administration promoters) almost exclusively as a rescue mission.[191] Within two days, the regime was overturned, the island secured, and American nationals rescued.

After an initially rocky period, the domestic response to the invasion was, for the most part, in keeping with the hopes and expectations of moderators inside the administration. News of the invasion initially brought a sharp restraint narrative backlash that dominated the national discussion from editorial pages to Capitol Hill. Different parts of the restraint narrative (i.e., blame, existential danger, and moral) echoed across the political landscape. "Immoral," "illegal," "wasteful," "invader," "oppressor," "and "mission impossible" were ways many in Congress described it.[192] Of the forty-four statements made on Capitol Hill in the first two days of the operation, twenty-nine (66%) condemned it. Echoing other restraint narrative themes, charges of executive branch deception and overreach were prevalent across the political discourse. "The concern for 1,000 Americans . . . seems to have been speculative at best," commented the *New York Times*, implying something more sinister afoot, "[The invasion] demonstrates to radicals in Central America that only logistics and not laws or treaties, will determine the means the United States is ready to employ against them."[193] Meese commented, "The uproar was nearly deafening."[194] "Snide, scathing and condemnatory," said Secretary of State Shultz, of the initial backlash.[195] "They said that I was trying to turn the Caribbean into 'another Vietnam,'" Reagan observed of the outcry.[196]

In order to tamp down these charges, the administration stuck closely to the moderator line, steering clear of Cold War justifications and focusing on hostages instead.[197] U.N. ambassador (and hardliner) Jean Kirkpatrick spoke, for instance, about Grenada at the United Nations on October 27. Shultz told her ahead of time to cast the invasion as resulting from "a unique set of circumstances," and not in east-west terms.[198] Like others in the administration, Kirkpatrick fell in line to help mute any sort of politically damaging restraint discourse. "The issue was not revolution, nor was it the type of government Grenada possessed," she said to the U.N. Security Council, of the reasons for the invasion, "[but instead] these very particular, very unusual, perhaps unique circumstances" of potential U.S. hostages.[199]

In the end, this public line had two important implications. First, as anticipated by pragmatists, it eventually worked to the administration's political advantage. On October 27, the first group of U.S. medical students arrived back in the

United States. With television cameras broadcasting live, a student walked off the plane, bent down and kissed U.S. soil. Students talked of the fear that they felt for their safety and thanked Reagan for rescuing them. Revelations over the next few days of large caches of Soviet military hardware and a contingent of several thousand Cuban troops on the island aided the administration's public image all the more. Not only were students rescued, but communism was stymied, which appealed to salient liberal narrative concerns.[200]

These developments flipped the political climate to the administration's advantage. Public opinion polls taken after October 27 showed 65 percent or more approved of the invasion.[201] On Capitol Hill, praise rang out as prior critics scrambled to correct themselves in order to get on the right side of the public mood. "President Reagan has been bolstered by the facts in defending his military intervention in Grenada," observed the *Columbus Journal*, "Reagan moved in time to prevent an Iran-style hostage crisis."[202] As hoped by administration officials, Grenada came to look, in short, like Mayaguez rather than Vietnam, which aided Reagan at home.

Second, forceful regime change in Grenada did not end the Vietnam syndrome, as some hardliners in the Reagan administration hoped. Nor, did it become a precedent for regime change wars in Central America or Africa, as critics feared. Why was this so? The answer again lies with the robust restraint narrative itself. "Fear of voter reprisal certainly played a large role in constraining President Reagan from proclaiming a grand Grenada doctrine," note a pair of scholars, "In the absence of public consensus about military interventions—even in areas deemed vital to U.S. security—Reagan would have risked electoral punishment if he had declared Grenada a precedent for future actions."[203] In essence, the restraint narrative pressure to define and justify Grenada narrowly as a one-off event had the unintended consequence of further validating the Vietnam syndrome. Grenada was an aberration, an exception that proved the power of the lesson at the center of the dominant restraint narrative of the day: no forceful regime promotion except in the most rare and compelling of circumstances. While political idiosyncrasies around the restraint narrative allowed Reagan space to invade Grenada, the restraint narrative postinvasion still maintained, therefore, its tight grip on the United States. As discussed more below, it constrained U.S. foreign policy through the remainder of the Cold War.

Alternative Explanations

Geopolitics

Realism anticipates that the liberal narrative weakens with rising threat perceptions and robust forceful regime change is most likely when a great power holds an overwhelming preponderance of power either regionally or globally. As with prior chapters, this argument faces problems in the late Cold War period. For starters, the opposite of what realists anticipate was the case for liberal narrative strength. As evident with the reaction to the Soviet invasion of Afghanistan, the nation's interest in defending liberal order abroad by stopping communism became more, not less, robust as Soviet geopolitical gains brought new (or better yet, renewed) perceptions of threats from abroad.

As to forceful regime promotion, the United States held a greater preponderance of power in Latin America than in other parts of the world. According to realists, this meant policymakers had greater freedom to use force, which was reflected in the fact that none inside the administration discussed possible war with the Soviets resulting from action in Grenada (or El Salvador). The problem for realism comes with explaining the variation between the Grenada and El Salvador cases. With the distribution of power in the 1980s conducive to robust forceful regime promotion, why was there military action in only Grenada, and not El Salvador or numerous other countries in Latin America at the time?[204] Answering this question requires us to look beyond realism. The political discourse around master narratives offers, as seen above, important leverage on topics like these.

Elite Polarization

The elite-polarization argument contends that the liberal narrative strengthens when policymakers become ideologically polarized. Forceful regime promotion becomes more likely under these conditions as well. Similar to realism, this argument also struggles to explain developments discussed in this chapter. Once deciding on war, President Lyndon Johnson was deeply committed to victory over communism in South Vietnam. He saw no value in and actively worked against the waning of public interest in promoting liberal order abroad that occurred during his presidency. Yet the liberal narrative weakened all the same. The liberal narrative also strengthened against the wishes of President Jimmy Carter. Like many elites, Carter was less ideologically polarized in the 1970s.[205] Yet he was forced by the national hysteria generated from Soviet geopolitical gains and the challenge of the 1980 presidential election to take up a more ideological, anticommunist tone. In short, liberal narrative strength did not follow elite polarization.

Elite polarization offers, at best, a mixed explanation of patterns of forceful regime promotion in these years. President Reagan and officials in his administration were deeply concerned about the spread of communism. This polarized temperament undoubtedly played a role in determining the stepped-up initiative in Central America to stop communism in places like El Salvador and Nicaragua. Increased military aid to the Salvadoran regime cannot be understood in full, then, without understanding the polarized temperament of Reagan officials.

But, on the big question of force, elite polarization alone offers an insufficient answer. Why was there robust forceful regime promotion in Grenada, but not El Salvador? Policy elites were polarized in this period and talked about combatting communism in both cases—this was the primary U.S. interest at stake in El Salvador. Yet there was no direct use of U.S. force there. Overall, what these two cases tell us, again, is that while ideological actors matter, their impact on policy is generally determined by another set of ideas—master narratives. The cases above demonstrate this. They show how competing discourses around robust master narratives elevated some elites inside the administration, while seriously diminishing others. This shaped, in turn, policy outcomes. Cases in this chapter demonstrate again, then, the explanatory benefits of the fuller ideational approach found in the master narrative argument. In short, we cannot understand patterns of forceful regime change here without it.

Master narratives helped determine patterns of U.S. forceful regime promotion in the late Cold War period, as seen with the cases of El Salvador and Grenada. The policy outcome in El Salvador represented a bargain between a strong liberal discourse and strong restraint discourse. The former gave the Reagan administration space to commit large sums of military aid and dispatch a small contingent of military advisors to El Salvador—both steps were taboo by restraint narrative standards. The latter prevented the direct use of force by the United States in El Salvador during the 1980s. As a jungle nation with an unpopular, nondemocratic government where the rationale for U.S. action was exclusively to fight communism, El Salvador looked too much like Vietnam to escape the constraints of the Vietnam syndrome. Costs for action loomed large for the Reagan administration, which precluded robust forceful regime promotion.

With Grenada, the master narrative landscape was distinct from Vietnam (and El Salvador) in ways that gave the Reagan administration political space to gamble on a full-scale regime change intervention in October 1983. Above all else, certain idiosyncrasies of this case precluded a strong restraint discourse from forming prior to or after the invasion started. Coupled with concerns about U.S. hostages, this lowered audience costs for military action in ways that allowed the administration to go forward with invasion. Overall, for both El Salvador and Grenada, the master narrative argument offers a strong account.

The political processes behind the regime promotion outcomes in El Salvador and Grenada were not unique to these two cases in the late years of the Cold

War. There were many instances into the early 1990s that looked like El Salvador, in particular. When a 1982 communist-inspired coup occurred, for instance, in Suriname, the Reagan administration ruled out direct U.S. force because it would be too "politically explosive at home," according to Secretary of State Shultz. Even a plan to provide only limited U.S. naval support to a Dutch-led invasion was shelved by the U.S. military because, as Shultz notes, they "were still seared by the Vietnam-experience." Military action in Chad, Sudan, the Philippines, and Panama was also circumvented by identical restraint-driven concerns during the Reagan administration.[206]

Reagan's successor, George H.W. Bush, dealt with the same constraints. Despite proclaiming the death of the Vietnam syndrome with the first Gulf War, Bush was deeply constrained by this restraint narrative. "There's not going to be any long drawn-out agony of Vietnam," Bush told his advisors, when he made his decision in the 1991 Gulf War not to continue to Baghdad in order to topple the regime of Saddam Hussein. He feared the nation would abandon him the way it did Lyndon Johnson.[207] Bush, of course, launched two full-scale regime promotion wars—Panama and Kuwait—during his time in office. Scholars agree that in both, it took extraordinary circumstances (narcotics in Panama and access to Middle East oil) to gamble against the Vietnam syndrome here.[208] Like Grenada, these cases tended again to be exceptions that proved the rule (or moral of the story), rather than instances that point to the irrelevance of the restraint narrative. Overall, the 1980s tell a clear story: master narratives profoundly shaped U.S. foreign policy in this period, especially when it came to forceful regime promotion.

REGIME CHANGE IN IRAQ
AND LIBYA

The 9/11 terrorist attacks and Arab Spring moved the Middle East and North Africa to the center of U.S. foreign policy in the 2000s. Forceful regime change played a major part here. This chapter explores two of the most prominent cases, the 2003 combat invasion of Iraq and the 2011 limited (air power only) intervention in Libya.

Conventional explanations of the Iraq War tend to focus overwhelmingly on elites, notably the ideology of neoconservatives or President George W. Bush's familial, religious, and financial interests.[1] This chapter offers a different argument than this. Following September 11 terrorist attack, the liberal narrative strengthened dramatically in the United States. In the Iraq case, this robust liberal narrative helped push the Bush administration toward a full-scale military invasion of Iraq, and also gave the administration a free hand to move the nation toward war once the administration decided on that course of action in 2002. Elites mattered here, no doubt. But they did so in a way that was highly determined by the robust liberal narrative.

In the case of Libya, the restraint narrative helps explain limited force. National disillusionment following the Iraq War generated a strong restraint narrative. This Iraq syndrome impacted President Barack Obama's approach to Libya. It raised audience costs for action in ways that compelled Obama to adopt a highly conscribed, backseat role militarily in the intervention to unseat the Gaddafi regime—a posture later dubbed "lead from behind."

Master Narratives at the Dawn of the Twenty-First Century

Across the 1990s, the liberal and restraint narratives weakened substantially. As trauma theory anticipates, change like this happens in event-driven contexts marked by declining threats and an end to major rivalry relationships. For the United States, the end to the Cold War brought a sense of triumphalism, a "new world order" marked by an unprecedented degree of U.S. predominance in the world. As part of this, the previously robust restraint narrative—the Vietnam syndrome—faded. President George H.W. Bush was chided extensively (i.e., storytelling by promoters), for example, at the end of the first Gulf War in 1991 for not continuing on to Baghdad to topple the Iraqi president Saddam Hussein. Members of the previously syndrome-laden Democratic Party led this charge, a fact that reflected and contributed to the broader change in the national mentality, toward a less constrained disposition about the use of force. As one reflection of this weakened restraint narrative in the 1990s, talk of peacekeeping and nation-building became more prominent again both across the public and in policy circles.[2]

The liberal narrative weakened in this period as well. The U.S. public celebrated the end of the Cold War and newly democratic governments in East-Central Europe. However, without a clear challenger around which to structure foreign policy, a sense of withdrawal and focus on the home front set in across the United States. Public support for democracy promotion as a policy objective steadily declined over the decade. Likewise, a sharp public backlash over U.S. Marine deaths on a nation-building mission in Somalia set a tone for U.S. policy. Non-to-limited action in Rwanda, Bosnia, and Kosovo followed. In each instance, Clinton officials claimed the public's flagging idealism constrained policy options.[3] This reflected something broader: the weakened liberal narrative of the 1990s.

The 9/11 terrorist attack on the World Trade Center and the Pentagon dramatically changed this master narrative landscape, especially when it came to the liberal narrative. "This week's frontal assault on America is a collective trauma unlike any other in any of our lifetimes," observed the *San Francisco Chronicle*.[4] Historians, commentators, and newspapers from across the country captured the collective reaction, using terms like "shell-shocked," "siege mentality," "modern nightmare," and "searing memory" to describe national sentiment in the wake of the attacks.[5]

Trauma theory anticipates that in circumstances of a direct attack on a community, external trauma is so palpable that new master narratives emerge quickly and to some degree organically, without the prompting and prodding of identifiable actors. This happened to a large degree following 9/11. Out of the turmoil of the terrorist attack, a "new narrative literally fell from the sky on September 11" and "became embedded in the popular imagination," noted a pair of scholars.[6] Within hours of the attack the story of events (and, with that, the story's moral to stop terrorism and protect freedom) was everywhere in the public discourse. It came from members of Congress, television and print media, and eventually President Bush.[7]

The story had all the standard parts of a national security narrative, noting specific events, assigning blame, and setting a way forward to repair. In morning and afternoon sessions in the House of Representatives on September 11, one member after another from both parties expressed, for instance, horror at the attack, framing it in existential terms. "This was an attack on our Nation, its people, our democracy, and the rule of law," said Representative Barbara Lee (D-CA), "We must uphold our democratic principles, our laws, and our cherished beliefs." Others talked similarly of the United States as "the symbol of freedom and democracy around the world" coming under assault and the actions of 9/11 as "attacks [on] the freedom of our country."[8] Indicative of the event's trauma, references to another painfully emotional and searing attack on the United States—Pearl Harbor—were common in the storytelling as well.[9] Terrorists were roundly blamed for the attack as calls went up to punish not only those responsible but also the countries that harbored them (i.e., repair and moral). "This is war," declared House Majority Leader Dick Gephardt (D-MO), just after the attack, "We will do everything ... to make sure that terrorists never, ever again can create this mayhem, this chaos, this violence against our people." Many echoed similar themes on September 11: "we will not rest"; "a state of war exists"; "we must declare war"; and "we will hunt you down like the animals that you are."[10] Again, the existential aspect was evident in calls to defend not just the United States but liberalism in general. "We must rededicate ourselves to our principles," said Representative Steve King (R-IA). Representative Ileana Ros-Lehtinen (R-FL) declared emphatically, too, "democracy will always triumph over terrorism."[11]

On the evening of September 11, President Bush addressed the nation. He acknowledged the well-developed story about events that was already there: "I appreciate so very much the members of Congress who have joined me in strongly condemning these attacks." The president then proceeded to tell the near identical story as those on Capitol Hill and in the media. He framed the events of the day in existential terms and directly assigned blame. "Our way of life, our very freedom came under attack in a series of deliberate and deadly terrorist acts," Bush said to open the speech. He talked about the resolve of the nation and the bravery of first responders to the attacks. From there, he mirrored the day's conversation and issued a stern call for action. "America was targeted for attack because we're the brightest beacon for freedom and opportunity in the world," the president said, "And no one will keep that light from shining." The moral to the already standard story about 9/11 was there as well. Bush pledged to track down those responsible and noted that "we will make no distinction between the terrorists who committed these acts and those who harbor them."[12]

Beyond government circles, there was near-universal acceptance of the burgeoning liberal narrative. Media commentators talked of the events in existential terms, commenting, for instance, that the "powerfully symbolic buildings" the terrorists targeted are "quintessential symbols of liberal, free market, Western values" that reflected the U.S. commitment to "tolerance and freedom."[13] Again, Pearl Harbor was mentioned frequently and, as one scholar noted, the attack challenged "the basic feelings that our parents, our society, had worked from our birth to nurture in us."[14] The passion to act in defense of freedom (i.e. repair or moral) surged as well among the public. A mid-September poll found that 59 percent of Americans felt the United States should "mount a long-term war to eliminate terrorist groups world-wide," rather than simply attack the terrorists involved in 9/11.[15] In another survey, 64 percent favored sending U.S. ground troops to combat terrorists in Afghanistan.[16] There was also a swell of support for robust action, which meant more than the past practice of just "lobbing a few missiles" at terrorists. Instead, terrorist organizations (and their state sponsors) needed to be "de-capitated," noted one commentator—"an all-out war on terrorism" and a policy that "shows resolve soon," others said.[17] Members of Congress continued to echo these themes as well in the days after 9/11. On September 14, both houses of Congress passed a joint resolution authorizing the use of military force (AUMF) against terrorists. In the House debate on the measure, 185 of the 201 comments (85%) on the AUMF referenced American values, liberty, freedom, or other indicators of the liberal narrative.

On September 20, President Bush gave his most expansive public comments on 9/11 to that point in a nationally televised speech. The speech echoed and, at the same time, validated the burgeoning story about the attack with its central lesson to defend liberal order against radical Islam. "Bush had no need to rally the nation behind his cause," commented the *Atlanta Journal-Constitution*, on the speech, "We were already there . . . He delivered the message that Americans needed and wanted to hear."[18] The president began by affirming the existential challenge of 9/11. "Enemies of freedom committed an act of war against our country," Bush said, "They hate our freedoms . . . They are the heirs of the murderous ideologies of the twentieth century . . . fascism, and Nazism, and totalitarianism." Sounding the moral of the liberal narrative, the president laid out an expansive initiative to combat the new ideological challenge. Like communism during the Cold War, "terrorism" was now the monolithic foe. "Our war

on terror is with al-Qaida, but it does not end there," said the president, "It will
not end until every terrorist group of global reach has been found, stopped, and
defeated."[19]

Bush's liberal narrative call to action received near-unanimous approval from
all quarters. Senator Patrick Leahy (D-VT) commented on the national unity
behind Bush's effort at "protecting our liberties and rights as Americans."[20] Senator Carl Levin (D-MI) praised the national "resolve to track down, root out, and
relentlessly pursue the terrorists and those who shelter or harbor them," and Representative Tom Lantos (D-CA) called the war "a struggle that must take on terrorism wherever and however it appears."[21] Republicans in Congress echoed the
same themes. Newspapers did as well. In the days that followed the speech, editors and commentators repeatedly sounded the liberal narrative lesson of a broad
"global struggle" against terrorism. "'Freedom and fear are at war," Bush told
Congress, and there is no question the nation supports him," wrote the editors
of the San Francisco Chronicle, "We certainly do."[22] The battle against "extreme
strains of Islamic fundamentalism" is "war against a new "ism," said the scholar
and policy practitioner, Michael McFaul.[23] Public opinion surveys showed the
same temperament. In late September 2001, a plurality supported "taking military action to destroy terrorist networks around the world."[24] Democracy promotion became more popular too. In January 2002, 77 percent considered it
"very important" or "fairly important" for the United States to encourage more
democracy in the Middle East.[25] The trauma of 9/11 led to a national groundswell of collective, national support for defending liberal political order abroad.
Overall, the liberal narrative strengthened substantially in the early 2000s.

Regime Change in Iraq

Following the first Gulf War, U.S. relations with Saddam Hussein remained hostile. In 1991, the United States led the effort to create the United Nations Special
Commission (UNSCOM) to inspect and oversee the termination of Iraqi weapons of mass destruction (WMD). In 1998, Hussein suddenly ended cooperation with UNSCOM and kicked out all inspectors. The United States and Great
Britain responded with four days of airstrikes against Iraq. In 1998, President Bill
Clinton signed the Iraq Liberation Act, making regime change in Iraq official U.S.
policy. In the pre–9/11 period, the Bush administration worked to build international support for new sanctions against Hussein.[26]

Almost immediately after 9/11, a nascent liberal discourse for stronger action
against Iraq emerged in the United States. This happened, most important,
without any prompting from the Bush administration. Just after the attack,
promoters of many stripes (such as former CIA director James Woolsey, the

neoconservative scholar Laurie Mylorie, the *Guardian*, and reporters for *CBS News*) raised questions about Iraq's involvement in the attack.[27] Despite efforts by the administration to downplay attention to Iraq, Bush's September 20 outlining of a broad war that included state sponsors of terrorism led to calls from many quarters for regime change action not only against Afghanistan, but Iraq as well.[28] Arguments linking Iraq to the antiterrorism narrative emerged. "It is impossible to imagine the United States 'winning' this war in any meaningful sense while Saddam Hussein remains in power," noted the editors of the *Washington Post* in mid-September.[29] Powerful conservatives outside of government pushed for an invasion of Iraq. On September 20, a group that included the editors of the *New Republic* and *Weekly Standard* signed an open letter to Bush which threatened to brand the president guilty of "surrender in the war on terrorism" if the president did not make a "determined effort" to oust Saddam Hussein, "even if evidence does not link Iraq directly to the attacks."[30]

Across the late fall, talk of Iraq kept growing. Several anthrax attacks across the country in October caused a "public hysteria."[31] With little evidence of its source, a drumbeat of press stories speculated that the anthrax came from Iraq.[32] At a press conference on the one-month anniversary of the 9/11 attacks, the first question Bush faced, for instance, was whether Iraq would be the next target in the war on terror.[33] The fall of the Taliban government in Afghanistan on November 13 amplified public attention to Iraq still further. "The anger over September 11 seemed to demand more," observed the political writer Peter Baker, "Afghanistan was not enough."[34] In late 2001, the nation was in search of the next target. "Sept 11 taught us what terrorists can do," wrote the commentator Richard Cohen, on November 30, "Afghanistan taught us what we can do."[35] Headlines on the editorial pages of major newspapers—such as "War on Terror: What Next?" and "On to Phase II"—told the same story, of a nation on a mission.[36]

For "Phase II," Iraq stood tall in the national discourse. On November 6, Bush mentioned for the first time in public his administration's concerns about WMD falling into the hands of terrorists. Despite not singling out any specific countries in his remarks, White House Press Secretary Ari Fleischer fielded at that day's press briefing thirty-four questions about Iraq and WMDs.[37] In the following weeks, the drumbeat for regime change intensified. The *Chicago Tribune* talked of "Squeezing Saddam," while others, like former Clinton administration official Leon Furth wrote about the evidence needed to "create an open-and-shut case for finishing him [Hussein]."[38] The same themes were sounded on Capitol Hill. In December, one statement after another linked the liberal narrative to toppling Saddam Hussein. "September 11 has demonstrated that we must take resolute action to prevent disasters before they occur," argued Lantos, Iraq is the "next target in the war on terror."[39] Congressman Dana Rohrabacher (R-CA) charged that stopping Saddam's WMD program was the next "sequential battle against terror-ism."[40] "Let us act now," said Representative Lindsay Graham (R-SC), of taking out Hussein and Iraq's WMD program, "Have we learned anything from Sep-tember 11?"[41] Sentiments like these were mainstream by late 2001. A late Novem-ber poll found that 74 percent of the U.S. public supported sending troops to "remove Saddam Hussein from power"; 61 percent believed that success against terrorism required Hussein's removal from power; and 72 percent believed that Iraq aided al Qaeda in the September 11 attacks.[42] In sum, by early 2002, a strong liberal discourse supported taking the war on terror to Iraq.[43]

This affected the Bush administration's policy toward Iraq in two important ways in late 2001. First, the robust liberal discourse around Iraq strengthened promoters (led by Vice President Dick Cheney) and weakened moderators (led by Secretary of State Colin Powell) inside the administration.[44] It opened space—"an opportunity," according to one White House official—for "hawks in the Bush Administration to press the war on terrorism forward."[45] As part of this, Powell especially went quiet in late 2001. When the State Department got wind in early December, for instance, that the *New York Times* was about to report that Powell was taking a softer line on Iraq than Secretary of Defense Donald Rumsfeld, it moved quickly to cut the story off. Deputy Secretary of State Richard Armit-age gave the *Times* a tough anti-Hussein interview on-the-record. Why? Powell worried about losing political capital if he looked soft on terrorism, and now, by extension, soft on Iraq. Better to fall in-step with the moral of the prevailing narrative than defy it.[46] As seen below, this kind of ducking became a theme for other moderators in 2002 and 2003. Here in late 2001, it helped promoters begin to more freely shape Iraq policy.[47]

Powell was not the only one worried about looking tough on terrorism. All Bush officials felt this way, which helps explain, second, how the 2001 liberal discourse around Iraq began to push the president and his advisors toward a regime change war in Iraq. From the first moments after the 9/11 attack, the administration scrambled to develop, sustain, and protect a liberal narrative image of looking tough on terrorism. Above all else, they worried about audi-ence costs for inaction. There are many examples. Nearly all of Bush's public appearances just after the attack (including his iconic visit to ground zero in New York City on September 14) were scripted to show a strong leader in tune with the national mood.[48] The September 20 speech reflected this too. Tasked with connecting the speech to national sentiments, Senior Advisor Karl Rove said that a presidency once "predicated on domestic issues was now, over-whelmingly, a national security one."[49] In the September 20 speech then, Bush wrapped himself in the moral of the robust liberal narrative. "I will not forget this wound to our country, or those who inflicted it," Bush pledged, "I will not yield—I will not rest—I will not relent in waging this struggle for the freedom and security of the American people."[50]

For the administration, looking tough on terrorism also meant countering public impressions of administration weakness. In the days after the attack, Bush officials went on the offensive, for example, after the president was described by several leading pundits as "occasionally wobbly," "somewhat tentative" and "shrunken in his clothes and understandably scared."[51] Rove spent much of September 12 calling reporters (some he did not even know) and Cheney appeared on news shows to kill impressions that Bush was weak. Press Secretary Ari Fleischer went so far as to warn critics, "In times like these people need to watch what they say, watch what they do."[52] Some at the time chided the administration for all this effort "to overcome the impression that Mr. Bush showed weakness." But for a tough-on-terrorism-obsessed administration, this was serious political business.[53] "Impressions harden quickly," observes Baker, "And if the memory of that day was of Bush in a seeming flight from danger, it could hobble his presidency."[54] It is for this same reason, in fact, that unlike FDR after Pearl Harbor, Bush refused in the months following 9/11 to set up an independent commission to explore how the attack happened.[55] According to one senior White House official, they wanted to avoid "the firestorms of anger," or blame, that could follow.[56] Better not to probe for mistakes and keep looking tough than cripple the administration politically with public impressions of weakness and missed opportunities that an independent counsel investigation might bring.[57]

Looking tough showed up in the administration's decisions for forceful regime change too. In Afghanistan, it meant not looking like Clinton. Administration officials felt that there "had been a pattern of weak responses" to terrorism during the Clinton years.[58] Bush was determined to be different. He was not interested, said Rice, in "lashing out with cruise missiles into tents."[59] Or, simply "pounding sand," as Bush said, repeatedly in policy debates.[60] In fact, Bush turned down the initial military options presented to him for Afghanistan because he thought they looked too weak, like Clinton. Limited action was not "good enough this time," said the president.[61] He wanted to "unleash holy hell" by getting U.S. boots on the ground.[62] In policy debates, Cheney said, "Air operations without boots on the ground could look weak."[63] Bush needed to look the part, to match the new, post–9/11 national story to fight terrorism.

This was the case with Iraq as well. For an administration so consumed by proving its mettle against terrorism to the American public, how could it not be affected by a burgeoning *public* discourse in 2001 that linked terrorism to Saddam Hussein's regime in Iraq? The answer: it couldn't. Iraq moved to center stage as the next stop in the war on terror, at least in part, to ensure the administration did not land on the wrong side of the liberal narrative—Bush was pushed toward using force to topple the regime in Iraq by audience costs for inaction.

This occurred around the single issue that dredged up the administration's weak-on-terrorism anxieties most profoundly from 2001 forward: a second terrorist attack with weapons of mass destruction. In the aftermath of 9/11, nothing worried the Bush administration more than this. The second-strike fear emerged immediately. It was one of the first things the Bush team discussed following the attack.[64] "What are you doing to stop the next attack?" Bush said, to Attorney General John Ashcroft and Director of the Federal Bureau of Investigation (FBI) Robert Mueller on September 14, "That's our new mission, preventing attacks."[65] Preventing a second terrorist strike remained a major preoccupation for the administration to the day Bush left office.[66] The WMD link to the second-strike fear became especially pronounced for Bush with the late 2001 anthrax scare. "There was a real, almost fatalistic concern that we were going to get hit again," said the vice president's deputy chief of staff, "In that atmosphere, the anthrax attack threw people for a loop."[67] It is difficult to overstate how powerful these WMD-second-strike concerns were for White House officials. They felt a "sense of mortal and existential danger," about it, notes Baker.[68] For some, it was an "obsession."[69]

Why so much worry over this? The answer involves more than simply protecting the nation. Politics surrounding the liberal discourse played a big role here too. In 2001 and after, the Bush administration knew that nothing could have made it look softer on terrorism—and, hence, more politically vulnerable—than a second terrorist attack, especially one with WMD. "There would have rightly been a different kind of second-guessing as Americans asked, "Why did you not do everything in your power to keep it from happening again?" Rice noted, of administration concerns about a second attack, "We couldn't fail."[70] The historian Timothy Naftali sums up the costs-for-inaction pressure on the administration. "Presidents are allowed only one 'Pearl Harbor' attack by the American people . . . Bush instinctively understood that his effectiveness as president depended on how quickly and comprehensively his administration responded to the attacks," notes Naftali, "It was clear, however, that there could be no more surprises in the United States."[71]

Fueled by the liberal narrative requirement to be tough on terrorism, the administration became consumed with worst case scenarios. Rice said that "repeating what everyone realized had been errors of omission and complacency" became an obsession.[72] The administration moved aggressively to avoid being "blindsided again."[73] To "underreact" was politically unacceptable.[74] Consequently, a panicked search to preempt the next attack set in. Every rock and stone had to be turned over in the liberal discourse, "look-tough" political climate of the post–9/11 period. "If there were another attack, how could they explain not doing everything in their power to prevent it?" Baker notes, *"Whatever it takes,* the men at Ground Zero had told Bush [a few days after 9/11]."[75]

This domestic political context brought Iraq to the fore.[76] After Bush learned on November 21 of contacts between Pakistani nuclear scientists and al Qaeda, the president asked Secretary of Defense Donald Rumsfeld about war plans for invading Iraq. If al Qaeda was buying, Iraq might be selling, he reasoned. "Get [General] Tommy Franks looking at what it would take to protect America by removing Saddam Hussein if we have to," Bush told Rumsfeld.[77]

From what we know, this marked Bush's first significant turn of attention to Iraq in the aftermath of the Afghan war.[78] It no longer seemed reasonable to leave in power a sworn enemy who might aid al Qaeda in acquiring WMD.[79] Looking strong on terrorism at home stood at the heart of this reasoning. Undersecretary of Defense Doug Feith captured this well:

> We wondered: What would President Bush tell the American people if [an] attack occurred, and the biological weapons agent were traced to Iraq? . . . How would Bush explain why he failed to connect the dots? . . . Could President Bush excuse himself by claiming he thought Saddam was . . . 'contained,'? Could the President say there was no need to worry about Saddam? The President could not honestly say any of those things.[80]

The robust liberal discourse around Iraq in late 2001 just at the point that Bush received news of the al Qaeda-nuclear scientist connection must have made concerns like these all the more pronounced for the administration. "We knew, why didn't you?" the public would demand to know, if there was a second strike involving Iraq.[81] The domestic fallout would have been devastating, essentially the administration's domestic political death knell. Bush certainly thought so. "This is how we're going to be judged," he told Rove, just after 9/11 about preventing a second/WMD attack.[82]

This second-strike/WMD nexus was an ever-present motivator for the administration down to the start of military operations against Iraq in 2003.[83] On the verge of the Iraq invasion, Bush said privately of an Iraq-aided terror attack, "I am just not going to be the president on whose watch that happens."[84] Better to move preemptively, Bush figured, than face the blame and potentially devastating political costs at home for inaction.[85] This happens in an environment marked by a robust liberal discourse. Baker sums it up well. "While Bush and Cheney had Iraq in their sights for a long time, they were responding to a public appetite for action," Baker notes, "For the first time in more than a generation, the country was willing to be assertive overseas."[86] Bush's fear of not measuring up to that assertiveness helped push him and the United States toward forceful regime change in Iraq.

Pushed to Act in Iraq: The Tarnished Image

While the second-strike worry set the Bush administration toward regime change starting in 2001, a new set of events in 2002 increased costs for inaction still further and accelerated Bush's rush to war. By early 2002, the combat victory in Afghanistan and prevention, to that point, of a second terrorist attack made antiterrorism a political strong suit for the president. Bush now measured up well against the moral of the liberal narrative to stop terrorism.[87] So much so in fact, that Rove told a meeting of the Republican National Committee (RNC) in the middle of January 2002 that GOP candidates should emphasize antiterrorism in the November elections. "We can go to the country on this issue," Rove said, "because they trust the Republican Party to do a better job of protecting and strengthening America's military might and protecting America."[88] Through the spring, however, a series of events started to tarnish Bush's liberal narrative image. The administration responded in ways that accelerated the national movement toward war, and, in the end, put the administration in a box politically that left Bush little choice but to pursue forceful regime change in Iraq.

Administration concerns about erosion in Bush's tough-on-terrorism image started to emerge in early 2002. Richard Berke of the *New York Times* reported that in January Bush advisors were having "extensive conversations about how long Mr. Bush can sustain his impressive popularity ratings."[89] Above all else, they worried that the political shine was coming off of Bush's strong antiterrorism image. Two factors in January contributed to this concern. First, the end of U.S. combat operations in Afghanistan meant that the war against terrorism was moving into a quiet stage, largely out of public view. This meant no more publicly visible, big-splash victories (like the fall of Kabul) to bolster Bush's image and center national attention on the GOP strength of antiterrorism.[90] Second, Democrats started charging the president with being disengaged on the economy, which still remained weak in the aftermath of September 11. Looking for their own strong suit for November, Democrats hoped to flip the national discussion away from terrorism—something that may be easier to do, reasoned the White House, with Afghanistan fading from view.[91] Overall, Bush was in danger of losing important domestic political ground in early 2002.

The spring brought a pair of developments that only made things worse in this respect for Bush. First, reports surfaced of administration mistakes in the search for al Qaeda leader, Osama bin Laden. In April, a *Washington Post* article detailed missed opportunities to get bin Laden in late 2001. A steady stream of critical media reports followed into the summer, all of which questioned Bush's leadership on terrorism.[92] An even more damaging development, came in May when a *New York Post* article with the headline "Bush Knew" revealed that Bush received warnings of terrorist attacks a month before September 11. Bush overlooked the warnings. Soon after the article's publication, news of other oversights came out too, including the fact that government officials ignored pre–9/11 FBI warnings of Middle Eastern men enrolled in U.S. flight schools.[93]

Seeing an opportunity to weaken Bush on terrorism, Democrats pounced.[94] "The President knew what?" Senator Hillary Clinton (D-NY) charged. "It is critically important we know . . . what happened and why actions were not taken," claimed Senator Christopher Dodd (D-CT), "Someone should have taken better action in my view."[95] Some insinuated a cover-up. "It is . . . very disturbing," said Congressman George Miller (D-CA), "This information has not been released to the American people or to the Congress of the United States for over 8 months."[96] The Bush administration's response made matters worse. Rice gave a defensive press briefing on May 17. The administration's stonewalling on Senate Majority Leader Tom Daschle's efforts to open an investigation into 9/11 also now amplified charges that the administration had something to hide.[97] "Bush had little to gain, and much more to lose, from a close look at his record on terrorism prior to September 11," notes one scholar, of how critics portrayed the administration's posture.[98]

The attacks tarnished Bush's liberal narrative image.[99] Two-thirds of the public said that the president should have revealed the missed information earlier, and 55 percent agreed that Bush should have issued hijack warnings in August 2001.[100] Commentators across the country were critical too. The *Chicago Tribune* joined others in chiding the White House for its secrecy: "It leaves exposed a weak flank in the Bush White House, a certain arrogant impatience with any questioning or criticism."[101] The *Washington Post* charged the administration with "a failure of imagination."[102] Some claimed Bush's 9/11 conduct should be an issue in the fall elections.[103] And many talked of how the incident hurt Bush's standing on terrorism. This "looks embarrassing enough to seriously damage the president's carefully crafted image of post-Sept. 11 brilliance," observed Clarence Page.[104] There was some truth here. By Memorial Day, only 35 percent of Americans thought the United States was winning the war on terror—a thirty-point decline from January.[105]

The 2002 damage to Bush's antiterrorism image—his political *sin quo non*—caused the administration to panic. "It bothered me," Bush admitted. It "rattled" others, according to administration insiders.[106] Fleischer talked, for instance, of the press "feeding frenzy" and how his own credibility was questioned.[107] The biggest fear, though, was audience costs for inaction that came with lost standing against the liberal narrative. "The White House is particularly worried the president will lose the political protection the fight against terrorism has brought him," one commentator said, of his conversations with Bush officials at the time.[108] Overall, Bush's ability to carry the liberal narrative mantle of fighting radical Islam was his political trump card. By the spring of 2002, that card started to disappear.

This impacted U.S. policy toward Iraq. By the summer of 2002, the administration needed a liberal narrative win—a way to re-establish its strong, antiterrorism image. For that, it turned to a public debate about removing Saddam Hussein from power.

Several pieces of important evidence support this argument. For starters, administration officials admitted that they viewed antiterrorism as a vital tool for success in the November elections. "There's a manipulation of the environment," said a White House strategist in December 2001, "They take advantage of the situation [i.e., war on terror developments] to achieve some [domestic] political objectives."[109] One indication of the politicization of antiterrorism was Rove's enhanced foreign policy role from late 2001 forward. In order to maintain bipartisanship, Bush initially chose not to include Rove in foreign policy discussions in the immediate aftermath of 9/11. That changed by 2002. "The degree of Mr. Rove's involvement underscores how world events have moved so much to the forefront of this White House, and how they have become so deeply intertwined with domestic policy," observed Richard Berke and David Sanger.[110]

Rove chimed in only on foreign policy issues that mattered to Bush's domestic political standing.[111] Iraq became one of those issues—a way to demonstrate administration action to off-set the political damage of the spring. As Rove put it, "9/11 had given Bush the leverage he needed in the political system."[112] Rove used that leverage to create a public drumbeat for war in Iraq. It started with Rove crafting the "axis of evil" language in Bush's 2002 State of the Union address that raised the specter of potential links between Iran, Iraq, and North Korea with terrorist organizations, like al Qaeda.[113] For Rove, this fit the administration's public image needs. It gave the country a new mission, he said, a bold vision to follow. The message to the country was "we can't go back to sleep again," Rove said.[114] The speech had its desired effect, creating an "intense discussion," notes Frederik Logevall, that kept the national conversation riveted on Bush's strong suit: antiterrorism.[115]

In the spring, Rove was at it again. He was a central figure in the administration's effort to repair Bush's tarnished antiterrorism image over pre–9/11 intelligence failures. In policy debates at the time, Rove sided with promoters, like Cheney and Deputy Director of Defense Paul Wolfowitz, who wanted to press forward with war against Iraq.[116] Why? Again, it was about domestic politics. A tough stand on the Iraq-terrorism link could restore, as several observers note,

Bush's strong liberal narrative image at home and, in turn, bolster Republicans at the polls in November (i.e., avoid costs for inaction). As was the case in late 2001, the pressure to keep pace with the liberal narrative elevated promoters, like Rove, and pushed the administration to accelerate the national discussion about war with Iraq.[117]

The timing of the White House's 2002 turn to Iraq also suggests that domestic image repair was a big factor in administration thinking. Condoleezza Rice notes that Bush started talking about Iraq in a "different way" in late spring of 2002—that is at the apex of Bush's liberal narrative swoon at home, when Democrats were attacking most viscously over intelligence failures.[118] This suggests that Bush, like Rove, came to see Iraq as a way to shore up his image in this period—a move to "enhance his presidency," a top State Department official said.[119] The administration initiated its most sustained effort to draw public attention to Iraq starting in the summer of 2002. On June 1, Bush publicly laid out his doctrine of preemptive force, and soon after that, formed the White House Iraq Group to carry out a public relations campaign for congressional passage of an AUMF on Iraq. Again, the White House's antiterrorism image drove this.[120] The administration was gripped with a "he-man macho psychosis," said House Majority Leader Dick Armey (R-TX) in the fall of 2002, "where they felt the need to go out and shoot somebody to show they're the tough guy on the block."[121]

One final observation about timing also points to liberal narrative repair at work in the Bush administration's blitz toward war in 2002. Bush officials insisted on an AUMF vote before November. Why this timeline? The next section deals with this in more detail. Observers agree that a vote before November ensured the nation's attention centered on Iraq and terrorism (rather than the economy) almost right up to Election Day. The Iraq vote fit, then, with Rove's plan. "The campaign calendar was driving the timing of the vote on Iraq," observed Michael Isokoff and David Corn.[122] Peter Baker notes similarly, "As Karl Rove had urged, Bush and Cheney had taken their leadership of the war on terror to the voters."[123] In the end, the quick vote paid off for Bush. Republicans held onto the House and won back the Senate in November. Many observers agree that antiterrorism and Iraq were big issues on voters' minds on Election Day. Bush did, therefore, good liberal narrative image repair in the last half of 2002. In the process, he moved the nation closer to military action against Iraq.[124]

In doing this, the president, whether intended or not, also trapped himself into war against Iraq. Bush created "a box of his own making" in 2002 by helping build a robust liberal discourse around Iraq.[125] "The failure to take on Saddam after what the president said," observed Bush advisor Richard Perle, "would lead to a collapse of confidence."[126] By late 2002, there was no way for Bush to back down from confronting Saddam Hussein, especially given his interests in appearing tough on terrorism heading into the 2004 presidential campaign. Cheney admitted this. After all the political capital invested by the president in highlighting the Iraq threat running up to the AUMF vote, Cheney claimed that a choice not to use force against Hussein would have again made Bush look like Clinton, meaning tepid and indecisive.[127] "If he failed to stand firm now, after all the saber rattling, he would be revealed as a weak man, an ineffectual man," argued Logevall.[128] This was the worst of all possible outcomes for a president whose domestic political legitimacy rested, as Bush's did, on living up to the liberal narrative mantle. Like political fallout from a second terrorist strike, inaction after all of the administration's liberal narrative profile raising on Iraq would politically cripple the administration. In conventional audience cost terms, Bush was locked in by his public commitments. Even he admitted this. "I have to do this," Bush told Powell, of his decision in January 2003 to invade Iraq.[129] He had no choice. The liberal discourse around Iraq made sure of that.

Free Hand to Act in Iraq

In addition to pushing the Bush administration to act, the robust liberal narrative in the early 2000s also gave President Bush a free hand to pursue forceful regime change in Iraq. As mentioned already, Bush officials helped create a broad public discourse for war starting in 2002. It succeeded in doing so largely because of the robust liberal narrative. To go back to a previously used metaphor, if Bush was selling, the nation was buying.

As detailed already, the public was primed for regime change in Iraq as early as November 2001. By the middle of 2002, that generally still remained the case. Nine out of ten U.S. citizens continued to believe Saddam Hussein supported terrorist organizations intent on attacking the United States and a majority still thought Iraq was involved in 9/11. At the same time, questions remained about the necessity of war.[130] "Dick, I think you may have a big problem with public perceptions of a possible Iraq war," Senate Minority Leader Trent Lott told Cheney in August 2002, "The case hasn't been made as to why we should do it."[131] Lott and others wondered most about the timing: Why now? In light of this, members of Congress, among them influential Democrats, encouraged the president at a September 4 meeting to get out front and win over public support for the AUMF. Build a broad discourse for war, they suggested. "It's about weapons of mass destruction getting into the wrong hands," House Minority Leader Dick Gephardt (D-MO) told Bush, "They [the American people] don't see it . . . We need to make it graphic."[132]

The administration was already thinking this way, of course, before September 4. "Don't worry, we're about to fix all of that," Cheney responded, to Lott in August.[133] During the summer of 2002, administration officials settled on a message, that manipulated the liberal narrative in ways suggested by Gephardt. The public climate "favored the White House," observed McClellan, "since 9/11 remained fresh on the minds of Americans."[134] The liberal narrative offered a conducive environment. As Wolfowitz put it, the WMD-terrorism link was the "one issue that everyone agreed on."[135] Other possible arguments for war against Iraq were, thus, intentionally set aside out of concern that they would not resonate as well with the nation. "During the campaign for war," McClellan observes, "they emphasized the threat of WMD and the possible link between Iraq and terrorism." It was a "marketing choice," he added.[136]

So the marketing campaign began. The terrorism-WMD-Iraq link showed up everywhere in the administration's public comments. "Bush struck 9/11 like a gong in every fear-instilling speech about Iraq he could," said one observer.[137] This began, in fact, as early as mid-December 2001 when the administration started talking publicly about Iraq. "It is pretty well confirmed," Cheney said, on *Meet the Press* in December, "that Mohammed Atta [a 9/11 hijacker] met with a senior official of the Iraqi intelligence service in Czechoslovakia last spring."[138] The gong sounded time and again into 2002. Powell charged, in February, that there was "no doubt" Iraq was developing nuclear weapons.[139] On Capitol Hill in May, Rumsfeld said, "terrorist networks have relationships with terrorist states [i.e., Iraq] that have weapons of mass destruction."[140] Bush harped on the WMD-Iraq-terror link in the State of the Union address, June 1 preemption speech, and other statements across the spring.[141]

The link also showed up in administration discourse around the AUMF. In meetings with members of Congress, Bush and others detailed aluminum tubes purchased by Saddam for nuclear purposes; Saddam's attempts to acquire uranium from Niger; and Iraq's ties to al Qaeda.[142] As Isokoff and Corn note, "It was scary stuff—death labs on wheels, direct WMD attacks on America."[143] The ties to the moral of the prevailing liberal narrative could not have been stronger in these meetings. "Dick, how would you feel if you voted no on this and the Iraqis brought in a bomb and blew up half the people of San Francisco?" Cheney said, to a skeptical Dick Armey, in a late September meeting.[144] In public, administration officials pressed the same kind of liberal narrative message. "Imagine September 11 with weapons of mass destruction," Rumsfeld said on a Sunday talk show in early September.[145] In the weeks that followed, Bush repeatedly echoed the WMD-Iraq-terror link in dramatic fashion as well. In all instances, he drew attention to the lessons of the dominant post–9/11 story. "We will not allow any terrorist or tyrant to threaten civilization with weapons of mass destruction," the president stated in a speech on the one-year anniversary of the attack, "Now and in the future, Americans will live as free people, not in fear."[146] Bush hit the same theme the next day at the United Nations and then again in Cincinnati, Ohio a few days before the congressional AUMF vote.[147]

It was all part of a plan to use the liberal narrative to move the nation toward war. This explains, in fact, the administration's insistence on an AUMF vote before November. Inside the administration, Cheney apparently hatched the idea. "In an election year . . . it was simple," records Woodward, of Cheney's argument in a strategy meeting on September 1, "The President should demand quick passage of a resolution so voters would know before the election where every congressman and senator stood on Saddam Hussein and his dangerous regime." Rice seconded this, saying the "president had maximum leverage."[148] Another senior administration official noted that "congressmen facing reelection" would have to vote for the AUMF "to prove their war-waging machismo."[149] In short, master narratives are most powerful when they raise electoral concerns as discussed in chapter 1. The administration chose to use liberal narrative pressure this way (something it knew it all too well, of course, from its own second-strike and tarnished image concerns) to press Congress to go along with regime change in Iraq.

The strategy worked. By the end of 2002, there was widespread buy in to the WMD-Iraq-terror link. It "spooked us all," Lott said, of his briefing with Cheney. While not trusting the vice president, Daschle could not escape the thought: "What if they're right about this?"[150] Major newspapers from the *Los Angeles Times* to the *Chicago Tribune* and *Washington Post* endorsed war with Iraq, citing worries about WMDs and terrorism.[151] The same was the case on Capitol Hill, where the liberal narrative and its lessons saturated the debate among members of Congress. On the final day of the AUMF debate, for instance, sixteen of the seventeen Senators who spoke in support of the resolution mentioned 9/11 and/ or fears of WMDs falling into the hands of terrorists. In the House, eighteen of twenty-six speakers in the final debate mentioned the same. "Look no further than September 11, 2001," argued Congressman J.C. Watts (R-OK), in supporting the AUMF.[152] "Ours is a brave new post–9/11 world, a time and place where things are different," charged Senator Chuck Schumer (D-NY), "Hussein could either use or give to terrorists weapons of mass destruction."[153] The House voted 296 to 133 in favor of the AUMF. In the Senate, it passed 77 to 23.[154]

As the administration anticipated, the political weight of appearing tough on terrorism (i.e., audience costs for inaction) bore down on members of both houses. Prior to the Senate vote, a Senate Foreign Relations Committee staffer with reservations about the war urged Democrats, for instance, to read the National Intelligence Estimate on Iraq provided to Congress in October. In the end, only six followed his advice. The staffer explained the indifference of Democrats here in liberal narrative, cost-for-inaction terms: "We had an election coming up. The Democrats were afraid of being seen as soft on Saddam or on terrorism."[155] Others testified to the same. "We're in a tough spot," Gephardt told Democrats on October 2. "His message for us was implicit," Representative Jim McGovern said, of the meeting, "He did not want the Democrats to be blamed for the next attack."[156] As a 2004 presidential hopeful needing to look tough on terrorism given the robust liberal narrative, Gephardt felt that politically he had no other choice. He stood by Bush's side in the White House Rose Garden as the president formally requested the AUMF, then helped usher the necessary legislation through to passage in the House.[157] For some critics of the war, this was fateful. "The top Democrats were at their weakest when trying to show how tough they were," said Senator Lincoln Chafee (R-RI), who voted against the AUMF, "They were afraid that Republicans would label them soft in the post-September 11 world."[158] As it had done with Colin Powell in late 2001, the liberal discourse around Iraq with its costs for inaction effectively bludgeoned congressional moderates into submission.

The end result was a free hand, or "permissive context," that gave President Bush political space to launch a full-scale, regime change invasion of Iraq in March 2003.[159] The robust liberal narrative—what one commentator at the time called the "fertile ground [of] the post-Sept. 11 landscape"—stood at the center of it all.[160]

Disillusionment and the Iraq Syndrome

As seen already, the Bush administration justified the war in Iraq on the basis of WMDs and Saddam Hussein's ties to al Qaeda. Though a secondary factor in the lead up to the invasion, the administration added to these arguments that of democratization. "We will be greeted as liberators," Cheney said.[161] In the end, none of these justifications for war turned out to be true. Saddam Hussein had almost no weapons of mass destruction, his links to al Qaeda were limited, and the postwar chaos that emerged in Iraq looked nothing like a healthy democracy. These outcomes traumatized the U.S. public. Profound national disillusionment and a new restraint narrative set in that came to be reflected in the lessons of the Iraq syndrome.

After the fall of Baghdad, the Iraq Survey Group led the effort to locate WMD in Iraq. In a preliminary report in July 2003, the group concluded that nearly all of the evidence—aluminum tubes, mobile biological labs, and chemical weapons depots—used by the administration to justify the war was faulty. "We were almost all wrong—and I include myself here," said David Kay, head of the Survey Group.[162] Other parts of the story for war started to fall apart too. Reports surfaced that administration claims about Iraqi efforts to secure uranium from

Niger were false. When the CIA publicly verified this, a feeding frenzy began as the press started to deconstruct the entire Bush story for war.[163]

These stunning revelations opened the door for moderators to narrate a new story—a restraint narrative—about Iraq. All of the elements of existential challenge, blame and repair showed up in this new story. Bush came under heavy fire (i.e., blame) for lying to the nation and abusing executive power (i.e., illiberal/ existential challenge). Charges like these came from everywhere. Members of Congress talked of Bush "suppressing the truth about Iraq" and claimed "Americans have been victims of lies, deceptions, and distractions."[164] Democrats were most vocal here, calling almost immediately for an independent investigation. Republicans joined in too. "I'm not pleased," said GOP senator Pat Roberts (KS), in October 2003, "Did they mislead us, or did they simply get it wrong? Whatever the answer, it's not good."[165] Concerned as ever about its public image, the White House double-downed on the WMD story, rather than admit mistakes.[166] In light of the Kay and Duelfer findings, this only fueled speculation of deceit. "A full-fledged shout-fest was under way among pundits, politicos, and cable talking heads" by fall 2003, observed Isokoff.[167] This part of the moderator story that focused on blame and deception gained broader traction as well.[168] Editorials ripped into the administration: "It . . . highlights Bush's misuse of intelligence to justify the war in Iraq"; "Bush terribly misled the public"; "the chief argument for the Iraq war remains thoroughly discredited"; "the president's justification for war . . . was fabricated out of whole cloth"; and "the White House 'misled' Americans."[169] A 2005 poll indicated that 53 percent believed Bush deliberately misled the public about Iraq's WMD program. Sixty percent were "skeptical" about the White House's reasons for invading Iraq.[170]

WMD was not the only issue that helped generate public disillusionment and gave space for moderator storytelling. The postwar situation on the ground in Iraq sparked national anger and disdain as well. On May 1, 2003, Bush gave a speech on-board an aircraft carrier declaring the end of combat operations in Iraq. "Mission Accomplished," read a banner that hung behind the president. "It was a big mistake," Bush later admitted.[171] The chaos in Iraq that followed the speech looked nothing like an accomplished mission or the budding democracy that Bush promised. By late May, a full-blown Sunni insurgency emerged that targeted U.S. forces and the new Iraqi coalition government set up by the United States. The violence reached its climax following the bombing of the al-Askari Mosque in Samarra, one of the holiest sites of Shia Islam, in February 2006. The mosque bombing set off a widespread conflict between Sunni and Shia Muslims. U.S. forces now found themselves in the middle of a full-blown civil war inside Iraq.[172]

After the Samarra bombing in particular, the situation looked hopeless to U.S. citizens. Here again, moderators found an opening to storytell. As part of this, deceit and blame of the administration resurfaced. Similar to the national discussion around the first Tet offensive in Vietnam, moderators charged, among other things, that the administration's rosy picture of developments in Iraq was a lie that misled the nation. "I have not been told the truth over and over again by administration witnesses," charged Senator Bill Nelson (D-FL), "and the American people have not been told the truth."[173]

Added to this, moderators blamed the Arab world more broadly (and with that Bush for not better understanding the Arab world) for the U.S. problems in Iraq. "We have committed this nation to a very tough struggle in a brutally inhospitable place populated not by incipient democracy-lovers but by people who have for generations settled disputes with bullets and bombs," claimed one newspaper in 2004.[174] This kind of charge was widespread. Similar to the disillusionment over Vietnam in the 1970s, moderators claimed the Iraq enterprise now looked incapable of producing a liberal outcome. "Is this what 'freedom on the march' looks like, Mr. Speaker?" argued Congresswoman Lynn Woolsey (D-CA), "The administration's Iraq policy is a tragic blunder of historic proportions."[175] As one scholar noted of this period, the "unspeakable, politically incorrect conclusion creeping into the minds of many influential people in Washington is that the Middle East is 'incurable.'"[176] To this end, moderators in think-tanks and the wider scholarly community in the mid-2000s talked repeatedly of the unpreparedness of the region for democracy.[177] These kinds of assessments resonated in new and deeper ways amid the disillusionment over Iraq.[178] Blame came from Republicans too. "The White House is completely disconnected from reality," Senator Chuck Hagel (R-NE) said in 2005, of the administration's optimistic view of democracy in the Middle East.[179] Polls reflected these sentiments. In 2006, 54 percent of Americans agreed that Bush "deliberately misled the American public" about Iraq and 55 percent believed the war was a mistake.[180] Overall, the moderator story of blame took hold broadly, helping to fuel deep public disillusionment.

This affected the master narrative landscape in the United States. For starters, it weakened the liberal narrative into the 2010s. While terrorism still concerned the U.S. public, the chaos in Iraq created a full-scale retreat in public support for promoting democracy and nation-building abroad. One poll found public support for democracy promotion fell from 52 percent in 2005 to 45 percent in 2006 to 37 percent in 2007.[181] "The U.S. public has become skeptical about promoting ideals abroad," observed a pair of scholars in early 2009.[182] In January of that year, newly elected president Barack Obama gave voice to the weakened liberal narrative in his first major address to Congress. "A cynical and doubtful" mood exists, the president said, about "shaping our world for good."[183]

Disillusionment had another master narrative impact as well. "The Iraq syndrome is coming," predicted a political scientist in 2007.[184] He was right. The Iraq War left a profound mark in the form of a robust restraint narrative on the collective psyche of the U.S. public. It "looms over" and "haunts" the United States to the current day.[185]

This Iraq syndrome embodied the entire moderator story of blame and existential danger as well as an important final piece: moral. The moral showed up in 2006 and beyond with a chorus of voices from across the political spectrum demanding the withdrawal of U.S. troops from Iraq. Some made the pitch indirectly, charging that Iraqi boots on the ground needed to replace U.S. forces. "It is time for the Iraqis to send in their own troops to take out the Shia militias and the Sunni insurgents," said Representative Ric Keller (R-FL).[186] "I support a responsible redeployment of our troops," said Representative Adam Schiff (D-CA), "so Iraqis are forced to take primary responsibility for securing and governing their country."[187] Others were more direct about the lessons of Iraq: "get our folks out of Iraq"; "Americans overwhelmingly want to see our troops begin to come home"; and "bring our troops home."[188] While some conservatives worked to defend Bush, many others joined the "no-boots-on-the-ground" club. Influential columnists like William F. Buckley and George Will claimed the war was a colossal mistake. To varying degrees, they and other conservatives railed against the folly of trying to militarily restructure other countries in general. In doing so, some tried to distance themselves and the Republican Party from it. "The so-called neo-con architects of this unnecessary war have led people down a primrose path in the opposite direction of . . . every traditional conservative position," argued Representative John Duncan (R-TN).[189] For all of these moderators and many others like them the big moral to the story was the same: avoid military action to topple and/or rebuild governments abroad.

In the late 2000s, this restraint narrative lesson took hold of the nation. Set on avoiding a repeat of the Iraq trauma, the Iraq syndrome prizes foreign policy limits.[190] In this vein, scholars and other commentators use terms like "timidity," "giant hesitation," "period of retreat," and "legacy of wariness and weariness" to describe the restraint narrative impact on the national temper toward policy abroad.[191] Parallels to the post-Vietnam period have been common in describing the Iraq syndrome. "The words *Middle East*, much as the term *Vietnam*, has come to mean being stuck in a foreign policy and military quagmire," notes David Rothkopf.[192]

Like its post-Vietnam predecessor, the "never again" component of the Iraq syndrome has meant more than anything else a deep public aversion to deploying American forces abroad, especially in large combat operations like Iraq.[193] To this end, common terms in the national discourse, like "no boots on the ground" and "war weariness," are pillars of the post-Iraq national discourse that reflect the robust restraint narrative.[194] "It's going to be 20 years before we go there again with boots-on-the-ground interventions," observed Lt. Col. John Nagle (ret) in 2013, "The American people, I think, are going to have a real hard time buying it, and we're going to have a hard time feeding it to them next time."[195] Polling data backs this up. By late 2006, the desire to get boots out of the Middle East started to show up. One exit poll on Election Day in November 2006 found that 55 percent wanted to begin withdrawing troops from Iraq immediately.[196] In 2009, 63 percent of the U.S. public supported withdrawing "all troops as soon as possible."[197]

The power and presence of the restraint narrative were evident in policy decisions during Bush's last two years in office. For instance, when Bush announced a surge of troops in Iraq to calm the sectarian violence, he faced a syndrome-driven wave of near-unanimous opposition to the move. Sixty-one percent of the U.S. public said they opposed the surge, and 54 percent wanted a full withdrawal within twelve months.[198] Members of Congress on both sides of the aisle expressed opposition, what one commentator called a "bipartisan scolding."[199] "Are you listening, Mr. Bush," noted the editorialist Tony Norman, "We don't believe you. This war is over. We lost."[200] In the end, Bush was forced to bend to the "no-boots" mentality of the nation by leaking word of an anticipated withdrawal date for all U.S. forces in order to get Congress to vote in favor of funding the troop surge.[201]

Iraq was not the only place the syndrome showed up. In June 2007, Bush turned down what he considered a tone-deaf proposal (i.e., out-of-step with the restraint narrative moral) from Cheney to bomb Syria for its presumed development of a nuclear reactor.[202] The syndrome affected policy toward Iran as well. When King Abdullah of Saudi Arabia pressed Rice and new Secretary of Defense Robert Gates, for a U.S. military strike against Iran in 2007, Gates shut the idea down with lessons at the center of the Iraq syndrome. "The American people would not stand for it," Gates told Abdullah, "In fact, he [Bush] would be impeached."[203]

Finally, the restraint narrative was on full display in the 2008 presidential elections. Every presidential candidate tried to align themselves with the lessons of the robust restraint narrative. On this score, Republicans ran away from Bush. "I'm not a carbon copy of President Bush," Mitt Romney claimed, during the GOP primaries. "Absolutely not," snapped Mike Huckabee, when asked if he supported Bush's vision for democracy promotion in the Middle East.[204] Democrats, like Senator Barack Obama, structured their entire campaigns around being the "un-Bush." Obama essentially wrapped himself in the Iraq syndrome, touting at nearly every campaign stop his long-standing opposition to the Iraq War. He tied himself to the narrative's moral of no boots on the ground too. "I opposed this war from the start," Obama said, when announcing his candidacy, "America, it's time to start bringing our troops home."[205] Obama promised full troop withdrawal within sixteen months of becoming president and an end to nation-building in general.[206] The appeal to syndrome themes helped him defeat two initial supporters of the Iraq War, Senator Hillary Clinton (D-NY) and Senator John McCain (R-AZ), on the way to the White House. A period of national pullback followed that shaped U.S. responses to regime crises overseas for the next eight years of Obama's administration. Libya serves as a prime example.

Libya

Barack Obama structured his Middle East policy around the Iraq syndrome and its collectively powerful lessons of restraint. "Iraq put handcuffs on us," said a State Department official during the Obama presidency, "It was a constant ghost hanging over everything."[207] Above all else, this restraint narrative pressed the administration toward a more minimalist foreign policy. In planning the 2010 troop surge in Afghanistan, for instance, Obama repeatedly referenced the lessons of Iraq as he turned down proposals from his military advisors for a robust nation-building operation. "Stan, if this were 2003, maybe we could do a counterinsurgency strategy," he told General Stanley McChrystal, "Maybe I would have done that, but it's 2009 and we're long past that point." Obama then added that "there is still no appetite here for us doing" even the shorter-term, lighter-footprint surge that his administration eventually undertook.[208] Afghanistan was not the only place that the moral of the restraint narrative mattered in the early Obama years. It also led to Obama's rejection of a 2001 proposal from the Pentagon to create a permanent force for stability operations. "After Iraq and Afghanistan, Obama was determined to get the United States out of the nation-building business," David Sanger explains, of the decision.[209]

The Iraq syndrome also deeply affected the administration's approach to the Arab Spring, including its response to the 2011 regime crisis in Libya.[210] Above else, the limited, backseat role that the United States took militarily in unseating Muammar Gaddafi's government in Libya was a direct product of a strong restraint discourse that developed in the United States around this case.

A popular uprising in Libya began on February 15, 2011. Gaddafi responded with force to maintain order and regain lost ground, especially around the rebel stronghold of Benghazi.[211] These events sparked a wide debate in the United States. On the one hand, many felt the need to take action in order to prevent a humanitarian disaster. Inside the Obama administration, advocates for this position included Ambassador to the United Nations Susan Rice, Special Assistant

ver and, eventually, Secretary of State Hillary Clinton. From the
Power, in particular, argued that it was critical to avoid another
the United States stood by and did nothing to stop a genocide.[212]

romoters outside the administration, that included Senators John
McCain and Joseph Lieberman as well as the Senate Foreign Relations Committee chair John Kerry, took a similar line.[213] "We ought to be considering a wide-
range of responses," argued Kerry, in early March.[214] Sympathy for the Libyan
rebels and calls for action came from other quarters too. Editorials in the *New
York Times*, *Washington Post*, *San Francisco Chronicle*, *Los Angeles Times*, and
other major newspaper joined a chorus of commentators who criticized Obama's
tepid response to the Arab Spring to that point and called, as a result, for a firmer
stand against Gaddafi. By early March, promoters advocated a range of options
from sanctions to aiding the rebels to a NATO-led no-fly zone to prevent a genocide in Libya.[215]

The impulse to act was tempered, on the other hand, by the Iraq syndrome.
The moral to the story here—that is, avoid "another Iraq"—was everywhere in
the public discourse around Libya. Moderators inside the administration, especially Secretary of Defense Robert Gates, played a big part in helping to fan this
discourse. Gates went public with his skepticism about using force against Gaddafi's regime in late February.[216] "In my opinion, any future defense secretary
who advises the president to again send a big land army into Asia or into the
Middle East or Africa should 'have his head examined,'" Gates said, in a speech on
February 25.[217] A few days later, he criticized "loose talk" about intervention, saying that a no-fly zone is "a big operation in a big country," with the potential for
escalation to a larger war.[218] Comments like these sparked caution that came to
saturate the wider public discourse by early March. "This nation could overthrow
Khadafy if it liked," observed the *Denver Post*, "Our troops toppled far more for-
midable regimes in Kabul and Baghdad only to discover that the nation-building
exercise that followed . . . created a military quagmire for years to come."[219] Others
commented about the "unpredictability" of military action and said that "force
should be off the table"—"don't want to do that again," said one observer.[220] "The
truth is that after Iraq, we just don't have a realistic option of invading another
Arab country with oil," said another.[221]

Promoters were thrown onto the defensive by this restraint discourse. Some
backpedaled on their positions, while most were forced to clarify the limits of
what they sought to do in Libya. They scrambled to come back in line with the
restraint narrative. "It's not going to be like Iraq," Kerry said, on March 6 of a no-
fly zone. Senate Minority Leader Mitch McConnell echoed this too. We need to
take action "short of sending our own military personnel."[222] "No one is talking

about introducing U.S. ground forces a la Afghanistan or Iraq," observed the *Wall Street Journal*, which supported a strong position against Gaddafi.[223] Limits like these reflected broader opinion. Polls in mid-March showed that while the public supported a multilateral no-fly zone over Libya, 65 percent opposed the "U.S. military getting involved with the situation in Libya" and 74 percent were concerned the United States might be "getting embroiled in a long-term conflict."[224] Overall, any sort of sentiment to protect Libyans in ousting a long-time dictator was muted by the Iraq syndrome.[225]

The White House was well aware of the growing public attention to Libya and, within that, the restraint narrative discourse. In early March, an administration official said that Libya had become a "water cooler issue," meaning a part of everyday conversation that dredged up public worries about another Iraq.[226] Internally, Gates and a cohort of other moderators took advantage of this and pressed restraint narrative themes. At meetings with Obama and other national security advisors into the weekend of March 12 and 13, Gates harped on the lessons of Iraq as he warned repeatedly, for instance, of postwar chaos in Libya and that, along these lines, the opposition may be more interested in sectarian objectives or, still worse, inspired by al Qaeda.[227] Obama's political advisors urged caution as well, reminding Obama that he had been elected to get the United States out of wars in the Middle East, not start new ones.[228] "We think about Iraq analogies all the time," said a senior administration official, of the internal deliberations in early March.[229] Overall, the moral of the prevailing restraint narrative bore down upon the White House, raising audience costs for action considerably.

The combination of the humanitarian impulse among Obama's advisors and the Iraq syndrome played a major part in Obama's March 15 decision for military action in Libya. The former provided the impetus to act, while the latter set limits on how to act. Obama's policy choice, then, came to match the mixed messages of the domestic discourse at the time around Libya.

By mid-March, a slaughter was on the horizon. Gaddafi's forces were moving unabated toward Misrata, with the Libyan dictator promising to punish not just the rebels but the city's residents. This had a big impact on Obama. "That's just not who we are," the president said, of standing by while civilians were massacred.[230] He worried that inaction might kill the Arab Spring uprisings as well as hurt U.S. credibility and his own reputation given his promises about defending human rights.[231] As a result, Obama asked Rice to put forward a UN resolution calling on member states to prevent, by force if necessary, a humanitarian disaster in Libya. He, then, authorized the U.S. military to take part in the multilateral effort.[232]

This was not to be a boots-on-the ground, combat invasion like Iraq, however. The restraint discourse of the Iraq syndrome made certain of that. The administration worked to ensure that force against Gaddafi would look like anything but another Iraq. This meant, above all else, a highly conscribed military operation for the United States involving a support role to a coalition of states using air power only, what eventually became labelled "lead from behind."[233]

Drawing on syndrome themes, Gates helped most in driving the administration to this militarily limited posture. During the meetings on March 15, the secretary of defense took a firm position against intervention. He pressed hardest on the point about postwar chaos. The United States would end up "owning" what came next in Libya, Gates argued. Above all else, he harped on a potential "stalemate," meaning another Iraq-like quagmire with sectarian conflict.[234] This argument played on the administration's worst fears—notably, the domestic political peril of an intervention that strayed from restraint narrative lessons. No one wanted to "own" Libya the way the U.S. did Iraq. In fact, there was a kind of surreal element to the entire Libyan issue for most administration officials. "I can't believe we are about to debate taking military action in another Islamic nation," a senior member of Obama's national security team told a reporter, days before the March 15 debate.[235] On March 10, Clinton testified on Capitol Hill about the "owning it" concerns too. "It's easy for people to say," she warned, in reference to talk about a simple military operation, "You use, you know, your men and women; you go out and do it and then you take the consequences if something bad happens."[236] Another administration official who took part in the deliberations stated simply, "There was a certain wariness to get involved militarily in a third Muslim country."[237]

This restraint discourse impacted Obama's decision on Libya. In response to Gates, Obama committed not to put U.S. boots on the ground. "America's involvement must be limited in scope and finite in time," the president said to his advisors on March 15. As Sanger observes, "In this post-Iraq age . . . [Obama] was not going to send ground troops into a third conflict."[238] He also agreed to two other steps intended to limit the U.S. role even further so as to avoid another Iraq. First, the United States would take the lead at the start of the air campaign for a short period ("days not weeks," Obama said, to his advisors) in order to take out Gaddafi's air defense system, then U.S. forces would move into a support role for its NATO and Arab allies to maintain the no-fly zone.[239] In order to match the public's syndrome temperament, the president made this limited, multilateral approach a prerequisite for action, in fact. "If they're willing to sign up to this," Obama said, to Rice about the United Nations and U.S. allies, "then we'll move forward."[240] In this vein, Gates later admitted that the Arab League's request for and willingness to contribute to outside intervention in Libya was a big factor in Obama's policy choice—it allowed Obama to adopt a limited approach, thus bringing policy in line with the prevailing restraint discourse. "Had the Arab League not voted that, there might have been a different outcome . . . in our decision," Gates said.[241] In short, the restraint discourse helped limit an already limited U.S. military role to "lead from behind," which offered important political protection at home for the administration.

Second, Obama bowed to the restraint narrative in how he publicly justified the mission. Notably, the stated goal of the mission in public was intentionally restricted to preventing a humanitarian disaster, and not regime change.[242] This move was more than just semantics. Coupled with the military limits on the operation, the humanitarian justification limited the U.S. role and responsibilities in ways that ensured the United States did not "own" Libya once Gaddafi was ousted. Multilateralism meant the invasion was not just a "U.S. thing," while the limited humanitarian goal (and not regime change) meant that what came after the coalition prevented a slaughter in Libya (i.e., satisfied the mission's humanitarian justification) was not Washington's responsibility, either.[243] "We didn't want to get sucked into an operation with uncertainty at the end," an administration official said, drawing parallels to Iraq, "How it turns out is not on our shoulders."[244] Another national security aid agreed: "we're not around on the ground, where we breed resentment . . . It's up to the Libyans."[245]

Together, these three moves—no U.S. combat troops, lead from behind, and no regime change—allowed Obama to take on the intervention by lessening the political danger (or, audience costs for action) of crossing the restraint narrative moral of "no more Iraqs." It was the "anti-Iraq" war, said one government official—"more like the 1991 gulf war than the 2003 Iraq war," said another observer close the White House.[246] Like Grenada in the prior chapter, Libya was, therefore, an exception that proved the power of the syndrome rule. "Call if we can help," David Sanger notes, of the prevailing tone in the Obama approach to Libya, "It was a philosophy that seemed to match the national mood."[247]

Indeed, that was the case. When announcing the war to the public on March 19, Obama harped on the lesson at the center of the restraint narrative. "I also want to be clear about what we will not be doing," the president said, "The United States is not going to deploy ground troops to Libya."[248] Through late March, administration officials used terms like "days not weeks" and "no boots on the ground" repeatedly in public to reinforce the president's message.[249] In the end, this helped calm the nerves of a jittery nation, fearful of another Iraq. "I like what I heard," said Representative Mike Rogers (R-MI) of Obama's promises about the limited U.S. role.[250] Overall, the president successfully fit U.S. military action in Libya into the national temperament which in 2011 was dominated by the Iraq syndrome. The end result was (as expected in a robust restraint narrative environment) an extremely limited regime change intervention in Libya.

Alternative Explanations

This section explores the strengths and weaknesses of several alternative explanations for forceful regime change in Iraq and Libya.

Geopolitics

Realism anticipates that the use of robust force for regime promotion is most likely when threat perceptions are low, which occurs most often when great powers hold a preponderance of power. On one level, this argument seems a valid explanation of Iraq and Libya. At the time of the Libyan regime crisis, the United States still had approximately 150,000 troops in Iraq and Afghanistan—a far smaller number of overseas deployed personnel than in 2003 when the Iraq War started.[251] Added to this, realists point to the rise of China across the 2000s as a new counterweight to the United States globally.[252] Arguably, realists would expect, then, robust forceful regime change to be most likely in the case of Iraq rather than Libya—the United States had a greater preponderance of power at the time of the former than the latter.

The biggest problem with this argument is timing. Most date China's emergence as a counterweight to the United States to the early 2000s.[253] If this is the case, why did the Iraq invasion occur in 2003 and not sooner, when the United States held an even greater preponderance of global power? This question becomes all the more puzzling when one considers that in 2003 the United Sates was also fighting the war in Afghanistan—there was no such comparable U.S. troop deployment in the 1990s. Overall, something more than just a preponderance of power accounts for regime change in Iraq.

The same can be said about Libya. In the years since the Libyan operation, the United States has withdrawn all combat troops from Iraq and most from Afghanistan. Furthermore, systemic economic weaknesses have slowed China's rise. Hence, the U.S. preponderance of power has arguably increased since 2011. Yet the United States shows no greater willingness to take on large-scale, forceful regime change invasions, like Iraq, than it did at the time of the Libyan operation.[254] Syria exemplifies this most. The regime crisis there has produced the kind of humanitarian nightmare that Obama officials worried about in Libya in 2011. Yet the United States has taken almost no action to stop the violence or remove the regime of the Syrian president Bashar al-Assad.

Why? Many cite the restraint narrative lessons found in the Iraq syndrome, not the relative power of the United States globally or in the Middle East region. Unlike Libya, other states have been unwilling to shoulder the burden of military action in Syria. This has raised all the worst possible syndrome fears of owning Syria (i.e., high costs for action) for all politicians in the United States. "He [Obama] sees a conflict like Iraq, where our hopes of doing good can be overwhelmed by the reality of getting into the aftermath," a senior administration official said, of Obama's restraint in 2013.[255] Overall, realism helps account for some features of the Iraq and Libya cases, but fails to offer as comprehensive an explanation of patterns of forceful regime change as the master narrative argument.

Elite Polarization

According to the stand-alone elite polarization argument, the likelihood of robust forceful regime promotion increases as elites become ideologically polarized due to either great power wars or regime crises abroad involving ideological rivals. This argument sheds interesting light on the Iraq and Libyan cases. President Bush and officials in his administration were clearly polarized in the early 2000s. They viewed combatting terrorism in ideological terms.[256] Perhaps more than any other case in this book, elites in the Bush administration also used, as detailed above, their positions of authority to push the nation toward war in Iraq. At one level, then, elite polarization offers a good explanation in this case.

The main challenges for the polarization argument comes with fine-grained policy issues, like the timing of regime change and how the administration managed to move the nation toward war in Iraq. As to timing, John Owen contends that U.S. policy elites became polarized around radical Islam in the early to mid-1990s.[257] Across this same period, there were also numerous regime crises inside Iraq. This being the case, why did full-scale regime change in Iraq not come until 2003? This puzzle reaches into the Bush years too. Neoconservatives lobbied for a more forceful approach toward Iraq during the first nine months of the Bush administration. But they found no receptive ears among Bush, Cheney, Rice, or Powell in that period.[258] What flipped the switch toward action and made the opinions of neoconservatives more mainstream within the administration? A focus on elite polarization alone cannot answer this. The master narrative argument steps in here. As discussed above, the trauma of 9/11 and the politics surrounding the liberal narrative pressed in on Bush in ways that elevated Iraq in the calculations of policy elites. That same master narrative landscape also mattered to how Bush was able to lead the nation to war. Without the robust liberal narrative that followed 9/11, it is hard to imagine that Bush or any other president could have convinced Congress and the American public to invade Iraq. Overall, the strong liberal narrative of the early 2000s played a critical part in accentuating the beliefs of and creating a political opportunity space for polarized elites in the lead up to robust forceful regime change in Iraq. Again, without understanding this master narrative landscape, elite polarization alone faces limitations in explaining robust forceful regime change in Iraq.[259]

The same kinds of issues arise for the elite polarization argument with Libya. Elite polarization remained high into the 2010s, largely because of continued fears about radical Islam.[260] On this score, Obama agreed to the 2010 surge in Afghanistan due to fears that a resurgent Taliban might aid al Qaeda. The new challenge of the Islamic State (ISIS) to regimes in Iraq and Syria, along with ISIS attacks on European and U.S. soil, have spiked elite polarization all the more. The puzzle for the elite argument is that despite all of this polarization, regime promotion in Libya (as well as other cases, like Syria) remained militarily limited. Elite polarization alone struggles to explain this. Along with concerns about a humanitarian disaster, polarization may have contributed some to the impulse for action in Libya. As far as the choice to *limit* action here, the Iraq syndrome, as discussed above, seems the key determinant. In general, the Iraq and Libya cases suggest that it is better to understand the important intersection between collective elite and national dispositions in order to build a more comprehensive ideational explanation of forceful regime promotion. The master narrative argument takes a step in that direction.

Counterarguments

Finally, it is important to consider a set of counterarguments, related to partisanship, the strength of the U.S. economy, and international credibility. Arguably, one can assume that as the economy strengthens, states are more likely to pursue major military commitments abroad, like robust forceful regime change, and vice versa. To this argument's credit, the more robust 2003 invasion of Iraq came at a point of greater economic strength than Libya. All the same, timing is a big problem for the strength-of-the-economy argument. While the U.S. economy was performing better at the time of Iraq relative to Libya, why did the Iraq invasion not come sooner, when the economy was even stronger during the boom of the 1990s? Likewise, as the U.S. economy has strengthened since 2011, why so much regime promotion restraint, like in Syria? Strength of the economy cannot explain this variation as well as the master narrative argument.

Partisanship offers another possible counterargument. Along these lines, the fact that Bush was a Republican and Obama a Democrat might explain the different outcomes in Iraq and Libya. This argument has some merit: Democrats

were more prone to multilateral solutions, like Libya, and Republicans toward unilateral military action, like Iraq. The partisanship argument breaks down, though, with a closer look at the cases. Congressional Democrats (including leaders like Gephardt and Daschle) voted in large numbers for the war in Iraq. Likewise, no Republicans called for combat operations in Libya. Instead, many endorsed Obama's multilateral, lighter-footprint operation or opposed the use of force altogether. If Republicans are unilateralists and Democrats multilateralists, what trumped party tendencies here? Again, master narratives offer a strong account. Many Democrats went along with the Iraq War for fear of looking weak on terrorism, and Republicans took positions on Libya that lined up with lessons at the center of the Iraq syndrome. Overall, partisanship might explain some aspects of promoter/moderator efforts to make political gains in the Iraq and Libya cases. On its own, this argument offers little explanatory power over the central puzzle here of robust military action in Iraq and limited action in Libya.

Lastly, concerns about international credibility or reputation had little impact on U.S. decisions in Iraq and Libya. As seen already, reputation affected Obama's decision some to act in Libya (though not on the issue of how much force to use). With regard to Iraq, George W. Bush showed almost no concern for international reputation. He faced stiff opposition from nearly all allies in Europe in the run-up to and during the Iraq War. Yet Bush pressed forward all the same. Bush faced similar opposition to the 2007 surge, and again moved forward regardless.[261]

In the 2000s, the United States pursued regime change in Iraq and Libya. It used full-scale combat operations in the former and limited force in the latter. This chapter demonstrates that master narratives played a major part in both decisions. In the former, a robust, post–9/11 liberal discourse around Iraq generated costs for inaction that sent the Bush administration looking for both new threats and ways to sustain its politically valuable antiterrorism image. In this context, Iraq moved to the center of policymaking for Bush. That same narrative also gave the administration space—a free hand—to build the public case for war with Iraq once the administration decided on that course of action in 2002. In the case of Libya, the Obama administration chose a limited, lead-from-behind role largely because of a second master narrative—the Iraq syndrome. A burgeoning restraint discourse sparked by moderators inside and outside the administration raised costs for action in ways that severely limited the U.S. military role in the Libyan crisis.

Like many others in this book, these cases—especially Iraq—have left an indelible and almost entirely negative mark on the U.S. body politic and the

Middle East at-large. How do we prevent this from happening again? The answer is complex. As seen above, it involves much more than blaming individual leaders and, thus, electing the right people to office. Instead, we need to know something more about managing the politics of master narratives—both the pressures applied to policymakers and the impulses of elites to use master narratives for their own political gain. The final chapter takes up this issue.

THE IMPLICATIONS OF MASTER NARRATIVE POLITICS

Forceful regime promotion has been one of the most common, destructive, and controversial military objectives pursued by great powers since the turn of the twentieth century. The United States has been, furthermore, a leading participant in these kinds of wars. This chapters reviews the findings in the prior chapters and, then, explores the implications for contemporary U.S. foreign policy.

The Explanations

This book finds that the master narrative argument explains forceful regime change in U.S. foreign policy better than two leading alternatives, realism and elite ideology. Statistical results discussed in chapter 2 demonstrate this to be the case broadly in U.S. foreign policy from 1900 to 2011. Table 7.1 tells a similar story. It offers a picture of evidence from eight case studies, designating the extent to which each case fits the expectations of different alternative arguments. "Partial" refers to cases where outcomes matched some, but not all, expectations of a certain explanation.

Realism

Realism anticipates that robust forceful regime promotion is most likely when a state possesses a preponderance of power either globally or in a certain region(s) of the world. Table 7.1 demonstrates that forceful regime promotion

TABLE 7.1 Predictions and outcomes in U.S. regime promotion cases

	REALISM	ELITE IDEOLOGY	MASTER NARRATIVES
Korea	No	No	Yes
China	Yes	Yes	Yes
Cuba	No	Partial	Yes
Vietnam	No	No	Yes
El Salvador	No	No	Yes
Grenada	Yes	Yes	Yes
Iraq	No	Partial	Yes
Libya	Yes	No	Yes

did not generally follow these realist expectations. The United States pursued its most robust invasions in cases (i.e., Korea, Vietnam, and Iraq) where it held no major preponderance of power. In Korea and Vietnam, policymakers knew that they risked a wider great power war, but went ahead with robust military action all the same. In Iraq, the United States clearly held more power than others in the international system, but still faced the rising power of China and an ongoing war in Afghanistan that, at the least, made a full-scale invasion less likely at this point than in prior years when a preponderance of U.S. power was even greater. Overall, then, the three largest regime promotion wars conducted by the United States since World War II make little sense from a realist perspective.

The puzzle for realism is compounded still further with U.S. decisions for military restraint. Washington refrained from full-scale invasions in regime crises (notably, El Salvador and Cuba) that occurred in Latin America during the Cold War. This was the one region of the world where the United States held an overwhelming preponderance of power at the time. If there was any place, therefore, that full-scale military operations should have been employed, it was here. This restraint, then, makes little sense as well for realists. The fact that full-scale force was used, furthermore, in Grenada raises more questions than answers. Notably, what allowed or pushed leaders toward robust military action here, but not other places in the region? Overall, something other than a preponderance of power seems more important to explain forceful regime change behavior.

Despite these weaknesses in the preponderance of power argument, realists may retort that there is a shift in power at the center of the master narrative argument that makes the case for realism in another way. Most notably, change in liberal narrative strength depends on the geopolitical gains and power of other states in the international system—power appears to be the central explanatory variable for one of the two main narratives at the center of this book, realists might contend.

As discussed in chapter 1, claims like these oversimplify the master narrative argument. They miss, above all else, the vital role of identity in explaining which geopolitical changes do and do not matter. More to the point, the master narrative argument contends that change in liberal narrative strength turns on geopolitical shifts involving *ideologically distant states*. It took geopolitics combined with German *autocracy* in the 1910s, German *fascism* in the 1930s, Soviet *communism* in the 1940s and al Qaeda's *radical Islam* to spark periods of the most significant strengthening in the liberal narrative between 1900 and 2011. Absent that ideological distance, liberal narrative strengthening does not generally occur. There was no surge in passion, for instance, inside the United States to defend liberal order when Great Britain used force to retake the Falkland Islands in 1983—a shared liberal identity meant the United States did not see Britain as a threat. Overall, geopolitics indeed matter, but only as a function of identity, which gives meaning to power in ways, then, that contrast sharply with how realists conceptualize threats in international politics.[1]

As mentioned in the introduction, realist factors present, of course, some important boundary conditions to the master narrative argument. States are not likely to pursue forceful regime promotion, for instance, in cases of highest security, and great power status seems a pre-requisite of sorts for states to consider regime promotion wars. These important boundary conditions aside, realism still offers, as the cases and statistical analysis in this book demonstrate, a generally weak account of patterns of forceful regime change in U.S. foreign policy over the last century or more.

Elite Ideology

The main argument in this book brings together elements of elite ideology and public narratives to offer a more holistic ideational approach to explain patterns of forceful regime promotion. In order to demonstrate the necessity of this argument, the book tested throughout a stand-alone elite-ideology account of forceful regime promotion. This elite-based argument contends that robust force is most likely when leadership elites, especially the president, become ideologically animated or polarized. Limited force or nonintervention is most likely when elites are either not polarized at all, or when polarized leaders reason that broader geopolitical costs are too high for action in a regime crisis (strategic costs essentially trump ideological preferences).[2]

As table 7.1 indicates, this argument fares about as well as realism. Of the three most militarily robust cases (Korea, Vietnam, and Iraq), the elite argument finds only partial strength in just one instance—Iraq. In the Korea and Vietnam cases, the presidents and some of their closest aides held strong strategic preferences against intervention, but went ahead with robust military action anyway. With Iraq, leader polarization undoubtedly contributed to regime change. The "partial" label here results from the timing of this decision. Elites had been polarized since the early 1990s and there were several regime crises in Iraq over this time. In addition, President George W. Bush turned aside internal pressure for a more forceful stand against Iraq in 2001, both before and just after 9/11. With all of the right elite-ideology conditions in place, then, why did robust action come so much later, in 2003? What pushed the Bush administration toward forceful regime change here? Elite ideology alone struggles to answer this.

Cases like China and Grenada appear to offer the strongest support for the elite-based argument—in the former, elites followed through on their preference of strategic restraint and in the latter followed through on their ideological preferences for a robust invasion. The puzzle for the elite argument here centers, of course, on cross-case variation. Leaders held similar strategic (Korea) and ideological (El Salvador) preferences around other cases at the same time, but did not follow through on those preferences. Something other than elite dispositions must have allowed leaders, then, to follow their preferences in some instances of regime crisis abroad and not others. A case like Cuba adds to this puzzle still further. Here, President John Kennedy preferred nonintervention, wanting instead to normalize relations with Cuba. While Kennedy chose against robust military action as the elite argument anticipates, his approval of the covert Bay of Pigs invasion clearly contradicted his preferences.

Overall, the case studies in this book raise doubts about the ability of a stand-alone elite-based account to help us understand the more fine-grained policy decisions related to patterns of forceful regime change. This does not mean, of course, that elite dispositions are irrelevant. Instead, the findings in this book suggest that the impact of elite ideology on policy is contextualized, or heavily conditioned, by other important factors, notably master narratives.

Master Narratives

As table 7.1 indicates, the master narrative argument offers a strong explanation of patterns of forceful regime promotion in the U.S. foreign policy. In sharp contrast to conventional explanations, broad national stories centered around the moral of either promoting/protecting liberal order or constraining the use of force abroad play a vital role in explaining why the United States sometimes uses robust military operations for regime promotion, and at other times chooses inaction or lesser means for these same ends. Master narratives prove a major reason behind, then, some of the largest, most controversial wars since the turn of the twentieth century.

The master narrative argument breaks new ground theoretically in three ways. First, as mentioned already, it develops a more holistic ideational account of forceful regime promotion by bringing together both elite-based and broader collective ideas. The argument starts, in fact, with elites. When deciding about force for regime promotion ends, leaders in the United States specifically look first through the lens of their own ideological/strategic preferences. But that alone only gets us so far. Because, in addition to their own ideological/strategic lens, leaders also look, most important, through a second lens—the lens of master narratives. Their decisions about force are shaped in profound ways by the political costs and benefits generated by master narrative discourses around specific cases of regime crisis abroad. Leaders in democratic states, especially, care deeply about not just their own preferences, but their standing with the broader public as well due to concerns about reelection and securing other parts of their policy agenda.

These two sets of ideas—elite ideology and master narratives—intersect in two different ways to shape policy outcomes. Sometimes, master narrative discourses line-up with, and thus allow leaders to follow, their preferred course of action. This was the case with China and Grenada. In each instance, presidents found a master narrative context that was conducive to their particular interests. A weakened liberal discourse allowed President Harry Truman to follow his preferred course of nonmilitary action in China. Likewise with Grenada, a weak restraint discourse and strong liberal narrative allowed President Ronald Reagan to follow his preferred course of robust military action.[3] Overall, in each of these cases, these two different sets of ideas—one elite-based, the other collective or national—worked hand-in-hand (i.e., as mutually necessary and sufficient conditions) to explain outcomes.

In a second type of cases, master narratives tend to be the primary driver of policy. Here, master narrative-based political pressure generally trumps the ideological/strategic dispositions of leaders altogether, pushing them in directions they would prefer not to go.

This helps explain the many cases in table 7.1 that do not match-up well with the stand-alone, elite-ideology argument. A robust liberal discourse pressed President Truman, for instance, to invade Korea, and cross the 38th parallel. Johnson's decision for escalation in Vietnam came for similar reasons. In both cases, the political weight of master narratives pushed these leaders to act in ways that contradicted their preferences. A similar kind of strengthened liberal discourse also helps explain the domestic political pressure (from late 2001 forward) that the

Bush administration felt to invade Iraq as well as why Kennedy allowed the Bay of Pigs invasion to go forward at all despite his preference against any use of force. In other cases, the restraint narrative had similar constraining effects, by pushing leadership elites toward limited military action or inaction in ways that contradicted the leader's ideological sentiments. A strong restraint discourse around El Salvador and Nicaragua prevented, for example, the Reagan Administration from pursuing the more robust military action in Central America that many preferred at the time. In general, cases like these—from Korea to El Salvador and Iraq—make sense only with the master narrative argument.[4]

Overall, what these pushed-to-act cases demonstrate is that in many instances of U.S. forceful regime promotion—including some of the largest and most important cases of the twentieth and twenty-first centuries—master narratives tend to be more of a necessary and sufficient condition in the decision-making process. Elites matter in certain ways here (see note), but the main driver and explanatory variable for policy outcomes are master narratives and the discourses, more specifically, that form around those master narratives.[5] In the final analysis, the master narrative argument significantly expands our understanding of patterns of forceful regime change in U.S. foreign policy.

In doing so, the argument also lays the foundation for new areas of research. In addition to raising questions, of course, about how master narratives might affect other kinds of foreign policy issues, the findings here raise several interesting lines of potential inquiry about forceful regime change as well. John Owen draws attention, for instance, to how transnational elite polarization leads to certain structural outcomes, like shortwaves of especially intense periods of interstate military action for forceful regime change ends.[6] Given the importance of master narratives to explain patterns of forceful regime change in U.S. foreign policy, it seems logical to ask how master narratives might also contribute to these shortwaves. Do they facilitate and constrain this kind of behavior, working alongside of and, at times, contradicting elite dispositions? If so, how? Along these lines, could master narratives also become transnational in ways that shape these structural dynamics of forceful regime promotion? Exploring these kinds of questions could further deepen our understanding of forceful regime promotion in world politics.

Forceful regime promotion by nondemocratic states represents another potential area of research. Some find that public opinion matters to foreign policymaking in nondemocracies.[7] Could broad public narratives impact, then, the foreign policy, and forceful regime change behavior, of nondemocratic states? Processes in nondemocracies related to how narratives form and impact leaders would likely be different than in a democracy, like the United States, and could vary even across different types (i.e., personalist or military) of nondemocratic regimes. Nonetheless, it seems altogether possible that master narrative politics of some sort could affect nondemocratic foreign policy.

The second major addition that the master narrative argument makes relates to our understanding of the formation and sources of national security narratives, especially in U.S. foreign policy. The leading work on this subject focuses largely on rhetorical style (i.e., the components of storytelling by heads of state) to explain narratives.[8] The argument in this book builds on this work by turning to cultural trauma in order to offer a more systematic, event-driven account of narratives that explains how events intersect with state identity to generate, contextualize, and privilege certain stories relative to others to become dominant collective narratives. Storytelling matters, then, but only when it matches up well with the right kind of event-driven political opportunity structure, notably external trauma for stories that strengthen the liberal narrative and internal trauma for those that strengthen the restraint narrative.

This theoretical turn has significant implications. Above all else, it helps explain the emergence and formation of vitally important narratives—the liberal and restraint narratives—in U.S. foreign policy that leading work struggles to explain. The master narrative argument also offers a more precise explanation of the timing of narrative formation/change than currently exists. Finally, attention to cultural trauma allows us to understand why it is that similar kinds of stories keep strengthening and weakening over time in U.S. foreign policy, showing up essentially as dominant or "master" narratives. All of these implications are important for one central reason: they help us better understand not only national security narratives, but also how and when those narratives shape specific policy outcomes.

The policy relevance of narratives is the third major theoretical addition that this book makes. The leading account of security narratives offers no explanation of narrative impact on state behavior. This book makes important advances, then, by drawing special attention to the social construction of master narrative discourses that come to shape policy at times. It demonstrates, more specifically, how different kinds of agents build varying types of discourses around robust master narratives. Worried about the domestic costs of being at odds with the powerful narratives behind these discourses, U.S. leaders tend to bring policy in line with prevailing master narrative sentiments, even when it contradicts their own preferences. Overall, this argument offers clear predictions and new directions, therefore, for understanding how narratives shape policy, especially forceful regime change decisions.

The argument makes other theoretical contributions as well. As discussed in prior chapters, these master narrative discourses matter because they raise audience costs, specifically costs for action (restraint discourse) or costs for inaction (liberal discourse). Leaders in democratic states are especially sensitive to these kinds of costs, building policy around them. Audience costs offer a powerful framework, then, for understanding how master narratives shape policy.

By the same token, the master narrative argument also makes two important additions to the audience-cost literature that suggest again new directions for future research. First, the master narrative argument expands our understanding of the processes under which audience costs form. Current literature finds audience costs emerge when heads of state in democracies make public commitments to some course of action.[9] Master narrative audience costs form in ways that are generally different from this, however, notably again, through this process of social construction that involves the discourses that agents build around robust master narratives. By developing a framework for understanding these discourses, the master narrative argument offers a new, more sociological way by which to understand the sources of audience costs that reaches beyond the current literature's narrow attention to public commitments alone.

Second, this discourse-centric approach demonstrates that audience costs can be far more varied than the current literature allows, leading as a result to a varied set of policy outcomes. To this end, audience costs are not, as traditionally conceived, simply binary in nature (i.e., costs or no costs) that result in binary policy outcomes (i.e., action or no action). Instead, the research in this book demonstrates that agent-driven discourses can generate audience costs along a spectrum or continuum, which leads, as a result, to a wide variety of audience-cost-driven policy outcomes. This was evident in several cases in this book. A strengthened liberal discourse around China in 1950 produced audience costs for inaction that pushed President Truman, for instance, to far greater cooperation with the Chinese Nationalists than he preferred. Those audience costs were not so high (like Korea)that Truman felt compelled to pursue a full military invasion to stop the spread of communism in China.[10] In essence, similar kinds of audience costs (i.e., liberal narrative-generated audience costs in this case) were not just "either/or" so to speak, but took different forms along a continuum; policy varied accordingly. Through its attention to choices that agents make about the master narrative discourses they build, this book offers, again, a way of theoretically understanding how audience costs like these, of varying strength, can form. The extension of this kind of theorizing to other issue areas and other types of audience costs will likely lead us to find that audience costs have a far wider and varied impact on decision making than is currently realized.

Overall, the research in this book expands our theoretical and empirical understanding of national security narratives in important ways, especially with respect to the foreign policy of the United States.

Master Narratives beyond U.S. Foreign Policy

Is the story this book tells unique to the United States, perhaps a function of so-called U.S. exceptionalism or other idiosyncrasies of U.S. democracy? Some might answer in the affirmative, arguing that liberalism and politics generally are so unique in the United States that other democratic states in Europe or Asia, especially, may not be subject to the same kinds of master narrative-driven policy outcomes.[11] While there likely is some truth here, this section offers several plausibility probes in British foreign policy that suggest master narratives—specifically, the restraint and liberal narratives—may also play an important role, at times, in the foreign policy of other democratic great powers beside the United States.

GREAT BRITAIN AND WORLD WAR II

British entrance into World War II is a prominent case of master narratives shaping policy. After promises from British Prime Minister Neville Chamberlain that appeasement would ensure peace in Europe, Nazi Germany's violation of the Munich Accords with the March 1939 invasion of Czechoslovakia traumatized the British public in ways that dramatically strengthened the liberal narrative in Britain. Promoter stories about the dangers of German expansionism and the need to protect liberal order found especially fertile ground. "Like water dripping on a stone, their voices suddenly broke through the crust of incredulity," observes A.J.P. Taylor of longstanding advocates for a tougher, more ideological line toward Hitler, "They seemed to have been proved right; and the 'appeasers' wrong."[12] Almost overnight, a panicked British public came to see Germany as an ideological menace on the rise in Europe. Newspapers showed the national temper, calling German action "a monstrous outrage" and talking of "the force with which [Hitler] has enslaved the Czech people." Calls to defend liberal order (i.e., moral) overwhelmed the political discussion. "Collective security must be organized, and that without delay, on a broad firm base of democratic principles," charged the *Liverpool Daily Post*. Appeasement was dead, claimed the *Daily Herald*, lying next to "the dust of the body of what was once free Czechoslovakia."[13]

In a story that parallels Truman's experience in Korea and Johnson's in Vietnam, promoters used this newly strengthened liberal narrative to attack Chamberlain for being weak on fascism. The day after the Czech invasion members of Parliament (MPs) grilled the prime minister. One commented, for example, on Chamberlain's "remarkable state of detachment" amid the "black death of totalitarian aggression" that was engulfing Europe. This kind of promoter discourse was everywhere across Britain by mid-1939.[14]

Facing rising audience costs for inaction, Chamberlain scrambled to keep pace with the burgeoning liberal discourse. "Chamberlain undoubtedly had been through a period of intense stress," observes the historian William Rock, "and the pressure exerted on him by Parliament and the press had made a deep imprint."[15] Above all else, the prime minister took steps to prevent further political damage at home by working to stop further German expansion to the East. Coming in line with the liberal discourse, he charged that Britain would not sacrifice peace for "the liberties that we have enjoyed for hundreds of years."[16] As a result, Britain (along with France) made a firm commitment in late March 1939 to protect the independence of Poland.[17] It was a fateful decision. The German invasion of Poland six months later left Britain no option but to respond with force. "The British government were trapped not so much by their guarantee to Poland, as by their previous relations with Czechoslovakia," observes Taylor, "They could not go back on their word again, if they were to keep any respect . . . with their own people."[18] In the end, the robust liberal discourse forced Chamberlain into commitments and eventually military action that constituted regime promotion wars in East-Central Europe, which as it turned out marked the start of World War II as well.

GREAT BRITAIN AND KOREA

For Britain, regime promotion in Korea in 1950 tells a similar story. Like the United States, North Korea's invasion stunned the British public and was interpreted in existential terms, as a challenge to liberal order. Newspapers across the country and political spectrum presented North Korean action as "part of an international communist scheme." Public surveys showed strong support for the need to "draw the line somewhere" against Soviet expansionism with many believing Soviet intentions were, as one survey respondent claimed, to "swamp the world."[19] There was unanimous support across the political spectrum for action. "If Russia were to succeed in splitting the Anglo-American alliance, the whole of the free world would lie open to forcible subjection to Communism," charged Anthony Eden, the leader of the minority Conservative Party, in his call for robust action in Korea, "That is the supreme consideration which must be ever present in our minds."[20] Winston Churchill and many other conservative MPs echoed the same theme.[21]

For his part, Prime Minister Clement Atlee wasted no time in bringing British policy in line in with this strong liberal discourse. He immediately painted Korea as evidence that communism was on the move and pledged support to the U.S.-led effort to save South Korea. Atlee did not want to fall on the wrong side of the liberal discourse and face Chamberlain's fate, in particular. "In the 1930s, Neville Chamberlain had done too little too late to match the Nazi buildup," observes the historian Callum MacDonald, "The Labour government, determined to avoid the same mistake, increased the arms budget under the impact of Korean fighting."[22] The firm position that Atlee's government took in Korea came with wide public support. A Gallup survey in July 1950 found that two out of three surveyed approved of policy toward Korea, with even Labour supporters turning in a 62 percent favorable rating.[23] Later in the year, 63 percent of the British public approved sending British troops to Korea and surveys also found strong support for crossing the 38th parallel.[24] Overall, a robust liberal narrative played an important part, it appears, in the British decision to participate in regime promotion in Korea.

GREAT BRITAIN AND THE RUSSIAN CIVIL WAR

Finally, like the United States, master narratives also played a part in restraining British regime promotion behavior at certain points in time. A classic example here is Britain's participation in the Russian civil war in the wake of World War I. Chapter two demonstrated how the liberal narrative weakened substantially in the United States following the war, due in part, as trauma theory expects, to the decline of Germany as an ideological challenger. The same kind of weakening in liberal narrative strength happened in Great Britain as well. One major manifestation of this was the expansive peace movement that emerged in Britain shortly after the war. Here, moderators narrated around a message of "no more war" that tapped into a general "war weariness," or a deep public urge to focus on the home front.[25] As ideological challenges receded, this moderator story became the new collective sentiment, according to historians, across Britain and most other major European countries at the time.[26]

The weakened liberal narrative seemed to profoundly affect British efforts at regime change in the Soviet Union. British troops entered Russia to support the anticommunist rebel movement at the high tide of liberal narrative strength in 1918 during the last days of World War I. By the spring of 1919, British (along with Allied policy in general) began to shift. Reflecting the peace movement, disillusionment began to settle in among the public toward British participation in the Russian civil war.[27] At a vital juncture in March when the British Cabinet needed to decide whether or not to escalate from a more limited to full-scale intervention, this discourse around a weakened liberal narrative resulted in an eventual full withdrawal by Britain short of military victory. A memo from the Russian ambassador at Paris pointed to national temperament as the reason: "The present policy of Allied governments with regard to intervention is explained by the existing extremely complicated political situation and by the opposition of the parties of the left as well as of the broad masses."[28] In sum, a weakened liberal narrative appeared to help generate high audience costs for forceful regime promotion in the Soviet Union following World War I. This helps explain, most important, why British involvement in regime promotion in Russia never escalated to full-scale invasion, as well as why the British eventually abandoned forceful regime change here altogether.

These British examples of master narratives at work are not isolated cases among democracies other than the United States. France went through its own liberal narrative surge on the road to World War II; during the Korean War, one scholar notes that the "cold war climate" in New Zealand set the stage for that country's contribution to the war effort; a strengthened liberal narrative in Europe following the September 11 terrorist attack brought many NATO countries to support and participate in the 2001 U.S.-led invasion of Afghanistan; and, finally, like the United States, disillusionment over the Iraq War strengthened restraint narratives in Europe, leading to more hesitancy among NATO states in the last decade to use robust military force in the Middle East.[29] Overall, this glimpse into other democracies suggests that, while different in ways perhaps from the United States, master narratives could play an important, yet underappreciated role, in the foreign policies of other democratic great powers as well. Further study seems warranted here.

Assessing Master Narrative Politics and Ways Forward

What are we to make of the politics of master narratives? Is policy driven by master narratives good for U.S. security and the common good? The answer to this question is mixed, with most cases (especially those involving the liberal narrative) in this book falling to the negative side of the ledger. That being the case, how do we control the politics of master narratives?

The Pros and (Mostly) Cons of Master Narrative Politics

The impact of master narratives on policy is not always bad. A burst of liberal narrative energy in the early 1940s awakened an overly restrained U.S. public to enter World War II. Europe and Asia were saved, as a result, from German/Japanese imperialism and a course set for the socio-political and economic development in those regions of the world that has been good for the United States and international order in general over the past sixty years. Restraint narratives can have an especially positive effect on policy. Most would agree that the choice by the United States not to commit to large-scale military operations in Central America due to restraints from the Vietnam syndrome was a good policy outcome in the 1980s. Likewise, the Iraq syndrome has produced a healthy degree of restraint in U.S. policy toward the Middle East in the 2010s, preventing a return to large combat invasions in response to the Arab Spring uprisings or emergence of the Islamic State.[30]

By and large, though, positive cases like these seem more the exception than the norm, especially when it comes to the liberal narrative as seen with the major instances of forceful regime promotion since World War II. Arguably, when master narratives play a leading role in policy formation, the outcomes are not always favorable for the affected countries or U.S. security.[31] There are several ways in which we see this.

For starters, the pressures to either act with bold resolve or do little-to-nothing that come with a robust liberal or restraint narrative often generate varying degrees of short-sightedness among policymakers. Certain motivated biases, especially wishful thinking, tend to set in among policy elites, which produces largely negative policy outcomes.[32] A robust liberal discourse in the late 1940s around U.S. policy in Asia, for instance, led the Truman Administration into the wishful thinking that it could unify the Korean peninsula without invoking a response from China or the Soviet Union. This miscalculation resulted in the deaths of nearly 37,000 U.S. combat personnel over a territory in Asia that U.S. policymakers at the time deemed strategically insignificant and a terrible place to fight a land war. Korea pales, of course, in comparison to the destructiveness of Vietnam. Here again, the same kind of robust liberal discourse about standing tough against communism in Asia led the Johnson Administration to abandon its own best judgment for the wishful thinking that the United States could build a stable government in South Vietnam. 58,000 U.S. combat personnel and millions of Vietnamese, Laotians, and Cambodians died in futility as a result. The war also nearly split American society in two. Finally, the 2003 Iraq War highlights that the negative impact of a robust liberal discourse is not a relic of the past, but alive and well in the twenty-first century. The Bush administration's impassioned effort to sustain a domestic image of being tough on terrorism as a means to ensure electoral victories in 2002 and 2004 led to wishful thinking about both Iraqi weapons of mass destruction and the prospects for a stable, democratic postwar Iraq. Rather than strategic gains for the United States, the war destabilized Iraq, fueled Islamic terrorism, and upset the balance of power in the region to Iran's advantage.

This draws attention to another negative implication of master narratives politics. The aftermath of regime promotion wars motivated by the liberal narrative is usually not that positive. As witnessed with Middle East cases and Indochina after the Vietnam War, regime promotion wars sometimes create political vacuums in their wake that lead to a breakdown of domestic institutions and, subsequently, extreme violence. In these conditions, local populations are arguably worse off in terms of personal safety and material security than prior to the regime promotion invasion.[33]

Finally, the most important overarching (and negative) implication of master narrative politics involves the narrowing of policy options available to decision makers. To this end, the decision-making context for policy elites becomes less pluralistic when master narratives play an especially prominent role in the policy process. Voices that advocate healthy, middle-range policy options are often silenced, leading again to largely undesirable outcomes. While not going so far as to press leaders to adopt robust military action, a still powerful liberal discourse in the China and Cuba cases prevented the pursuit of better, middle-range policy options in both instances. With China, the liberal discourse marginalized State Department supporters of normalization with Mao Zedong and led to a hostile approach instead.[34] The United States, subsequently, lost a potential counterweight to Soviet power in Asia and set a course of anticommunist policies in the region that directly contributed to Korea and Vietnam. Cuba tells a similar story. Here, the liberal discourse pushed JFK into the failed Bay of Pigs invasion, which directly contributed to the Cuban Missile Crisis and decades of U.S.-Cuban hostility that produced little significant benefit for the United States or the Cuban people.

Although generally not as strategically damaging, restraint narratives can have similar kinds of de-pluralizing, and hence narrowing, effects that produce less than desirable policy outcomes at times. Syria and Libya exemplify this. The Iraq syndrome has arguably allowed both the humanitarian crisis in Syria to grow worse and new security challenges to grow for Europe and the United States as a result. Above all else, fears of getting dragged into "another Iraq" prevented the especially restraint-sensitive Obama administration from building a multilateral coalition to take steps—like setting up refugee safe havens inside Syria or creating humanitarian corridors to Turkey—that, while far short of a ground invasion, held the potential to do some good to limit human suffering and reduce refugee flows. These kinds of middle-range policies were common in the nonrestraint 1990s for dealing with similar humanitarian crises in the Balkans and Iraq.[35] With Syria, however, all talk about safe havens has been largely taboo. Obama used the public's restraint-driven worries about another Iraq in Syria as a way to pursue a hands-off policy that lined up with his own post-Iraq caution.[36] President Donald Trump has done much the same. Again, there is a great deal that is good about this restraint—Syria has not become "another Iraq" for the United States. By the same token, the humanitarian disaster in Syria has produced nearly 400,000 deaths and a massive refugee crisis.[37] This outcome might have been at least, ameliorated if the grip of the Iraq syndrome did not narrow, or allow for the narrowing, of policy debate to the most minimal of options in Syria.

Post-Gaddafi Libya offers a similar story. At a critical September 2012 juncture of government consolidation in Libya, the political firestorm created by the attacks on the U.S. consulate at Benghazi caused the Obama administration to pull the plug entirely on all aid programs in Libya. In order to avoid the political firestorm that would come with the loss of more American lives (Benghazi occurred just two months before U.S. elections, i.e., looming audience costs), Obama canceled a set of nonmilitary initiatives to assist government reforms, organize budgets, and train the Libyan armed forces. Here again, these middle-range policies, that did not involve the direct use of U.S. force, were abandoned due to worries over a potential "witch hunt" at home.[38] The implications of this are important. The U.S./European failure to provide nonmilitary assistance after Gaddafi's fall helped accelerate a new set of humanitarian challenges as Libya becomes a failed state and potential new home for terrorist organizations. Again, this kind of nonpluralistic, and frankly uncreative, policy narrowing happens when robust master narratives are especially prominent in the policymaking process.

Managing the Politics of Master Narratives

With such negative implications, how do we control the politics of master narratives? The answer that the research in this book suggests is complex and expansive. As seen already, the politics of master narratives involve the interaction between certain kinds of traumatic events and storytelling by influential agents. These agents, first, frame those events in ways that cause narratives to strengthen then, second, sometimes use those strengthened narratives to build discourses for and against certain policies, like forceful regime promotion. In general, managing the politics of master narratives has less to do with events than it does with these agents and their responses to those events. Trauma-generating events are nearly impossible to control. There was nothing the United States could have done to prevent or alter events, like the 1940s Soviet aggression in East-Central Europe or 1968 TET offensive, which sparked major changes to the master narrative landscape. What can be controlled, however, is how polities—and most important, influential agents within those polities—respond to those events and use master narratives. Agents are, no doubt, shaped by their times, hence by narratives and major events. But they also exercise a great deal of independence, meaning they possess a capacity for self-control and general restraint.[39] And here is where managing the politics of master narratives takes place.

This process requires, more specifically, an approach to foreign policy that involves a high degree of what some scholars call "reflexivity," meaning intentional self-reflection that questions broad, conventional postulates while also allowing for more attention to the complex and contingent aspects of different policy situations.[40] This kind of "focus on remaking ourselves" opens space for more policy pluralism that helps break the stranglehold of master narrative politics.[41] Reflexivity in the domain of master narratives demands two interrelated things specifically: first, a broad excavation of narratives when powerful and, second, responsible political discourse by leading foreign policy voices (notably, promoters and moderators), especially at points of foreign policy crises abroad.

EXCAVATING MASTER NARRATIVES

Excavating master narratives involves a broad national discussion that unearths core assumptions about and questions the efficacy of master narratives as guiding principles for how to think about the world and the making of foreign policy. This kind of excavation of robust social norms and beliefs is nothing new in democratic societies, like the United States. There are constant, ongoing debates in the public dialogue about the rightness and boundaries of conventional expectations. Over the past sixty years, widely accepted collective assumptions about the right role for women and minorities, in particular, have changed dramatically in western societies. This has happened largely because taken-for-granted social standards have been challenged by activists, political pundits, and public intellectuals using history and real-world events to tell stories that point to inequality and core problems brought by extant social values and narratives.[42]

This kind of broad excavation of master narratives in the realm of foreign policy is imperative, but also largely absent historically in the United States. Even with the trauma of the Vietnam War, a robust liberal narrative reflected in the "tough-on-communism" mantra remained largely unquestioned, for instance, in U.S. foreign policy through the late 1980s (see chapters 2 and 5). A similar lack of narrative excavation has marked the post–9/11 period as well. The tumultuous national conversation around U.S. foreign policy since 2003 has focused criticism almost exclusively on presidential policy and decision making, like Bush's mistakes in Iraq or Obama's shortcomings in post-Gaddafi Libya and Syria.[43] This misplaced blame overlooks altogether, however, the powerful narratives reflected in mantras, like "stop terrorism" and "no more Iraqs," that were a core part of the poor or questionable policy decisions made by these presidents (and many other presidents like them). Those narratives remain unexcavated.

There needs to be more of a national conversation here to bring about narrative excavation. More specifically, pundits, public intellectuals, policy elites, and editorialists of all political persuasions must focus greater attention on master narratives, in essence to understand the history of master narratives in U.S. foreign policy that this book uncovers and to use that as a basis to bring these narratives to light and critically assess them.[44] Given its contribution to destructive and over-expansionist policies in the past, this especially needs to be the case with the liberal narrative. Excavation here must center, for instance, on a rethinking of the kind of threat faced with Islamic terrorism. Since 9/11, the prevailing national assumption across the United States has been that groups like al Qaeda and now ISIS pose an existential challenge, capable of disrupting or bringing down western civilization.[45] National assumptions like these need excavating. History can be useful here. We need to talk openly about the damage from Korea to Vietnam and Iraq of allowing overly simplistic mantras like "stop communism" or "tough on terrorism" to dictate policy. This broad excavation must focus on more recent history too. From 9/11 to bombings in Paris and Brussels, terrorist attacks have not led to existential crises in any of these cases. Governments and societies have remained intact, life has gone on for citizens in all states targeted by these attacks.

Overall, this kind of liberal narrative excavation will help reset the national conversation and public expectations in ways that moderate the response to the next major foreign policy shock, which could be another terrorist attack, at some point, on U.S. soil. By contextualizing attacks like these away from existential challenges, narrative excavation allows the public more space to take a deep breath in ways that can give leaders important space to avoid over-simplification of policy problems and wishful thinking that has led to over-reaction and unnecessarily aggressive policies in the past. Excavation of the liberal narrative landscape in the present is more likely to yield more measured, middle-range policy responses in the future that result in better managing the problem of terrorism (or other possible challenges, like a rising China).

RESPONSIBLE POLITICAL DISCOURSE

A higher degree of reflexivity also requires more responsible political discourse from important actors engaged in policy debates. As this book demonstrates time and again, choices by these influential agents (promoters and moderators) are often based on near-term political opportunism and ideological zeal, at the expense or to the detriment of the broader national interest or any sense of the common good. This kind of irresponsible political discourse plays on powerful master narratives in ways that over-simplifies and de-pluralizes policy debates. Again, some of the worst possible policy outcomes have followed. In 1950 and 1964, Republicans used the liberal narrative, for instance, to paint Democrats as weak on communism in order to gain an advantage in coming elections— Korea and Vietnam followed.[46] In the 1960 presidential campaign, Democratic nominee John F. Kennedy one-upped Vice President Richard Nixon by appealing to the liberal narrative with a stiff anticommunist position on Castro's Cuba—the hapless Bay of Pigs invasion followed. In 2002, Democrats and Republicans both tried to use a hyper-charged, post–9/11 policy context to make political gains by looking tough on terrorism—Iraq followed.

Overall, this kind of political opportunism needs to end. Master narratives and the trauma-generating events that often give rise to robust narratives should not be used as political wedges in the game of U.S. politics. Moderators and especially promoters need, again, to learn from history. Near-term political gains using robust master narratives not only produce negative policy outcomes, they also do not leave promoters and moderators who successfully employ these tactics in the most favorable light historically. As author of the 1950s "Red Scare," Joseph McCarthy is viewed with infamy in the same way that modern-day neoconservatives find themselves in a political wasteland following the Iraq War, which is a nearly identical position to isolationists after Pearl Harbor. Overall, this kind of negative historical legacy is the plight of many promoters and some moderators who use (and sometimes abuse) the master narrative landscape of U.S. foreign policy.

There is a good reason for this, which brings us back to the argument at the heart of this book. When promoters and moderators hijack the master narrative environment to their advantage, they upset a certain kind of pragmatic-idealist equilibrium at the core of the United States' liberal identity. This book tells a story that is all about this equilibrium. The United States finds woven into its national DNA an interest in shaping the world for good, in essence a natural inclination to protect and promote liberal political order abroad. Yet just as pronounced within that DNA is a skepticism about overreach for liberal ends, especially when it involves the expenditure of blood and treasure for seemingly liberal goals that may not turn out to be so liberal or strategically beneficial in the end. When moderators and promoters use the mantras (for instance, "weak on communism" or "no more Iraqs") of a given master narrative environment to their advantage, they narrow the policy debate to one side of the national DNA or the other in ways that sets the stage for their own long-term failure and ostracism. George W. Bush and neoconservatives went too far toward a militarized idealism in the same way that 1930s isolationists tilted too much to the extreme of valueless and illiberal retrenchment. Each paid a deep political price for their extremes.[47]

Moderators and promoters would be well-served to learn from cases like these. Moderation by these agents, especially at points of crisis abroad, is vital. It will open the door to a more pluralistic policymaking context and with that a road toward creative, middle-range policy outcomes for the United States. The overall result will be a foreign policy that bends in the direction of restraint with a modest vision for and tempered actions toward liberal goals abroad. Responsible political discourse, then, ensures healthy debate and healthy policy. Above all else, it places the United States in a position to better respond to international crises, to be a less traumatized and more sober nation in its foreign policy. In the end, that will be good—for U.S. security, international stability, and human flourishing in general.

Notes

INTRODUCTION: MASTER NARRATIVES AND FORCEFUL REGIME CHANGE

1. I use the phrases "regime promotion" and "regime change" interchangeably. For examples of the conventional arguments, see John M. Owen, IV, *The Clash of Ideas in World Politics: Transnational Networks, States, and Regime Change, 1510–2010* (Princeton: Princeton University Press, 2010) and Michael C. Desch, "America's Illiberal Liberalism," *International Security* 32, no. 3 (2007/8): 18–19.

2. Alexander B. Downes and Jonathan Monten, "Forced to Be Free? Why Foreign Imposed Regime Change Rarely Leads to Democratization," *International Security* 37, no.4 (2013): 90–131. Added to this, democracy rarely follows in the state targeted by forceful regime change.

3. Antifascism, anticommunism, and antiterrorism are "liberal" because they derive from and protect national identity, or liberalism in democratic states (see chapter 1).

4. Ronald R. Krebs, *Narrative and the Making of US National Security* (Cambridge: Cambridge University Press, 2015). As discussed more in chapter 1, existing work on national security narratives (such as Krebs's important study) also struggles to explain the recurring strength of the liberal and restraint narratives over time, their specific temporal manifestations, as well as how and when narratives in general impact policy decisions.

5. Jeffrey C. Alexander et al., eds., *Cultural Trauma and Collective Identity* (Berkeley: University of California Press, 2004). Dominic Tierney, *How We Fight: Crusades, Quagmires, and the American Way of War* (Lincoln: University of Nebraska Press, 2012). Dominic Tierney offers a fascinating, broad overview of similar dynamics to the liberal and restraint narrative in U.S. foreign policy. My conceptualization of these phenomena as narratives, attention to trauma, and discussion about policy application offers more specificity about how, when, and why the restraint and liberal narratives change along with a more predictive account of when and how these narratives shape specific policy outcomes.

6. This is a core part of how liberal states identify themselves but is not a statement on how perfectly or unselfishly they pursue these goals abroad.

7. Geopolitics matter as a function of ideology and identity, not just power. See chapter 1.

8. These moments of robust liberal narrative are when U.S. exceptionalism is most pronounced.

9. The Iraq syndrome also gave Obama political space to pursue a more militarily limited approach to countering terrorism.

10. Owen, *Clash of Ideas*, 26.

11. Bruce W. Jentleson and Ariel E. Levite, "The Analysis of Protracted Foreign Military Intervention," in *Foreign Military Intervention: The Dynamics of Protracted Conflict*, ed. Ariel E. Levite et al. (New York: Columbia University Press, 1992), 5–8, 18–19 and Micah Zenko, *Between Threats and War: U.S. Discrete Military Operations in the Post–Cold War World* (Palo Alto: Stanford University Press, 2010). Another category of limited would be cases where combat troops are inserted for training and support roles of local armies/militias, but are intentionally constrained from fighting in ways synonymous with

a conventional combat role. The argument in this book offers predictions for why leaders choose either limited or robust military action generally, but makes no predictions for what specific types of force leaders will choose to use within those two broad categories. A strong restraint discourse is expected to push a leader toward limited military action, for instance, but the leader's subsequent choice for a *specific type* of limited action (say covert operations instead of air power, or vice versa) will be more historically contingent, potentially shaped by the restraint discourse but likely shaped by factors other than master narrative discourses as well.

12. Between 1900 and 2001, the United States participated in (and usually led) twenty-seven interventions, compared with the Soviet Union (nineteen), Britain (ten), and France (eight).

13. Jeffrey W. Legro, *Rethinking the World: Great Power Strategies and International Order* (Ithaca: Cornell University Press, 2005), 5.

14. Legro, *Rethinking the World*, 5; Krebs, *Narrative*, 21; Emile Durkheim, *The Rules of Sociological Method*, 8th ed. (Glencoe: Free Press, 1950), 1–28.

15. Phillip Selznick, *Leadership in Administration: A Sociological Interpretation* (New York: Harper and Row, 1957), 14–16, 38–42 and Joanne Martin, *Culture in Organizations: Three Perspectives* (New York: Oxford University Press, 1992).

16. On the distinction between collective opinion and aggregate individual opinion, see Charles Taylor, "Interpretation and the Sciences of Man," *Review of Metaphysics* 25, no. 1 (1971): 3–51. For work demonstrating the impact of collective ideas on public opinion, see Judith Goldstein, *Ideas, Interests, and American Trade Policy* (Ithaca: Cornell University Press, 1993), chapters 1 and 4 and Legro, *Rethinking the World*, chapters 1 and 3. Goldstein demonstrates, for example, how dominant ideas about protectionism shaped voter preferences in the 1932 election, leading President Franklin Roosevelt to eschew his own preferences for liberalization and campaign on protectionist policies instead.

17. Benjamin Page and Robert I. Shapiro, *The Rational Public: Fifty Years in Americans' Policy Preferences* (Chicago: University of Chicago Press, 1992), 13–16, 362–66.

18. Louis Klarevas, "The 'Essential Domino' of Military Operations: American Public Opinion and the Use of Force," *International Studies Perspectives* 3, no. 4 (2002): 417–37. Leaders pay close attention to public opinion (especially when it comes to the use of force), hence, *ceteris paribus*, one can assume they pay close attention to collective beliefs, like master narratives, as well.

19. Jerome Bruner, *Making Stories: Law, Literature, Life* (New York: Farrar, Straus and Giroux, 2002), 8, 31. See also Marie-Laure Ryan, "Story, Plot, and Narration," in *Narrative*, ed. David Herman (Cambridge: Cambridge University Press, 2007), 29.

20. Kenneth Burke, *A Grammar of Motives* (Berkeley: University of California Press, 1969), xv. In light of this, it makes sense that in Kenneth Burke's well-known descriptive pentad of narratives, "act" (what was done) and "scene" (when or where it was done) comprise the first two defining features of a narrative.

21. Thomas Berger, *Cultures of Antimilitarism: National Security in Germany and Japan* (Baltimore: Johns Hopkins University Press, 1998), 9; Ann Swidler, "Culture in Action: Symbols and Strategies," *American Sociological Review* 51, no. 2 (1986): 279; Elizabeth Kier, *Imagining War: French and British Military Doctrine between the Wars* (Princeton: Princeton University Press, 1997), 26; Mark L. Haas, *The Ideological Origins of Great Power Politics, 1789–1989* (Ithaca: Cornell University Press, 2005), 5–6.

22. Krebs, *Narrative*, 10; Jenny Edkins, *Trauma and the Memory of Politics* (Cambridge: Cambridge University Press, 2003), 88–89; Michael D. Jones and Mark K. McBeth, "A Narrative Policy Framework: Clear Enough to Be Wrong?" *Policy Studies Journal* 38, no. 2 (2010), 334; Maarten A. Hajer, "Discourse Coalitions and the Institutionalization of

Practice: The Case of Acid Rain in Britain," in *The Argumentative Turn in Policy Analysis and Planning*, ed. Frank Fischer et al. (Durham: Duke University Press, 1993), 44.

23. Ryan, "Story, Plot and Narration," 29. See also Hayden White, *The Content of the Form: Narrative Discourse and Historical Representation* (Baltimore: Johns Hopkins University Press, 1987), ix and Alasdair MacIntyre, *After Virtue: A Study in Moral Theory* (South Bend: University of Notre Dame Press), 194–96, 201.

24. Edkins, *Trauma and Memory*, 88; Ryan, "Story, Plot, and Narration" 28–30; Krebs, *Narrative*, 11; and Frank Kermode, "Secrets and Narrative Sequence," in *On Narrative*, ed. W.J.T. Mitchell (Chicago: University of Chicago Press, 1981), 80.

25. Burke, *A Grammar of Motives*, xv.

26. Hajer, "Discourse Coalitions," 45.

27. Krebs, *Narrative*, 13.

28. Bruner, *Making Stories*, 20, 31.

29. Jones and McBeth, "A Narrative Policy Framework," 341.

30. Victor Turner, "Social Dramas and Stories about Them," *Critical Inquiry* 7, no. 1 (1980), 167. See also Erving Goffman, *Frame Analysis: An Essay on the Organization of Experience* (New York: Harper Colophon Books, 1974), 504.

31. Krebs, *Narrative*, 13.

32. Jeffrey C. Alexander, "Toward a Theory of Cultural Trauma," in *Cultural Trauma*, ed. Alexander et al., 12; Elliott G. Mishler, "Models of Narrative Analysis: A Typology," *Journal of Narrative and Life History* 5, no. 2 (1995), 88; and Jonathan Shay, *Achilles in Vietnam: Combat Trauma and the Undoing of Character* (New York: Simon and Schuster, 1995), 3–4.

33. Alexander, "Toward a Theory," 12–15.

34. Jones and McBeth, "A Narrative Policy Framework," 340.

35. Barry Posen, *The Sources of Military Doctrine: France, Britain and Germany Between the World Wars* (Ithaca: Cornell University Press, 1984), 13.

36. Stephen G. Brooks and William C. Wohlforth, *America Abroad: The United States' Global Role in the 21st Century* (New York: Oxford University Press, 2016), 5–6, 11–13. Stephen Brooks and Bill Wohlforth note that factors like master narratives can affect the choices leaders make about grand strategy.

37. As detailed in chapter 1, the fact that elites mattered here does not contradict this book's argument since that argument develops a more holistic ideational account that brings together two different types of beliefs—elite ideology and master narratives. The conditions that lead to change in these beliefs differ in important ways, making them two generally distinct social phenomena.

38. Changes like these are not a function of partisanship either, see chapter 6.

39. Bruce Russett, *Controlling the Sword: The Democratic Governance of National Security* (Cambridge, MA: Harvard University Press, 1990), 93. This work by agents is important because the specifics of foreign policy developments are generally distant for the public in democratic states.

40. Michael Tomz, "Domestic Audience Costs in International Relations: An Experimental Approach," *International Organization* 61, no. 4 (2007): 821.

41. Mathew Levendusky and Michael Horowitz, "When Backing Down Is the Right Decision: Partisanship, New Information, and Audience Costs," *Journal of Politics* 74, no. 2 (2012): 323.

42. The failure of moderators to argue against military action when the restraint narratives is strong leads to a weak restraint discourse, giving leaders political space at home to gamble on robust forceful regime change if they so prefer. This was the case with Reagan's decision to invade Grenada.

1. THE LIBERAL NARRATIVE, RESTRAINT NARRATIVE, AND PATTERNS OF FORCEFUL REGIME CHANGE

1. Some may consider the experience of the 2003 Iraq War so searing that a similar type of war is unlikely to happen again. The discussion below explains why this reasoning can be incorrect.

2. John M. Owen, IV, *The Clash of Ideas in World Politics: Transnational Networks, States, and Regime Change, 1510–2010* (Princeton: Princeton University Press, 2010), 32–66. For other work on elite ideology, see Mark L. Haas, *The Ideological Origins of Great Power Politics, 1789–1989* (Ithaca: Cornell University Press, 2005) and Henry Nau, *Conservative Internationalism: Armed Diplomacy under Jefferson, Polk, and Reagan* (Princeton: Princeton University Press, 2013).

3. For the broader discussion, see Kenneth N. Waltz's *Man, the State, and War: A Theoretical Analysis* (New York: Columbia University Press, 1959), 231–34, 238, and his *Theory of International Politics* (New York: Random House, 1979), 12–22.

4. This may be the case for other democratic great powers at different points in time as well, see chapter 7.

5. Owen argues that geopolitics explain restraint in periods of high polarization. When polarization is high, leadership elites (i.e., a head of state and his/her inner circle) sometimes deny their own polarization if they believe that military intervention could spark a counter-intervention and/or much wider great power war (Owen, *Clash of Ideas*, 43–46). Like elite polarization, this strategic argument also struggles to explain cross-case variation as explored in the chapters to follow. Sometimes, leaders find political space to follow their better strategic judgments, at other points not as they get pushed into forceful regime change despite their strategic concerns.

6. Sometimes nonleadership elites especially help develop master narrative discourses, but here too the choices to do so by these elites (and, most important, whether or not those discourses matter to policy) is a function of master narratives, not qualities related to elites and their ideology.

7. Ronald R. Krebs, *Narrative and the Making of US National Security Policy* (Cambridge: Cambridge University Press, 2015), 31–65. In Krebs's argument, presidential authority solves the standard collective ideation problem, see Jeffrey W. Legro, "The Transformation of Policy Ideas," *American Journal of Political Scientists* 44, no. 3 (2000): 419–32.

8. Krebs, *Narrative*, 31–65, 122–72, 191–265.

9. Krebs, *Narrative*, 25, 59.

10. There is some evidence of this with the post–9/11 antiterrorism narrative as well even.

11. For Wilson, see Arthur Link, *Woodrow Wilson and the Progressive Era, 1910–1917* (New York: Harper and Brothers Publishers, 1954), chapters 8 and 10; Ernest R. May, *The World and American Isolation, 1914–1917* (Cambridge: Harvard University Press, 1959), 132–70, 418–33; Daniel M. Smith, ed., *American Intervention, 1917: Sentiment, Self-Interest, or Ideals?* (Boston: Houghton Mifflin, 1966), 26–28, 96, 107–8, 180–90. For Truman, see chapter 3. Eventually both were pushed by political pressure to adopt narrative language in their public comments. But, this still leaves the question of narrative origins unanswered—in short, where did the narrative that pushed them to speak out come from?

12. See chapters 5 and 6, for examples. Krebs, *Narrative*, 26, 67–68, 75, 223–24. Krebs refers to some of these narratives as "narratives" but never explores their origins, presumably because, one is left to conclude, none of them fit his argument.

13. Krebs, *Narrative*, 4, 94–97; Legro, "Transformation of Policy Ideas."

14. Krebs, *Narrative*, 60–61. Indicative of the limited role events play in Krebs's argument, Krebs offers no theory of unsettled times and only the broadest of parameters for measuring when times are unsettled. Consequently, presidential rhetoric (which receives extensive attention in Krebs's account) takes center stage theoretically in the argument. In the absence of a theory of unsettled times, Krebs's argument is also more descriptive than predictive since we cannot know when narratives will change or form without first knowing when, how, and why times become unsettled. This limits the argument's ability to explain policy—like forceful regime change—in any predictable way across time.

15. For examples, see Michael D. Jones and Mark K. McBeth, "A Narrative Policy Framework: Clear Enough to Be Wrong?" *Policy Studies Journal* 38, no. 2 (2010): 334–41; Jerome Bruner, *Making Stories: Law, Literature, Life* (New York: Farrar, Straus and Giroux, 2002), 6, 11–16; Hayden White, *The Content of the Form: Narrative Discourse and Historical Representation* (Baltimore: Johns Hopkins University Press, 1987), 7–11, 21–22; Maarten A. Hajer, "Discourse Coalitions and the Institutionalization of Practice: The Case of Acid Rain in Britain," in *The Argumentative Turn in Policy Analysis and Planning*, ed. Frank Fischer et al. (Durham: Duke University Press, 1993), 63; Margaret R. Somers, "Narrativity, Narrative Identity, and Social Action: Rethinking English Working-Class Formation," *Social Science History* 16, no. 4 (1992): 591–616; Marco Verweij et al., "Clumsy Solutions for a Complex World: The Case of Climate Change," *Public Administration* 84, no. 4 (2006): 817–43.

16. Many scholars avoid or overlook how event-driven context helps not only disrupt the political/ideational environment but also establish the dominance of certain kinds of ideas/beliefs/stories over others (even Legro's more sophisticated work on ideational structure fails to capture this). To some extent, this is surprising. Despite some differences across cases, a striking feature of the empirical findings in this literature are general *similarities* in ideational outcomes across different countries facing *similar* kinds of event-driven challenges. The strategic challenges in Europe of the 1910s led, for instance, to the same kind of strengthened collective story to defend liberal order (over and against powerful isolationist ideas) as similar strategic challenges did in the 1940s and later on in the Cold War. This similar-event-similar-outcome dynamic shows up repeatedly in work on economic crises in the extant literature as well. See, for example, Legro, "Transformation of Policy Ideas"; Legro, "Whence American Internationalism," *International Organization* 54, no. 2 (2000): 253–89; Jack Goldstone, "Ideology, Cultural Frameworks, and the Process of Revolution," *Theory and Society* 20, no. 4 (1991): 405–53; Peter Gourevitch, *Politics in Hard Times: Comparative Responses to International Economic Crises* (Ithaca: Cornell University Press, 1986), 12, 28; Judith Goldstein, *Ideas, Interests and American Trade Policy* (Ithaca: Cornell University Press, 1993), 12; and Frank R. Dobbin, "The Social Construction of the Great Depression: Industrial Policy During the 1930s in the United States, Britain and France," *Theory and Society* 22, no. 1 (1993): 1–56.

17. Krebs, *Narrative*, 84–85. A weakening of isolationist sentiment and national acceptance of ideological dangers abroad reflected the changing narrative landscape before storytelling.

18. Krebs, *Narrative*, 68–79. Lend-lease came, for instance, prior to FDR's storytelling and U.S. full engagement in the war only after the narrative fully settled-in in December 1941—hence, the importance of better specifying narrative change. As to the events, some (notably, German invasion of Denmark and Norway) also affected the timing and content of FDR's storytelling, raising the point again of how events matter to shaping narrative content.

19. The underspecification of unsettled times plays into this. When theory centers on presidential rhetoric, it naturally leads one's analysis to focus on the temporal idiosyncrasies of different narratives, rather than any sort of cross-temporal similarities.

20. Jeffrey W. Legro, *Rethinking the World: Great Power Strategies and International Order* (Ithaca: Cornell University Press, 2005). For a similar kind of argument that focuses on casualties in war, see Christopher Gelpi, Peter D. Feaver, and Jason Reifler, *Paying the Human Cost: American Public Opinion and Casualties in Military Conflicts* (Princeton: Princeton University Press, 2009). Krebs's focus on positive policy outcomes (see above) is essentially a functionalist argument as well.

21. At many points in the following chapters, the liberal narrative scored functional victories, yet declined precipitously nonetheless. Examples include substantial narrative changes with the defeat of German autocracy in World Wars I and II; the U.S. military victory against the 1968 TET offensive in Vietnam; and the end of the Cold War. Functionalist accounts also cannot explain the resurgence in the strength of some collective beliefs, like the liberal narrative, at many other points in time.

22. Kai Erickson, *A New Species of Trouble* (New York: W.W. Norton, 1994), 184–89; Jeffrey C. Alexander, "Toward A Theory of Cultural Trauma," in *Cultural Trauma and Collective Identity*, ed. Jeffrey C. Alexander et al. (Berkeley: University of California Press, 2004), 10, 15; Neil Smelser, "Psychological and Cultural Trauma," in *Cultural Trauma and Collective Identity*, ed. Alexander et al., 41–42, 45; Arthur G. Neal, *National Trauma and Collective Memory: Major Events in the American Century* (Armonk, NY: M.E. Sharpe, 1998), 5.

23. Neil Smelser, "Psychological and Cultural Trauma," in *Cultural Trauma and Collective Identity*, ed. Alexander et al., 44.

24. Ronald L. Jepperson, Alexander Wendt, and Peter J. Katzenstein, "Norms, Identity, and Culture in National Security," in *The Culture of National Security: Norms and Identity in World Politics*, ed. Peter J. Katzenstein (New York: Columbia University Press, 1998), 54.

25. Smelser, "Psychological and Cultural," 36, 44. See also Alexander, "Toward a Theory," 1, 10; Neal, *National Trauma*, 3; Emma Hutchison, "Trauma and the Politics of Emotion: Constituting Identity, Security and Community After the Bali Bombing," *International Relations* 24, no. 1 (2010), 66.

26. Alexander, "Toward a Theory," 10.

27. Neal, *National Trauma*.

28. Smelser, "Psychological and Cultural," 36, 39; Alexander, "Toward a Theory," 10–12; Piotr Sztompka, "Cultural Trauma: The Other Face of Social Change," *European Journal of Social Theory* 3, no. 4 (2000): 452.

29. Neil J. Smelser, *Theory of Collective Behavior* (New York: Free Press, 1962), 67, 81–83.

30. Jennifer Mitzen, "Ontological Security in World Politics: State Identity and the Security Dilemma," *European Journal of International Relations* 12, no. 3 (2006): 342, 345–46.

31. Alexander, "Toward a Theory," 10.

32. Smelser, "Psychological and Cultural," 38.

33. Legro, *Rethinking the World*, chapter 1.

34. Alexander, "Toward a Theory," 10. On political opportunity structure, see Sydney Tarrow, *Power in Movement: Social Movements, Collective Action and Politics* (Cambridge: Cambridge University Press, 1994), 118–23, 130.

35. In times of trauma, audiences measure different stories less by whether or not they have all the component parts of a story and more by whether or not those stories speak appropriately into the pain created by events. On the standard account, see Krebs, *Narrative*, 5, 44–45.

36. C. William Walldorf Jr., *Just Politics: Human Rights and the Foreign Policy of Great Powers* (Ithaca: Cornell University Press, 2008), chapter 4.

37. For similar psychological processes, see Yuen Foong Khong, *Analogies at War: Korea, Munich, Diem Bien Phu and the Vietnam Decisions of 1965* (Princeton: Princeton, NJ, 1992).

38. Alexander, "Toward a Theory," 11.

39. For another example, see K.M. Fierke, "Whereof We Can Speak, Thereof We Must Not be Silent: Trauma, Political Solipsism, and War," *Review of International Studies* 30, no. 4 (2004): 486.

40. In their attention to affirmation, blame and repair, these narratives generally reflect the main elements of story (act, scene, agent, agency, and purpose) discussed in the introduction and in Kenneth Burke, *A Grammar of Motives* (Berkeley: University of California Press, 1969), xv.

41. Alexander, "Toward a Theory," 11–15; Smelser, "Psychological and Cultural," 38–39, 52–53.

42. Neal, *National Trauma*, 5, 23, 201; Smelser, "Psychological and Cultural," 45; Smelser, *Theory of Collective Behavior*, 67, 81–83; chapter 5.

43. Ron Eyerman, "Cultural Trauma: Slavery and the Formation of African American Identity," in *Cultural Trauma and Collective Identity*, ed. Alexander et al., 63.

44. Erickson, *A New Species*, 184–89; Smelser, "Psychological and Cultural" 41–42, 45; Alexander, "Toward a Theory," 15; Neal, *National Trauma*, 5.

45. Many scholars apply trauma theory to nation-states. For examples, see Neal, *National Trauma*; Hutchison, "Trauma and the Politics"; and Smelser, "September 11, 2001, as Cultural Trauma," in *Cultural Trauma and Collective Identity*, ed. Alexander et al., 264–82.

46. The fact that the restraint narrative strengthens under conditions related to the liberal narrative does not reflect some sort of secondary status for it nor support arguments about historical sequencing (Frank Klingberg, *Cyclical Trends in American Foreign Policy Moods: The Unfolding of America's World* (Lanham, MD: University Press of America, 1983). Strong restraint narratives do not always follow robust liberal narratives and change in the strength of both master narratives does not occur on predictable cycles (see figures 2.1, 2.2, and 2.7 in chapter 2). Hence, we need a better specified explanation of master narrative formation and change. The theoretical intersection of the liberal and restraint narratives should not surprise us since both find their roots in liberal identity. Despite this common touch point to liberalism, the liberal and restraint narratives are still distinct social phenomena with distinct properties and causes.

47. Smelser, "Psychological and Cultural," 36, 45.

48. Neal, *National Trauma*, 17, 22, and 69–71 and Smelser, "September 11," 270.

49. Michael W. Doyle, "Liberalism and World Politics," *American Political Science Review*, 80, 4 (December 1986), 1161.

50. Walldorf, *Just Politics*, 9–10.

51. John M. Owen, IV, *Liberal Peace, Liberal War: American Politics and International Security* (Ithaca: Cornell University Press, 1997), 23. See also Haas, *Ideological Origins*.

52. The motivations of promoters and moderators varies. While some are ideological purists, politicians especially can be more calculating. Sometimes, they storytell because it yields political advantages over an opponent or opposing party/coalition. At other points, they storytell to keep pace with an already strengthening narrative, so as not to look out step with the public.

53. This is not synonymous with a realist conception of threats. Simply because an ideational argument includes an element of geopolitics, does not mean that it somehow cedes ground to (or, masks for) realism. A realist account of threats centers *exclusively* on

geopolitics: threats emerge when other states take steps to increase their power (see Waltz, *Theory of International Relations*). In the external trauma argument, threat is not a function of geopolitics alone, but instead geopolitics *and* identity. Geopolitical changes that contribute to external trauma are only those that involve gains by ideologically distant (in this case, illiberal) great powers. Identity shifts in power cause, then, a natural identity reaction, notably the strengthening of the liberal narrative. Geopolitics *woven through* the lens of identity and domestic contestation explain threat perceptions. For similar arguments, see Owen, *Clash of Ideas*; Haas, *Ideological Origins*; and Stephen M. Walt, *The Origins of Alliances* (Ithaca: Cornell University Press, 1987), 1–50. Walt similarly combines material and ideational factors, at points, to explain state threat perceptions.

54. Smelser, "Psychological and Cultural," 36, 45. Direct attacks produce an "instinctual impulse" of concern about "society's existence" that strengthens master narratives.

55. Bruce Russett, *Controlling the Sword: The Democratic Governance of National Security* (Cambridge: Harvard University Press, 1990), 93. This is due in part to the distances of foreign policy from most citizens.

56. Paul Pierson, "Increasing Returns, Path Dependence, and the Study of Politics," *American Political Science Review* 94, no. 2 (2000): 251–67.

57. This process of narrative strengthening shares some similarities with elite polarization in that geopolitics matter, which is not surprising since elites and the broader public share the same identity, in this case liberalism. There are important differences here too, though, since polarization (i.e., elite) and master narratives (i.e., public) are ideas at two different levels of analysis. The factors affecting master narratives but not polarization include: geopolitical shifts other than regime crises and great powers wars; distance of geopolitical challenges; social carriers in developing the trauma process; and geopolitical decline of rivals as well as disillusionment which affect the liberal narrative and create restraint narratives (i.e., pathways 2 and 3). These different processes matter to the *timing* of change for master narratives (which can differ from polarization), which effect, in turn, the *timing* and *substance* of policy outcomes.

58. *Promotion* and *protection* are two sides of the same coin, linked together by their shared connection to liberal identity. Protection-based variants (like anticommunism) are an outgrowth of liberalism intended to prevent damage to the state by stopping the spread of ideologies that harm identity. Protection-based narratives are best categorized, then, as "liberal" narratives. For a similar argument, see Haas, *Ideological Origins*.

59. For similar processes, see Jeffery T. Checkel, *Ideas and International Political Change: Soviet/Russian Behavior and the End of the Cold War* (New Haven: Yale University Press, 1997), 9–12.

60. Benjamin I. Page and Robert Y. Shapiro, *The Rational Public: Fifty Years of Trends in Americans' Policy Preferences* (Chicago: University of Chicago Press, 1992), 185–94 and Jerome Bruner, *Mandate from the People* (New York: Duell Sloan Pearce, 1944), 15–16. Returning to Krebs, what mattered most to explain the slow emergence of the liberal narrative was not related to something unique to FDR (he and other internationalists told the right story as promoters), but instead this series of validating events that over time made the internationalist story the new collective wisdom. This is critical to explain the timing, substance, and process of narrative formation and change.

61. Again, contra-realism, geostrategic decline that matters is decline by an ideologically distant (in this case illiberal) power.

62. Alexander, "Toward a Theory," 22–23. Trauma theorists refer to this as collective "calming down."

63. Emile Durkheim, *Suicide: A Study in Sociology* (Glencoe, IL: Free Press, 1951), 246 and Sztompka, "Cultural Trauma," 458.

64. Smelser, "Psychological and Cultural," 36.

65. Sztompka, "Cultural Trauma," 458; and Smelser, "Psychological and Cultural," 52–53.

66. This kind of instrumentalism does not mean that policy elites alone determine the content of the liberal narrative, only that they use it to justify certain policy ends at times. Theodore J. Lowi, *The End of Liberalism: The Second Republic of the United States*, 2nd ed. (New York: W.W. Norton, 1979), 127–63.

67. The Abu Ghraib prison abuses in Iraq contributed in similar ways to disillusionment in the early to mid-2000s.

68. Smelser, "Psychological and Cultural," 41–43; Eyerman, *Cultural Trauma: Slavery and the Formation of African American Identity* (Cambridge: Cambridge University Press, 2004), 2.

69. Restraint narratives weaken through a process similar to pathway two above. Since restraint narratives are trauma-specific (and with that, temporally linked to specific rivalry periods), new eras in foreign policy often create a collective sense that restraint narratives are now less relevant, or lessons that apply to a different time. Restraint narratives weaken or lose their collective grip on the nation entirely here, especially when promoters narrate around new identity threats abroad. On ideational decline, see Maurits van der Veen, *Ideas, Interests, and Foreign Aid* (Cambridge: Cambridge University Press, 2011) and Neta Crawford, *Argument and Social Change in World Politics: Ethics, Decolonization, and Humanitarian Intervention* (Cambridge: Cambridge University Press, 2002).

70. Alexander Wendt, *Social Theory of International Politics* (Cambridge: Cambridge University Press, 1999), 77–88.

71. Among the leading works, see James D. Fearon, "Domestic Political Audiences and the Escalation of International Disputes," *American Political Science Review* 88, no. 3 (1994): 577–92; Fearon, "Signaling Foreign Policy Interests," *Journal of Conflict Resolution* 41, no. 1 (1997): 68–90; Michael Tomz, "Domestic Audience Costs in International Relations: An Experimental Approach," *International Organization* 61, no. 4 (2007): 821–40; Mathew Levendusky and Michael Horowitz, "When Backing Down Is the Right Decision: Partisanship, New Information, and Audience Costs," *Journal of Politics* 74, no. 2 (2012): 323–38.

72. Tomz, "Domestic Audience Costs," 821.

73. Fearon, "Domestic Political Audiences" 577.

74. Levendusky and Horowitz, "When Backing Down," 323.

75. Levendusky and Horowitz, "When Backing Down," 323; Fearon, "Domestic Political Audiences." The vast majority of work here focuses on these kinds of audience costs for inaction.

76. Jack S. Levy et al., "Backing Out or Backing In? Commitment and Consistency in Audience Cost Theory," *American Journal of Political Science* 59, no. 4 (2015): 988–89.

77. Fearon, "Domestic Political Audiences," 583.

78. Fearon, "Domestic Political Audiences," 583.

79. Sometimes, commitments by presidents contribute to master narrative audience costs, but in most instances they do not and in some cases (i.e., Reagan in Central America, chapter 5) presidential commitments help produce audience costs *against*, rather than in support of, commitments. For some who talk about and critique the audience cost literature along these and other lines, see Jack Snyder and Erica D. Borghard, "The Cost of Empty Threats: A Penny, Not a Pound," *American Political Science Review*, 105, no. 3 (2011): 437–56; and Stephen M. Walt, "Rigor or Rigor Mortis: Rational Choice and Security Studies," *International Security* 23, no. 4 (1999): 5–48.

80. On the power of collective discourses, see Stephen Ellingson, "Under the Dialectic of Discourse and Collective Action: Public Debate and Rioting in Antebellum Cincinnati," *American Journal of Sociology* 101, no. 1 (1995): 107. These discourses contribute to

the analogies leaders draw upon in making foreign policy decisions, see Khong, *Analogies at War*, chapter 1.

81. Owen, *Clash of Ideas*, 32–36. These kinds of agents can include elites, especially nonleadership elites like other politicians, policy experts, social leaders, and policy commentators. Some of them (i.e., "promoters") resemble Owen's transnational ideational networks (TINs), while others ("moderators) do not. Unlike Owen's argument, these agents operate in a highly conscribed narrative context that affects much of what they do and how they matter. On the former, master narratives impact agent choices about how and whether to build discourses at all, which contrasts with Owen's account that expects TINs as ideological purists to be unwavering in advocating for their cause. The next section discusses how master narratives leverage some discourses over others in policy debates.

82. Walldorf, *Just Politics*, 19–20.

83. Ernest R. May, *The World and American Isolation, 1914–1917* (Cambridge: Harvard University Press, 1959), 430.

84. On these dynamics, see Doug McAdam, "Micromobilization Contexts and Recruitment Activism," in *From Social Structure to Action: Comparing Social Movement Research Across Cultures*, ed. Bert Klandermans et al. (London: JAI Press 1988), 131.

85. Thomas J. Christensen, *Useful Adversaries: Grand Strategy, Domestic Mobilization, and Sino-American Conflict, 1947–1958* (Princeton: Princeton University Press, 1996), 72–73.

86. Pamela E. Oliver and Gerald Marwell, "Mobilizing Technologies for Collective Action," in *Frontiers in Social Movement Theory*, ed. Aldon D. Morris et al. (New Haven: Yale University Press, 1992), 252.

87. Walldorf, *Just Politics*, 20.

88. In this and all other pathways below, leaders fear that robust narrative discourses could shape voter preferences. For a discussion, see Richard Sobel, *The Impact of Public Opinion on U.S. Foreign Policy Since Vietnam: Constraining the Colossus* (New York: Oxford University Press, 2001), 11–12; and V.O. Key, *Public Opinion and American Democracy* (New York: Alfred A Knopf, 1961), 14.

89. James Irving Matray, *The Reluctant Crusader: American Foreign Policy in Korea, 1941–1950* (Honolulu: University of Hawaii Press, 1985), 236–51; Campbell Craig and Frederik Logevall, *America's Cold War: The Politics of Insecurity* (Cambridge: Belknap Press of Harvard University Press, 2009), 117.

90. Karl Bermann, *Under the Big Stick: Nicaragua and the United States since 1848* (Boston: South End Press, 1986), 183–94 and L. Ethan Ellis, *Frank B. Kellogg and American Foreign Relations, 1925–1929* (Westport, CT: Greenwood Press, 1974), 23–85.

91. In this kind of discourse context, President Bill Clinton found more space to set policy (i.e., Haiti) but was also constrained by the weak liberal narrative in many instances (Rwanda and the Balkans). For examples, see Sarah E. Kreps, "The 1994 Haiti Intervention: A Unilateral Operation in Multilateral Clothes," *Journal of Strategic Studies* 30, no. 3 (2007): 449–74; Henry F. Carey, "U.S. Domestic Politics and the Emerging Humanitarian Intervention Policy: Haiti, Bosnia, and Kosovo," *World Affairs* 164, no. 2 (2001): 72–82; Sobel, *The Impact of Public Opinion*, chapters 12 and 13.

92. Jepperson, Wendt, and Katzenstein, "Norms, Identity and Culture," 56; and Finnemore, *The Purpose of Intervention: Changing Beliefs about the Use of Force* (Ithaca: Cornell University Press, 2003), 6.

93. Ronald Reagan, *An American Life* (New York: Simon and Schuster, 1990), 471–79.

94. The case-study chapters consider counterarguments about partisanship, the economy, and prestige.

95. Owen, *Clash of Ideas*, 42, see also 37. For added support to this argument, see Adam J. Berinsky, "Assuming the Costs of War: Events, Elites, and American Public Support for

Military Intervention," *Journal of Politics* 69, no. 4 (2007): 975–97. For U.S. elite attitudes about democracy promotion, see Tony Smith, *America's Mission: The United States and the Worldwide Struggle for Democracy in the Twentieth Century* (Princeton: Princeton University Press, 1994).

96. John J. Mearsheimer, *Why Leaders Lie: The Truth about Lying in International Politics* (New York: Oxford University Press, 2011), 55.

97. Waltz, *Theory of International Politics*; Morton A. Kaplan, *System and Process in International Politics* (Huntington: Robert K. Krieger, 1975); and Walt, *Origins of Alliances*.

98. Owen, *Clash of Ideas*, 73–75. Owen dispels these realist arguments in detail.

99. Michael C. Desch, "America's Illiberal Liberalism," *International Security* 32, no. 3 (2007/8): 18–19. For a similar argument that brings attention to psychological dynamics as well, see Robert Jervis, "The Remaking of a Unipolar World," *Washington Quarterly* 29, no. 3 (2006): 7–19.

100. Realists of all stripes—notably, offensive, defensive, and neoclassical—share these same expectations, which many discuss in the broader context of democracy promotion by democratic great powers. See, for example, Christopher Layne, "Kant or Cant: The Myth of the Democratic Peace," in *The Peril of Anarchy: Contemporary Realism and International Security*, ed. Michael E. Brown et al. (Cambridge: MIT Press, 1995), 329; John J. Mearsheimer, "Back to the Future: Instability in Europe after the Cold War," in *The Peril of Anarchy*, 121–24; Randall Schweller, "U.S. Democracy Promotion: Realist Reflections," in *American Democracy Promotion: Impulses, Strategies, and Impacts*, ed. Michael Cox et al. (Oxford: Oxford University Press, 2000), 41; Barry R. Posen, *The Sources of Military Doctrine: France Britain and Germany Between the Wars* (Ithaca: Cornell University Press, 1984), 58, 80.

101. Desch, "America's Illiberal Liberalism."

102. The realist arguments about liberal narrative strength offer opposite predictions but are both consistent with extant realist scholarship.

103. In each of the selected cases, the source of regime crisis was not created by the United States directly. For example, regime crisis in South Vietnam came from the North Vietnamese/ Vietcong infiltration; and in Iraq, it came from Kurdish and Shia forces in northern and southern Iraq that on occasion across the 1990s and early 2000s tried to challenge Saddam Hussein's regime.

104. Jeffrey K. Olick, *The Politics of Regret: On Collective Memory and Historical Responsibility* (New York: Routledge, 2007), 22.

105. Walldorf, *Just Politics*, 14–16 and 36–37.

106. Gary King, Robert O. Keohane, and Sidney Verba, *Designing Social Inquiry* (Princeton: Princeton University Press, 1994), chapter 6.

107. Stephen Van Evra, *Guide to Methods for Students of Political Science* (Ithaca: Cornell University Press, 1997), 56–67.

2. THE BROAD PATTERNS

1. Appendices are available at https://www.willwalldorf.com. For codebooks, see Appendix B. John M. Owen, IV, *The Clash of Ideas in World Politics: Transnational Networks, States, and Regime Change, 1510–2010* (Princeton: Princeton University Press, 2010). This list of cases comes from Owen. As Owen notes some of these interventions may have included interests in addition to regime promotion, which does not take away from the fact that they were still regime promotion cases. The United States had certain geostrategic interests in combatting the Axis powers in World War II, for example. Regime promotion goals stood alongside of and augmented these objectives from the start of each intervention. For this reason, leading studies consider these cases, and others like them, regime promotion cases.

2. Emile Durkheim, *The Rules of Sociological Method*, 8th ed. (Glencoe, IL: Free Press, 1950), 1–28. See also Jeffrey W. Legro, "Whence American Internationalism," *International Organization* 54, no.2 (2000): 256 and Charles Taylor, "Interpretation and the Sciences of Man," *Review of Metaphysics* 25, no. 1 (1971): 3–51.

3. Jeffrey K. Olick, *The Politics of Regret: On Collective Memory and Historical Responsibility* (New York: Routledge, 2007), 22. This assessment parallels the conversation about collective and public opinion in the introduction. Broad collective ideas and beliefs, like master narratives, can be reflected in survey data at times. By the same token, given the ontological differences between master narratives (collective) and public opinion (aggregate individual), survey data is best used in tandem with other more reliable measures of collective phenomena as with the historical case studies in the chapters to follow.

4. See examples in Ole R. Holsti, *Public Opinion and American Foreign Policy* (Ann Arbor: University of Michigan Press, 2007).

5. Durkheim, *The Rules*, 27–28; Olick, *The Politics of Regret*, 21–22; and Kimberly A. Neuendorf and Paul D. Skalski, "Quantitative Content Analysis and the Measurement of Collective Identity," in *Measuring Identity: A Guide for Social Scientists*, ed. Rawi Abdelal et al. (Cambridge: Cambridge University Press, 2009), 203–36.

6. John Markoff, "Suggestions for the Measurement of Consensus," *American Sociological Review* 47, no. 2 (1982): 290–98. See also Neuendorf et al., "Quantitative Content Analysis," 211.

7. Legro, "Whence American Internationalism," 256–57.

8. Jeffrey W. Legro, *Rethinking the World: Strategies and International Order* (Ithaca: Cornell University Press, 2005), 52. See also Frank Klingberg, *Cyclical Trends in American Foreign Policy Moods: The Unfolding of America's World* (Lanham, MD: University Press of America, 1983). Modern presidents poll test every facet of the State of the Union address in order to ensure broad appeal. Presidents in earlier eras did the same with surveys of editorial opinion.

9. Joshua W. Busby and Jonathan Monten, "Without Heirs? Assessing the Decline of Establishment Internationalism in U.S. Foreign Policy," *Perspectives on Politics* 6, no. 3 (2008): 451–72.

10. The papers include the *New York Times, Chicago Tribune, St. Louis Post-Dispatch, Los Angeles Times, Dallas Morning-News, San Francisco Chronicle, Richmond Times-Dispatch*, and the *Washington Post*.

11. Legro, "Whence American Internationalism"; Neuendorf et al., "Quantitative Content Analysis," 205; and Ted Hopf, *Social Construction of International Politics: Identities and Foreign Policies, Moscow, 1955 and 1999* (Ithaca: Cornell University Press, 2002), 24; Ronald R. Krebs, *Narrative and the Making of US National Security* (Cambridge: Cambridge University Press, 2015), 195–97.

12. Mark D. West, ed., *Theory, Method, and Practice in Computer Content Analysis* (Westport, CT: Ablex, 2001); J. Samuel Fitch, "The Garrison State in America: A Content Analysis of Trends in the Expectation of Violence," *Journal of Peace Research* 22, no. 1 (1985): 31–45. Many agree that high numbers of references to keywords in a certain policy domain reflects the audience's interest in a robust pursuit of goals in that policy area.

13. John Tures, "The Democracy-Promotion Gap in American Public Opinion," *Journal of American Studies* 41, no. 3 (2007): 557–79, 562–63; Francis Fukuyama and Michael McFaul, "Should Democracy be Promoted or Demoted?" *Washington Quarterly* 31, no. 1 (2007–8): 24. These and related terms were used extensively, for instance, by President George W. Bush in State of the Union addresses between 2002 and 2005, a period when opinion polls showed solid support for democracy promotion abroad (hovering between fifty-five and seventy percent). In fact, at the point of Bush's 2002 "axis of evil" speech,

70% of the public supported democracy promotion and editorials in leading national newspapers on the left and right agreed with Bush. As these poll numbers declined later in the decade, so did value terms in State of the Union addresses.

14. For more on terms here across time, see Appendix A. We counted terms related to democracy, freedom, *and* human rights because they stem from liberal values at the center of the U.S. identity and, inherently, involve the domestic political and social order of other states. See, for instance, Jennifer Windsor, "Advancing the Freedom Agenda: Time for Recalibration?" *Washington Quarterly* 29, no. 3 (2006): 28.

15. For the complete list, contact the author.

16. "Free" is a good example of a possible double entendre, whose meaning needed interpretation in the text and could not be included in the computer counts. If "free" referred to political freedom (i.e., "free speech" or "free press"), we counted it. If it referred to something like "free trade," we did not count it, since this is a reference to economics, not politics.

17. Jeffrey W. Legro, "Whence American Internationalism," 256 and Krebs, *Narrative*, 195–97.

18. Legro, "Whence American Internationalism," 253–89. This sample size adequately captures what it is intended to capture. Initially, we coded only four newspapers, which yielded a total of 256 editorials. The statistical results with the expanded dataset of 484 editorials are virtually identical to the earlier findings with the smaller sample size from four newspapers.

19. William R. Thompson, "Identifying Rivals and Rivalries in World Politics," *International Studies Quarterly* 45, no. 4 (2001): 562.

20. Thompson, "Identifying Rivals and Rivalries in World Politics," 562–64. There was some subjectivity for the coders, especially on start and end dates of the restraint narrative, which is common as Thompson notes when coding secondary historical sources. We limited subjectivity to the best extent possible by using multiple coders and a clear set of coding rules. See Appendix A.

21. Owen, *The Clash of Ideas*; Correlates of War Project, *Intra-State War Dataset*, version 4.1 (Ann Arbor: University of Michigan, 2007).

22. In figure 2.1, a scale was used to demonstrate the liberal narrative for the sake of presentation. The narrower date range (1913 to 2011) is for presentation as well. For a discussion, see Appendix A.

23. Klingberg, *Cyclical Trends*.

24. Samuel Huntington, *American Politics: The Promise of Disharmony* (Cambridge, MA: Belknap Press of Harvard University Press, 1981), chapters 1 and 8.

25. As discussed in Appendix A, the State of the Union address measure is on a 0 to 7 scale of the liberal narrative, while the editorial measure is on a –1 to 2 scale.

26. See, for instance, Ole R. Holsti and James N. Rosenau, "Cold War Axioms in a Post-Vietnam Era," in *Change in the International System*, ed. Ole R. Holst et al. (Boulder, CO: Westview Press, 1980), 276–87.

27. Selig Adler, *The Isolationist Impulse: Its Twentieth-Century Reaction* (London: Abelard-Schuman, 1957), 40. Tony Smith, *America's Mission: The United States and the Worldwide Struggle for Democracy in the Twentieth Century* (Princeton: Princeton University Press, 1994), 5–6.

28. Cited in William C. Widenor, *Henry Cabot Lodge and the Search for an American Foreign Policy* (Berkeley: University of California Press, 1980), 227.

29. Stephen Sestanovich, *Maximalist: America in the World from Truman to Obama* (New York: Alfred A. Knopf, 2014), 10; Campbell Craig and Frederik Logevall, *America's Cold War: The Politics of Insecurity* (Cambridge: Belknap Press of Harvard University Press, 2009), 144 and 214.

30. "America Aroused," *New York Times*, January 13, 1980; Richard J. Walton, "Reeling Backward," *New York Times*, January 10, 1980; Stanley Karnow, "The End of American Exceptionalism," *Sun* (Baltimore), April 28, 1980.

31. Smith, *America's Mission*, 207.

32. Amy Zalman and Jonathan Clarke, "The Global War on Terror: A Narrative in Need of a Rewrite," *Ethics and International Affairs* 23, no. 2 (2009): 101.

33. Tures, "The Democracy-Promotion Gap," 562.

34. Alan Dawley, *Changing the World: American Progressives in War and Revolution* (Princeton: Princeton University Press, 2003), 294; Stuart I. Rochester, *American Liberal Disillusionment: In the Wake of World War I* (University Park: Pennsylvania State University Press, 1977), 71.

35. Cited in Hans Kohn, *American Nationalism: An Interpretive Essay* (New York: Macmillan, 1957), 207. Smith, *America's Mission*, 119–20.

36. Cited in Fred Turner, *Echoes of Combat: The Vietnam War in American Memory* (New York: Anchor Books, Doubleday, 1996), 32.

37. David Chandler, "Culture Wars and International Intervention: An 'Inside/Out' View of the Decline of National Interest," *International Politics* 41, no. 3 (2004): 360.

38. Suzanne Katzenstein and Jack Snyder, "Expediency of the Angels," *National Interest*, 100 (2009): 58–67. See also Natan Sharansky and Ron Dermer, "The Case for Freedom," *American Spectator* 40, no.4 (2007): 36; and Francis Fukuyama and Michael McFaul, "Should Democracy be Promoted or Demoted?" *Washington Quarterly* 31, no. 1 (2007–8): 24.

39. Threat and disillusionment were coded on a 0–3 scale in both the State of the Union addresses and editorials. See chapter 1 and Appendix A.

40. Stephen M. Walt, *The Origins of Alliances* (Ithaca: Cornell University Press, 1987); John Lewis Gaddis, *The Long Peace: Inquiries into the History of the Cold War* (Oxford: Oxford University Press, 1989); and Paul Kennedy, *The Rise and Fall of Great Powers: Economic Change and Military Conflict from 1500 to 2000* (New York: Random House, 2000). For other sources, see Craig and Logevall, *America's Cold War*; Julian E. Zelizer, *Arsenal of Democracy: The Politics of National Security—From World War II to the War on Terrorism* (New York: Basic Books, 2012).

41. Warren I. Cohen, *The American Revisionists: The Lessons of Intervention in World War I* (Chicago: University of Chicago Press, 1967), 50.

42. Hans Kohn, *American Nationalism: An Interpretive Essay* (New York: Macmillan, 1957), 207.

43. George Ball cited by George C. Herring, *America's Longest War: The United States and Vietnam, 1950–1975* (Philadelphia: Temple University Press, 1986), 3.

44. Edward P. Morgan, *The 60s Experience: Hard Lessons About Modern America* (Philadelphia: Temple University Press, 1991), 161.

45. Ronald Asmus, "The Democrats' Democracy Problem," *Washington Post*, July 17, 2007.

46. State of the Union, Address before a Joint Session of the Congress on the State of the Union (1971, 2006, 2007, 2011), http://www.presidency.ucsb.edu/ws/index.php?pid=3110.

47. There is a process involving agents or social carriers that is tested more extensively in the case studies to follow.

48. Smith, *America's Mission*, 5–6, 10, and 119–20; Lester D. Langley, *The United States and the Caribbean in the Twentieth Century* (Athens: University of Georgia Press, 1982), 118–34; Dana G. Munro, *The United States and the Caribbean Republics, 1921–1933* (Princeton: Princeton University Press, 1974), 187–267.

49. Michael T. Klare, *Beyond the "Vietnam Syndrome": U.S. Interventionism in the 1980s* (Washington, DC: Institute for Policy Studies, 1981), 1; Anthony Lake, ed. *The Vietnam Legacy: The War, American Society and the Future of American Foreign Policy* (New York: New York University Press, 1976).

50. Mueller, "Iraq Syndrome Redux," *Foreign Affairs*, June 18, 2014, www.foreignaffairs.com/articles/141578/John-Mueller/Iraq-Syndrome-Redux; Dana Stuster, "The Iraq Syndrome: A Decade Later, What Lessons Haven't We Learned from the War in Iraq that We Should?" *Foreign Policy*, March 19, 2013, www.foreingpolicy.com/articles/2013/03/19the_iraq_syndrome.

51. Cited in Gayle Tzemach Lemmon, "Iraq's Do-Nothing Legacy," DefenseOne.com, www.defenseone.com/ideas/2014/13/iraqs-do-nothing-legacy/80908.

52. Brian M. Pollins and Randall L. Schweller, "Linking the Levels: The Long Wave and Shifts in U.S. Foreign Policy, 1790–1993," *American Journal of Political Science* 43, no. 2 (1999): 431–64.

53. See Appendix A for a discussion of how these competing arguments are measured.

54. "Threat Level" refers to national threat perceptions associated with the master narrative argument and the realist alternative in tables 2.3, 2.4, and 2.5.

55. The estimation methodology here is OLS. When conducting least squares regressions with time series, the presence of serially correlated errors can bias results. Autocorrelation typically produces overstated t-statistics due to the downward bias of standard errors, increasing the possibility of type one errors. Initial OLS regressions with the model specified above reveal that autocorrelation is indeed present for the State of the Union address data (autocorrelation was checked for using the Portmanteau/Box-Ljung Q test and by examining the correlogram of residuals). Hence, an AR(1) correction to the State of the Union address and Editorial regressions was employed to remove biases of autocorrelation on our t-statistics.

56. No collinearity issues existed in any models.

57. The lagged dependent variable illustrates that the effects of all of the independent variables on the liberal narrative will persist for a significant amount of time.

58. Endogeneity has the potential to be a problem in these OLS regressions since our measures of liberal narrative and threat level come from text. Specifically, it is possible that discussions of threat were followed by discussions of values and vice versa. Hence, the threat variable may produce biased results in the OLS regressions due to potential feedback between threat and the liberal narrative. This was addressed with instrumental variables (IV) to re-estimate our OLS regressions, where we instrument for threat level. With good instruments, the implementation of IV regressions is typically straightforward, using estimators such as two stage least squares (2SLS). However, some claim that the presence of heteroskedasticity makes 2SLS estimator inefficient (although still consistent). The estimator that offers both consistent and efficient estimation, even in the presence of heteroskedasticity, is the generalized method of moments (GMM) estimator. Hence, we proceeded with GMM in order to address endogeneity. Given the power of GMM as an estimator, it is standard practice in macroeconomic research to use lagged dependent variables as instruments. Doing the same here, lagged values of our dependent variable were created to instrument for threat level. Intuitively, if the regressors are dated time period t and the instruments are dated time period $t-1$, this means that the instruments are orthogonal to the threat level that occurs in time period t. In other words, the timing of the instruments precedes the timing of the potential endogenous regressors in the equation, which therefore allows for their use as instruments. See Christopher F. Baum, Mark E. Schaffer, and Steven Stillman, "Instrumental Variables and GMM: Estimation and Testing," *Stata Journal* 3, no. 1 (2003): 1–31; Lars P. Hansen, "Large Sample Properties of

Generalized Method of Movements Estimators," *Econometrica* 50, no. 3 (1982): 1029–54; Manuel Arellano and Stephen Bond, "Some Tests of Specification for Panel Data: Monte Carlo Evidence and an Application to Employment Equations," *Review of Economic Studies* 58, no. 2 (1991): 277–97; Manuel Arrelano and Olympia Bover, "Another Look at the Instrumental Variable Estimation of Error-components Models," *Journal of Econometrics* 68, no. 1 (1995): 29–51.

The models were estimated with GMM to deal with endogeneity. For the GMM estimation, the primary instruments used were two lags of the suspected endogenous independent variable, as well as two lags of each of the competing variables for which our regression controls. The estimation weighting matrix in the GMM procedure was heteroskedastic and autocorrelation (HAC) consistent, with the Bartlett kernel and Newey-West fixed bandwidth. The GMM results indicated that endogeneity was not a problem for the models in table 2.4. Finally, a Hausman test, which is a test of the endogeneity of the regressor suspected of biasing our OLS results was conducted. Rejection of the null under the Hausman test (based on the p-value for the Hausman test) implies that there is evidence of endogeneity—nonrejection implies no evidence of endogeneity issues. The Hausman tests in table 1 yielded p-values larger than 0.10, meaning nonrejection of the null hypothesis of the Hausman test. Hence, while endogeneity may theoretically be an issue, there appeared to be no biases in the OLS results. This adds confidence in the OLS findings. See Jerry A. Hausman, "Specification Tests in Econometrics," *Econometrica* 46, no. 6 (1978): 1251–71.

59. Though the lagged dependent variable was not significant in these models, it was included anyway for the sake of consistency with the models in table 2.4 and due to the fact that autocorrelation existed in the models found in tables 2.5.

60. In other specifications of the models in tables 2.4 and 2.5, controls for major exogenous shocks during the twentieth and twenty-first century were included. In the State of the Union address data, none were significant. With the editorials, the Cold War and 9/11 appeared to depress the liberal narrative. Since this does not affect the statistical significance of the variables of interest nor augment the explanatory power of the model, they were not included in these final models in order to enhance degrees of freedom.

61. Strength of the economy was assessed in multiple ways in the models, using logged gross domestic product (GDP), inflation, and recession data in other specifications. In all instances and regardless of the combination of these variables used, the economic variables showed no statistical significance. Recession data was included in all models (including those below on military intervention) because this variable gave the best results among the economic variables. It also captures both GDP and Inflation in a single variable, which helped increase the degrees of freedom in our models. Recession data available from National Bureau of Economic Research's Business Cycle Dating Committee, http://www.nber.org/cycles/recessions.html.

62. See Appendix B for how variables in the competing explanations were measured. The models did not control for opportunities to intervene that result from regime crises in any given year. The absence of this control did not invalidate or change the findings, however. First, unlike the other alternatives controlled for in our models, there is no good theoretical reason to expect that an increase in opportunities would lead to an increase in regime change interventions (in fact, the opposite could be the case—more crises could lead to decisions to avoid or limit engagement in messy situations abroad). Second, and related, regime crises occur annually all over the world, meaning there are always opportunities for U.S. regime promotion at any moment. What is important to understand are the factors that lead to decisions to take advantage of some opportunities and not others. On this score, two of the explanations included in the model—the polarization and master narrative arguments—anticipate that effective opportunities will be mediated in

their impact on forceful regime promotion by the ideological distance of states involved in the regime crisis (polarization argument) or the strength of narratives and agent-driven discourses (narrative argument). Determining how opportunities matter, then, between these competing explanations is a qualitative issue that the case studies in later chapters address.

63. See Appendix B for all military intervention coding.

64. No good theoretical reasons exist, by contrast, for testing lagged versions of the other variables in the model, including restraint narratives. As discussed in chapter one, disillusionment and the restraint narrative have an especially searing impact on collective thinking. Consequently, moderators can build politically salient restraint discourses against military action far more quickly than promoters can build liberal discourses capable of producing impetus toward military action. When coupled with the fact that nonmilitary action is generally easier than military action for a democratic polity to make given the sacrifices to the nation involved in using force, a strong restraint narrative/discourse should have a more immediate impact on decisions for or against force. This explains our decision not to lag the restraint narrative in our models.

65. No collinearity issues were present in these analyses.

66. The Hausman test in the GMM models indicated that endogeneity was not an issue. Again, the lagged dependent variable demonstrated that the effects of all of the independent variables on military interventions would persist for a significant portion of time.

67. The Hausman test in the GMM results indicated that endogeneity was not a problem for any models in table 2.7.

68. This is also not terribly surprising, since theoretically, it is anticipated that military action, including regime change wars, can contribute to disillusionment and threat perceptions that, in turn, affect liberal narrative strength.

69. Legro, "Whence American Internationalism," 256–57.

70. The case study chapters add depth to the discussion of many of these periods.

71. For historical examples, see Benjamin I. Page and Robert Y. Shapiro, *The Rational Public: Fifty Years of Trends in Americans' Foreign Policy* (Chicago: University of Chicago Press, 1992), 185–94.

72. The point here is not that elites *exclusively* reflect broad narratives. As discussed in the chapters to follow, they sometimes play important roles as promoters and moderators. But in this role they are also deeply constrained by the field of play set by narratives. Elites neither get what they always argue for, nor are they the sole determinants of those narratives. The findings in tables 2.4 and 2.5 reinforce this.

73. For those that argue editorials are similar to State of the Union addresses since they too are written by elites, the same conclusions can be drawn.

74. Robert Jervis, "The Remaking of a Unipolar World," *Washington Quarterly* 29, no. 3 (2006): 7–19 and Michael C. Desch, "America's Illiberal Liberalism," *International Security* 32, no. 3 (2007/8): 18–19.

3. REGIME CHANGE IN KOREA AND CHINA

1. The end of isolationism meant the restraint narrative was weak in this period. For space reasons, this chapters focuses less on this change.

2. Campbell Craig and Frederik Logevall, *America's Cold War: The Politics of Insecurity* (Cambridge: Belknap Press of Harvard University Press, 2009), 60–66 and Melvin Small, *Democracy and Diplomacy: The Impact of Domestic Politics on U.S. Foreign Policy, 1789–1994* (Baltimore: Johns Hopkins University Press, 1996), 83.

3. Frederik Logevall, "A Critique of Containment," *Diplomatic History* 28, no. 4 (2004): 493. Stephen J. Whitfield, *The Culture of the Cold War*, 2nd ed. (Baltimore: Johns Hopkins Press, 1996), chapters 1–4.

4. "Red Tide At Flood," *Atlanta Constitution*, February 27, 1948; "Only Full Reconstruction Can Save This One World," *San Francisco Chronicle*, March 13, 1947; and "Once Again A President Gives Grave Counsel," *Courier-Journal* (Louisville), March 18, 1948.

5. Athan Theoharis, *Seeds of Repression: Harry S. Truman and the Origins of McCarthyism* (Chicago: Quadrangle Books, 1971), 200.

6. "Mr. Truman and Mr. Wallace," *New York Times*, September 15, 1946.

7. George H. Gallup, *The Gallup Poll: Public Opinion 1935–1971*, vol. 1 (New York: Random House, 1972), 587, 640, and 682.

8. "American-Russian Suspicion," *Milwaukee Journal*, March 1, 1946. See also "The Loyalty Probe Record," *San Francisco Chronicle*, March 1, 1948.

9. David Halberstam, *The Best and the Brightest* (New York: Random House, 1972), 108. For one of many other examples, see Whitfield, *The Culture of the Cold War*, vii.

10. Craig and Logevall, *America's Cold War*, 67–73; Greg Herken, *The Winning Weapon: The Atomic Bomb in the Cold War, 1945–1950* (New York: Alfred A. Knopf, 1980), 129–30.

11. Craig and Logevall, *America's Cold War*, 68 and Herken, *The Winning Weapon*, 129.

12. "What's Russia's Goal," *New York Times*, February 17, 1946; "The Red Riddle," *New York Times*, March 10, 1946; "Where Is Russia Going?" *Milwaukee Journal*, February 24, 1946.

13. "Mr. Churchill's Message," *New York Times*, March 6, 1946; "The Loan Would Serve the Purpose Ideally," *Courier-Journal*, March 7, 1946.

14. "American-Russian Suspicion"; "Of Grave Concern," *Charlotte Observer*, February 19, 1946; "Not Safe Even in All Home Hands," *Charlotte Observer*, February 23, 1946.

15. "Where Is Russia Going?" See also "Nasty Question," *Charlotte Observer*, February 22, 1946.

16. *Congressional Record*, 79th Cong., 2nd Sess., 1946, 92, pt. 1: A968.

17. *Congressional Record*, 79th Cong., 2nd Sess., 1946, 92, pt. 1: A644 and 1227.

18. *Congressional Record*, 79th Cong., 2nd Sess., 1946, 92, pt. 2, 1576.

19. See for instance, Craig and Logevall, *America's Cold War*, 67. Deborah Welch Larson *Origins of Containment: A Psychological Explanation* (Princeton: Princeton University Press, 1985), 250–301. To sustain cooperation with Moscow, Truman initially rejected the more combative approach recommended in the February 1946 Long Telegram and the September 1946 Clifford-Elsey Report.

20. Cited by H. Bradford Westerfield, *Foreign Policy and Party Politics: Pearl Harbor to Korea* (New Haven: Yale University Press, 1955), 208–9.

21. *Congressional Record*, 79th Cong., 2nd Sess., 1946, 92, pt. 2: 2265.

22. In order, *Congressional Record*, 79th Cong., 2nd Sess., 1946, 92, pt. 1: A649.

23. *Congressional Record*, 79th Cong., 2nd Sess., 1946, 92, pt. 1: A703.

24. *Congressional Record*, 79th Cong., 2nd Sess., 1946, 92, pt. 1: 1227.

25. *Congressional Record*, 79th Cong., 2nd Sess., 1946, 92, pt. 1: A703.

26. *Congressional Record*, 79th Cong., 2nd Sess., 1946, 92, pt. 1: A845.

27. Cited by Westerfield, *Foreign Policy and Party Politics*, 209.

28. Logevall, "A Critique of Containment," 491. Republicans were a minority in Congress, demonstrating the political power of the shifting liberal narrative.

29. Larson, *Origins of Containment*, 258; John Lewis Gaddis, *Strategies of Containment: A Critical Reappraisal of Postwar American Security Policy* (Oxford: Oxford University Press, 1982), 284, 304–6, 312–15.

30. Robert J. Donovan, *Conflict and Crisis: The Presidency of Harry S. Truman, 1945–1948* (New York: W.W. Norton, 1977), 185.

31. James Byrnes, "U.S.-Soviet Tensions Build," http://www.history.com/speeches/us-soviet-tension-builds. Larson, *Origins of Containment*, 258–59. To look tough

at home, Truman also used a battleship to take the recently deceased Turkish ambassador home to Turkey.

32. Craig and Logevall, *America's Cold War*, 67–73; Small, *Democracy and Diplomacy*, 82–83.

33. Reprinted in *Major Problems in American Foreign Policy, Volume II: Since 1914*, ed. Dennis Merrill et al., 7th ed. (New York: Wadsworth Publishing, 2009), 195–97.

34. Westerfield, *Foreign Policy and Party Politics*, 209.

35. Anne O'Hare McCormick, "The Stiffening Attitude toward Russia," *New York Times*, March 2, 1946.

36. James Reston, "Have We a New Foreign Policy?" *Washington Post*, March 3, 1946.

37. "'Toward a Good Understanding,'" *San Francisco Chronicle*, March 7, 1946.

38. "Mr. Churchill's Plea," *Chicago Tribune*, March 7, 1946; "Let's Hang Together—Churchill," *Los Angeles Times*, March 7, 1946; and "Joint Anglo-American Defense," *Milwaukee Journal*, March 7, 1946.

39. Logevall, "A Critique of Containment," 493. Ronald R. Krebs, *Narrative and the Making of US National Security* (Cambridge: Cambridge University Press, 2015), 191–264.

40. Larson, *Origins of Containment*, 291.

41. "Mr. Truman has Done the Inevitable Thing," *Courier-Journal*, September 21, 1946.

42. "Henry Wallace's Letter," *Milwaukee Journal*, September 18, 1946. See also "A Dignified Valedictory and a Ray of Hope," *Courier-Journal*, September 22, 1946.

43. Gallup, *The Gallup Poll*, vol. 1, 604.

44. Small, *Democracy and Diplomacy*, 90; Westerfield, *Foreign Policy and Party Politics*, 212–13.

45. Larson, *Origins of Containment*, 291. "Did I catch hell," Truman commented privately of the liberal narrative backlash he felt for initially supporting Wallace's speech.

46. Larson, *Origins of Containment*, 262–67. See also Craig and Logevall, *America's Cold War*, 73–76.

47. "The Truman Doctrine, 1947," reprinted in *Major Problems in American Foreign Policy*, 220–21.

48. Gallup, *The Gallup Poll*, vol. 1, 636–67.

49. "Only Full Reconstruction," 14.

50. "Seeing it Through," *Washington Post*, March 15, 1947.

51. *Rochester Democratic and Chronicle* and *Philadelphia Inquirer* cited by "Extracts from American Editorial Comment on President Truman's Speech," *New York Times*, March 13, 1946; "America's New World Role," *St. Louis Post-Dispatch*, March 13, 1947; "Always Remember—Congress is You," *Atlanta Constitution*, March 13, 1947.

52. "The Red Question," *Chicago Tribune*, March 15, 1947.

53. "'Editorial Reaction to Current Issues,' Greek Situation, Parts I and II, March 19, 1947," Harry S. Truman Library and Museum online archives, http://www.truman library.org/whistlestop/study_collections/doctrine/large/documents/index.php? documentdate=1947-03-19&documentid=4-8&pagenumber=1.

54. Richard M. Freeland, *The Truman Doctrine and the Origins of McCarthyism: Foreign Policy, Domestic Politics and Internal Security, 1946–1948* (New York: New York University Press, 1985), 88; Thomas J. Christensen, *Useful Adversaries: Grand Strategy, Domestic Mobilization, and Sino-American Conflict, 1947–1958* (Princeton: Princeton University Press, 1996), 51.

55. Theoharis, *Seeds of Repression*, 31.

56. Soviet gains beyond 1947 reinforced the liberal narrative all the more.

57. Henry R. Nau, *Conservative Internationalism: Armed Diplomacy under Jefferson, Polk, Truman, and Reagan* (Princeton: Princeton University Press, 2013), 149–61.

58. Gallup, *The Gallup Poll*, vol. 1, 601–2. A poll found that "Foreign policy, relations with Russia" was the top response when voters were asked what should be discussed in the November elections.

59. Cited by Zelizer, *Arsenal of Democracy*, 66; see Logevall, "A Critique of Containment," 491. Truman tried to invoke it as well. Larson, *Origins*, 300–301.

60. Cited by Zelizer, *Arsenal of Democracy*, 66.

61. Freeland, *The Truman Doctrine*, 77–78.

62. Freeland, *The Truman Doctrine*, 82; Zelizer, *Arsenal of Democracy*, 67 and Halberstam, *The Best and Brightest*, 109.

63. Cited by Robert Dallek, *Harry S. Truman* (New York: Times Books, 2008), 54.

64. Logevall, "A Critique of Containment," 491–92.

65"Draft Suggestions for the President's Message to Congress on the Greek Situation, March 3, 1947," Subject File J.M. Jones Papers, Harry S. Truman Library and Museum online archives, http://www.trumanlibrary.org/whistlestop/study_collections/doctrine/large/documents/index.php?documentdate=1947-03-03&documentid=6-9&pagenumber=1.

66. Christensen, *Useful Adversaries*, 49 and Freeland, *The Truman Doctrine*, 96–97.

67. Cited by Freeland, *The Truman Doctrine*, 96 and Christensen, *Useful Adversaries*, 50.

68. "Draft Suggestions for the President's Message."

69. "Draft Suggestions for the President's Message"; "Meeting Notes, ca. 1947," Subject File, J.M. Jones Papers, Harry S. Truman Library and Museum online archives, http://www.trumanlibrary.org/whistlestop/study_collections/doctrine/large/documents/index.php?documentdate=1947-02-00&documentid=8-4&pagenumber=1; "Memo for the file, re: drafting of the President's Message to Congress, March 12, 1947," Subject File, J.M. Jones Papers, Harry S. Truman Library and Museum online archives, http://www.trumanlibrary.org/whistlestop/study_collections/doctrine/large/documents/index.php?documentdate=1947-03-12&documentid=7-2&pagenumber=1.

70. Cited by Freeland, *The Truman Doctrine*, 99–100. More realpolitik advisors were pushed aside, see Nau, *Conservative Internationalism*, 148.

71. Krebs, *Narrative*, 39–41. Krebs misses the extent to which traumatic events and an already strengthening liberal narrative pressed Truman into this role as promoter.

72. Small, *Democracy and Diplomacy*, 82–83. See also Christensen, *Useful Adversaries*, chapter 3.

73. Whitfield, *The Culture of the Cold War*, vii.

74. Freeland, *The Truman Doctrine*, 99–100.

75. Tang Tsou, *America's Failure in China, 1941–50* (Chicago: University of Chicago Press, 1963), 127–288, 352–63, and 428; Nancy Bernkopf Tucker, *Patterns in the Dust: Chinese-American Relations and the Recognition Controversy, 1949–1950* (New York: Columbia University Press, 1983); Robert J. Donovan, *Conflict and Crisis: The Presidency of Harry S. Truman, 1945–1948* (New York: W.W. Norton, 1977), 26–27 and 39–49; Robert J. Donovan, *Tumultuous Years: The Presidency of Harry S. Truman, 1949–1953* (New York: W.W. Norton, 1982, 75.

76. Thomas J. Christensen, *Useful Adversaries*, chapters 3 and 4.

77. Ross Y. Koen, *The China Lobby in American Politics* (New York: Octagon Books, 1974), 49–55; Westerfield, *Foreign Policy and Party Politics*, 262.

78. Koen, *The China Lobby*, 58–59.

79. Koen, *The China Lobby*, 73; Christensen, *Useful Adversaries*, 59.

80. Tsou, *America's Failure*, 451–52; Lewis McCarol Purifoy, *Harry Truman's China Policy: McCarthyism and the Diplomacy of Hysteria, 1947–1951* (New York: New Viewpoints, 1976), 64–68.

81. Westerfield, *Foreign Policy and Party Politics*, 261; Koen, *The China Lobby*, 89; and Robert E. Herzstein, *Henry R. Luce, Time, and the American Crusade in Asia* (Cambridge: Cambridge University Press, 2005), 89–90.

82. Tsou, *America's Failure*, 449. See also Herzstein, *Henry R. Luce*, 81–85.

83. Cited by Tsou, *America's Failure*, 466, 468–69.

84. Tsou, *America's Failure*, 449, 464–65, and 468–70.

85. Purifoy, *Harry Truman's China Policy*, 65–68 and Christiansen, *Useful Adversaries*, 75.

86. Christiansen, *Useful Adversaries*, 74–75.

87. Purifoy, *Harry Truman's China Policy*, 67–68.

88. Cited by Christensen, *Useful Adversaries*, 65.

89. Cited by Christiansen, *Useful Adversaries*, 67.

90. Purifoy, *Harry Truman's China Policy*, 57.

91. John Stewart Service cited by Nancy Bernkopf Tucker, *China Confidential: American Diplomats and Sino-American Relations, 1945–1996* (New York: Columbia University Press, 2001), 62–63.

92. Christiansen, *Useful Adversaries*, 64 and Tsou, *America's Failure*, 453.

93. Koen, *The China Lobby*, 88–89; Tsou, *America's Failure*, 456–61.

94. Cited by Purifoy, *Harry Truman's China Policy*, 68; cited by Christensen, *Useful Adversaries*, 62.

95. Christiansen, *Useful Adversaries*, chapter 3.

96. Freeland, *The Truman Doctrine*, 335.

97. Christensen, *Useful Adversaries*, 60–62. Even Christensen, who makes the vote-swapping argument, admits the importance of the liberal narrative here. Purifoy, *Harry Truman's China Policy*, 68 and Freeland, *The Truman Doctrine*, 200. Some in the administration saw this ideological trap before the speech.

98. Cited by Christensen, *Useful Adversaries*, 66, 70. Marshall agreed (emphasis added).

99. Westerfield, *Foreign Policy and Party Politics*, 346–47.

100. Christiansen, *Useful Adversaries*, 81–82 and Ronald L. McGlothlen, *Controlling the Waves: Dean Acheson and U.S. Foreign Policy in Asia* (New York: W.W. Norton, 1993), 93–94.

101. Tsou, *America's Failure*, 363. See also David Halberstam, *The Coldest Winter: America and the Korean War* (New York: Hyperion, 2007), 239–40.

102. Both cited by Tsou, *America's Failure*, 363.

103. Tsou, *America's Failure*, 363.

104. Tsou, *America's Failure*, 363.

105. Freeland, *The Truman Doctrine* 110. Halberstam, *The Coldest Winter*, 243. Luce talked about these constraints.

106. "America's Greatest Decision," *Los Angeles Times*, March 13, 1947.

107. "Always Remember—Congress is You," *Atlanta Constitution*, March 13, 1947.

108. George H. Gallup, *The Gallup Poll: Public Opinion 1935–1971*, vol. 2 (New York: Random House, 1972), 818, 853, 887, 919, 930.

109. Christiansen, *Useful Adversaries*, 72–73 and Purifoy, *Harry Truman's China Policy*, 60–62.

110. Donovan, *Tumultuous Years*, 76. Koen, *The China Lobby*, 16.

111. Halberstam, *The Coldest Winter*, 343–44; Ronald J. Caridi, *The Korean War and American Politics: The Republican Party as a Case Study* (Philadelphia: University of Pennsylvania Press, 1968), 12; Purifoy, *Harry Truman's China Policy*, 104; Dallek, *Harry S. Truman*, 102.

112. Paul. G. Perpaoli Jr., *Truman and Korea: The Political Culture of the Early Cold War* (Columbia: University of Missouri Press, 1999), 24.

113. Robert Griffith, *The Politics of Fear: Joseph R. McCarthy and the Senate* (Lexington: University Press of Kentucky, 1970), 74; and Caridi, *The Korean War and American Politics*, 12.

240 NOTES TO PAGES 91–93

114. Thomas C. Reeves, "Introduction," in *McCarthyism*, ed. Thomas C. Reeves (Malabar: Robert E. Krieger, 1989) 3; and Christensen, *Useful Adversaries*, 115.

115. Cited by Guangqui Xu, *Congress and the U.S.-China Relationship, 1949–1979* (Akron: University of Akron Press, 2007), 23. Zelizer, *Arsenal of Democracy*, 91–92.

116. Herzstein, *Henry R. Luce*, 101–11; Robert M. Blum, *Drawing the Line: The Origins of the American Containment Policy in East Asia* (New York: W.W. Norton, 1982), 66–67; Donovan, *Tumultuous Years*, 36–39, 76–77.

117. Tucker, *Patterns in the Dust*, 166.

118. Herzstein, *Henry R. Luce*, 126–31. These charges gained added salience when Acheson publicly defended his long-standing friendship with Alger Hiss.

119. Cited by Craig and Logevall, *America's Cold War*, 123 and E. J. Kahn Jr., *The China Hands: America's Foreign Service Officers and What Befell Them* (New York: Viking Press, 1975), 213.

120. Cited by Kahn, *The China Hands*, 212–13. See also Herzstein, *Henry R. Luce*, 127–29.

121. George Kennan, "Persecution Left and Right," in *McCarthyism*, ed. Reeves, 88; Seymour Martin Lipset, "An Instrument Rather than A Creator," in *McCarthyism*, ed. Reeves, 132.

122. "Bombs Over China," *Washington Post*, February 11, 1950; "Conflict of Loyalties," *Washington Post*, January 27, 1950 and "The Personal Equation," *Washington Post*, March 28, 1950.

123. "Don't Look under the Rug, Says Acheson," *Los Angeles Times*, January 14, 1950 and "The Quality of Friendship," *Los Angeles Times*, January 27, 1950.

124. "What Policy for Peace?" *San Francisco Chronicle*, June 24, 1950.

125. Herzstein, *Henry R. Luce*, 109.

126. Gallup, *The Gallup Poll*, vol. 2, 852.

127. Gallup, *The Gallup Poll*, vol. 2, 911–12. Those numbers strengthened in time. Reeves, "Introduction," 3.

128. Steven Casey, *Selling the Korean War: Propaganda, Politics and Public Opinion in the United States, 1950–1953* (Oxford: Oxford University Press, 2008), 15; Cabell Phillips cited by Whitfield, *The Culture of the Cold War*, 38; Christensen, *Useful Adversaries*, 113–14.

129. Thomas Stokes, "Washington with Thomas Stokes," *Charlotte Observer*, April 5, 1950; Purifoy, *Harry Truman's China Policy*, 69–74.

130. Christensen, *Useful Adversaries*, 86–90; McGlothlen, *Controlling the Waves*, 111–12; Purifoy, *Harry Truman's China Policy*, 178–79, 181–82, 204–5.

131. Nancy Bernkopf Tucker, *China Confidential: American Diplomats and Sino-American Relations, 1945–1996* (New York: Columbia University Press, 2001), 64–65 and Kahn, *The China Hands*, 206–8, 224–25.

132. Truman especially hated bringing Dulles in given his work for Dewey in 1948. See William Whitney Stueck Jr., *The Road to Confrontation: American Policy toward China and Korea, 1947–1950* (Chapel Hill: The University of North Carolina Press, 1981), 145–46; John Lewis Gaddis, *The Long Peace: Inquiries into the History of the Cold War* (New York: Oxford University Press, 1987), 85.

133. Halberstam, *The Coldest Winter*, 326.

134. "What Policy for Peace," 10.

135. "Toward Policy in Asia," *New York Times*, June 23, 1950.

136. "'We are Playing for Keeps,'" *Milwaukee Journal*, March 13, 1950.

137. Burton I. Kaufman, *The Korean War: Challenges in Crisis, Credibility, and Command* (Philadelphia: Temple University Press, 1986), 45.

138. "Isolationists Mislead Stalin," *Milwaukee Journal*, June 27, 1950.

139. "The Beginning of World War III?" *Atlanta Constitution*, June 26, 1950.

140. "Distant Thunder in Korea," *San Francisco Chronicle*, June 27, 1950 and "The Cold War—(Delete Cold)," *San Francisco Chronicle*, June 28, 1950.

141. *Congressional Record*, 81st Cong., 2nd Sess., 1950, 96, pt. 7: 9146–305.

142. Eric F. Goldman, *The Crucial Decade: America, 1945–1955* (New York: Alfred A. Knopf, 1959), 157.

143. "The Beginning of World War III," 12 and "Ground Troops Move in," *New York Times*, July 1, 1950.

144. *Congressional Record*, 81st Cong., 2nd Sess., 1950, 96, pt. 7: 9238–243, 9271. See also Purifoy, *Harry Truman's China Policy*, 201; Goldman, *The Crucial Decade*, 170; and Caridi, *The Korean War*, 39–50.

145. Zelizer, *Arsenal of Democracy*, 99 and Stueck, *The Road to Confrontation*, 194.

146. James Irving Matray, *The Reluctant Crusader: American Foreign Policy in Korea, 1941–1950* (Honolulu: University of Hawaii Press, 1985), 236–51 and Stueck, *The Road to Confrontation*, 177–202.

147. Craig and Logevall, *America's Cold War*, 117.

148. Zelizer, *Arsenal of Democracy*, 99. See also Dallek, *Harry S. Truman*, 106 and Small, *Democracy and Diplomacy*, 93.

149. Freeland, *The Truman Doctrine*, 349.

150. Cited by Purifoy, *Harry Truman's China Policy*, 232.

151. Small, *Democracy and Diplomacy*, 93.

152. Cited by Donovan, *Tumultuous Years*, 209–10.

153. Donovan, *Tumultuous Years*, 194 and 202.

154. Donovan, *Tumultuous Years*, 215 and Matray, *The Reluctant Crusader*, 250–51.

155. Donovan *Tumultuous Years*, 200–201 and Stueck, *The Road to Confrontation*, 186–87.

156. Stueck, *The Road to Confrontation*, 187.

157. Stueck, *The Road to Confrontation*, 177–84.

158. Ellen Schrecker, *Many Are the Crimes: McCarthyism in America* (Boston: Little, Brown, 1998), 158–59.

159. Cited by Casey, *Selling the Korean War*, 32–33.

160. Matray, *The Reluctant Crusader*, 246.

161. Casey, *Selling the Korean War*, 20.

162. Casey, *Selling the Korean War*, 28.

163. Cited by Halberstam, *The Coldest Winter*, 99.

164. Halberstam, *The Coldest Winter*, 99.

165. Cited by Christiansen, *Useful Adversaries*, 123, 128–30.

166. Cited by Donovan, *Tumultuous Years*, 197–98.

167. Marquis Childs, "Far East Decision," *Washington Post*, June 28, 1950.

168. Christensen, *Useful Adversaries*, 136.

169. Tucker, *Patterns in the Dust*, 196.

170. Halberstam, *The Coldest Winter*, 369. See also Gaddis, *The Long Peace*, 87.

171. Donovan, *Tumultuous Years*, 205. See also Freeland, *The Truman Doctrine*, 350.

172. Cited by Matray, *The Reluctant Crusader*, 244.

173. Christensen, *Useful Adversaries*, 133–37 and Gaddis, *The Long Peace*, 82–87.

174. Christensen, *Useful Adversaries*, 136 and McGlothlen, *Controlling the Waves*, 128.

175. Freeland, *The Truman Doctrine* 350.

176. Purifoy, *Harry Truman's China Policy*, xiii–xiv.

177. *Congressional Record*, 81st Cong., 2nd Sess., 1950, 96, pt. 1: 153, 155.

178. *Congressional Record*, 81st Cong., 2nd Sess., 1950, 96, pt. 1: 170.

179. *Congressional Record*, 81st Cong., 2nd Sess., 1950, 96, pt. 1: 298.

180. *Congressional Record*, 81st Cong., 2nd Sess., 1950, 96, pt. 1: 390.

181. Xu, *Congress*, 40–49 and Blum, *Drawing the Line*, 178–84.

182. Koen, *The China Lobby*, 99 and Xu, *Congress*, 42–45.

183. *Congressional Record*, 81st Cong., 2nd Sess., 96, pt. 1: 166. See also Blum, *Drawing the Line*, 178–84.

184. *Congressional Record*, 81st Cong., 2nd Sess., 96, pt. 1: 169.

185. *Congressional Record*, 81st Cong., 2nd Sess., 96, pt. 1: 298, 155.

186. *Congressional Record*, 81st Cong., 2nd Sess., 96, pt. 1: 298, 165; Christensen, *Useful Adversaries*, 122–23. Public ambivalence about using force in China and the need to continue to appeal to cost-cutting Republicans explains the limits here.

187. Christiansen, *Useful Adversaries*, 135.

188. "Memorandum of Conversation, by the Ambassador at Large (Jessup)," *Foreign Relations of the United States, 1950*, volume 7 (Washington, DC: U.S. Government Printing Office, 1950), 159.

189. Cited by Gaddis, *The Long Peace*, 87.

190. "Democracy Takes Its Stand," *New York Times*, June 28, 1950; *Congressional Record*, 81st Cong., 2nd Sess., 96, pt. 7: 9154–544.

191. Christensen, *Useful Adversaries*, 128–30 and Blum, *Drawing the Line*, 196.

192. Goldman, *The Crucial Decade* 170.

193. Halberstam, *The Coldest Winter*, 138–68.

194. Casey, *Selling the Korean War*, 100; Dallek, *Harry S. Truman*, 108.

195. Gallup, *The Gallup Poll*, vol. 2, 943.

196. "Freedom Crusade on the March," *Milwaukee Journal*, September 19, 1950.

197. "Will We Lose the Peace Again?" *Atlanta Constitution*, September 28, 1950.

198. "For a United Korea," *St. Louis Post-Dispatch*, September 29, 1950; "For a Free, Secure Korea," *San Francisco Chronicle*, September 19, 1950; "What Our Role Will Be in a Post-War Korea," *Courier-Journal*, October 3, 1950.

199. "We Come to the Bridge in Korea," *Los Angeles Times*, September 28, 1950.

200. Zelizer, *Arsenal of Democracy*, 101–2; Craig and Logevall, *America's Cold War*, 132–35; and Caridi, *The Korean War*, 52–53.

201. Casey, *Selling the Korean War,* 38–39, 75.

202. Cited by Casey, *Selling the Korean War*, 78.

203. Caridi, *The Korean War*, 53–54.

204. Caridi, *The Korean War*, 218 and Zelizer, *Arsenal of Democracy*, 104.

205. Cited by Kaufman, *The Korean* War, 51.

206. Casey, *Selling the Korean War,* 83.

207. Cited by Halberstam, *The Coldest Winter*, 326.

208. Cited by Christensen, *Useful Adversaries*, 191.

209. George F. Kennan, *Memoirs*, vol. 2 (Boston: Little, Brown, 1972), 75.

210. Casey, *Selling the Korean War*, 98.

211. Small, *Democracy and Diplomacy*, 118.

212. Caridi, *The Korean War*, 83–84. See also Stueck, *The Road to Confrontation*, 221–22, 231; Craig and Logevall, *America's Cold War*, 118.

213. Halberstam, *The Coldest Winter*, 327–29.

214. "Draft Memorandum Prepared by the Policy Planning Staff," *Foreign Relations of the United* States, 1950, vol. 7 (Washington, DC: U.S. Government Printing Office, 1950), 472.

215. Harry S. Truman, *Years of Trial and Hope*, vol. 2 (Garden City, NY: Doubleday, 1956), 334–35.

216. Acheson cited by Casey, *Selling the Korean War*, 97. See also Stueck, *The Korean War*, 53; Halberstam, *The Coldest Winter*, 323–34.

217. Cited by Freeland, *The Truman Doctrine*, 355.

218. Stueck, *The Korean War*, 75–76.

219. Both cited by Halberstam, *The Coldest Winter*, 331.

220. Cited by Donovan, *Tumultuous Years*, 271 and 275.

221. Dean Acheson, *Present at the Creation: My Years at the State Department* (New York: Norton, 1969), 446.

222. Cited by Halberstam, *The Coldest Winter*, 324.

223. Cited by Casey, *Selling the Korean War*, 100.

224. Stueck, The *Road to Confrontation*, 231.

225. Small, *Democracy and Diplomacy*, 94.

226. Stueck, The *Road to Confrontation*, chapter 6.

227. Herzstein, *Henry R. Luce*, 148–52; Craig and Logevall, *America's Cold War*, 120–21 and 130–31.

228. Christensen, *Useful Adversaries*, 67 and 134–35.

229. Christensen, *Useful Adversaries*, 67–68; Gaddis, *The Long Peace*, 80–81; and Freeland, *The Truman Doctrine*, 341–42.

230. Donovan, *Tumultuous Years*, 108.

231. Freeland, *The Truman Doctrine*, 358; and Stueck, *The Korean War*, 43.

232. Matray, *The Reluctant Crusader*, 247–48.

233. Tucker, *China Confidential*, 85–86.

234. Halberstam, *The Coldest Winter*, 329–30; Stueck, *The Road to Confrontation*, 204–6; and Casey, *Selling the Korean War*, 100.

235. John M. Owen, IV, *The Clash of Ideas in World Politics: Transnational Networks, States, and Regime Change, 1510–2010* (Princeton: Princeton University Press, 2010), chapter 6; Nau, *Conservative Internationalism*, chapter 6.

236. Owen, *The Clash of Ideas in World Politics*, 43–46.

237. Of course, Truman and Acheson did not get all they preferred (i.e., full disengagement from Chiang).

238. Tucker, *Patterns in the Dust*, 186 and Christensen, *Useful Adversaries*, chapters 3, 4, 134–35.

239. Tucker, *Patterns in the Dust*, 58 and James Peck, *Washington's China: The National Security World, The Cold War, and the Origins of Globalism* (Amherst: University of Massachusetts Press, 2006), 65–66.

240. Donovan *Tumultuous Years*, 200–201; Stueck, *The Road to Confrontation*, 186–87; and Matray, *The Reluctant Crusader*, 236.

241. Small, *Democracy and Diplomacy*, 93.

242. Purifoy, *Harry Truman's China Policy*, 232.

243. Small, *Democracy and Diplomacy*, 83; Christensen, *Useful Adversaries*, 39–40; Jeffrey W. Legro, *Rethinking the World: Great Power Strategies and International Order* (Ithaca: Cornell University Press, 2005), chapter 3.

4. REGIME CHANGE IN CUBA AND VIETNAM

1. Jim Rasenberger, *The Brilliant Disaster: JFK, Castro, and America's Invasion of Cuba's Bay of Pigs* (New York: Scribner, 2011) and George C. Herring, *America's Longest War: The United States and Vietnam, 1950–1975*, 2nd ed. (Philadelphia: Temple University Press, 1986).

2. Campbell Craig and Frederik Logevall, *America's Cold War: The Politics of Insecurity* (Cambridge, MA: Belknap Press of Harvard University Press, 2009), 150 and George H. Gallup, *The Gallup Poll: Public Opinion, 1935–1971*, vol. 3 (New York: Random House, 1972), 1243.

3. Julian E. Zelizer, *Arsenal of Democracy: The Politics of National Security—From World War II to the War on Terrorism* (New York: Basic Books, 2010), 122–37.

4. Craig and Logevall, *America's Cold War*, 152; Douglas C. Foyle, *Counting the Public In: Presidents, Public Opinion and Foreign Policy* (New York: Columbia University Press, 1999), 83–107.

5. Foyle, *Counting the Public In*, 113–20; Zelizer, *Arsenal of Democracy*, 138–42; Craig and Logevall, *America's Cold War*, 174–76; Robert A. Divine, *The Sputnik Challenge* (New York: Oxford University Press, 1993).

6. Cited by Zelizer, *Arsenal of Democracy*, 139; Robert Weisbrodt, *Maximum Danger: Kennedy, the Missiles, and the Crisis of American Confidence* (Chicago: Ivan R. Dee, 2001), 22; Foyle, *Counting the Public In*, 117. Like Truman in the 1940s, the Eisenhower administration tried to dampen the surge of liberal narrative passion, which stands against elite polarization and realist arguments.

7. Cited by Robert A. Divine, *Foreign Policy and U.S. Presidential Elections, 1952 and 1960* (New York: Franklin Watts, 1974), 188.

8. Zelizer, *Arsenal of Democracy*, 139.

9. Cited by Divine, *Sputnik*, 198.

10. Cited by Craig and Logevall, *America's Cold War*, 174.

11. Divine, *Sputnik Challenge*, 199–205; Divine, *Foreign Policy*, 191–92.

12. Robert Dallek, *An Unfinished Life: John F. Kennedy, 1917–1963* (Boston: Little, Brown, 2003), 350.

13. "American National Election Study 1960 (Pre-Election)," *University of Michigan Survey Research Center,* September 12–November 7, 1960, iRoper Center, https://roper center.cornell.edu.

14. Weisbrodt, *Maximum Danger*, 12–13.

15. Weisbrodt, *Maximum Danger*, 32–34; Divine, *Foreign Policy*, 213–14, 220, and 250.

16. "Crisis in the Cold War," *New York Times*, May 9, 1960; William S. White, "Danger to the Free World," *News and Observer* (Raleigh), July 4, 1960. For other examples, see editorials in *The Denver Post, Louisville Courier, Washington Post, Milwaukee Journal, St. Louis Post-Dispatch,* and *Los Angeles Times*.

17. *Congressional Record*, 86th Cong., 2nd Sess., 1960, 106, pt. 8: 9803–4, 10395, 10624.

18. *Congressional Record*, 86th Cong., 2nd Sess., 1960, 106, pt. 8: 12740.

19. Rasenberger, *The Brilliant Disaster*, 17.

20. Divine, *Foreign Policy*, 221.

21. *Congressional Record*, 86th Cong., 2nd Sess., 1960, 106, pt. 10: 12820.

22. *Congressional Record*, 86th Cong., 2nd Sess., 1960, 106, pt. 10: 12940, 13330, A3415.

23. *Congressional Record*, 86th Cong., 2nd Sess., 1960, 106, pt. 8: 9803–4.

24. *Congressional Record*, 86th Cong., 2nd Sess., 1960, 106, pt. 8: 10756–71, 10785–87; and pt. 10: 12820–22

25. *Congressional Record*, 86th Cong., 2nd Sess., 1960, 106, pt. 10: 12778, see also 12820–22; JFK in Divine, *Foreign Policy*, 209–10.

26. *Congressional Record*, 86th Cong., 2nd Sess., 1960, 106, pt. 8: A4316.

27. *Congressional Record*, 86th Cong., 2nd Sess., 1960, 106, pt. 8: 13708.

28. *Congressional Record*, 86th Cong., 2nd Sess., 1960, 106, pt. 10: 13330; and pt. 8: 10394.

29. Divine, *Foreign Policy*, 211.

30. Gallup, *Gallup Poll*, 1673 and 1738.

31. Divine, *Foreign Policy*, 236.

32. "The Bear's Embrace," *Washington Post*, July 11, 1960; "As the World Changes," *St. Louis Post-Dispatch*, June 13, 1960; *Congressional Record*, 86th Cong., 2nd Sess., 1960, 106, pt. 10: A5009–10.

33. Divine, *Sputnik Challenge*, 221.

34. Cited by Divine, *Sputnik Challenge*, 211. See also Gallup, *Gallup Survey*, 1675; Weisbrodt, *Maximum Danger*, 14.

35. Rasenberger, *Brilliant Disaster*, 78.

36. Cited by Divine, *Foreign Policy*, 191, 209–10.

37. Divine, *Foreign Policy*, 235–56.

38. Divine, *Foreign Policy*, 258–60.

39. Divine, *Foreign Policy*, 265.

40. See, for instance, "Senator Kennedy and the Islands," *Los Angeles Times*, October 18, 1960; Weisbrodt, *Maximum Danger*, 34.

41. Arthur Schlesinger, *A Thousand Days: John F. Kennedy in the White House* (Boston: Houghton Mifflin, 1965), 225.

42. Weisbrodt, *Maximum Danger*, 32–34.

43. Schlesinger, *Thousand Days*, 224.

44. Cited by Rasenberger, *Brilliant Disaster*, 92 and Weisbrodt, *Maximum Danger*, 20.

45. Cited by Rasenberger, *Brilliant Disaster*, 92.

46. Rasenberger, *Brilliant Disaster*, 94; Weisbrodt, *Maximum Danger*, 35–36.

47. Weisbrodt, *Maximum Danger*, 18.

48. Howard Jones, *The Bay of Pigs* (New York: Oxford University Press, 2008), 14–33.

49. Jones, *The Bay of Pigs*, 32–33.

50. Dallek, *Unfinished Life*, 342.

51. Dallek, *Unfinished Life*, 350; Schlesinger, *Thousand Days*, 226.

52. Schlesinger, *Thousand Days*, 226.

53. Lawrence Freedman, *Kennedy's Wars: Berlin, Cuba, Laos, and Vietnam* (New York: Oxford University Press, 2000), 124.

54. Rasenberger, *Brilliant Disaster*, 146.

55. Cited by James G. Blight et al., eds., *The Bay of Pigs Invasion Reexamined* (Boulder, CO: Lynn Rienner, 1998), 64.

56. Piero Gleijeses, "Ships in the Night: The CIA, the White House, and the Bay of Pigs," *Journal of Latin American Studies* 27, no. 1 (1995): 17–18.

57. Rasenberger, *Brilliant Disaster*, 130. JFK's pledge during the campaign helped generate these audience costs.

58. *Foreign Relations of the United States [FRUS]*, vol. 10 (Washington, DC: United States Government Printing Office, 1997), doc. 24, 46–52.

59. *FRUS*, doc. 30, 61.

60. Rasenberger, *Brilliant Disaster*, 126.

61. *FRUS*, doc. 40, 90.

62. *FRUS*, doc. 46, 103–4.

63. Schlesinger, *Thousand Days*, 242, 249–50; Freedman, *Kennedy's Wars*, 127–37; Rasenberger, *Brilliant Disaster*, 139–40.

64. *FRUS*, doc. 61, 148.

65. *FRUS*, doc. 81, 187–88.

66. Thomas G. Paterson, "Fixation with Cuba: The Bay of Pigs, Missile Crisis, and Covert War Against Fidel Castro," in *Kennedy's Quest for Victory: American Foreign Policy, 1961–1963*, ed. Thomas G. Paterson (New York: Oxford University Press, 1989), 126.

67. *Congressional Record*, 86th Cong., 2nd Sess., 1960, 107, pt. 2: 2706–8.

68. *Congressional Record*, 86th Cong., 2nd Sess., 1960, 107, pt. 3: 3451–52.

69. *Congressional Record*, 86th Cong., 2nd Sess., 1960, 107, pt. 5: 5502–4, 5507.

70. *Congressional Record*, 86th Cong., 2nd Sess., 1960, 107, pt. 5: A2401.

71. Rasenberger, *Brilliant Disaster*, 170. "Castro doesn't need agents over here," said Kennedy, "All he has to do is read our papers."

72. "Invasion of Cuba," *Washington Post*, April 18, 1961.

73. "Cuba in Torment," *New York Times*, April 16, 1961; "Revival of a Revolution," *Los Angeles Times*, April 18, 1961; and "U.S. Favors Cuban Rebels," *Milwaukee Journal*, April 18, 1961.

74. Gallup, *Gallup Poll*, 1681 and "Gallup Poll (AIPO)," *Gallup Organization*, July 16–21, 1960, iRoper Center, https://ropercenter.cornell.edu.

75. Freedman, *Kennedy's Wars*, 145.

76. Schlesinger, *Thousand Days*, 257–78.

77. *FRUS*, vol. 10, doc. 219, 527.

78. Cited by Freedman, *Kennedy's Wars*, 128.

79. Cited by Gleijeses, "Ships in the Night," 26.

80. Cited by Dallek, *Unfinished Life*, 358.

81. Cited by Blight et al., *Bay of Pigs*, 65.

82. Rasenberger, *Brilliant*, 127–65 and Blight et al., *Bay of Pigs*, 83–155.

83. Freedman, *Kennedy's Wars*, 145.

84. Jones, *Bay of Pigs*, 83. See also Rasenberger, *Brilliant Disaster*, 131; and Trumbull Higgins, *The Perfect Failure: Kennedy, Eisenhower, and the CIA at the Bay of Pigs* (New York: W.W. Norton & Co., 1987), 119.

85. Cited by Freedman, *Kennedy's Wars*, 140.

86. No evidence suggests the Korea syndrome factored in here.

87. *Congressional Record*, 87th Cong., 1nd Sess., 1961, 107, pt. 4: 5192

88. *Congressional Record*, 87th Cong., 1nd Sess., 1961, 107, pt. 3: 3053.

89. *Congressional Record*, 87th Cong., 1nd Sess., 1961, 107, pt. 3: 3419–20.

90. *Congressional Record*, 87th Cong., 1nd Sess., 1961, 107, pt. 5: 5986–87.

91. Rasenberger, *Brilliant Disaster*, 152–53.

92. Divine, *Foreign Policy*, 269–70.

93. "Gallup Poll (AIPO)," July 1960. Divine, *Foreign Policy*, 268–70.

94. This list includes the *Los Angeles Times, New York Times, Chicago Tribune, Washington Post, Atlanta Constitution, San Francisco Chronicle, The Milwaukee Journal, Denver Post, Raleigh News and Observer*, and *St. Louis Post-Dispatch*.

95. Cited in *Congressional Record*, 87th Cong., 1nd Sess., 1961, 107, pt. 4: 4734.

96. "Dark Doings in the Caribbean," *Charlotte Observer*, April 11, 1961; "No Proxy War in Cuba," *St. Louis Post-Dispatch*, April 13, 1961; "U.S. Has big Stakes in Cuban Invasion," *Denver Post*, April 18, 1961; "Call to Arms," *Washington Post*, April 12, 1961.

97. "Government Helps to Clarify Problem in Cuba; Solution Still Elusive," *Denver Post*, April 16, 1961.

98. Rasenberger, *Brilliant Disaster*, 113–312; Freedman, *Kennedy's Wars*, 123–38; Blight et al., *The Bay of* Pigs, 59–132.

99. *FRUS*, doc. 38, 81–88; *FRUS*, doc. 45, 95–99.

100. Mac Bundy in *FRUS*, doc. 47, 107.

101. *FRUS*, doc. 86, 197.

102. Rasenberger, *Brilliant Disaster*, 152–53.

103. Schlesinger, *Thousand Days*, 286.

104. *FRUS*, doc. 86, 201.

105. *FRUS*, doc. 86, 201.

106. Freedman, *Kennedy's Wars*, 140.

107. Jones, *Bay of Pigs*, 74–75.

108. Schlesinger, *Thousand Days*, 259.

109. Schlesinger, *Thousand Days*, 259.

110. Higgins, *Perfect Failure*, 121–22.

111. The Revolutionary Council never landed, foreclosing any opportunity to call for U.S. help.

112. Rasenberger, *Brilliant Disaster*, 311–18; Schlesinger, *Thousand Days*, 286. For specific examples, *Congressional Record*, 87th Cong., 1nd Sess., 1961, 107, pt. 5: A2798–99, A2807, SA2808–9.

113. *Congressional Record*, 87th Cong., 1nd Sess., 1961, 107, pt. 5: 6594–97.

114. UPI, "Goldwater Talks Intervention," *Courier-Journal* [Louisville], April 23, 1961.

115. W.H. Lawrence, "President Calls Top Advisors," *New York Times*, April 20, 1961.

116. *Congressional Record*, 87th Cong., 1nd Sess., 1961, 107, pt. 5: A2804–5.

117. For example, "Hard Lessons in Cuba," *St. Louis Post-Dispatch*, April 21, 1961.

118. Gallup, *Gallup Poll*, 1717.

119. "Kennedy Picks New Cold War Weapons to Assure the Nation's Survival," *Denver Post*, April 21, 1961.

120. Schlesinger, *Thousand Days*, 288.

121. Dallek, *Unfinished Life*, 369.

122. Dallek, *Unfinished Life*, 370.

123. "No Punch, But Neat Footwork," *Chicago Tribune*, April 25, 1961.

124. Cited by Rasenberger, *Brilliant Disaster*, 272.

125. Rasenberger, *Brilliant Disaster*, 284–87.

126. Lloyd C. Gardner, *Pay Any Price: Lyndon Johnson and the Wars for Vietnam* (Chicago: Ivan R. Dee, 1995), chapters 4 and 5.

127. Cited by Rasenberger, *Brilliant Disaster*, 317, 337.

128. Cited by Leslie H. Gelb and Richard K. Betts, *The Irony of Vietnam: The System Worked* (Washington, DC: Brookings Institution Press, 1979), 185.

129. Cited by Gardner, *Pay Any Price*, 73.

130. Cited by Gelb and Betts, *Irony of Vietnam*, 222. Eisenhower faced similar pressure, see Herring, *America's Longest War*, 45–56.

131. "Harris Survey," *Louis Harris & Associates*, September 1–28, 1963, iRoper Center, https://ropercenter.cornell.edu.

132. Doris Kearns, *Lyndon Johnson and the American Dream* (New York: Harper & Row, 1976), 247–48 and Gelb and Betts, *Irony of Vietnam*, 205–12.

133. "Break in Saigon," *Oregonian*, November 2, 1963; "Messy Business in Vietnam Increases Hope for Victory," *Charlotte Observer*, November 3, 1963; "Saigon after the Storm," *New York Times*, November 7, 1963.

134. William Conrad Gibbons, *The U.S. Government and the Vietnam War: Executive and Legislative Roles and Relationships, Part II: 1961–1964* (Princeton: Princeton University Press, 1986), 219.

135. Cited by Gibbons, *The U.S. Government and the Vietnam War*, 220.

136. Robert David Johnson, *Congress and the Cold War* (Cambridge: Cambridge University Press, 2006), 109; *Congressional Record*, 88th Cong., 2nd Sess., 1964, 110, pt. 3: 3279 and pt. 9, 11603.

137. Gelb and Betts, *Irony of Vietnam*, 213.

138. Cited by Gibbons, *U.S. and Vietnam War*, part II, 209 and Kearns, *Lyndon Johnson*, 251.

139. Cited by Gibbons, *U.S. and Vietnam War*, part II, 99.

140. Gibbons, *U.S. and Vietnam War*, part II: 99–100.

141. Frederik Logevall, *Choosing War: The Lost Chance for Peace and the Escalation of the War in Vietnam* (Berkeley: University of California Press, 1999), 82–84, 91–92.

142. Gibbons, *U.S. and Vietnam War*, part II, 215, 217.

143. Cited by Logevall, *Choosing War*, 92.

144. Cited by Gibbons, *U.S. and Vietnam War*, part II, 216.

145. Gibbons, *U.S. and Vietnam War*, part II, 216–18 (emphasis added).

146. Robert Dallek, *Flawed Giant: Lyndon Johnson and His Times, 1961–1973* (New York: Oxford University Press, 1998), 102.

147. Cited by Dallek, *Flawed Giant*, 101.

148. Cited by Gardner, *Pay Any Price*, 95, 113.

149. Dallek, *Flawed Giant*, 101; Kearns, *Lyndon Johnson*, 251–53; Gelb and Betts, *Irony of Vietnam*, 110–11; Logevall, *Choosing War*, 77.

150. Cited by Logevall, *Choosing War*, 101–11.

151. Gardner, *Pay Any Price*, 117.

152. *Congressional Record*, 88th Cong., 2nd Sess., 1964, 110, pt. 4: 3279, 4326.

153. *Congressional Record*, 88th Cong., 2nd Sess., 1964, 110, pt. 4: 4780–82.

154. *Congressional Record*, 88th Cong., 2nd Sess., 1964, 110, pt. 4: 4986.

155. "Answer in Viet-Nam: More Dollars," *Chicago Tribune*, March 19, 1961; "McNamara on Viet-Nam," *Washington Post*, March 27, 1961; "Policy of Retreat," *Oregonian*, March 27, 1961; "Fulbright Does a Service," *Milwaukee Journal*, April 5, 1961.

156. Cited by Logevall, *Choosing War*, 195.

157. *Congressional Record*, 88th Cong., 2nd Sess., 1964, 110, pt. 11: 3279, 14792.

158. *Congressional Record*, 88th Cong., 2nd Sess., 1964, 110, pt. 9: 3279, 11522.

159. James Reston, "Washington: The Politics of Vietnam," *Washington Post*, June 16, 1965; "The Viet-Nam Dilemma," *Washington Post*, June 17, 1965.

160. *Congressional Record*, 88th Cong., 2nd Sess., 1964, 110, pt. 11: 14792–93.

161. "Our Credibility in Laos," *New York Times*, May 29, 1964. For others, see "Reality in Indochina," *Des Moines Register*, June 23, 1964.

162. The thirty-three statements opposing war came from only six members of the House and Senate.

163. Dallek, *Flawed Giant*, 145.

164. Cited by Kearns, *Lyndon Johnson*, 252.

165. Kearns, *Lyndon Johnson*, 253.

166. Cited by Dallek, *Flawed Giant*, 145–46.

167. Logevall, *Choosing War*, 171; Dallek, *Flawed Giant*, 144–46.

168. Cited by Gardner, *Pay Any Price*, 117, 119.

169. Gardner, *Pay Any Price*, 124.

170. Cited by Dallek, *Flawed Giant*, 147.

171. Dallek, *Flawed Giant*, 146.

172. Gibbons, *U.S. and Vietnam War*, part II, 266–73.

173. Dallek, *Flawed Giant*, 145.

174. Stanley Karnow, *Vietnam: A History* (New York: Viking Press, 1983), 326.

175. Dallek, *Flawed Giant*, 149–50, Logevall, *Choosing War*, 196–97; Karnow, *Vietnam*, 268–77; Frank E. Vandiver, *Shadows of Vietnam: Lyndon Johnson's War* (College Station: Texas A&M University Press, 1997), 21–24. The second attack was likely fabricated to give Johnson a chance to look tough on communism in Vietnam.

176. Cited by Gibbons, *U.S. and Vietnam War*, part II, 289.

177. Cited by Gardner, *Pay Any Price*, 135.

178. Dallek, *Flawed Giant*, 150.

179. Dallek, *Flawed Giant*, 150.

180. Cited by Vandiver, *Shadows of Vietnam*, 25.

181. Vandiver, *Shadows of Vietnam*, 25; Gibbons, *U.S. and Vietnam War*, part II, 294–96; Dallek, *Flawed Giant*, 154–55.

182. William Conrad Gibbons, *The U.S. Government and The Vietnam War: Executive and Legislative Roles and Relationships, Part III: January–July 1965* (Princeton: Princeton University Press), 11; and Dallek, *Flawed*, 153–54.

183. *Congressional Record*, 88th Cong., 2nd Sess., 1964, 110, pt. 14: 18336, 18399, 18407.

184. Gibbons, *U.S. and Vietnam War*, part II, 313.

185. All cited by Gibbons, *U.S. and Vietnam War*, part II, 327, 315.

186. House discussion mirrored the Senate but lasted only forty minutes.

187. Herring, *America's Longest War*, 123. See also Karnow, *Vietnam*, 395; Gardner, *Pay Any Price*, 138.

188. "Harris Survey," *Louis Harris & Associates*, October 1–31, 1964, iRoper Center, https://ropercenter.cornell.edu. See also Logevall, *Choosing War*, 205–6 and Herring, *America's Longest War*, 123.

189. Arthur Krock, "'Make-Believe Vocabulary' in Drivers Tones," *New York Times*, April 2, 1964. Some pressed air power, but no one advocated ground troops.

190. Logevall, *Choosing War*, 250–51; Brian VanDeMark, *Into the Quagmire: Lyndon Johnson and the Escalation of the Vietnam War* (New York: Oxford University Press, 1991), 29–30.

191. Gardner, *Pay Any Price*, 153.

192. Logevall, *Choosing War*, 240–70; VanDeMark, *Into the Quagmire*, 28–32.

193. Gibbons, *U.S. and Vietnam War*, part II, 375–82; Vandiver, *Shadows of Vietnam*, 88–91.

194. Cite Dallek, *Flawed Giant*, 244 and VanDeMark, *Into the Quagmire*, 47–49.

195. See Joseph Alsop's "The World He Never Made," *Washington Post*, November 30, 1964; "Accepting Defeat," *Washington Post*, December 23, 1964; "Johnson's Cuba II," *Washington Post*, December 30, 1964.

196. Gibbons, *U.S. and Vietnam War*, part III, 82–83.

197. VanDeMark, *Into the Quagmire*, 47.

198. Both in Gibbons *U.S. and Vietnam War*, part III, 41.

199. Both cited by Gibbons *U.S. and Vietnam War*, part II, 395.

200. Cited by Gibbons *U.S. and Vietnam War*, part III, 48.

201. Cited by Gardner, *Pay Any Price*, 166–67.

202. Cited in Gardner, *Pay Any Price*, 167. On the Kennedy factor, see Dallek, *Flawed Giant*, 247; VanDeMark, *Into the Quagmire*, 59; Kearns, *Lyndon Johnson*, 253–59.

203. Cited by Gardner, *Pay Any Price*, 167.

204. Cited by David Halberstam, *The Best and the Brightest* (New York: Random House, 1972), 530.

205. Cited by Dallek, *Flawed Giant*, 247.

206. Cited by Kearns, *Lyndon Johnson*, 263.

207. Cited by Vandiver, *Shadows of Vietnam*, 31.

208. Cited by Kearns, *Lyndon Johnson*, 260.

209. Gibbons, *U.S. and Vietnam War*, part III, 83–90.

210. Gardner, *Pay Any Price*, 182.

211. Cited by Dallek, *Flawed Giant*, 255.

212. Cited by Gibbons, *U.S. and Vietnam, War*, part III, 161–65.

213. Cited by VanDeMark, *Into the Quagmire*, 101.

214. Gibbons, *U.S. and Vietnam War*, part III, 73, 145; Robert Dallek, "Lyndon Johnson and Vietnam: The Making of a Tragedy," *Diplomatic History* 20, no. 2 (1996): 148.

215. Cited by "U.S. Counter-Strike Supported," *Los Angeles Times*, February 10, 1965.

216. "A Great Speech," *Chicago Tribune*, February 27, 1965.

217. Joseph Alsop, "Quoting the Odds," *Washington Post*, February 15, 1965.

218. James Reston, "Washington: The Larger Implications of Vietnam," *New York Times*, April 25, 1965.

219. Roscoe Drummond, "Weakness Would Alienate Public," *Charlotte Observer*, May 3, 1965. See also Dallek, "Lyndon Johnson and Vietnam," 148.

220. VanDeMark, *Into the Quagmire*, 109, 113; Karnow, *Vietnam*, 417–18.

221. Cited by Gardner, *Pay and Price*, 220. VanDeMark, *Into the Quagmire*, 203–4.

222. All cited by VanDeMark, *Into the Quagmire*, 216, 154, 162.

223. Cited by Vandiver, *Shadows of Vietnam*, 130, see also 124–26.

224. VanDeMark, *Into the Quagmire*, 163–64.

225. "The President Readies for War, But Offers Peace Without Bloodshed," *Atlanta Constitution*, July 29, 1965.

226. "War in Vietnam," *Sun* (Baltimore), July 29, 1965.

227. "More Men to Viet Nam," *Des Moines Register*, July 29, 1965. For similar comments, see *Los Angeles* Times, *Milwaukee Journal, New York Times, Charlotte Observer*, and *Oregonian*.

228. Scholars agree. Gelb and Betts, *Irony of Vietnam*, 13–25, 202–3, 221–23; VanDeMark, *Into the Quagmire*, 212–21; Dallek, *Flawed Giant*, 277–80; and Kearns, *Lyndon Johnson*, 259 and 284.

229. Kearns, *Lyndon Johnson*, 264.

230. Kearns, *Lyndon Johnson*, 270.

231. Gardner, *Pay Any Price*, 54; Gibbons *U.S. and Vietnam War*, part III, 60.

232. Rasenberger, *Brilliant Disaster*, 318, 327.

233. Freedman, *Kennedy's Wars*, 132–33.

234. Cited by Rasenberger, *Brilliant Disaster*, 284.

235. John M. Owen, IV, *The Clash of Ideas in World Politics: Transnational Networks, States, and Regime Change, 1510–2010* (Princeton: Princeton University Press, 2010), 186–96.

236. As seen above, even JFK did some of what he did not want due to liberal narrative pressure. He preferred no invasion at all.

237. Rasenberger, *Brilliant Disaster*, 129–31; Schlesinger, *Thousand Days*, 276.

238. Herring, *America's Longest War*, 115.

239. Cited by Jones, *Bay of Pigs*, 68.

240. Rasenberger, *Brilliant Disaster*, 129–31.

241. Cited by VanDeMark, *Into the Quagmire*, 101; Logevall, *Choosing War*, 244–47.

5. REGIME CHANGE IN EL SALVADOR AND GRENADA

1. Tom Engelhardt, *The End of Victory Culture: Cold War America and the Disillusioning of a Generation* (Amherst: University of Massachusetts Press, 1998), 3–6 and David W. Levy, *The Debate Over Vietnam* (Baltimore: Johns Hopkins University Press, 1991), 30.

2. Cited by Fred Turner, *Echoes of Combat: The Vietnam War in American Memory* (New York: Anchor Books, Doubleday, 1996), 19–20.

3. Turner, *Echoes of Combat*, 19.

4. Charles DeBenedetti, *An American Ordeal: The Antiwar Movement of the Vietnam Era* (Syracuse, NY: Syracuse University Press, 1990) and Todd Gitlin, *The Sixties: Years of Hope and Days of Rage* (Toronto: Bantum Books, 1987).

5. Interview available at http://www.youtube.com/watch?v=hNYZZi25Ttg.

6. Turner, *Echoes of Combat*, 22.

7. George C. Herring, *America's Longest War: The United States and Vietnam, 1950–1975* (Philadelphia: Temple University Press, 1986), 192 and Levy, *The Debate Over Vietnam*, 145–46.

8. Engelhardt, *The End of Victory Culture*, 202.

9. Engelhardt, *The End of Victory Culture*, 187–90.

10. Charles E. Neu, "The Vietnam War and the Transformation of America," in *After Vietnam: Legacies of a Lost War*, ed. Charles E. Neu (Baltimore: Johns Hopkins University Press, 2000), 18.

11. Engelhardt, *The End of Victory Culture*, 187–90.

12. Cited by Engelhardt, *The End of Victory Culture*, 201–3.

13. Levi, *The Debate Over Vietnam*, 145.

14. Herring, *America's Longest War*, 192.

15. John Leo, "Cleric, Classified 1A After Protest, Refuses Draft," *New York Times*, April 16, 1968; L. James Binder, "The Agony of the U.S. Army," *New York Times*, November 30, 1971.

16. Leo, "Cleric, Classified"; Binder, "The Agony of the U.S. Army"; "Winding Down the Rhetoric," *Wall Street Journal*, November 13, 1969.

17. John Allen Long, "Antiwar Spectrum," *Christian Science Monitor*, April 26, 1968.

18. Levy, *The Debate Over Vietnam*, 41–53; Engelhardt, *The End of Victory Culture*, 9–10; Michael Charlton and Anthony Moncrieff, *Many Reasons Why: The American Involvement in Vietnam* (New York: Hill and Wang, 1978), 155–56.

19. Margaret Halsey, "Topics: Selective Morality and Citizen Loyalty," *New York Times*, April 27, 1968.

20. Irving Howe, "The New 'Confrontation Politics' Is a Dangerous Game: The Idea Is to Prod," *New York Times*, October 20, 1968.

21. Paul W. Valentine, "U.S. Workers Stage Antiwar Protest," *Washington Post*, May 5, 1972.

22. Valentine, "U.S. Workers Stage Antiwar Protest."

23. Engelhardt, *The End of Victory Culture*, 202, 21–29.

24. Turner, *Echoes of Combat*, 18.

25. Herring, *America's Longest War*, 192.

26. Edward P. Morgan, *The 60s Experience: Hard Lessons about Modern America* (Philadelphia: Temple University Press, 1991), 161.

27. Valentine, "U.S. Workers Stage," A3.

28. "New Bombing Revives Antiwar Protests," *New York Times*, December 23, 1972.

29. Cited in "New Bombing Revives Antiwar Protests."

30. "Chomsky Tells of Trip to Hanoi: Antiwar Activist Also Visited Laos on 2-Week Journey," *New York Times*, May 20, 1970.

31. Binder, "The Agony of the U.S. Army." For similar assessments, see Guenter Levy, *America in Vietnam* (Oxford: Oxford University Press, 1978), 435 and Norman Podhoretz, *Why We Were in Vietnam* (New York: Simon Schuster, 1982), 12–14.

32. Levy, *The Debate Over Vietnam*, 151.

33. Turner, *Echoes of Combat*, 130.

34. *Congressional Record*, 91st Cong., 1st Sess., 1969, 115, pt. 6: 7772–73, 7782.

35. *Annual Message on the State of the Union*, January 22, 1971, http://www.presidency.ucsb.edu/ws/index.php?pid=3110.

36. Richard Nixon, *The Real War* (New York: Warner Books, 1980), 114–15, 96.

37. David Chandler, "Culture Wars and International Intervention: An 'Inside/Out' View of the Decline of National Interest," *International Politics* 41, no. 3 (2004): 360; Lewis Sorely, *Arms Transfers Under Nixon: A Policy Analysis* (Lexington: University of Kentucky, 1983), 30; Henry Kissinger in Ben J. Wattenberg, "Is There a Crisis of Spirit in the West? A Conversation with Dr. Henry Kissinger and Senator Daniel P. Moynihan," *Public Opinion*, 1, no. 2 (1975): 4; Daniel P., Moynihan, "The Politics of Human Rights," *Commentary* 64, no. 2 (1977): 25.

38. Irving Kristol, "Consensus and Dissent in US Foreign Policy," in *The Vietnam Legacy: The War, American Society and the Future of American Foreign Policy*, ed. Anthony Lake (New York: New York University Press, 1976), 83.

39. Michael T. Klare, *Beyond the "Vietnam Syndrome": U.S. Interventionism in the 1980s* (Washington, DC: Institute for Policy Studies, 1981), 1; Graham T. Allison, Ernest R. May and Adam Yarmolinsky, "Limits to Intervention," in *After Vietnam: The Future of American Foreign Policy*, ed. Robert W. Gregg et al. (Garden City, NY: Anchor Books 1971), 55–57; Philip L. Geyelin, "The Vietnam Syndrome," in *Vietnam in Remission*, ed. James F. Veninga et al. (College Station: Texas A&M University Press, 1985), 76.

40. Long, "Antiwar Spectrum."

41. Dr. George H. Gallup, *The Gallup Poll: Public Opinion 1972–1977*, vol. 1 (Wilmington: Scholarly Review Resources, 1978), 468–90.

42. Dennis A. Gilbert, *Compendium of American Public Opinion* (New York: Facts on File Publications, 1988), 164–65.

43. Stanley Karnow, "After Vietnam, Americans Want an Assurance of Success," *Sun* (Baltimore), October 20, 1980. Other scholars note the same. Jerel A. Rosati, "The Domestic Environment," in *Intervention in the 1980s: U.S. Foreign Policy in the Third World*, ed. Peter J. Schraeder (Boulder, CO: Lynne Rienner, 1989), 155–56; Jon Western, *Selling Intervention and War: The Presidency, the Media, and the American Public* (Baltimore: John Hopkins University Press, 2005), 100–102; Kai P. Schoenhals and Richard A. Melanson, *Revolution and Intervention in Grenada: The New Jewel Movement, the United States and the Caribbean* (Boulder, CO: Westview Press, 1985), 117–27.

44. Cited by Paul Y. Hammond et al., *The Reluctant Supplier: U.S. Decisionmaking for Arms Sales* (Cambridge: Oelgeschlager, Gunn, and Hain, 1983), 47 and Richard F. Grimmett, "The Roles of Security Assistance in Historical Perspective," in *U.S. Security Assistance: The Political Process*, ed. Ernest Graves et al. (Lexington, MA: Lexington Books, 1985), 39. See also Lewis Sorely, *Arms Transfers under Nixon: A Policy Analysis* (Lexington: University of Kentucky Press, 1983), 5–7; Leslie H. Gelb and Richard K. Betts, *The Irony of Vietnam: The System That Worked* (Washington, DC: Brookings Institution Press, 1979), 360.

45. "A Handle on Arms Sales," *Washington Post*, November 28, 1975.

46. Rowland Evans and Robert Novak, "Foreign Aid Bargaining," *Washington Post*, April 28, 1976.

47. Stephen S. Rosenfeld, "American Intervention and Influence," *Washington Post*, May 2, 1975.

48. Cynthia J. Arnson, *Crossroads: Congress, the President and Central America, 1976–1993*, 2nd ed. (University Park: Pennsylvania State University Press, 1993), 11 and Ernest Graves, "Implications for the Future of Security Assistance as an Instrument of Defense and Foreign Policy," in *U.S. Security Assistance*, 170–71.

49. Cited by Steven A. Hildreth, "Perceptions of U.S. Security Assistance, 1959–1983: The Public Record," in *U.S. Security Assistance*, 68 and 57.

50. Evans and Novak, "Foreign Aid."

51. On the resolution, see Robert David Johnson, *Congress and the Cold War* (Cambridge: Cambridge University Press, 2006), 190–93; Graves, "Implications for the Future," 170–71.

52. *Congressional Record*, 93rd Cong., 1st Sess., 1973, 119, pt. 17: 25082.

53. *Congressional Record*, 93rd Cong., 1st Sess., 1973, 119, pt. 17: 25105.

54. *Congressional Record*, 93rd Cong., 1st Sess., 1973, 119, pt. 17: 25105, 21595.

55. *Congressional Record*, 93rd Cong., 1st Sess., 1973, 119, pt. 19: 24537, 25083, 25094.

56. "A Dividing Line," *Los Angeles Times*, November 8, 1973; "War Powers Veto Overridden," *Chicago Tribune*, November 10, 1973; "Congress Asserts Itself," *Des Moines Register*, November 10, 1973; and "War Powers," *Atlanta Constitution*, July 20, 1973.

57. Piero Gleijeses, *Conflicting Missions: Havana, Washington, and Africa, 1959–1976* (Chapel Hill: University of North Carolina Press, 2002), 328–32, 353–62.

58. "Angola," *New York Times*, November 3, 1975.

59. "The Struggle for Angola," *Chicago Tribune*, November 25, 1975.

60. "Angola," *Washington Post*, December 23, 1975.

61. *Congressional Record*, 94th Cong., 1st Sess., 1975, 121, pt. 31: 40533.

62. *Congressional Record*, 94th Cong., 1st Sess., 1975, 121, pt. 31: 41632.

63. *Congressional Record*, 94th Cong., 1st Sess., 1975, 121, pt. 31: 41625, 40465.

64. *Congressional Record*, 94th Cong., 1st Sess., 1975, 121, pt. 32: 41626.

65. Gleijeses, *Conflicting Missions*, 332.

66. Johnson, *Congress and the Cold War*, 221–24; Klare, *Beyond the "Vietnam Syndrome,"* 3.

67. See "Gerald R. Ford: The Mayaguez Affair," http://www.presidentprofiles.com/Kennedy-Bush/Gerald-R-Ford-The-mayaguez-affair.html; Gallup, *The Gallup Poll*, vol. 1, 456–57.

68. Chandler, "Culture Wars," 360.

69. Both cited by Wattenberg, "Is there a Crisis," 8 and 4–5.

70. Gallup, *The Gallup Poll*, vol. 1, 55–56.

71. James J. Kilpatrick, "U.S. Must Block Soviet Domination of Angola," *Sun*, December 2, 1975.

72. John Ehrman, *The Rise of Neoconservatism: Intellectuals and Foreign Affairs, 1945–1994* (New Haven: Yale University Press, 1995), 110–11.

73. Cited by Ehrman, *The Rise of Neoconservatism*, 107.

74. Cited by Ehrman, *The Rise of Neoconservatism*, 114.

75. Cited by Klare, *Beyond the "Vietnam Syndrome,"* 4.

76. "Stuck on the Horn," *Washington Post*, January 13, 1978; "Keeping Cool on Ethiopia," *New York Times*, February 3, 1978; "A Wild Gamble," *Chicago Tribune*, February 9, 1978; Steven Rattner, "Jackson Criticizes Carter's Moves on Foreign and Domestic Matters," *New York Times*, February 6, 1978.

77. "Satan Russia," *Los Angeles Times*, December 30, 1979 and "End of a Second Honeymoon," *Sun*, January 3, 1980.

78. Johnson, *Congress and the Cold War*, 251–52. See also Richard Walton, "Reeling Backward," *New York Times*, January 10, 1980; Tim Wicker, "The Way to Get Tough," *New York Times*, January 8, 1980; Edward N. Luttwak, "A 'Hands-Off' U.S. Policy on Afghanistan? No," *New York Times*, January 6, 1980; Francis Fitzgerald, "Muskets and Gunboats," *New York Times*, January 9, 1980.

79. Jack Nelson, "Reagan Pledges Stronger America," *Los Angeles Times*, July 18, 1980.

80. Richard J. Whalen, "It's Time to Reverse Our Retreat and Resume the Cold War," *Washington Post*, January 20, 1980; and Rudy Abramson, "Kennedy Warns of Growing 'War Hysteria,'" *Los Angeles Times*, February 2, 1980.

81. David Kline, "1931. 1936. 1980?" *New York Times*, January 10, 1980; Richard J. Walton, "Reeling Backward," *New York Times*, January 10, 1980.

82. "The Turnaround," *Dallas Morning News*, January 25, 1980.

83. Stanley Karnow, "The End of American Exceptionalism," *Sun*, April 28, 1980.

84. E.J. Dionne Jr., "Surveys Find Crises Stir Militant Mood," *New York Times*, February 5, 1980.

85. "America Aroused," *New York Times*, January 13, 1980; "Caging the Bear," *Sun*, January 1, 1980.

86. Klare, *Beyond the "Vietnam Syndrome,"* 9 and Johnson, *Congress and the Cold War*, 247.

87. Norman Podhoretz, *The Present Danger: "Do We Have the Will to Reverse the Decline of American Power?"* (New York: Simon & Schuster, 1980), 86–87.

88. Gilbert, *Compendium of Public Opinion*, 169.

89. Gilbert, *Compendium of Public Opinion*, 164–65.

90. C. William Walldorf Jr., *Just Politics: Human Rights and the Foreign Policy of Great Powers* (Ithaca: Cornell University Press 2008), 156–58.

91. Arnson, *Crossroads*, 64–65 and Walldorf, *Just Politics*, 157–58.

92. Cited by Arnson, *Crossroads*, 56.

93. "Saving El Salvador," *News and Observer* (Raleigh), March 4, 1981.

94. All cited by William M. LeoGrande, *Our Own Backyard: The United States in Central America, 1977–1992* (Chapel Hill: University of North Carolina Press, 1998), 87–88.

95. Dario Moreno, *U.S. Policy in Central America: The Endless Debate* (Miami: Florida International University Press, 1990), 113–14; Edwin Meese III, *With Reagan: The Inside Story* (Washington, DC: Regnery Gateway, 1992), 237; Western, *Selling Intervention*, 137; Hall Gulliver, "Vietnam South of the Border," *Atlanta Constitution*, February 27, 1981; Mary McCrory, "Reagan Not Reading El Salvador Mail," *Atlanta Constitution*, March 10, 1981.

96. Arnson, *Crossroads*, 58–59; Meese, *With Reagan*, 237; and Gulliver, "Vietnam South of the Border."

97. "The Next 'Vietnam'?" *Des Moines Register*, February 24, 1981.

98. "Aid to El Salvador," *Atlanta Constitution*, March 18, 1981.

99. Mary McGrory, "Hearing Echoes of Vietnam," *The Charlotte Observer*, February 25, 1981; "Psychodrama in El Salvador," *New York Times*, February 27, 1981.

100. Thomas G. Patterson, "Presidential Address: Historical Memory and Illusive Victories: Vietnam and Central America," in *The United States and the Vietnam War: Significant Scholarly Articles*, ed. Walter Hixson (New York: Garland, 2000), 72.

101. "EL Salvador and Vietnam," *Wall Street Journal*, March 5, 1981. See also Laurence Silberman, "El Salvador is *Not* Vietnam," *Los Angeles Times*, March 4, 1981.

102. George H. Gallup, *The Gallup Poll: Public Opinion 1981* (Wilmington: Scholarly Resources Review, 1982), 63.

103. William M. LeoGrande, *Central America and the Polls: A Study of U.S. Public Opinion Polls on U.S. Foreign Policy toward El Salvador and Nicaragua under the Reagan Administration* (Washington, DC: Washington Office on Latin America, 1987), 10; Edward Walsh, "Reagan Gets First Public Backlash—on Salvador Policy," *Washington Post*, March 27, 1981.

104. Don Oberdorfer, "Battling the Ghosts of Vietnam," *Washington Post*, March 1, 1981; Arnson, *Crossroads*, 5–6; LeoGrande, *Our Own Backyard*, 102; and Patterson, "Presidential Address," 85.

105. Subcommittee on Foreign Operations and Related Agencies of the House Committee on Appropriations, *Foreign Assistance and Related Programs Appropriations for 1982*, 97th Cong., 1st Sess., 24 March 1981: 283.

106. For many examples, see Arnson, *Crossroads*, 5, 57; Klare, *Beyond the "Vietnam Syndrome*," 13–14.

107. Walldorf, *Just Politics*, 157–60.

108. Cited by Johnson, *Congress and the Cold War*, 265.

109. Arnson, *Crossroads*, 71–74.

110. Bill Peterson, "Reagan Plea Rejected, Senate Votes Terms for Salvadoran Aid," *Washington Post*, September 25, 1981; Arnson, *Crossroads*, 4–6.

111. Alexander M. Haig Jr., *Caveat: Realism, Reagan, and Foreign Policy* (New York: Macmillan, 1984), 95–96.

112. Cited by LeoGrande, *Our Own Backyard*, 82–83. Caspar W. Weinberger, *Fighting for Peace: Seven Critical Years in the Pentagon* (New York: Warner Books, 1990), 31–32.

113. Cited by Lou Cannon, *President Reagan: The Role of a Lifetime* (New York: Public Affairs, 2000), 298.

114. Cannon, *President Reagan*, 163–64; 298; 301–2.

115. Cited in Cannon, *President Reagan*, 301–2. This reflected the military's own Vietnam syndrome.

116. Cited by LeoGrande, *Our Own Backyard*, 83.

117. Cannon, *President Reagan*, 198.

118. Weinberger, *Fighting for Peace*, 31–32; Haig, *Caveat*, 125, 128, and 130. Haig complained that Weinberger constantly harped on Vietnam and the escalation theme in NSC meetings as well as conversations between the two secretaries.

119. Cannon, *President Reagan*, 298.

120. Haig, *Caveat*, 127–28. See also Meese, *With Reagan*, 234.

121. Haig, *Caveat*, 127–28.

122. Cannon, *President Reagan*, 293

123. LeoGrande, *Our Own Backyard*, 90.

124. Cited by Patterson, "Presidential Address," 84.

125. Cited by LeoGrande, *Our Own Backyard*, 101.

126. Cited by Hedrick Smith, *The Power Game: How Washington Works* (New York: Random House, 1988), 350–51.

127. Bob Scheiffer and Gary Paul Gates, *The Acting President* (New York: E.P. Dutton, 1989), 125.

128. Cited by LeoGrande *Central America*, 4 and 101; Smith, *The Power Game*, 351; and Cannon, *President Reagan*, 163.

129. Scheiffer and Gates, *The Acting President*, 125. Haig complained of a "guerilla campaign" inside the White House.

130. Arnson, *Crossroads*, 72–73.

131. Cited in Arnson, *Crossroads*, 116–17.

132. Cited by Ehrman, *The Rise of Neoconservatism*, 145–47.

133. LeoGrande, *Our Own Backyard*, 175–76.

134. George P. Shultz, *Turmoil and Triumph: My Years as Secretary of State* (New York: Charles Scribner's Sons, 1993), 297, 299; LeoGrande, *Our Own Backyard*, 194–95.

135. Walldorf, *Just Politics*, 159.

136. Cited by Shultz, *Turmoil and Triumph*, 292.

137. Cited in Shultz, *Turmoil and Triumph*, 292.

138. Cited by LeoGrande, *Our Own Backyard*, 214. Reagan advisors followed up with a blitz of blame-related arguments against Congress.

139. Gilbert, *Compendium Public Opinion*, 170–71.

140. Cited by Arnson, *Crossroads*, 129.

141. *Congressional Record*, 98th Cong., 1st Sess., 1983, 129, pt. 8: 10138

142. Arnson, *Crossroads*, 129. See also *Congressional Record*, 98th Cong., 1st Sess., 1983, 129, pt. 8: 10148, 10409–16.

143. Arnson, *Crossroads*, 153–57.

144. "El Salvador's 9-to-5 War," *New York Times*, March 9, 1983.

145. Gilbert, *Compendium of Public Opinion*, 170–71.

146. LeoGrande, *Central America*, 19.

147. Anthony Lewis, "Why Are We in Vietnam?" *New York Times*, March 6, 1983; "Honduras and Vietnam," *Chicago Tribune*, October 11, 1983; *Congressional Record*, 98th Cong., 1st Sess., 1983, 129, pt. 8: 10406.

148. LeoGrande, *Our Own Backyard*, 198.

149. "Yanquiology," *New York Times*, May 15, 1983; Arnson, *Crossroads*, 2.

150. LeoGrande, *Our Own Backyard*, 204–8 and Arnson, *Crossroads*, 129.

151. Shultz, *Turmoil and Triumph*, 297–99; LeoGrande, *Our Own Backyard*, 214–16.

152. Cited by LeoGrande, *Our Own Backyard*, 220–21.

153. Shultz, *Turmoil and Triumph*, 307 and 317.

154. Ronald Reagan, *An American Life* (New York: Simon & Schuster, 1990), 479.

155. Cited by LeoGrande, *Our Own Backyard*, 202, 214–15, 197. Reagan repeated the pledge twice in months to follow.

156. Clark was replaced as national security advisor by Bud McFarlane.

157. Shultz, *Turmoil and Triumph*, 344–45.

158. LeoGrande, *Our Own Backyard*, 221; and Arnson, *Crossroads*, 137–43.

159. Robert J. Beck, *The Grenada Invasion: Politics, Law, and Foreign Policy Decision-making* (Boulder, CO: Westview Press, 1993), 10–12; 25–31.

160. Beck, *Grenada Invasion*, 12–17.

161. Gary Williams, *US-Grenada Relations: Revolution and Intervention in the Backyard* (New York: Palgrave Macmillan, 2007), 30, 108.

162. Beck, *Grenada Invasion*, 98–99; Schoenhals and Melanson, *Revolution and Intervention*, 139; Russell Crandall, *Gunboat Democracy: U.S. Interventions in Dominican Republic, Grenada, and Panama* (New York: Rowman & Littlefield, 2006), 134–35.

163. Weinberger, *Fighting for Peace*, 107.

164. Cited by Crandall, *Gunboat Democracy*, 137.

165. Williams, *US-Grenada Relations*, 112.

166. Shultz, *Turmoil and Triumph*, 328.

167. Beck, *The Grenada Invasion*, 104–10; Shultz, *Turmoil and Triumph*, 326; Constantine C. Menges, *Inside the National Security Council: The True Story of the Making and Unmaking of Reagan's Foreign Policy* (New York: Simon & Shuster, 1988), 69–90.

168. Cited by Williams, *US-Grenada Relations*, 108.

169. Cited by Beck, *The Grenada Invasion*, 149 and Schoenhals and Melanson, *Revolution and Intervention*, 143.

170. Williams, *US-Grenada Relations*, 108.

171. Western, *Selling Intervention*, 114; Schoenhals and Melanson, *Revolution and Intervention*, 143.

172. On Capitol Hill, there were only two statements on Grenada during the crisis.

173. Brigitte Nacos, *The Press, Presidents, and Crises* (New York: Columbia University Press, 1990), 162.

174. Nacos, *The Press, Presidents, and Crises*, 161–65.

175. Western, *Selling Intervention*, 114–15, 124; Crandall, *Gunboat Democracy*, 138; Beck, *The Grenada Invasion*, 99.

176. Western, *Selling Intervention*, 122–23.

177. Cited in Western, *Selling Intervention*, 125. See also Menges, *Inside the National Security Council*, 58 and Michael K. Deaver, *Behind the Scenes* (New York: William Morrow, 1987), 147.

178. Williams, *US-Grenada Relations*, 132.

179. Weinberger, *Fighting for Peace*, 109.

180. Weinberger, *Fighting for Peace*, 109.

181. Beck, *The Grenada Invasion*, 98–99; Schoenhals and Melanson, *Revolution and Intervention*, 139.

182. Western, *Selling Intervention*, 124.

183. For example, see Western, *Selling Intervention*, 132

184. Cited in Western, *Selling Intervention*, 124; Klare, *Beyond the "Vietnam Syndrome,"* 13.

185. Meese, *With Reagan*, 217.

186. Cited by Weinberger, *Fighting for Peace*, 112.

187. Reagan, *An American Life*, 451.

188. Shultz, *Turmoil and Triumph*, 344–45.

189. Shultz, *Turmoil and Triumph*, 284.

190. Cited by Williams, *US-Grenada Relations*, 137–38.

191. For a good detailing, see Beck, *The Grenada Invasion*, 55–61; and Schoenhals and Melanson, *Revolution and Intervention*, 148–50. Hardliners were infuriated that "restoring democracy" was not mentioned.

192. *Congressional Record*, 98th Cong., 1st Sess., 1983, 129, pt. 21: 29400, 29407, 29405.

193. "Which Threat Is Grenada," *New York Times*, October 26, 1983. See also "Why Invade Grenada?" *Chicago Tribune*, October 26, 1983.

194. Meese, *With Reagan*, 219–20.

195. Shultz, *Turmoil and Triumph*, 339.

196. Reagan, *An American Life*, 456.

197. Beck, *The Grenada Invasion*, 55–57.

198. Cited in Beck, *The Grenada Invasion*, 209–10.

199. Cited by Schoenhals and Melanson, *Revolution and Intervention*, 148–50.

200. Schoenhals and Melanson, *Revolution and Intervention*, 156–58; and Nacos, *The Press, President*, 181.

201. Bruce W. Jentelson, "The Prudent Public: Post Post-Vietnam American Opinion on the Use of Military Force," *International Studies Quarterly* 36, no. 1 (1992): 49–74 and Schoenhals and Melanson, *Revolution and Intervention*, 153–54.

202. Cited by Schoenhals and Melanson, *Revolution and Intervention*, 160, 154–56.

203. Schoenhals and Melanson, *Revolution and Intervention*, 159–69.

204. Barry P. Posen and Steven W. Van Evra, "Reagan Administration Defense Policy: Departure from Containment," in *Eagle Resurgent? The Reagan Era in American Foreign Policy*, ed. Kenneth A. Oye et al. (Boston: Little, Brown, 1987), 75–114. Some realists claimed Central America and the Caribbean carried little strategic value. This might help explain the El Salvador outcome, but Grenada still makes little sense.

205. John M. Owen, IV, *The Clash of Ideas in World Politics: Transnational Networks, States, and Regime Change, 1510–2010* (Princeton: Princeton University Press, 2010), 196.

206. Shultz, *Turmoil and Triumph*, 292–94 and 625; Cannon, *President Reagan*, 300.

207. Cited by Julian E. Zelizer, *Arsenal of Democracy: The Politics of National Security—From World War II to the War on Terrorism* (New York: Basic Books, 2010), 363–64, see also 364–87.

208. Eytan Gilboa, "The Panama Invasion Revisited: Lessons for the Use of Force in the Post Cold War Era," *Political Science Quarterly* 110, no. 4 (1995–96): 539–62; Crandall, *Gunboat Democracy*, chapter 4; and Zelizer, *Arsenal of Democracy*, chapter 15.

6. REGIME CHANGE IN IRAQ AND LIBYA

1. Jonathan Monten, "The Roots of the Bush Doctrine: Power, Nationalism, and Democracy Promotion in U.S. Strategy," *International Security* 29, no. 4 (2005): 112–56 and Robert Jervis, "The Remaking of a Unipolar World," *Washington Quarterly* 29, no. 3 (2006): 7–19.

2. Julian E. Zelizer, *Arsenal of Democracy: The Politics of National Security—From World War II to the War on Terrorism* (New York: Basic Books, 2010), 376–80.

3. Zelizer, *Arsenal of Democracy*, 386–90, 401–5, 422–25; Ole R. Holsti, *Public Opinion and American Foreign Policy* (Ann Arbor: University of Michigan Press, 2007), 120–24, 270–74; Richard Sobel, *The Impact of Public Opinion on U.S. Foreign Policy Since Vietnam: Constraining the Colossus* (New York: Oxford University Press, 2001), 193–230.

4. "Time out to Deal with Trauma," *San Francisco Chronicle*, September 13, 2001.

5. Michael Isokoff and David Corn, *Hubris: The Inside Story of Spin, Scandal, and the Selling of the Iraq War* (New York: Three Rivers Press, 2007), 79; Terry H. Anderson, *Bush's Wars* (New York: Oxford University Press, 2011), 73–74; "Answer Terror with Resolution," *Sun* (Baltimore), September 12, 2001; "U.S. Resolve: Unshattered," *Los Angeles Times*, September 12, 2001; and "The War against America," *New York Times*, September 12, 2001.

6. Amy Zalman and Jonathan Clarke, "The Global War on Terror: A Narrative in Need of a Rewrite," *Ethics and International Affairs* 23, no. 2 (2009): 101.

7. Ronald Krebs claims Bush created this narrative. In reality, the robust liberal narrative in this period was well-formed by the time Bush spoke on September 11 and, especially, by September 14 when Krebs says Bush did his most relevant storytelling. In fact, Krebs's own account indicates Bush was pushed to take-up storytelling to some degree by the already robust liberal narrative that formed quickly here outside the administration (Krebs, *Narrative*, 150–52). Because of this, it is difficult to say that the strengthening liberal narrative here resulted from fearmongering or polarization. It was also not caused by a sudden 2001 shift in power to the U.S.'s advantage, since U.S. relative power was declining with China's rise.

8. *Congressional Record*, 107th Cong., 1st Sess., 2001, 147, pt. 12: 16774, 16754.

9. *Congressional Record*, 107th Cong., 1st Sess., 2001, 147, pt. 12: 16797.

10. *Congressional Record*, 107th Cong., 1st Sess., 2001, 147, pt. 12: 16763, 16753–56.

11. *Congressional Record*, 107th Cong., 1st Sess., 2001, 147, pt. 12: 16753–54.

12. "Text of Bush's Address," http://edition.cnn.com/2001/US/09/11/bush.speech.text/.

13. "Time Out to Deal with Trauma," *San Francisco Chronicle*, September 13, 2001; Thomas Freedman, "What Would World War III Require of US?" *Charlotte Observer*, September 13, 2001; "U.S. Resolve: Unshattered," *Los Angeles Times*, September 12, 2001.

14. Steve Chapman, "What We Lost—and What We Will Keep," *Chicago Tribune*, September 12, 2001; David J. Rothkopf, *National Insecurity: American Leadership in an Age of Fear* (New York: Public Affairs, 2014), 4.

15. "Gallup/CNN/USA Today Poll: Terrorism Reaction Poll # 3," *Cable News Network and USA Today*, September 21–22, 2001, iRoper Center, https://ropercenter.cornell.edu.

16. "Harris Interactive Survey # 07: Terrorism," *Time Magazine and Cable News Network*, September 27–28, 2001, iRoper Center, https://ropercenter.cornell.edu.

17. Kelly Alexander Jr., "Let's Declare Open Season on Terrorists," *Charlotte Observer*, September 13, 2001; "War without Illusion," *Charlotte Observer*, September 16, 2001; "Preparing the Blow," *Washington Post*, September 18, 2001.

18. "President Sounded All the Right Notes," *Atlanta Journal-Constitution*, September 21, 2001.

19. Cited in *Congressional Record*, 107th Cong., 1st Sess., 2001, 147, no. 123: S9553–55.

20. Cited in *Congressional Record*, 107th Cong., 1st Sess., 2001, 147, no. 123, 1748–49.

21. Cited in *Congressional Record*, 107th Cong., 1st Sess., 2001, 147, no. 123: 17481, 17465.

22. "Bush Exudes Strength," *San Francisco Chronicle*, September 21, 2001.

23. Michael McFaul, "To Fight a New 'ism,'" *Washington Post*, September 22, 2001.

24. "Pew Research Center Poll: Response to Terrorism Poll," *Pew Research Center for the People & the Press*, September 21–25, 2001, iRoper Center, https://ropercenter.cornell.edu.

25. "Pew Research Center Poll: January News Interest Index--Politics/Television/Iraq," *Pew Research Center for the People & the Press*, January 9–13, 2002, iRoper Center, https://ropercenter.cornell.edu.

26. "Iraq Weapons Inspections Fast Facts," http://www.cnn.com/2013/10/30/world/meast/iraq-weapons-inspections-fast-facts/; Michael R. Gordon and General Bernard E. Trainor, *Cobra II: The Inside Story of the Invasion and Occupation of Iraq* (New York: Vintage Books, 2007), 14–16; Richard N. Haas, *War of Necessity, War of Choice: A Memoir of Two Iraq Wars* (New York: Simon & Schuster, 2009), 175–80; Bob Woodward, *Plan of Attack* (New York: Simon & Schuster, 2004), 19–23.

27. Donald Rumsfeld, *Known and Unknown: A Memoir* (New York: Sentinel, 2011), 422; Isokoff and Corn, *Hubris*, 79–80.

28. Peter Baker, *Days of Fires: Bush and Cheney in the White House* (New York: Anchor Books, 2013), 146–47.

29. "Afghanistan," *Washington Post*, September 15, 2001.

30. Cited in Frank Rich, *The Greatest Story Ever Sold: The Decline and Fall of Truth in Bush's America* (London: Penguin Books, 2006), 28.

31. "Fears of Anthrax and Smallpox," *New York Times*, October 7, 2001.

32. Scott McClellan, *What Happened: Inside the Bush White House and Washington's Culture of Deception* (New York: Public Affairs, 2008), 110–11; Ari Fleischer, *Taking Heat: The President, the Press, and My Years in the White House* (New York: HarperCollins, 2005), 197–98.

33. Fleischer, *Taking Heat*, 197.

34. Baker, *Days of Fire*, 191; Rothkopf, *National Insecurity*, 30–31.

35. Richard Cohen, ". . . And Now to Iraq," *Washington Post*, November 30, 2001.

36. "War on Terror: What Next?" *Los Angeles Times*, November 27, 2001; Robert Kagan, "On to Phase II," *Washington Post*, November 27, 2001.

37. Fleischer, *Taking Heat*, 215.

38. Leon Furth, "Not the Most Urgent Goal," *Washington Post*, November 27, 2001.

39. *Congressional Record*, 107th Cong., 1st Sess., 2001, 147, pt. 123: 27062.

40. *Congressional Record*, 107th Cong., 1st Sess., 2001, 147, pt. 123: 27064–65.

41. *Congressional Record*, 107th Cong., 1st Sess., 2001, 147, pt. 123: 27066–67.

42. "Gallup/CNN/USA Today Poll: November Wave 2: Terrorism/Anthrax/Cloning," *Cable News Network and USA Today*, November 26–27, 2001, iRoper Center, https://ropercenter.cornell.edu; "ABC News/Washington Post Poll: Terrorism/Flying," *ABC News/Washington Post*, December 18–19, 2001, iRoper Center, https://ropercenter.cornell.edu; and Baker, *Days of Fire*, 191.

43. Rich, *Greatest Story*, 40. Bush did little to create this. His first overt public warning about Saddam Hussein came on November 29.

44. Other leading promoters included Deputy Director of Defense Paul Wolfowitz, Defense Secretary Donald Rumsfeld, and Undersecretary of Defense Doug Feith.

45. McClellan, *What Happened*, 127–30; Timothy Naftali, "George W. Bush and the 'War on Terror,'" in *The Presidency of George W. Bush: A First Historical Assessment*, ed. Julian E. Zelizer (Princeton: Princeton University Press, 2010), 73. Baker, *Days of Fire*, 178–79. Cheney in particular was described by insiders as having "a fever" about Iraq.

46. Woodward, *Plan of Attack*, 38–39.

47. Woodward, *Plan of Attack*, 148–49.

48. Woodward, *Plan of Attack*, 136–37.

49. Karl Rove, *Courage and Consequence: My Life as a Conservative in the Fight* (New York: Simon & Schuster, 2010), 272 and 287.

50. *Congressional Record*, 107th Cong., 1st Sess., 2001, 147, pt. 123: S9555

51. David S. Broder, "A New Reality for George W. Bush," *Washington Post*, September 13, 2001; Richard Cohen, "Taking Command," *Washington Post*, September 22, 2001.

52. Rich, *Greatest Story*, 29–30.

53. "Demands of Leadership," *New York Times*, September 13, 2001.

54. Baker, *Days of Fire*, 133.

55. Baker, *Days of Fire*, 25–27.

56. McClellan, *What Happened*, 117. Bush officials also knew the political damage to Clinton from independent investigations.

57. Jane Mayer, *The Dark Side: The Inside Story of How the War on Terror Turned into a War on American Ideals* (New York: Random House, 2009), 26; Woodward, *Plan*, 24.

58. Woodward, *Plan of Attack*, 30.

59. Condoleezza Rice, *No Higher Honor: A Memoir of My Years in Washington* (New York: Crown, 2011), 80.

60. Rice, *No Higher Honor*, 80; Baker, *Days of Fire*, 137; Rumsfeld, *Known and Unknown*, 359.

61. Cited in Woodward, *Bush*, 26.

62. Cited in Woodward, *Bush*, 26 and Rumsfeld, *Known and Unknown*, 359.

63. Bob Woodward, *Bush at War* (New York: Simon & Schuster, 2002), 159, 168, 278–80.

64. Woodward, *Bush at War*, 346; Baker, *Days of Fire*, 122–24.

65. George W. Bush, *Decision Points* (New York: Crown, 2010), 144–45; Mayer, *Dark Side*, 33

66. Elisabeth Bumiller, *An American Life: A Biography* (New York: Random House, 2007), 111–12.

67. Baker, *Days of Fire*, 163.

68. Baker, *Days of Fire*, 170. Mayer, *Dark Side*, 5 and Bumiller, *American Life*, 168–69.

69. Bumiller, *American Life*, 168–69.

70. Rice, *No Higher Honor*, 103–4; 88.

71. Naftali, "George W. Bush," 63–64.

72. Paraphrased Bumiller, *American Life*, 168–69.

73. Mayer, *Dark Side*, 5.

74. Woodward, *Plan of Attack*, 47.

75. Baker, *Days of Fire*, 164.

76. Bumiller, *American Life*, 169.

77. Baker, *Days of Fire*, 178–79; Woodward, *Plan of Attack*, 3.

78. Baker, *Days of Fire*, 144–45; Woodward, *Plan of Attack*, 25. Bush had suspicions about Hussein on September 11, but initially turned aside all pressure, from neoconservatives especially, to consider using force.

79. Baker, *Days of Fire*, 161.

80. Douglas J. Feith, *War and Decision: Inside the Pentagon at the Dawn of the War on Terrorism* (New York: HarperCollins, 2008), 216.

81. For a similar assessment, see Michael J. Gerson, *Heroic Conservatism: Why Republicans Need to Embrace America's Ideals (And Why They Deserve to Fail If They Don't)* (New York: HarperCollins, 2007) 128–29.

82. Woodward, *Plan of Attack*, 91.

83. Karen Hughes, *Ten Minutes from Normal* (New York: Viking 2004), 282–83; Isokoff and Corn, *Hubris*, 23; Woodward, *Plan of Attack*, 159–60.

84. Cited in Baker, *Days of Fire*, 252.

85. McClellan, *What Happened*, 111–12.

86. Baker, *Days of Fire*, 191.

87. "CBS News/New York Times Poll: Bush/Enron/Parties/War on Terrorism," *CBS News and New York Times*, January 21–24, 2002, iRoper Center, https://ropercenter.cornell.edu.

88. Cited in Baker, *Days of Fire*, 184.

89. Cited in Rich, *Greatest Story*, 42.

90. Cited in Frederik Logevall, "Anatomy of an Unnecessary War: The Iraq Invasion," in *Presidency of George W. Bush*, 104.

91. Baker, *Days of Fire*, 183.

92. Rich, *Greatest Story*, 42–46.

93. Bumiller, *American Life*, 180.

94. Jeff Zeleny, "Some Democrats See Peril in Criticizing Bush Actions," *Chicago Tribune*, May 19, 2002, 11.

95. Cited in *Congressional Record*, 107th Cong., 1st Sess., 2001, 148, pt. 63: 8039–40.

96. Cited in *Congressional Record*, 107th Cong., 1st Sess., 2001, 148, pt. 63: 7914.

97. Bumiller, *American Life*, 180; Rich, *Greatest Story*, 47–48; Mayer, *Dark Side*, 26.

98. Mayer, *Dark Side*, 26–27.

99. Bumiller, *American Life*, 180.

100. Zeleny, "Some Democrats See Peril"; Debra J. Saunders, "Who Knew?" *San Francisco Chronicle*, May 21, 2002.

101. "America's Raucous Democracy," *Chicago Tribune*, May 18, 2002.

102. "A Failure of Imagination," *Washington Post*, May 19, 2002.

103. "Distractions and Diversions," *New York Times*, May 21, 2002.

104. Clarence Page, "Call A Truce in the Sept. 11 Blame Game," *Chicago Tribune*, May 19, 2002.

105. Logevall, "Anatomy of an Unnecessary War," 103–4.

106. Baker, *Days of Fire*, 199.

107. Fleischer, *Taking Heat*, 238.

108. Page, "Call A Truce," 7. See also E.J. Dionne, "Get to the Truth," *Washington Post*, November 21, 2001.

109. Cited in Rich, *Greatest Story*, 42.

110. Richard L. Berke and David E. Sanger, "Some in Administration Grumble as Aide's Role Seems to Expand," *New York Times*, May 13, 2002.

111. See Berke and Sanger, "Some in Administration Grumble."

112. Cited in Woodward, *Plan of Attack*, 90.

113. Woodward, *Plan of Attack*, 90.

114. Cited in Woodward, *Plan of Attack*, 91.

115. Logevall, "Anatomy of an Unnecessary War," 95.

116. Berke and Sanger, "Some in Administration," 1.

117. Logevall, "Anatomy of an Unnecessary War," 103–4; Rich, *Greatest Story*, 44–55.

118. Cited in Bumiller, *American Life*, 171.

119. Haas, *War of Necessity*, 169.

120. Bumiller, *American Life*, 171; Anderson, *Bush's Wars*, 104; Isokoff and Corn, *Hubris*, 29.

121. Isokoff and Corn, *Hubris*, 23.

122. Isokoff and Corn, *Hubris*, 30.

123. Baker, *Days of Fire*, 228.

124. Baker, *Days of Fire*, 214–15, 228; Woodward, *Plan of Attack*, 168–69.

125. Rich, *Greatest Story*, 62.

126. Cited in Logevall, "Anatomy of an Unnecessary War," 112.

127. Woodward, *Plan of Attack*, 262.

128. Logevall, "Anatomy of an Unnecessary War," 112.

129. Woodward, *Plan of Attack*, 270–71.

130. McClellan, *What Happened*, 120–21.

131. Baker, *Days of Fire*, 210.

132. Cited in Woodward, *Plan of Attack*, 170.

133. Baker, *Days of Fire*, 210.

134. McClellan, *What Happened*, 120.

135. Cited in McClellan, *What Happened*, 130.

136. McClellan, *What Happened*, 131.

137. Rich, *Greatest Story*, 218.

138. Anderson, *Bush's Wars*, 96.

139. Woodward, *Plan of Attack*, 103.

140. Anderson, *Bush's Wars*, 100.

141. Cited in Woodward, *Plan of Attack*, 119–20.

142. Seymour M. Hersh, *Chain of Command: The Road from 9/11 to Abu Ghraib* (New York: HarperCollins, 2004), 203–4; Isokoff and Corn, *Hubris*, 117.

143. Isokoff and Corn, *Hubris*, 117

144. Baker, *Days of Fire*, 220–21.

145. Anderson, *Bush's Wars*, 106; Isokoff and Corn, *Hubris*, 35; Bumiller, *American Life*, 191–92.

146. Anderson, *Bush's Wars*, 107.

147. Isokoff and Corn, *Hubris*, 42.

148. Woodward, *Plan of Attack*, 168.

149. Cited in Rich, *Greatest Story*, 58. See also McClellan, *What Happened*, 12.

150. Cited in Isokoff and Corn, *Hubris*, 32.

151. "The Wrong Resolution," *Los Angeles Times*, October 11, 2002; What the War Resolution Means," *Chicago Tribune*, October 11, 2002; "Irrefutable," *Washington Post*, February 6, 2003.

152. *Congressional Record*, 107th Cong., 2nd Sess., 2002, 148, pt. 133: 20248.

153. *Congressional Record*, 107th Cong., 2nd Sess., 2002, 148, pt. 133: 20248.

154. Baker, *Days of Fire*, 226–27.

155. Isokoff and Corn, *Hubris*, 137.

156. Cited in Isokoff and Corn, *Hubris*, 128.

157. Baker, *Days of Fire*, 223–24; Woodward, *Plan of Attack*, 201.

158. Logevall, "Anatomy of an Unnecessary War," 110.

159. Logevall, "Anatomy of an Unnecessary War," 108–12.

160. Bob Deans, "A Halting Go-Ahead on Iraq," *Atlanta Journal-Constitution*, October 13, 2002.

161. Cited in Baker, *Days of Fire*, 253, see also 290–91.

162. Cited in Isokoff and Corn, *Hubris*, 348, see also 206–9.

163. Rich, *Greatest Story*, 210. See also Isokoff and Corn, *Hubris*, 228–32, 248–54.

164. *Congressional Record*, 108th Cong., 2nd Sess., 2004, 150, pt. 121: H7941; 150, pt. 126: H8643; 150, pt.11: 11, 291, 292; pt. 126: H8643.

165. Cited in Isokoff and Corn, *Hubris*, 328, 226–30.

166. Isokoff and Corn, *Hubris*, 214, 250–51, 289–91; Baker, *Days of Fire*, 280.

167. Isokoff and Corn, *Hubris*, 324.

168. Baker, *Days of Fire*, 425.

169. "Down in the Gutter," *St. Louis Post-Dispatch*, October 3, 2003; "The Nuclear Bomb That Wasn't," *New York Times*, October 4, 2004; "A Bluff That Worked Too Well," *Los Angeles Times*, October 8, 2004; "Our Opinions," *Atlanta Journal-Constitution*, October 8, 2004; and "Flawed Intel and UN Booty" *Chicago Tribune*, October 7, 2004.

170. Isokoff and Corn, *Hubris*, 395; Adam Nagourney and Janet Elder, "Bush's Rating Falls to Its Lowest Point, New Survey Finds," *New York Times*, June 29, 2004.

171. Baker, *Days of Fire*, 269.

172. Baker, *Days of Fire*, 447–49.

173. Cited in Rice, *No Higher Honor*, 547.

174. "Our Opinions," *Atlanta Journal-Constitution*, April 2, 2004.

175. *Congressional Record*, 109th Cong., 2nd Sess., 2006, 152, pt. 23: H423.

176. Moises Naim, "Missing Link: Casualties of War," *Foreign Policy* 44 (2004): 95.

177. Barbara Ann J. Rieffer and Kristan Mercer, "Democracy Promotion: The Clinton and Bush Administrations," *Global Society* 19, no.4 (2005): 407; Steven Heydemann, "Upgrading Authoritarianism in the Arab World," Saban Center for Middle East Policy at the Brookings Institution, 2007, http://www.brookings.edu/research/papers/2007/10/arabworld; Edward Mansfield and Jack Snyder, "Prone to Violence: The Paradox of the Democratic Peace," *National Interests*, no. 82 (2005/6): 41–43; and Laurence Whitehead, "Losing 'the Force'? The 'Dark Side' of Democratization after Iraq," *Democratization* 16, no. 2 (2009): 215–42, 221; G. John Ikenberry and Anne-Marie Slaughter, *Forging a World of Liberty under Law* (Princeton: Woodrow Wilson School of Public and International Affairs, 2006), 19–20.

178. Thomas Carothers, "The 'Sequencing' Fallacy," *Journal of Democracy* 18, no. 1 (2007): 12–27.

179. Cited in Baker, *Days of Fire*, 294.

180. "Time/SRBI Poll" *Time Magazine*, October 3–4, 2006, iRoper Center, https://ropercenter.cornell.edu; Isokoff and Corn, *Hubris*, 425.

181. Francis Fukuyama and Michael McFaul, "Should Democracy be Promoted or Demoted?" *Washington Quarterly* 31, no. 1 (2007–8): 24.

182. Suzanne Katzenstein and Jack Snyder, "Expediency of the Angels," *National Interest*, no. 100 (2009): 58–67.

183. "Address before a Joint Session of the Congress on the State of the Union," February 24, 2009, http://www.presidency.ucsb.edu/ws/index.php?pid=3110.

184. Christopher J. Fettweis, "Post-Traumatic Iraq Syndrome," *Los Angeles Times*, June 12, 2007.

185. Gayle Tzemach Lemmon, "Iraq's Do-Nothing Legacy," DefenseOne.com, www.defenseone.com/ideas/2014/13/iraqs-do-nothing-legacy/80908; "Ten Years After," *New York Times*, March 19, 2013.

186. *Congressional Record*, 110th, 1st Sess., 2007, 153, pt. 6: H398.

187. *Congressional Record*, 109th Cong., 2nd Sess., 2006, 152, pt. 46: H1707.

188. *Congressional Record*, 110th, 1st Sess., 2007, 153, pt. 6: H349, S412, S414.

189. *Congressional Record*, 109th Cong., 2nd Sess., 2006, 152, pt. 3: H849, also 152, 23, H424; Baker, *Days of Fire*, 478–79.

190. James Dobbins, "Learning Curve," *Foreign Policy*, March 13, 2013, http://foreignpolicy.com/2013/03/13/learning-curve-3/; John Mueller, "Iraq Syndrome Redux," *Foreign Affairs*, June 18, 2014, https://www.foreignaffairs.com/articles/iraq/2014-06-18/iraq-syndrome-redux.

191. "U.S. Foreign Policy Challenges Ahead," *Diane Rehm Show*, National Public Radio, March 13, 2013, http://thedianerehmshow.org/shows/2013-03-13/us-foreign-policy-challenges-ahead.

192. Rothkopf, *National Insecurity*, 239.

193. "U.S. Foreign Policy Challenges Ahead."

194. Max Boot, "The Iraq Syndrome," *Weekly Standard*, Jan 28, 2013, http://www.maxboot.net/articles/112-the-iraq-syndrome.html; J. Dana Stutser, "The Iraq Syndrome," *Foreign Policy*, March 19, 2013, http://foreignpolicy.com/2013/03/19/the-iraq-syndrome/.

195. Cited in Stutser, "The Iraq Syndrome."

196. Baker, *Days of Fire*, 509.

197. "CNN/ORC Poll # 2009-006: Economy/International Relations," *Cable News Network*, April 3–5, 2009, iRoper Center, https://ropercenter.cornell.edu.

198. Baker, *Days of Fire*, 525; Isokoff and Corn, *Hubris*, 428.

199. Dana Milbank, "The Secretary vs. the Senators," *Washington Post*, January 12, 2007.

200. Tony Norman, "Have You No Decency, Mr. President?" *Pittsburgh Post-Gazette*, January 12, 2007.

201. Baker, *Days of Fire*, 556–57.

202. Baker, *Days of Fire*, 551–53; Robert M. Gates, *Duty: Memoirs of a Secretary at War* (New York: Vintage Books, 2015), 171–77, 190.

203. Gates, *Duty*, 182–85; Rice, *No Higher Honor*, 624–25.

204. Cited in Baker, *Days of Fire*, 568, 599, see also 600–607.

205. Cited in Rothkopf, *National Insecurity*, 123.

206. Bob Woodward, *Obama's Wars* (New York: Simon & Schuster, 2010), 776.

207. Cited in Lemmon, "Iraq's Do-Nothing Legacy."

208. Cited in Woodward, *Obama's Wars*, 329–30. See also Rothkopf, *National Insecurity*, 175–80.

209. David Sanger, *Confront and Conceal: Obama's Secret Wars and Surprising Use of American Power* (New York: Crown, 2012), 355–56.

210. Rothkopf, *National Insecurity*, 279.

211. Christopher S. Chivvis, *Toppling Qaddafi: Libya and the Limits of Liberal Intervention* (Cambridge: Cambridge University Press, 2014), 53.

212. Michael Hastings, "Inside Obama's War Room," *Rolling Stone*, October 13, 2011, http://www.rollingstone.com/politics/news/inside-obamas-war-room-20111013; James Mann, *The Obamians: The Struggle Inside the White House to Redefine American Power* (London: Viking, 2012), 289.

213. Mann, *Obamians*, 289.

214. David L. Sanger and Thom Shanker, "Gates Warns of the Risks of Imposing No-Flight over Libya," *New York Times*, March 3, 2011.

215. "Stopping Qaddafi," *New York Times*, February 25, 2011; "Dictator's Delusion," *San Francisco Chronicle*, March 1, 2011; "No to a No-Fly Zone in Libya." *Los Angeles Times*, March 2, 2011; "Grounding Mr. Gaddafi," *Washington Post*, March 3, 2011.

216. Mann, *Obamians*, 286–88.

217. Cited in Martin S. Indyk et al., *Bending History: Barack Obama's Foreign Policy* (Washington, DC: Brookings Institution Press, 2012), 161; Chivvis, *Toppling Qadaffi*, 38–40.

218. Cited in Chivvis, *Toppling Qadaffi*, 28; "No to a No-Fly," 24.

219. "Libya Isn't Our Battle to Fight," *Denver Post*, March 8, 2011.

220. Chivvis, *Toppling Qadaffi*, 28; "No to a No-Fly," 24; "Zakaria: U.S. Should Not Go It Alone," *CNN*, March 2, 2011, http://www.cnn.com/video/data/2.0/video/bestoftv/2011/03/02/exp.arena.libya.nofly.zone.cnn.html.

221. Nicholas D. Kristof, "Here's What We Can Do to Tackle Libya," *New York Times*, March 3, 2011.

222. "Face the Nation," *CBS News*, March 6, 2003, http://www.cbsnews.com/htdocs/pdf/FTN_030611.pdf. See also Kerry, John. "Libya: An Iraq Redux?" *Washington Post*, March 11, 2011.

223. "Obama's Libyan Abdication," *Wall Street Journal*, March 7, 2011.

224. "Fox News Poll: Obama/Budget deficit/Union rights/Nuclear power: March 2011," Fox News, March 14–16, 2011, iRoper Center, https://ropercenter.cornell.edu; "Quinnipiac University Poll, Mar, 2011," *Quinnipiac University Polling Institute*, March 22–March 28, 2011, iRoper Center, https://ropercenter.cornell.edu.

225. Ethan Chorin, *Exit the Colonel: The Hidden History of the Libyan Revolution* (New York: Public Affairs, 2012), 211.

226. Chivvis, *Toppling Qadaffi*, 43.

227. Chivvis, *Toppling Qadaffi*, 38–40, 55–57.

228. Rothkopf, *National Insecurity*, 281.

229. David E. Sanger, "Seeking Lessons from the Iraq War. But Which Ones?" *New York Times*, March 20, 2013.

230. Sanger, *Confront and Conceal*, 245.

231. Sanger, *Confront and Conceal*, 344–45.

232. Scott Wilson and Joby Warrick, "Obama's Shift toward Military Action," *Washington Post*, March 19, 2011.

233. Chivvis, *Toppling Qadaffi*, 65–67; Mann, *Obamians*, 301.

234. Hastings, "Inside Obama's War Room"; Chivvis, *Toppling Qadaffi*, 55–57.

235. Cited in Sanger, *Confront and Conceal*, 338.

236. Karen DeYoung and Edward Cody, "U.S. Plans to Send Aid Team to Libya," *Washington Post*, March 11, 2011.

237. Hastings, "Inside Obama's War Room."

238. Sanger, *Confront and Conceal*, 346–47.

239. Hastings, "Inside Obama's War Room"; Sanger, *Confront and Conceal*, 345–47; Mann, *Obamians*, 293–95; Elisabeth Bumiller and David D. Kirkpatrick, "Obama Threatens Military Action against Qaddafi," *New York Times*, March 19, 2011; Helen Cooper and Steven Lee Myers, "Shift by Clinton Helped Persuade President to Take a Harder Line," *New York Times*, March 19, 2011.

240. Cited in Sanger, *Confront and Conceal*, 346–47.

241. David Ignatius, "Mr. Reality Check on the Middle East," *Washington Post*, March 23, 2011.

242. Mann, *Obamians*, 298–99.

243. Hastings, "Inside Obama's War Room."

244. Cited in Bill Kristol, "Give War a Chance," *Weekly Standard* 16, no. 28 (April 4, 2011), 7–8.

245. Cited in Sanger, *Confront and Conceal*, 355.

246. Hastings, "Inside Obama's War Room"; Cooper and Myers, "Shift by Clinton."

247. Sanger, *Confront and Conceal*, 354.

248. Karen DeYoung, "U.S. Takes on Support Role as Allies Mobilize for No-Fly Zone," *Washington Post*, March 19, 2011.

249. Indyk et al., *Bending History*, 163; Karen DeYoung and Peter Finn, "Questions Are Raised about Involvement, Goals," *Washington Post*, March 21, 2011.

250. DeYoung, "U.S. Takes on Support."

251. Ben Rhodes, "Infographic: Troop Levels in Afghanistan and Iraq," https://www.whitehouse.gov/blog/2011/06/23/infographic-troop-levels-afghanistan-and-iraq.

252. Christopher Layne, "This Time It's Real: The End of Unipolarity and *Pax Americana*," *International Studies Quarterly* 56, no. 1 (2012): 203–14.

253. Layne, "This Time It's Real."

254. Debates about the Islamic State center only on a higher degree of limited military action, notably and increase in special operations forces (not combat troops) in a forward, mostly advisory position.

255. Sanger, "Seeking Lessons." For an insider's perspective that reflects the same, see Derek Chollet, *The Long Game: How Obama Defied Washington and Redefined America's Role in the World* (New York: Public Affairs, 2016), 1–26, 127–34.

256. Rumsfeld, *Known and Unknown*, 353 and 355.

257. John M. Owen, IV, *The Clash of Ideas: Transnational Networks, States, and Regime Change, 1510–2010* (Princeton: Princeton University Press, 2010), 230–37.

258. Woodward, *Plan of Attack*, 13–22.

259. Some might wonder if master narratives simply helped open space here to move toward war, while it was neoconservatives in the administration (like Paul Wolfowitz) who pushed not just for war but regime change war in Iraq, meaning elite polarization would still be the main driver of policy. This argument faces two problems. First, the liberal narrative discourse around Iraq that developed in late 2001 (which was not encouraged by Bush officials) was not just a generic call for war. Instead, it embodied a specific and widely accepted demand for *regime change*. Second, when Bush and others talked in early 2003 about being trapped into regime change, they were not referring to pressure from elites but about the price (i.e., audience costs) the president would pay with the public for backing down—again a function of master narratives, not elites alone.

260. Rothkopf, *National Insecurity*, 4, 123–24.

261. Baker, *Days of Fire*, 189; Anderson, *Bush's Wars*, 93, 98.

7. THE IMPLICATIONS OF MASTER NARRATIVE POLITICS

1. Others note something similar, see Mark L. Haas, *The Ideological Origins of Great Power Politics, 1789–1989* (Ithaca: Cornell University Press, 2005).

2. John M. Owen, IV, *The Clash of Ideas in World Politics: Transnational Networks, States, and Regime Change, 1510–2010* (Princeton: Princeton University Press, 2010).

3. Parallel cases (Korea and El Salvador) where master narrative discourses blocked elites from following their preferences demonstrate just how important master narratives are to explaining Grenada and China.

4. These cases are not rare. Other similar U.S. cases include Mexico and Nicaragua (1920s), Cuba (1920s), Laos (1964), Dominican Republic (1965), Suriname (1982), Philippines (1980s), Chad and Sudan (1980s), Iraq (1991), and Afghanistan (2001). Even in the cases of China (aid to the Nationalists) and Grenada (continued postinvasion deference to the Vietnam syndrome) leaders got pushed by master narratives into policies they did not prefer.

5. As expected by the master narrative argument, nonleadership elites (and even some elites inside government) sometimes help build discourses. While the independent choices of these actors to do so are important, master narratives are still usually the central variable at work here. Narratives often shape elite decisions about whether or not to build discourses and sometimes determine choices about how robust discourses should be (i.e. in terms of their demands for or against force). Master narratives also determine, even more importantly, when and if those discourses shape policy. From Korea to Cuba, Vietnam, El Salvador, and Iraq, the strength of master narratives was the key factor that determined which elite arguments and wider discourses became salient and shaped leader decisions. Presidents were moved most not by qualities (like rhetorical style or ideological passion) of elite promoters/moderators themselves, but instead by the master-narrative-driven domestic (especially electoral) costs associated with certain discourses. Coupled with the fact that leaders choose to act in ways they prefer not to in pushed-to-act cases, this is another reason that it is appropriate to say that the master narrative dynamics offer in instances like these more of a necessary and sufficient set of conditions to explain policy outcomes.

6. Owen, *The Clash of Ideas*.

7. Jessica L.P. Weeks, *Dictators at War and Peace* (Ithaca: Cornell University Press, 2014).

8. Ronald R. Krebs, *Narratives and the Making of US National Security* (Cambridge: Cambridge University Press).

9. James D. Fearon, "Domestic Political Audiences and the Escalation of International Disputes," *American Political Science Review* 88, no. 3 (1994): 577–92; Fearon, "Signaling Foreign Policy Interests," *Journal of Conflict Resolution* 41, no. 1 (1997): 68–90.

10. The Cuba case demonstrates the impact of other similar mid-range audience costs.

11. For instance, Louis Hartz, *The Liberal Tradition in America: An Interpretation of American Political Thought Since the Revolution* (Orlando: Harcourt Books, 1955).

12. A.J.P. Taylor, *The Origins of the Second World War* (New York: Simon & Schuster, 2005), 202.

13. William R. Rock, *Appeasement on Trial: British Foreign Policy and Its Critics* (New York: Archon Books, 1966), 207–8, 214.

14. All cited in Rock, *Appeasement on Trial*, 204–5.

15. Rock, *Appeasement on Trial*, 212.

16. Cited by Taylor, *The Origins*, 205.

17. Taylor, *The Origins*, 209–22.

18. Taylor, *The Origins*, 214.

19. All cited by J.H. Hoare, "British Public Opinion and the Korean War," *Papers of the British Association for Korean Studies*, vol. 2 (London: Center for Korean Studies, School of Oriental and African Studies, 1992), 13.

20. Cited by David Carlton, *Anthony Eden: A Biography* (London: Penguin Books, 1981), 287.

21. Martin Gilbert, *"Never Despair": Winston Churchill, 1945–1965* (London: William Heinemann, 1988), 537.

22. Callum MacDonald, "Great Britain and the Korean War," in *The Korean War: Handbook of the Literature and Research*, ed. Lester B. Brune (Westport, CT: Greenwood Press, 1996), 101.

23. Cited by Hoare, "British Public Opinion," 12.

24. Hoare, "British Public Opinion," 16; *British Political Opinion 1937–2000: The Gallup Polls*, ed. Anthony King (London: Politico's, 2001), 322.

25. Peter N. Stearns, *Peace in World History* (London: Routledge, 2014), 262–64.

26. David Cortright, *A History of Movements and Ideas* (Cambridge: Cambridge University Press, 2008), 60–62.

27. Leonid I. Strakhovsky, *Intervention at Archangel: The Story of Allied Intervention and Russian Counter-Intervention in North Russia, 1918–1920* (New York: Howard Fertig, 1971), 172–73.

28. Cited in Strakhovsky, *Intervention at Archangel*, 171.

29. Jeffrey Gray, "Australia, New Zealand, and the Korean War," in *The Korean War*, 121 and John Peterson, "Europe, America, and 11 September," *Irish Studies in International Affairs* 13 (2002), 23–42.

30. For example, see Dana Milbank, "On Syria, U.S. Military Leaders Offer Only Timidity," *Washington Post*, December 9, 2015.

31. Unlike the liberal narrative, the restraint narrative historically does more good than harm to policy. When it proves detrimental to policy, it does so in one of two ways. First, it can lead to a hardened commitment to inaction abroad that clouds the ability of policymakers to think about the broader national interest in ways that causes strategic damage (i.e., the slow response to the rise of Nazi Germany). Second, the restraint narrative can prevent consideration of even the most minimal steps to address human suffering and humanitarian crises abroad that are both acceptable to most scholars (even those most committed to restraint) and often healthy for U.S. foreign policy given the country's liberal identity, which must be effectively managed or accommodated by any grand strategy, including one centered on restraint. On humanitarian intervention as a part of a restraint grand strategy, see Barry R. Posen, "The Case for Restraint," *American Interest* 3, no. 2 (2007): 14–15.

32. Robert Jervis, Richard Ned Lebow, and Janice Gross Stein, *Psychology and Deterrence* (Baltimore: Johns Hopkins University Press, 1985), 25–26.

33. Healthy democratic government is often lacking as well. See Alexander B. Downes and Jonathan Monten, "Forced to Be Free? Why Foreign-Imposed Regime Change Rarely Leads to Democratization," *International Security* 37, no. 4 (2013): 90–131.

34. Thomas J. Christensen, *Useful Adversaries: Grand Strategy, Domestic Mobilization, and Sino-American Conflict, 1947–1958* (Princeton: Princeton University Press, 1996), 86.

35. Iraq was eventually invaded, but only after the master narrative context changed following 9/11, which again reinforces the point about the negative implications of liberal narrative politics.

36. David E. Sanger, "Seeking Lessons from the Iraq War. But Which Ones?" *New York Times*, 20 March 2013, A1 and Sanger, *Confront and Conceal: Obama's Secret Wars and Surprising Use of American Power* (New York: Crown, 2012), 361–63.

37. On the strategic dangers of refugee crises, see Sarah K. Lischer, *Dangerous Sanctuaries: Refugee Camps, Civil War, and the Dilemmas* (Ithaca: Cornell University Press, 2006).

38. Kim Ghattas, "Hillary Clinton Has No Regrets about Libya," foreignpolicy.com, http://foreignpolicy.com/2016/04/14/hillary-clinton-has-no-regrets-about-libya/; Posen, "The Case for Restraint," 14–15; and Downes and Jonathan Monten, "Forced to Be Free?" 90–131. The kinds of programs Obama canceled are limited and offer, thus, a preferable alternative to democracy promotion by force. Arguably, Obama's first and primary mistake in Libya lay with expanding what had been a properly limited humanitarian intervention (i.e., multilateral with the United States in a support role) into a regime change intervention. Given both the poor U.S. track record of postwar success with regime change in general and Obama's recognition that a robust restraint narrative would constrain even the most minimal postwar U.S./international engagement to aid with institution building in Libya, staying away from regime change was the better course. U.S. participation in regime change also contributed to Libya becoming a failed state.

39. For a similar point, see Lene Hansen, *Security as Practice: Discourse Analysis and the Bosnian War* (London: Routledge, 2006), 212.

40. Jack L. Amoureux, *A Practice of Ethics for Global Politics: Ethical Reflexivity* (London: Routledge, 2016), 1–2.

41. Amoureux, *A Practice of Ethics for Global Politics*, 9.

42. Others in international relations make similar parallels. See Hansen, *Security as Practice*, 19–20.

43. For an example, see Richard Cohen, "Of Pride, Falls—and Obama's Foreign Policy," *Washington Post*, May 9, 2016.

44. Hansen, *Security as Practice*, 212.

45. Among others, Republican presidential nominee Donald Trump used this narrative repeatedly in his 2016 campaign for the White House.

46. On Joseph McCarthy's opportunism, see Richard Fried, "The Discovery of Anti-communism," in *McCarthyism*, ed. Thomas C. Reeves (Malabar, FL: Robert E. Krieger, 1989), 20.

47. In the post-Iraq period, restraint discourse around different crises abroad continues to generate healthy restraint in U.S. foreign policy, especially when it comes to the initiation of major new combat operations for regime change. The danger (like that faced by interwar isolationists) comes with poor management of master narrative politics. Nonjudicious, overuse of the restraint narrative that bends policy too distinctly away from ideological/moral content can create space for a robust liberal narrative backlash capable of crowding out healthy restraint-based policies. A version of this happened around Obama's quick, complete 2011 withdrawal of U.S. forces from Iraq. The president's desire to fulfill a campaign promise centered on the restraint narrative drove this move. The subsequent rise of the Islamic State sparked a domestic wave of liberal narrative criticism

charging that Obama failed to grasp the danger of "radical Islamic terrorism." Trump subsequently drew on this in the 2016 campaign in ways that then boxed Trump as president into continuing the U.S. troop presence in both Afghanistan and Iraq/Syria. Overall, Obama's overuse of the restraint narrative set the stage for this liberal narrative backlash in ways that has slowed progress toward healthy U.S. retrenchment from longstanding Middle East wars. Obama's drawdown from Iraq was right and necessary, but among other things, a slower withdrawal might have prevented this scenario from playing out and dampened the domestic political pressure that appears to have locked the United States into longer term military commitments than are strategically useful and beyond what either Obama or Trump preferred.

Index

Acheson, Dean, 85–86, 89–90, 95, 98, 103, 104
Afghanistan policy and War: in Cold War master narrative, 148; in Iraq policy, 172, 177, 194, 200; Iraq syndrome in, 189; in Libya policy, 194; NATO participation in, 210; post-9/11 demands for action in, 170–71
Africa, 26–27, 168
Africa policy, 145–46, 147–48. *See also* Libya policy
agents (social carriers), 6–7, 14–15, 16, 29–30, 34–36, 45, 228n81
agent stories, 6–7, 22, 24, 25–27, 213
Aiken, George, 128
air force/power, 95, 125–29, 192
al-Askari Mosque bombing, 185–86
Alexander, Jeffrey, 25, 27
Alliance for Progress (Kennedy), 114–15
al Qaeda, 173, 176, 177–78, 182, 184, 215. *See also* Islam, radical; terrorism
Alsop, Joseph, 130
Angola policy, 145–46, 147
anthrax scare (2001), 175
antifascism narrative of international engagement, 22–23. *See also* liberal narrative
antiterror image, 1–2, 174, 175–76, 177–81, 182–84, 211. *See also* terrorism/antiterrorism
antiwar discourse, 8, 16, 32, 140–43, 150
apartheid, South African, 26–27
appeasement, 89, 91–92, 207
Arab Spring, 189–90, 191
Armey, Dick, 180, 182
Armitage, Richard, 173
Ashcroft, John, 175
Asia, 91–93, 94, 99, 104–5, 123–24, 126–30, 132, 211–12. *See also* China policy; Korea policy; Vietnam policy and War
Atlee, Clement, 208–9
audience costs for action/inaction: in Britain, on Nazi Germany, 208; in China policy, 77, 88–90, 91, 206; in Cuba policy, 116–18; in El Salvador policy, 40, 151, 152–54, 155–57, 165; in Grenada policy, 139, 157, 158–59, 160–63, 165; in Iraq policy, 173–74, 176–77,

178–79, 181, 182–84; in Korea policy, 37, 94, 102, 103–4; in patterns of forceful regime change, 15, 16, 33–34, 35, 37, 38–40, 75; in Russian Civil War policy, 209–10; in Syria policy, 195; in Taiwan policy, 97, 98–99; in Vietnam policy, 123–25, 126–28, 129, 131–32, 137
AUMF (authorizing use of military force) in Iraq, 170, 180–84
"axis of evil" speech (Bush), 179

Baker, James, 152, 153–54, 174, 176–77
Ball, George, 125, 131–32
Bay of Pigs invasion, 5, 109, 114–22, 202, 204, 212
Beirut, Lebanon, Marine Corps bombing, 159–60
beliefs, collective, 9–10, 24–27, 44, 47–49, 50–51, 75, 203, 214–15
Benghazi, Libya, 189–90, 213
Ben Suc (Vietnam), razing of, 140
Ben Tre (Vietnam), burning of, 140
bin Laden, Osama, 177–78. *See also* al Qaeda
bipartisanship, 49, 97, 116–17, 122, 128, 179, 188
Bishop, Maurice, 158
Bissell, Richard, 115–16
blame: for 9/11 attacks, 169–71; in 1960s master narrative, 110–12; in 1980s master narrative, 147; in anti-Vietnam war discourse, 141–43; in Cold War narratives, 79–81, 83; for Iraq, 185; for the loss of China, 91–92; in narrative of events, 11–12; in narrative strength, 27, 29, 31, 44–45
Bradley, Omar, 97, 100
Brewster, Owen, 88
Bridges, Stiles, 99, 117, 121
Brooke, Edward, 145
Buckley, William F., 187
Bullitt, William, 88
Bundy, McGeorge "Mac," 117–18, 124, 128, 131, 132, 137
Bundy, William, 127, 130
Bush, George H. W., and administration, 8, 16, 166, 168

restraint discourse in, 3–4, 7–8, 16, 73–74; special operations in, 8; support roles in, 8–9, 192–93; in Vietnam policy, 129, 137. *See also* China policy; Cuba policy; El Salvador policy; Libya policy; Syria; Taiwan policy

normative commitments. *See* elite ideological polarization

norms, social, 10, 11–13, 31, 141–43, 214–15. *See also* beliefs, collective

North Africa. *See* Libya policy

North Atlantic Treaty Organization and master narratives, 210

Obama, Barack, and administration, 5, 8, 33, 186, 188–94, 268n38

O'Donnell, Kenny, 118, 128

O'Mahony, Joseph, 95

opinion polls. *See* public opinion

Ottinger, Richard, 143

Owen, John, 17–19, 41, 105, 136, 195, 204, 222n5

Panama, 166

partisanship, 5, 196–97

patterns of forceful regime change: alternative explanations for, 40–42; audience costs in, 15, 16, 33–34, 75; changes of intervention type in, 46; conventional wisdom on, 75–76; defined, 8; elite ideology and polarization in, 17–19, 39; event-driven context in, 35, 223n16; liberal narrative strength in, 52–61; master narrative argument on, 17–24; master narrative impact on, 14–16, 24–40, 61–64, 69–74; measuring of, 48–52; trauma theory on, 64–69

Pearl Harbor, 170

Percy, Charles, 149–50, 151

Perle, Richard, 180

Pleiku airbase bombing (Vietnam), 131–32, 137

pluralism in policymaking, 213–14, 216–17

political opportunity structure: Cold War anticommunist panic in, 79; liberal narrative in, on Iraq, 195–96; for moderator discourse on Vietnam, 141; in patterns of forceful regime change, 26–27, 29–30, 35, 36, 38; and storytelling, in national security narratives, 205

political price. *See* audience costs for action/inaction

political space, narrative-generated: in Cuba policy, 120, 136; in Grenada policy, 157–58, 163, 165; in Iraq policy, 173; in patterns of regime change, 19, 37, 38; in Taiwan policy, 99–100; in Vietnam policy, 136; weak narratives in, 39

Powell, Colin, 173

power, relative: in Asia, 104–5; of China, in Iraq and Libya policy, 194–95; in Cuba and Vietnam policies, 134, 135; in El Salvador and Grenada policies, 163–64; in geopolitical policies, 41–42, 134, 135; in Iraq and Libya policy, 194–95; in realism, 199–201; in regime change, 8–9

Power, Samantha, 189–90

pragmatism, 156, 160–61, 216

predicting forceful regime change, 36–40

Present Danger, Committee on, 147

presidents: abuse of authority by, 142, 162, 185; commitments of, in audience costs, 206; commitments of, in restraint discourse, 227n79; executive-branch authority, 19–20, 142, 145, 162, 185; mistakes by, 177–78, 180; in patterns of regime change, 19–23; statements of, in quantifying threat and disillusionment, 51–52. *See also* executive-branch authority; name of president; State of the Union addresses

Press Intelligence, Division of (DPI), 84

pressure, narrative-generated: in China policy, 89–92, 93, 106, 107; collective beliefs and stories in, 9–10; in Cuba policy, 115–21; in decision-making, 3, 4–5; in elite dispositions, 203–4; in El Salvador policy, 149–50, 155–56; in forceful regime change, 1–5, 9, 13–17, 18–19; in Grenada policy, 159, 163; in Iraq policy, 175–76, 179–80, 183; in Korea policy, 93–97, 101–4, 106, 107; in liberal narrative strength, 1947–1949, 85–86; in patterns of regime change, 19, 47–48, 73–74; in predicting forceful regime change, 38–40; in Taiwan policy, 97–98; in Vietnam policy, 122–34. *See also* audience costs for action/inaction

prestige, international: in China and Korea policies, 95–96, 106–7; in Cuba and Vietnam policies, 120–21, 136–37; in Iraq and Libya policies, 197. *See also* image

promoters/promoter discourse. *See* liberal narrative discourse

promotion model/index, 52, 69–74